KNOWLEDGE IN THE MAKING

JOAN DELFATTORE

Knowledge in the Making

ACADEMIC FREEDOM AND
FREE SPEECH IN AMERICA'S SCHOOLS
AND UNIVERSITIES

Yale

UNIVERSITY PRESS

NEW HAVEN & LONDON

Published with assistance from the foundation established in memory of
Philip Hamilton McMillan of the Class of 1894, Yale College.

Set in Scala and Scala Sans type by
The Composing Room of Michigan, Inc.
Printed in the United States of America.

Library of Congress Cataloging-in-Publication Data
DelFattore, Joan, 1946–
Knowledge in the making : academic freedom and free speech in
America's schools and universities / Joan DelFattore.
p.   cm.
Includes bibliographical references and index.
ISBN 978-0-300-11181-1 (alk. paper)
1. Educational law and legislation—United States.   2. Freedom of
speech—United States.   3. Academic freedom—United States.
I. Title.
KF4124.5.D45 2010
344.73'078—dc22   2010019280

A catalogue record for this book is available from the British Library.

This paper meets the requirements of ANSI/NISO Z39.48–1992
(Permanence of Paper).

10 9 8 7 6 5 4 3 2 1

To my cousin Chuck Rohde; his wife, Barbara; and their wonderful children and grandchildren. We are born into our families and choose our friends. Thanks for being both.

Where there is much desire to learn, there of necessity will be much arguing, much writing, many opinions; for opinion in good men is but knowledge in the making.

—John Milton, "Areopagitica"

CONTENTS

PREFACE

AT ALL LEVELS OF EDUCATION, FROM KINDERGARTEN through graduate school, public schools and universities must address the issues raised by the expression of controversial views. What is the ideal balance between the majority's right to make decisions, directly or through its representatives, and the individual's right to dissent? When constituencies clash over what should be taught or published, whose views prevail or should prevail, and on what basis? If decisions reflect the interplay of multiple constituencies, how should the control be shared? The answers to such questions are likely to be different for elementary and secondary (K–12) schools, on the one hand, and universities, on the other. Far from drawing a bright line between them to avoid dealing with these differences, it is imperative that we consider public education as a whole in order to determine how, and how successfully, it deals with controversial ideas at each level. Most significantly, what is it teaching not only about the content of particular disputes but about the best ways to handle differences of opinion on sensitive subjects?

I explore such questions by means of case studies involving four areas of controversy. The first of these is the politically and emotionally charged issue of race, which provides an opportunity to consider what happens when faculty and students say things that conflict, or are perceived to conflict, with important school or university initiatives. Such incidents illustrate the delicate balance between the institution's right to promote certain ideas in its own voice and its obligation to respect academic freedom and the free-speech rights of individuals. The book offers a similar treatment of disputes over the expression of controversial opinions about homosexuality. Following this consideration of matters of personal identity, the discussion moves on to conflicts over the teaching of evolution. How do populism and beliefs about religion affect decisions involving course content, student work, and faculty research? Among other things, the analysis addresses the meaning of religious neutrality in public education and the role of personal belief in dealing with matters that are subject to empirical testing.

The final area of controversy that I discuss is politics—in particular, the accusation that public universities are hotbeds of liberalism in which the academic freedom of conservative faculty and the free-speech rights of conservative students are insufficiently protected. Representative case studies, such as the debate over a legislative proposal known as the Academic Bill of Rights, facilitate an analysis of the allocation and use of power in the academy. To what extent, for instance, do the faculty in particular content areas conflate their own orthodoxy of thought with the definition of the discipline itself? And what rights do students have, or should they have, when instruction conflicts with their personal views? The book concludes with a discussion of *Garcetti v. Ceballos* (2006), a Supreme Court decision that broadened the power of government employers to regulate what employees say in the course of their jobs. The implications of *Garcetti* for professors in public universities and, to a lesser extent, for teachers in K–12 schools loom large in current discussions of academic freedom and free-speech rights in public education.

Although the rulings of federal courts give school and university administrators the authority to discourage controversial speech, we must look elsewhere for the motivations that may impel them to do so. Among the chief culprits is a powerful and growing cultural current that drives political leaders, media voices, and the general public into increasingly polarized positions. Pundits glory in their ability to spin the truth, to promulgate half-truths, and to create unfounded concern, all in the service of bringing about a desired outcome at any cost. Braying, bawling, and name-calling drown out thoughtful discussion, and concessions to fair play are equated with weakness and treachery. Fueling this cultural drive toward polarization is the dismissal of moderation as something other than newsworthy. Reason and open-mindedness do not sell. In this cultural environment, it is not surprising that K–12 school officials, university administrators, political officeholders, and even some faculty and students mistakenly consider vigorous debate to be inherently incompatible with civility, mutual respect, and good order. They may also be influenced by adherents of polarization who seek to squelch any discussion that does not serve the truth as they see it. In either situation, the fundamental fallacy is the belief that controversy weakens an educational system by distracting students and faculty from pursuing appropriate educational goals. Controversy is, in reality, one of the pillars on which the advancement of knowledge rests.

To be sure, it is possible to be so open-minded that one's brains fall out, but the willingness to hear all sides of an argument and to concede a seat at the table to those with whom one disagrees is not in itself a character flaw or evidence of mental weakness. There is no inconsistency in holding—and upholding—an opinion without ridiculing, minimizing, or suppressing opposing views. The difficulty of implementing that philosophy in public schools and even in universities—and indeed, there is some doubt about whether it is possible to do so—makes an informed understanding of academic freedom and free speech more essential today than ever before. Only when we come to grips with the issues underlying the treatment of controversial expression throughout our system of public education, kindergarten through graduate school, can we hope to explore the implications of existing policies and practices for the development of future generations and for this nation's commitment to providing world-class education.

ACKNOWLEDGMENTS

AS A PROFESSOR IN A PUBLIC UNIVERSITY, even more than as the author of this book, I am grateful to the American Association of University Professors (AAUP) for its long and effective advocacy for a view of higher education in which faculty bear the primary responsibility for teaching and scholarship and have a voice in academic decisionmaking. From Edwin R. A. Seligman, chair of the committee that produced the *Declaration of Principles on Academic Freedom and Academic Tenure* in 1915 to Robert M. O'Neil, chair of the subcommittee that wrote *Protecting an Independent Faculty Voice* in 2009, nationally renowned scholars have found in the AAUP an avenue for leadership in the advancement of academic freedom. On more than one level, it is their work that has made this book possible.

I would also like to thank the English Department at the University of Delaware for its long-standing, if sometimes bemused, support of my choice of a scholarly career outside traditional literary studies. In addition to accepting such work in fulfillment of my research obligations, my colleagues have provided encouragement in such forms as travel funds and opportunities to teach my scholarship. That is, alas, not yet an industry standard, and I feel fortunate to be experiencing it. With respect to this particular book, I thank the department as a whole and its 2004–9 chair, Stephen A. Bernhardt, for myriad forms of collegiality and support.

The opinions expressed in this book are those of the author, who does not speak for the University of Delaware.

1

A Seat at the Table

Coercion is natural; freedom is artificial. Freedoms are socially engineered spaces in which parties engaged in specified pursuits enjoy protection from parties who would otherwise naturally seek to interfere in those pursuits. One person's freedom is therefore always another person's restriction: we would not have even the concept of freedom if the reality of coercion were not already present.

— Louis Menand, "The Limits of Academic Freedom"

IF "[O]NE PERSON'S FREEDOM IS . . . always another person's restriction," as Louis Menand suggested, then any discussion of *what* academic freedom is must consider *whose* it is. The invocation of academic freedom signals a claim to control the parameters of discourse: not only the right to determine whether certain material should be included but also the authority to establish the principles on which such decisions are to be made. Inevitably, the efforts of any constituency or individual to exercise control can be successful only at the expense of competitors whose understanding of academic freedom would produce a different result.

Even the definition of academic freedom reflects a struggle among constituencies. As a term of art, it applies to universities and university faculty.[1] The extent to which it is constitutionally protected is open to discussion, but it is firmly established as a professional standard. Its underlying premise is that in any system of higher education that aspires to be a world leader, decisions about what and how to teach, how to conduct research and interpret the results, and how to evaluate scholarly or creative work must be made by specialists in the relevant fields rather than by university officials, state legislators, or other nonexperts. For the same reason, academic freedom also protects the right of faculty within a university to share in its governance, which may include voting on such matters as the appointment of department chairs, the hiring of new faculty members, and decisions about promotion and tenure. Used in this sense, it does not apply to teachers in elementary or secondary (K–12) schools or to students at any level, nor does it extend to parents, politicians, taxpayers, advocacy groups, or community activists.

As a matter of general usage, the term "academic freedom" is employed much more comprehensively. Its most obvious use is to describe the ability of K–12 teachers to exercise their professional discretion in teaching, interacting with students, and carrying out other elements of their jobs. The term is also applied to the ability of students to say what they like, to influence their instruction, and to receive information. Most extensively, it is used to describe any constituency's claim to freedom of speech with respect to any education-related matter. As its scope broadens, this popular understanding of academic freedom becomes indistinguishable from generic free-speech rights, and its only function is to signify that the topic of discussion involves some aspect of education. The academic freedom of university professors is rooted in the social benefits to be gained from the unfettered exercise of their content-area expertise, and its use with respect to K–12 teachers is based on their pedagogical and academic background. By contrast, claims to academic freedom by students and the general public rest primarily on the assertion that the claimant has the same right as anyone else to express and receive ideas.

What's in a Name?

In view of the tangle of meanings attached to the concept of academic freedom, the first order of business must be to sort out the terminology. Limiting academic freedom to universities and excluding K–12 schools— particularly when that is done by scholars who are themselves professors— is, of course, vulnerable to the accusation of professorial snobbery. In reality, however, it reflects genuine differences inherent in the two kinds of academic employment. Although some senior-high-school honors classes may approach and indeed reach the university level in content and technique, K–12 public schools as a whole transmit well-known and well-established information, and they foster critical and interpretive skills at a level appropriate for children who are younger than college students and who display a wider range of academic proficiency. Public schools are also tasked with inculcating "community values"—that is, whatever ideals the school board endorses as long as their promotion in public schools is not unconstitutional, as religious indoctrination would be. The governance structure of these schools is based on a long-standing conviction that public elementary and secondary education should reflect the will of the people as carried out by representatives who are answerable, directly or indirectly, to the voters. Accordingly, the authority to decide what is taught in K–12 public schools rests not with individual teachers nor with the faculty as a whole but with school boards that are either elected or appointed by elected officials.

To be sure, teachers in some districts may be so intimately involved in selecting instructional materials, developing and revising curricula, and implementing teaching methodologies that, collectively if not individually, they have effective control of instruction. Some school boards may also encourage teachers to generate, disseminate, and experiment with new ideas in the pedagogy of their fields and may even release teachers from some of their classroom obligations for this purpose. If, however, conditions within a district alter—perhaps because the demographics of the local population change, because a new superintendent or school board takes office, because an activist community group targets a particular issue, or because new conditions are attached to eligibility for federal funding—the fact that ultimate authority rests with the board may become all too clear. When lawsuits concerning the control of educational content reach the courts, teachers may be astonished to learn that state and local school boards can indeed tell them what to teach and how to teach it.

The situation is different in public universities because their core functions within the society are different. University students, most of whom are legally adult, are presumed to be less impressionable and more capable of dealing with controversial and complex ideas than are K–12 students. No one is forced to attend any particular institution or even to enroll in college, and students choose their own majors and many of their own courses or sections of courses. University professors as a group hold more advanced degrees than K–12 teachers do, and they present their disciplines at a higher level. Moreover, although academic freedom applies to university faculty as teachers, it arose out of their role as researchers. Unlike K–12 schools, universities are expected to develop new knowledge and to produce the next generation of experts whose task it will be to carry on the questioning, challenging, and debating necessary to advance human understanding. For this reason, university faculty who are experts in their fields—*because* they are experts in their fields—have responsibility for shaping and carrying out their research programs, disseminating the results, and determining what and how to teach within their areas of expertise. They are also expected to push the boundaries of orthodoxy and accepted knowledge and to experiment with cutting-edge concepts that may cause discomfort to other experts and possibly to some segments of the public. To fulfill these responsibilities, they must be free to pursue truth wherever they believe it may lead, to disseminate what is learned, and to debate about the meaning and significance of new information in order to determine what is able to withstand informed challenge and what must fall to better arguments. Guarantees of academic freedom are not meant to provide privilege or status to professors but to create the conditions that enable universities to fulfill functions that differ materially from those of K–12 education.

Because academic freedom carries a substantive meaning in relation to universities that is not paralleled in K–12 schools, I use that term in its specialized sense except when quoting or paraphrasing the statements of other people. The ability of K–12 teachers to make their own decisions about what and how to teach and about other aspects of their jobs is described as the exercise of professional discretion. For the same reasons, I do not apply the term "academic freedom" to the free expression of students, politicians, advocacy groups, community activists, parents, and other members of the public. The intent is not to deny or minimize their undoubted right to free speech but to be clear about what is at issue in each situation. Indicating that a particular statement does not fall under the heading of academic freedom does not suggest either that the speech is of low value or that it does not enjoy constitutional protection.

In view of these differences, it is not surprising that the academic freedom of university faculty, the professional discretion of K–12 teachers, and the free-speech rights of students and others are not often discussed in the same scholarly works. More commonly, books and articles delve into such elements as the background, legal standing, and political status of one of these constituencies, referencing the others—if at all—to provide points of comparison and contrast. Although there is much to be said for this approach as a means of exploring case law and public policy in each area, there is also room for a more comprehensive discussion of the expression of controversial ideas in the curriculum, in faculty research, and in other campus speech by faculty and students at all levels. Differences between various constituencies and academic environments, no matter how significant in themselves, should not be permitted to obscure the interconnectedness and interdependence of public education as a whole. The vast majority of students in public universities have experienced K–12 public education, and an important function of public universities is to prepare teachers for K–12 public schools. More fundamentally, public education as a social institution, wholly or partially supported by public funds and regulated to a greater or lesser extent by elected officials, represents certain cultural values and imperatives. Important among these is the need to deal effectively and equitably with the intense differences of opinion that are the inevitable product of a society that is at once free and highly diverse.

As the epigraph by Menand indicates, conflicts over what may or must be said in the context of public education reflect a perception on the part of each participating constituency that its claim to control the discourse trumps the claims of other constituencies. Michael A. Olivas suggested that "how one characterizes classroom interactions is akin to turning a kaleidoscope in the light: From one perspective it is a professor's autonomy to teach how she sees fit; from another it is a student's right to learn in an environment free of harassing behavior; from yet another it is the Dean's duty to ensure that appropriate instruction is taking place; and finally, it may be the accrediting agency's responsibility to maintain uniform standards across institutions."[2] To the extent that one constituency prevails in a given situation, the others will almost inevitably feel that what they are likely to call their academic freedom, used in this context to describe the right to prevail in an education-related matter, is not adequately recognized.

Consider, for instance, disputes involving two science teachers, Roger DeHart and Rodney LeVake. Both taught biology in public high schools in the late 1990s, DeHart in the state of Washington and LeVake in Minnesota. Both challenged the theory of evolution and wished to present other explanations more in keeping with their religious views. Both stated that as qualified professionals, they were empowered to decide how to interpret their content field to their students. They also maintained that their academic freedom and that of their students required the presentation of alternatives to evolution.

As soon as these disputes became public, several constituencies came forward to challenge the teachers' claim that the right to determine what to teach rested with them. Prominent among these constituencies were national organizations representing the mainstream scientific community, which routinely interjects itself into disputes about science instruction by asserting something similar to control of a brand name. Accordingly, the National Academy of Sciences, the American Association for the Advancement of Science, and the National Center for Science Education denied that DeHart and LeVake had the authority to teach nontestable, supernatural explanations of the ultimate cause of life in biology classes.[3] In their view, such theories have a place in religion, philosophy, or social studies classes; indeed, they may even be true. Nevertheless, these organizations maintain, it is demonstrably incorrect and not a matter of viewpoint or opinion to describe such concepts as science. Parents in each of the affected school districts also joined the fray. Some of these parents allied themselves with the mainstream scientific community, asserting that their children's academic freedom included the right to learn accepted scientific theory and method. Others defined academic freedom in terms of participatory democracy: since evolution is presented in most biology classes, it is only fair to include opposing views.

In each of these disputes, the constituency that prevailed was the local school board. Based on decisions made or endorsed by each board, DeHart and LeVake were restricted in their teaching and removed from courses that included evolution. LeVake, represented by attorneys from the American Center for Law and Justice, sued on the ground that by preventing him from sharing his views on evolution with his students, school officials had violated his rights to free speech and freedom of religion.[4] The decision of the Court of Appeals of Minnesota was so predictable as to be, in some ways, the least interesting element of this discussion: "LeVake's responsibility as a public school teacher to teach evolution in the manner prescribed by the curriculum overrides his First Amendment rights as a private citizen."[5] This outcome was based on the well-established premise that school boards enjoy broad authority to determine the curriculum for K–12 schools as long as they do not stray into unconstitutional waters. Nevertheless, acknowledging the school board's legal right to have the final word does not preclude discussion of the procedures and priorities that should contribute to shaping that word. In addition to considering what the courts have said, it is important to reflect upon the logical and practical considerations involved in determining whose voices should be heard and heeded in order to foster the academic rigor and the free play of ideas appropriate to each level of American public education.

The Zen of Cat Herding

Histories of education sometimes trace the notion of unfettered inquiry back to Socrates, although at least in the short term, the outcome of his endeavors was not encouraging. By contrast, even the most draconian modern administrators recognize that poisoning the faculty, tempting as the prospect might appear, is likely to be considered excessive. A more immediate progenitor of the contemporary concept of academic freedom was Charles Darwin, whose work was a key factor in bringing about a widespread change in the understanding of research and of knowledge itself. The scientific revolution associated with Darwin took scientific inquiry out of the reach of amateurs, making it the province of highly educated specialists. Over time, experts in all academic disciplines joined their scientific brethren in declaring that university-level academic work must be assessed by peers in the field because administrators, trustees, and other nonexperts lack the background to understand it. Moreover, teaching and research must be disinterested in the sense that they represent the true state of knowledge at any given time. Ideas should not be gerrymandered, exaggerated, or suppressed to reinforce an ideological preconception or to justify a particular practical outcome.

The leading exponent of academic freedom in American universities is the American Association of University Professors (AAUP), a university faculty union whose stated purpose is "to advance academic freedom and shared governance, to define fundamental professional values and standards for higher education, and to ensure higher education's contribution to the common good."[6] Shortly after its foundation in 1915, the AAUP declared that the ability of professors to carry out their duty to their institutions and to society at large "requires that our universities shall be so free that no fair-minded person shall find any excuse for even a suspicion that the utterances of university teachers are shaped or restricted by the judgment, not of professional scholars, but of inexpert and possibly not wholly disinterested persons outside of their ranks."[7] The principles of academic freedom enunciated in several successive AAUP documents are incorporated into faculty contracts or university policy statements in the vast majority of secular universities, public or private, and in many religious institutions.[8] Indeed, in the absence of a commitment to free inquiry, it is difficult to see how a twenty-first-century university could credibly seek recognition as an intellectual leader.

Ronald Dworkin, a prominent philosopher of law, elaborated upon one of the AAUP's justifications for academic freedom when he observed that professors "are less likely to act from nakedly political or ideological motives than are those whose power it insulates them from."[9] If this system worked perfectly, university faculty would function as highly qualified and disinterested knowledge-seekers, tolerant of dissent and error within reasonable bounds and open to new ideas. In my own academic career, I have seen some of my colleagues go to great lengths in a sincere effort to meet those expectations. Nevertheless, professors are no more immune to human failings than administrators are, and the line between defining a discipline and establishing an orthodoxy is a fine one.

Under the current understanding of academic freedom, the faculty in each discipline are entrusted with the authority to determine its scope and its acceptable methodologies; to screen candidates for graduate study and thus for admission to the profession; to decide as peer reviewers whether scholarship is worthy of being published or presented at academic conferences; and to participate significantly in hiring, retaining, promoting, and dismissing faculty. Clearly, these decisions must rest on commonly understood standards and expectations. Otherwise, the assessment of excellence and even the definition of the discipline itself would vary wildly with personal and regional preferences. More significantly, there would be nothing resembling the rigorous quality control necessary to sustain credibility and progress within an academic field. Nevertheless, in the name of maintaining high standards, professors may fall into the error of defining "good" work as that which conforms to patterns of thought or methodology that are not inherent in the discipline but merely represent the assumptions of the majority. As Louis Menand pithily observed, "Giving departments and disciplines the freedom to determine their own course of action means giving professors the freedom to interfere with one another's professional designs."[10] Even more pithily, he commented, "Disciplinarity makes us stupid."[11]

Prominent among scholars who address the effects of professorial choice on the shape of academic disciplines is Cary Nelson, Jubilee Professor of Liberal Arts and Sciences and professor of English at the University of Illinois at Urbana-Champaign and, at this writing, president of the AAUP. Like numerous other English professors, Nelson proposes the addition of certain works or types of works to the so-called literary canon based on a broadening and democratization of the standards by which literature is judged. Beyond that, however, he treats the disciplinary struggles within his own content area not as an end in themselves but as a springboard to a fuller discussion of the politics and practices of American higher education. "I use my own discipline of English simultaneously as a representative case and as an exaggerated instance of forces at work widely in the humanities and throughout higher education," wrote Nelson. "More narrowly, I also use my own period specialization in modern American poetry repeatedly to show how a faculty member's teaching and historical research can have wider social implications and can be positioned in relation to contemporary debates."[12]

The dynamics of struggles such as those Nelson addresses within the field of English studies may be seen in a similar tug-of-war being conducted in university history departments. This debate is outlined here with an apology for the oversimplification that is inseparable from the need for brevity. On one side of this debate are traditional historians who believe that the discipline should continue to focus on events of national and world significance. The resulting emphasis on the activities of rich white males arises not from bias, they assert, but from objectivity. As a matter of inescapable historical truth, those were the people who participated in events critical to shaping the past and the present. It is this consideration, not a desire to favor any race, gender, or socioeconomic standing, that should drive decisions about what is worthy of scholarly study or of inclusion in the curriculum. With respect to the methodology of their discipline, traditional historians maintain that historical analysis should be based on a disinterested assessment of the available materials and not on a desire to promote any political or social ideology.

On the other side are social historians who focus on previously unrepresented or underrepresented groups, such as racial minorities, women, homosexuals, and the poor. In their view, the reflection of a political viewpoint in historical analysis is not only appropriate but unavoidable. What passes for a lack of ideology, they maintain, is in fact the promotion of traditional, conservative attitudes so deeply ingrained in the culture as to simulate neutrality. As this argument suggests, the two camps also disagree about whether there is any such thing as genuinely objective fact or truth. The question of academic freedom arises because each side accuses the other of bias in making hiring and promotion decisions, directing the work of graduate students, and evaluating material submitted for publication or for presentation at conferences. Consequently, each side sees itself as struggling to avoid being shut out of the kinds of activities necessary to build and maintain an academic career.

In an essay entitled "The New Advocacy and the Old," Gertrude Him-melfarb spoke as a traditional historian faced with a redefinition of her discipline's content and methodology. In her view, the primary threat that social historians represent is not that they study previously ignored populations but that they advance an ideological view of traditional history as "a reflection of the power structure, of the 'hegemonic' interests of the dominant class." Accordingly, she maintained, social historians reject not only the popes-and-kings approach to history but also the work of historians who wish to write about disadvantaged groups "in the traditional scholarly manner, as disinterested history rather than as an ideological cause—to be scholars rather than advocates." She laid the blame for these changes on the postmodernist movement, which "made advocacy seem more than a political ploy and gave it intellectual credibility and respectability." Specifically, she argued, postmodernists deny that "there is any such thing as knowledge, truth, reason, or objectivity." Instead, they suggest that those ideals are "not only unattainable but undesirable—that they are indeed authoritarian and repressive." In her view, this skepticism about the existence of objective truth is yet another example of an ideology based on "[t]he suspicion of reason as 'phallocentric,' of logic as 'logocentric,' of objectivity as 'patriarchal' or 'masculinist.'"[13]

Representing the other side of the debate is Joan W. Scott, a social historian who rejects what she views as the dominance of a traditional, androcentric model of historical analysis. Taking issue with the underlying assumptions of the AAUP statements of 1915 and 1940, she maintains that the absence of control by university administrators or by outside forces benefits the majority of professors within the discipline and militates against those whose work displeases the majority. "[T]he inseparable other side of that regulatory and enabling authority is that it ensures consensus by exclusion," she wrote. "And the grounds for exclusion can be, historically have been, *difference*—difference from some representative type . . . or difference from the reigning philosophical and methodological assumptions (about causality, say, or intentionality, or the transparency of fact in the writing of history)." In particular, she argued, caricaturing and denigrating postmodernism is intended to devalue the work of social historians and so to "bar from the field critics of foundational disciplinary premises." She found it particularly ironic when "the tables are sometimes turned as the defenders of orthodoxy invoke the protection of academic freedom against [their own] internal critics as if the critics were outsiders, effectively banishing them."[14]

This juxtaposition of Himmelfarb's essay with Scott's makes it clear that assigning decisions about research and teaching to specialists in the field does not ensure results that everyone will consider fair and neutral. Appropriately enough, the academic culture that arose from the Darwinian revolution depends quite a bit on the survival of the fittest, as anyone who attends English Department meetings can attest. It is unquestionably competitive, not only on an individual level but also with respect to warring viewpoints and subspecialties. Nevertheless, some of the disputes discussed in this book demonstrate instances in which those dynamics operate more even-handedly than either Himmelfarb or Scott acknowledged. "Many people feel, of course, that the machinery is not working properly because the professors no longer play fairly with one another, and work that doesn't fit the reigning paradigms doesn't get rewarded," Louis Menand wrote. "But work that doesn't fit the reigning paradigms has never been rewarded until it succeeds in persuading enough practitioners of its superiority to the work that does."[15] Whether this system is the best way to operationalize academic freedom at the university level is a matter for later discussion. At this point, the intent is merely to ensure that the terms of engagement are clear.

Although university faculty are generally at liberty to pursue their research and teaching subject to quality control by peers in their fields, two limitations should be noted: faculty do not govern all academic decisions, and the autonomy that they possess under the aegis of academic freedom is not infrequently challenged. State legislatures, which have the power to establish public colleges and universities, may define the intellectual scope and focus of such institutions; for instance, they may choose to found an agricultural college, a technical college, or a liberal arts school. They may also place legitimate conditions on state funding of higher education, such as stipulating that certain subsidies are to be used to promote study in a particular field. Under the principles of academic freedom as defined by the AAUP, state legislatures should not attempt to use their power of the purse to determine what professors may or may not teach or write, but not everyone shares the AAUP's view. In 2002, for instance, the Missouri state legislature cut the budget of the University of Missouri–Kansas City (UMKC) by $50,000 in retaliation for an article published in the *Journal of Homosexuality* by Harris Mirkin, an associate professor in the Political Science Department.[16] The measure's legislative sponsor, Representative Mark Wright (R–District 137), initially attempted to reduce the appropriation by more than $100,000—the estimated cost of Mirkin's salary and benefits. To

Wright's outspoken dismay, the university chancellor sided with the professor, and a subsequent effort to persuade the university's board to overrule the chancellor and dismiss Mirkin was equally unsuccessful.

Whereas state legislators bent on penalizing individual professors must generally pursue their goals by attempting to influence university officials, the officials themselves retain direct authority over many academic decisions even if they observe the AAUP standards of academic freedom. The degree of faculty involvement in university governance varies from one institution to another, but it is not unusual for faculty committees to make recommendations rather than binding decisions about hiring, promotion, tenure, and dismissal. These faculty recommendations carry sufficient weight to cause comment if they are disregarded without demonstrably good cause, and AAUP standards require that the reasons for overriding a faculty vote be clearly explained. Nevertheless, the final decision rests with the administration. Administrators may also influence faculty activity by reducing or eliminating programs, moving departments from one college to another, or changing faculty assignments. Nevertheless, direct attempts to regulate the content of teaching or research are usually blocked. In a case in point, a philosophy professor at the City College of New York was sanctioned for publications suggesting that intelligence varies with race. He sued in federal court and won. Similarly, when administrators at the University of Delaware attempted to prevent two education professors from receiving grants for work on race-based intelligence, an arbitrator upheld the faculty.

Elementary, My Dear Watson—and Secondary

Almost nothing that has been said so far applies to the likely conduct or outcome of disputes involving teachers in K–12 schools, whose work is subject to a high degree of regulation by school boards. As Donald Uerling summarized the situation in a 2000 article, "No court has found that public school teachers' First Amendment rights extend to choosing their own curriculum or classroom management techniques in contravention of school policy or dictates. Although teachers' out-of-class conduct, including their advocacy of particular teaching methods, is protected by the Constitution, their in-class pedagogical method is not protected by academic freedom."[17]

Justifications offered for this governance structure include the facts that K–12 students are young and impressionable, that school attendance is compulsory in elementary and secondary schools, and that students may have little if any choice about the school they attend or the classes they take. The high attrition rate among teachers increases the proportion of inexperienced personnel, and teacher shortages may result in the desperation-driven hiring of people who have not completed full or rigorous preparation programs. At best, K–12 teachers, as a group, have significantly less education than do university professors, particularly in the content fields they teach. The fundamental conceptualization and organization of K–12 public schools, which transcend any of these practical considerations, define them as instruments of the public and subject to the public will.

For all of these reasons, it makes sense for school boards, either elected or appointed by elected officials, to have authority over curriculum and other school-related speech. Nevertheless, from a policy perspective, there is a balance to be struck between these factors and the advantages to be gained when qualified and experienced K–12 teachers are able to exercise some degree of professional discretion in determining how to achieve the goals of K–12 education. As Kevin G. Welner observed, "If we accept the traditional view of schools as a vehicle for inculcating youth to accept shared values and norms . . . then we are likely to assign teachers a role with limited discretion and autonomy. If, however, we hold a more dynamic view of schools and society, we may see the need for greater teacher discretion and greater First Amendment protection. For instance, we may value the teaching of critical thinking or teacher professionalism and teacher-initiated innovation."[18] Donald Uerling made a similar point. "A teacher's 'academic freedom' in K–12 schools, as grounded in the First Amendment, is more myth than reality," he wrote. "Clearly, school officials have great constitutional latitude to regulate a teacher's academic expression in the school environment. But school boards and administrators must always be mindful that what is legally permissible may not always be educationally sound. Their rhetoric about the professionalism of teachers must be matched by their respect for the unique talents that teachers bring to their classrooms."[19]

Critics of the public schools also suggest that a school board's tight control of teachers' speech may be unfair to constituencies other than teachers. Welner, for instance, discussed the discontent of parents, particularly those in minority communities, who believe that the political clout necessary to have one's views represented in board-approved messages is not equally shared. Despite the appearance of democratic process in the exercise of authority by a school board that is directly or indirectly answerable to the voters, minorities may be marginalized if nothing can be said in the schools that differs from the majoritarian orthodoxy. Another consideration was raised by Karen C. Daly, who suggested that the rigid exercise of school-board control over teacher speech does a disservice to the students. "The right to hear contains two related components: the right of students to avoid indoctrination and the right to be exposed to a variety of ideas and viewpoints during the course of their education. Protection of teacher speech prevents the first right from being violated and enables the second right to be realized."[20]

Despite the reservations expressed by advocates of free speech for teachers, the school boards' authority to govern rests firmly on a long series of legal decisions. Such decisions typically reference the First Amendment to the U.S. Constitution, which states: "Congress shall make no law respecting an establishment of religion, or prohibiting the free exercise thereof; *or abridging the freedom of speech,* or of the press; or the right of the people peaceably to assemble, and to petition the Government for a redress of grievances" (emphasis added). The italicized portion, known as the Free Speech Clause, differs in its application depending on the nature of the speech, the identity of the speaker, and the circumstances under which it is uttered.[21] In the context of the present discussion, the salient distinction is that K–12 teachers cannot invoke their First Amendment right to free speech as individuals as a means of substituting their own judgment for that of the school board with respect to curriculum, teaching methods, or other aspects of K–12 instruction.

Underlying the authority of school boards is the premise that the messages delivered in K–12 public schools constitute the state's speech, not that of individual teachers. Among the many decisions that illustrate this point is *Miles v. Denver Public Schools* (1991). The case began when a ninth-grade student asked John Miles, a social studies teacher, whether the school had changed over time. Miles replied that the school was less clean and discipline more relaxed than in earlier years. As an example, he referred to a rumor that two students, one of whom he named, had engaged in a romantic tryst on the tennis court at lunchtime. The students involved in that incident and their parents complained to school officials, and Miles was placed on a four-day paid administrative leave while the district investigated. A letter of reprimand subsequently placed in his personnel file stated that his remark "displayed poor judgment" and that the alleged activity "was an inappropriate topic for comment in a classroom setting." He was warned to "refrain from commenting on any items which might reflect negatively on any individual members of our student body."[22] He sued, claiming that he had a right under the First Amendment to express his views in response to the student's question. The federal district court granted summary judgment in favor of the Denver school district, and the U.S. Court of Appeals for the Tenth Circuit agreed.

The basis for the outcome in *Miles* was a Supreme Court decision, *Hazelwood School District v. Kuhlmeier* (1988), upholding a high school principal's authority to censor stories written by students for the school newspaper. According to *Hazelwood*, school officials may control student speech that meets two standards: it is, or reasonably appears to be, sponsored by the school; and the school officials' actions "are reasonably related to legitimate pedagogical concerns."[23] On this basis, the Tenth Circuit decision in *Miles* states, "We are convinced that if students' expression in a school newspaper bears the imprimatur of the school, then a teacher's expression in the 'traditional classroom setting' also bears the imprimatur of the school. Based on the analysis in *Hazelwood*, we conclude Miles' expression during a ninth-grade government class must be treated as school-sponsored expression in a nonpublic forum for First Amendment purposes." Defending the propriety of using a decision that dealt with student speech, the court found "no reason to distinguish between the classroom discussion of students and teachers in applying *Hazelwood* here. A school's interests in regulating classroom speech—such as 'assur[ing] that participants learn whatever lessons the activity is designed to teach' and that students are not 'exposed to material that may be inappropriate for their level of maturity'—are implicated regardless of whether that speech comes from a teacher or student." The court concluded that the letter of reprimand served "legitimate pedagogical purposes," such as requiring teachers to behave in a professional manner, refrain from making statements inappropriate for the audience, respect the privacy of students, and refrain from embarrassing them before their peers. The court dismissed Miles' claim of academic freedom with the blunt statement that "the caselaw does not support Miles' position that a secondary school teacher has a constitutional right to academic freedom."[24]

A second case decided on the basis of *Hazelwood*, *Ward v. Hickey* (1993), arose when Toby Klang Ward, a biology teacher in Belmont, Massachusetts, engaged her ninth-grade students in a discussion of the abortion of fetuses with Down's syndrome. Ward, who was completing her third year as an untenured teacher, had excellent ratings and had already been proposed for reappointment with tenure. Shortly after the discussion of abortion, the school committee tabled the proposal to reappoint, which later failed on a tie vote. Ward filed suit in federal district court, lost, and turned to the U.S. Court of Appeals for the First Circuit. The standard the court applied was that "a school committee may regulate a teacher's classroom speech if: (1) the regulation is reasonably related to a legitimate pedagogical concern; and (2) the school provided the teacher with notice of what conduct was prohibited." Consistent with the Tenth Circuit decision in *Miles,* the First Circuit found that *Hazelwood* may be applied to speech by teachers as well as by students: "Like the newspaper [at issue in *Hazelwood*], a teacher's classroom speech is part of the curriculum. Indeed, a teacher's principal classroom role is to teach students the school curriculum. Thus, schools may reasonably limit teachers' speech in that setting."[25]

By the time the case reached the appeals court, Ward was not asserting that the school committee lacked the authority to exclude speech on abortion from biology classes. Rather, she relied on the premise that, in the court's words, "[e]ven if under [*Hazelwood*] a school may prohibit a teacher's statements before she makes them, however, it is not entitled to retaliate against speech that it never prohibited." The decision adds, "[W]e do not hold that a school must expressly prohibit every imaginable inappropriate conduct by teachers. . . . The relevant inquiry is: based on existing regulations, policies, discussions, and other forms of communication between school administration and teachers, was it reasonable for the school to expect the teacher to know that her conduct was prohibited?"[26] In the end, the court ruled against Ward without deciding that question because Ward had not raised it in a timely manner.

A final example of the use of *Hazelwood* in cases pertaining to the exercise of professional discretion by teachers is *Lacks v. Ferguson Reorganized School District R-2* (1998). Cecilia Lacks, an English teacher in St. Louis, Missouri, permitted the students in her writing classes to use profanity in their work. Divided into small groups, the class wrote and performed several plays, all of which were laced with such words as "fuck," "shit," "nigger," and "bitch." The plays were videotaped, and when the principal heard about the videotapes from a student, he conducted an investigation. Among other things, he discovered that Lacks had also permitted a student to read aloud to the class two profanity-laced, sexually graphic poems that he had written. The school board subsequently dismissed her for persistently violating a school-district policy banning student profanity, and she filed suit.

At the end of the trial in federal district court, a jury found that the school did not have a legitimate pedagogical interest in forbidding the use of pro-

fanity in creative writing assignments. Moreover, it accepted Lacks's assertion "that she thought that the board's policy on profanity applied only to
'student behavior' and not to students' creative assignments. She also argued that her teaching method, which she describes as the 'student-cen-
tered method' and which she explained at length at the hearing, required her
to allow her students creative freedom, which included the use of profanity.
Lacks could not say with certainty that she would be able to teach at Berkeley High School if her students were not given the freedom to use profanity in their creative activities." The U.S. Court of Appeals for the Eighth Circuit reversed both findings. While remarking that school officials might
have imposed a lesser penalty on Lacks, who had taught successfully in the
district since 1972, the court found that "[a] flat prohibition on profanity in
the classroom is reasonably related to the legitimate pedagogical concern of
promoting generally acceptable social standards."[27] The decision also notes
that Lacks had been repeatedly warned about the use of profanity in the
school newspaper, which she moderated, and that signs saying "No Profanity" were posted in her classroom.

The outcomes of *Miles, Ward,* and *Lacks* bear out Neal H. Hutchens' observation that "the degree of protection afforded by courts to teachers under
Hazelwood generally stands far removed from the kinds of speech protections associated with academic freedom. Instead, courts have generally relied on *Hazelwood* as a means to emphasize the authority of school authorities to control teachers' in-class speech."[28] Karen Daly agreed. "The net
effect of *Hazelwood* as applied is the subtle infantilization of teachers," she
wrote. "The expressive rights of teachers are placed on par with those available to students, with school administrators given the power to treat employees as if they were unruly children. . . . [T]he expansive nature of 'legitimate pedagogical concerns' creates the potential for excessive restrictions
as well. As interpreted by the lower courts, *Hazelwood* is increasingly hostile to the idea of teachers as reasonably autonomous professionals."[29]

A second test sometimes employed in cases involving the exercise of professional discretion by K–12 teachers derives from two Supreme Court decisions, *Pickering v. Board of Education* (1968) and *Connick v. Myers* (1983).
Marvin L. Pickering, a public-school teacher, wrote a letter to the editor of a
local newspaper criticizing the school board for spending too much money
on athletics and not enough on academics. The letter was written shortly
after the voters defeated a referendum to increase school taxes. The school
board, claiming that Pickering's assertions were false, dismissed him on

the ground that his letter had hampered the school district's ability to fulfill its functions. Ruling in favor of Pickering, the Supreme Court rejected the premise "that teachers may constitutionally be compelled to relinquish the First Amendment rights they would otherwise enjoy as citizens to comment on matters of public interest in connection with the operation of the public schools in which they work." Indeed, since teachers are likely to be well informed on this topic, "it is essential that they be able to speak out freely on such questions without fear of retaliatory dismissal."[30] Of particular importance was the Court's observation that "in a case such as the present one, in which *the fact of employment is only tangentially and insubstantially involved in the subject matter of the public communication made by a teacher,* we conclude that it is necessary to regard the teacher as the member of the general public he seeks to be" (emphasis added).[31] As the Court made clear, *Pickering* protects the right of public employees to speak freely on matters of public concern when they do so as citizens, outside the scope of the activities they undertake in return for their paychecks. Pickering's classroom speech and other job-related duties were not at issue.

With respect to the school board's claims, the Court weighed the need to keep the schools running smoothly against Pickering's interest in speaking out on a matter of public concern. It found that neither Pickering's accurate statements nor those he made in error substantially interfered with the functioning of the schools. Moreover, since his comments did not hinder his own performance or affect anyone with whom he regularly worked, his ability to do his job was not impaired. Under these circumstances, the Court concluded that "the interest of the school administration in limiting teachers' opportunities to contribute to public debate is not significantly greater than its interest in limiting a similar contribution by any member of the general public." The Court also observed that if the school board believed "that even comments on matters of public concern that are substantially correct . . . may furnish grounds for dismissal if they are sufficiently critical in tone, we unequivocally reject it."[32]

Fifteen years after *Pickering,* the Supreme Court decided *Connick v. Myers.* The case arose when an assistant district attorney, objecting to a transfer imposed on her by her supervisors, circulated a questionnaire soliciting her coworkers' views on their office's employment practices. When she was subsequently dismissed, her supervisors told her that although the primary reason was her refusal to accept the transfer, the questionnaire was also a factor. She thereupon sued, claiming that her right to distribute the questionnaire was protected under *Pickering*. The Supreme Court ruled against her. In the Court's view, only one item on the questionnaire—an inquiry concerning coerced participation in political campaigns—was of public concern. Other than that, the Court found, Connick's questioning of her supervisors' actions represented a matter of personal interest and was subject to discipline if her employer had reasonable cause to believe that it might interfere with the smooth working of the office. Compared with *Pickering*, *Connick* narrowed the range of speech deemed to be a matter of public concern, proportionately increasing the range of speech subject to regulation by the government employer.

Obviously, neither *Pickering* nor *Myers* is a perfect match for lawsuits involving claims by teachers that the First Amendment protects their in-class statements, selection of instructional materials, teaching methods, remarks to students, or decisions as moderators of extracurricular activities. The distinguishing element of *Pickering* is that it concerns something a teacher said as a private citizen outside the scope of his employment, and *Myers* did not address public schools at all. Nevertheless, a test derived from combining these two decisions is often employed in cases involving the professional discretion of K–12 teachers. Under the *Pickering/Connick* test, the speech of public employees may be constitutionally protected if it relates to a matter of public concern as defined in *Connick* and if, as in *Pickering*, the employee's free-speech rights are deemed to outweigh the employer's interest in maintaining the efficient functioning of the government entity. This test is sometimes applied in conjunction with another Supreme Court precedent, *Mt. Healthy City School District Board of Education v. Doyle* (1977). Under *Mt. Healthy*, even if public employees can demonstrate that speech covered by the First Amendment was a factor in an adverse job action, the employer can still prevail by showing that the action would have occurred for other reasons in the absence of the protected speech.

Among the K–12 cases decided under *Pickering/Connick* was *Kirkland v. Northside Independent School District* (1989), filed by an untenured high school teacher whose contract was not renewed. Timothy Kirkland taught history in San Antonio, Texas, for two years. School officials declined to renew his contract for a third year, citing poor teaching performance. Kirkland maintained that the real reason for his dismissal was his use of an unapproved supplemental reading list in his world history classes. Although the district provided both a reading list of its own and a procedure for requesting approval for alternate lists, Kirkland used neither. When he was notified of the nonrenewal of his contract, he sued on the ground that school officials were violating his free-speech rights by firing him for using an unapproved reading list. He maintained that the list constituted protected speech because it dealt with a matter of public concern: "blatant censorship of his ideological views. . . . Specifically, plaintiff urges that school officials cannot squelch nonconforming view-points regarding what should be taught in public classrooms."[33]

When Kirkland prevailed in a jury trial in federal district court, the school district took the case to the U.S. Court of Appeals for the Fifth Circuit. Citing *Connick*, the appeals court found that Kirkland's use of an unapproved reading list in his world history classes did not constitute speaking out on a matter of public concern. In response to his allegation that the matter of public concern was censorship by the school district, the court pointed out that school officials had not had any opportunity either to censor or to approve his reading list because he had not submitted it to them. Moreover, the court noted, many of the works on the list, which consisted almost entirely of fiction, were part of the English curriculum and already available in the school. The court further observed that Kirkland had said nothing about censorship until after he had been notified of the nonrenewal of his contract. "Contrary to Kirkland's suggestion," the decision states, "this case fails to present a matter of public concern with respect to censorship of reading material or a teacher's 'academic freedom.' Although the concept of academic freedom has been recognized in our jurisprudence, the doctrine has never conferred upon teachers the control of public school curricula."[34] Because Kirkland failed to show that he had spoken as a citizen on a matter of public concern, there was no need to balance his free-speech interest against the interests of the school district in establishing and enforcing procedures for the development of class reading lists.

Kirkland served as a precedent for another decision, *Boring v. Buncombe County Board of Education* (1998), which employed both *Hazelwood* and *Pickering/Connick* as precedents. Margaret Boring, who taught high school drama in Black Mountain, North Carolina, selected a controversial play, *Independence*, for use by her students. Written by Lee Blessing, the play depicts a dysfunctional family of daughters coping with a neurotic mother. When Boring's students performed it in a regional competition, they won seventeen of the twenty-one available awards. They subsequently performed it again for an English class at the school. A parent objected to its content, which prompted the principal to read the play. Having done so, his first response was to forbid the students to perform *Independence* at the state competition. Later, faced with protests from the parents of the student actors, he agreed to allow the play to be performed on condition that certain parts of it be omitted. The students went on to win second place at the state competition. Following another dispute with Boring over damage to a stage floor, the principal asked the superintendent of schools to transfer her to another school. The superintendent did so, citing her violation of the district policy relating to the selection of controversial material. Boring protested that at the time she selected the play, the policy pertained only to the choice of instructional materials for the classroom; dramatic performances were added later.

When an appeal to the board of education was unsuccessful, Boring sued on the ground that "her transfer was in retaliation for expression of unpopular views through the production of the play and thus in violation of her right to freedom of speech." The federal district court upheld the school officials, and the U.S. Court of Appeals for the Fourth Circuit agreed. Based on the definition of curriculum in *Hazelwood,* the court determined that the performance of the play qualified as part of the curriculum and that it could reasonably be perceived as a school-sponsored and school-approved activity. The court also found that "[t]he makeup of the curriculum of Owen High School is by definition a legitimate pedagogical concern. . . . If the performance of a play under the auspices of the school and which is part of the curriculum of the school, is not by definition a legitimate pedagogical concern, we do not know what could be." Having made this determination, the court cited *Connick* as the basis for ruling that Boring's situation "does not present a matter of public concern and is nothing more than an ordinary employment dispute. That being so, [Boring] has no First Amendment rights derived from the selection of the play *Independence.*"[35]

A similar line of reasoning applies to situations in which school authorities mandate or proscribe certain curricular materials or teaching methods. A case in point is *Bradley v. Pittsburgh Board of Education* (1990). Earl Bradley, a high school teacher in the Pittsburgh school district, developed a teaching technique known as Learnball. Bradley asserted that its purposes included student engagement, teamwork, and the promotion of classroom discipline and morale. It involved "a sports format, peer approval, dividing each class into teams, student election of team leaders and an assistant teacher, giving students responsibility for establishing class rules and grading exercises, and imposing a system of rewards such as radio playing and shooting baskets with a foam ball in the classroom."[36] Following a protracted battle with school authorities over his use of this method, Bradley was dismissed, and he failed in his legal attempt to win reinstatement.

Another teacher in the Pittsburgh school district, Diane Murray, also an advocate of Learnball, was told by school authorities to cease using that teaching method. She filed suit with Bradley as co-plaintiff, alleging that she had an academic-freedom right to use Learnball. Although she did not challenge the school board's authority to determine curriculum, she said that her use of Learnball did not affect the curriculum because it was a method of classroom management that could be applied to any content. She also alleged that her use of Learnball was a way "to express her positive personality, feelings, and philosophy to her students. In that regard . . . Learnball is a political statement on Murray's part." The U.S. Court of Appeals for the Third Circuit found it unnecessary to define the scope of a teacher's academic freedom because "no court has found that teachers' First Amendment rights extend to choosing their own curriculum or classroom management techniques in contravention of school policy or dictates." On this basis, the court declared, "it is undisputed that defendants have determined that Learnball is not an appropriate pedagogical method. They are entitled to make this determination. Murray has no right of academic freedom that extends to the choice of Learnball classroom management techniques despite the school's ban or that would render the ban unconstitutional." Based on *Pickering*, however, it found that the school board had no authority to penalize Murray for promoting Learnball when she was acting as a private speaker, as opposed to using it in her classroom. "[T]he School District's undisputed right to control the classroom curriculum does not extend to a right to control a teacher's proselytization of teaching methods. . . . Nor can a teacher suffer retaliation for criticism of school officials outside the classroom."[37]

The Supreme Court's decision in *Garcetti v. Ceballos* (2006), discussed in Chapter 9, went beyond the *Pickering/Connick* test by giving government employers sweeping control over speech uttered by employees in the pursuance of their job duties. Because the job-related speech of K–12 teachers was already subject to greater regulation than that of university faculty, this decision does not have the potential to have the same impact on them as on professors, but it is nonetheless significant.

And Now, a Word About Our Students

Although students are, by definition, not yet experts in their fields, and most of those in K–12 schools are not legally adults, they nonetheless enjoy some First Amendment protection. In brief, K–12 students have the right to express their personal views in ways that are not disruptive to the educational process, but their speech can be constrained with respect to activities sponsored or approved by the school. As adults, university students generally enjoy full First Amendment rights subject to reasonable time, place, and manner restrictions. For example, they may not be prevented from demonstrating against a university provost's decision to hold classes on Saturdays, but neither may they erupt into such a demonstration in the middle of math class or paint slogans on the provost's office wall—or on the provost.

Within the context of classroom instruction, the two most important free-speech rights enjoyed by students throughout the public-education system are the right to be free from coercive indoctrination and the right to be taught the subject matter of the course. With respect to the first of these, it is important to note that the students' right to freedom from coercive indoctrination does not prevent public universities or K–12 schools from promoting their own institutional views. Students, like the rest of the population, have no constitutional right never to hear ideas that they do not like, and with some exceptions—such as religious proselytizing—government entities may speak in their own voice to advocate certain viewpoints. Public schools and universities are, for instance, entitled and indeed required to promote racial equity. The distinction, which can be a fine one, is that the governing bodies of public schools and universities may craft and disseminate an institutional message as long as the students are neither compelled to express agreement nor prevented from expressing disagreement. They may be penalized for actions that violate school policy, such as spraying racist slogans on a student's dormitory door, but they may not be disciplined solely for expressing opposition to the ideological content of the institution's message.

In addition to being aware of institutional messages, students attend classes in which opinions are expressed. The ability of K–12 teachers to offer their own views may be constrained by school policy, but as a function of academic freedom, university professors are expected to share not only factual information but also their interpretations of it. In a course on twentieth-century American politics, for instance, a professor might legitimately draw conclusions about the long-term significance of Ronald Reagan's presidency and support them with evidence and arguments. Nevertheless, the instructor's sharing of knowledge, interpretations, and conclusions must not infringe upon another major function of education—the promotion of critical thinking—nor upon the students' right to hold their own beliefs. The students' obligation to learn the course material does not extend to sharing the instructor's view of it.

Nadine Strossen, professor at the New York Law School and former president of the American Civil Liberties Union, addressed this point in the following terms: "So long as advocacy is conducted within a classroom context of critical analysis and inquiry, it is completely consistent with constitutional and civil liberties values. But if advocacy is conducted within a classroom context of inculcation or indoctrination, it is inconsistent with those values."[38] The *Joint Statement on Rights and Freedoms of Students*, formulated by the AAUP in conjunction with national organizations of university students, expresses a similar view: "Students should be free to take reasoned exception to the data or views offered in any course of study and to reserve judgment about matters of opinion, but they are responsible for learning the content of any course of study for which they are enrolled." Moreover, the *Joint Statement* declares, "Student performance should be evaluated solely on an academic basis, not on opinions or conduct in matters unrelated to academic standards."[39] Although this statement focuses on universities, its principles apply throughout public education. Students in K–12 schools, as well as those in universities, have both an obligation to learn the course material and the right to disagree with the teacher's view of it, and ideological conformity should not be a factor in academic grading at any level.

Although controversial topics may be entirely appropriate to the classroom, they belong there only if they are germane to the subject matter of the course or, in K–12 schools, related to the established curriculum. Students attending class should not be turned into a captive audience for the instructor's irrelevant harangues. Faculty are free, as citizens, to participate in public discussions of controversial issues, but their professional responsibilities preclude them from dedicating any significant amount of class time to topics not germane to the course. This distinction is illustrated by Northwestern University's treatment of two of its faculty members. Arthur Butz, an associate professor of electrical engineering, is active in the Holocaust denial movement. In February 2006, for instance, he publicly commended President Mahmoud Ahmadinejad of Iran for stating that the Holocaust never happened. Nevertheless, nothing in the public record suggests that he has addressed this topic in his engineering classes, and he abides by the AAUP standard under which professors who speak as private citizens have a duty to make it clear that they are not speaking for the university. Moreover, since his field is electrical engineering and not modern European history, his views on the Holocaust are not subject to standards of professional competence or accountability. Administrators at Northwestern have taken no action against him, although they have expressed the opinion that his views are inaccurate and deplorable. By contrast, the contract of an adjunct instructor in Butz's department was not renewed after he ignored warnings to stop including the Holocaust in his engineering classes. Although he argued that he was counteracting Butz's well-known views by challenging engineering students to confront the moral responsibilities of their profession, his speech directly affected his teaching in a way that Butz's statements do not.

Outside class, students in public secondary schools and universities are entitled to freedom of speech as long as it is lawful and does not disrupt the orderly functioning of the institution. The same standards pertain to the formation and financial support of extracurricular student clubs. The federal Equal Access Act (EAA) of 1984, which applies to public secondary schools that accept federal funds and allow noncurricular clubs, forbids discrimination against any proposed student club "on the basis of the religious, political, philosophical, or other content of the speech at such meetings."[40]

Even before the Supreme Court upheld the EAA in *Board of Education of the Westside Community Schools v. Mergens* (1990), it struck down a policy under which the University of Missouri–Kansas City (UMKC) excluded a student religious club from campus on the ground that the university could not appear to promote religion. In declaring the policy unconstitutional in *Widmar v. Vincent* (1981), the Court found that the university's role was not to take responsibility for the speech of students in any club but to create a venue within which the students, as individuals, could express their personal views. Moreover, according to the Court, UMKC was home to such a wide variety of clubs representing so many topics and viewpoints that no reasonable observer would conclude that the university was endorsing all or any of them. A similar line of reasoning was evident in *Board of Regents of the University of Wisconsin v. Southworth* (2000), in which the Supreme Court upheld the university against students who objected to paying a student activity fee that supported student clubs with which they disagreed.[41]

As these examples suggest, any dispute over academic freedom, professional discretion by K–12 teachers, or the free speech of students involves a struggle within which various constituencies claim the right to control the discourse. Paradoxically, the only way for any constituency to feel entirely fulfilled would be to define everyone's choices in terms of the parameters established by the successful group. Disputes over controversial expression thus have no solution if "solution" is defined to mean an outcome with which everyone agrees. Benjamin Franklin wrote, "Without Freedom of Thought, there can be no such Thing as Wisdom; and no such Thing as publick Liberty, without Freedom of Speech."[42] It would be difficult to find anyone who opposes those sentiments in principle, but the challenge of determining what they mean in practice can surely make the fur fly.

2

Freedom and (or) Equality

He that would make his own liberty secure must guard even his enemy from oppression; for if he violates this duty he establishes a precedent that will reach to himself.
    —Thomas Paine, "Dissertations on First Principles of Government"

AS A BROAD STATEMENT OF PRINCIPLE, Paine's observation seems unlikely to arouse much controversy. In context, his point was that the atrocities following the French Revolution reflected the lack of a written constitution whose provisions would apply consistently to all citizens, regardless of which party held power at a particular time. The underlying premise, colloquially approximated by such expressions as "What's sauce for the goose is sauce for the gander" and "What goes around comes around," is widely shared, as is the belief that liberty depends upon the equitable enforcement of law. Nevertheless, as soon as the discussion moves from sentiment to application, conflicts arise in determining what "liberty" and "oppression" mean in practice.

In the context of this chapter, which deals with controversial speech about race, the Paine quotation may be interpreted to support either of two competing models. On one side of the debate, it can be used to defend speech codes and other proscriptions against hate speech. If members of the majority wish to be treated with respect and enjoy an opportunity to excel without being oppressed by a hostile environment, the argument runs, then as a matter of justice and equity, the same advantages must be extended to minorities. According to this line of reasoning, the achievement of this goal requires and justifies such measures as limiting the use of racist works in the curriculum and prohibiting racist language. On the other side of the debate, opponents of speech codes protest that if minorities value their ability to express their views freely, as they have done in civil rights protests and elsewhere, then they must not seek to suppress the free speech of people who wish to air racially antagonistic sentiments. In the first of these two interpretations, the liberty to be secured arises from the maintenance of a nonhostile environment, and the oppression to be avoided lies in the marginalization of minorities through a racially insensitive selection of instructional materials and racist campus speech. In the second interpretation, liberty is equated with the freedom to engage in the speech of one's choice on either side of a given issue, whereas oppression refers to the use of government power to restrict the utterance of certain words or to proscribe the expression of disfavored viewpoints, including racism.

Conflicts over the treatment of racist speech in public schools and universities might appear, at their most elementary level, to embody a tension between equality and liberty: tolerating racist speech diminishes equality, whereas restricting it abridges liberty. In reality, the situation is more complex because each side claims to represent a synthesis of the two values. Those who oppose governmental restrictions on the expression of racist views assert that the principle of free speech treats everyone equally by providing an across-the-board opportunity to air opinions fully, freely, and without constraint. To be sure, this argument runs, the government must uphold the equality of its citizens in a variety of ways through its *own* actions, but social equality must be achieved through the free marketplace of ideas, not by means of governmental suppression of the private speech of individuals.

Advocates of restrictions on racist speech deny that their quest for equality impinges upon any constitutional or moral right to free expression. Among other things, they point out that some speech acts, such as libel and harassment, are not protected under the First Amendment. In addition to maintaining that some racist speech falls within categories already subject to sanction, they argue that the very existence of such categories constitutes a precedent for restricting speech deemed harmful to the public good. In their view, racist speech has been (mis)classified as protected free expression only because the laws that restrict speech in the public interest have been enacted by the white population to protect such majoritarian concerns as property and professional reputation. Thus, they conclude, the assertion that the regulation of racist speech would abridge legitimate First Amendment rights is based not on principle but on majoritarian bias.

The debate over racist expression in public education involves two separate issues: the government's own speech about race and governmental attempts to limit the private speech of individuals. This juxtaposition illustrates the point that the government's speech about some issues, such as religion and race, is constrained by constitutional imperatives that do not extend to the speech of private individuals. With regard to race, government agencies, including public schools and universities, are required to enforce the equal protection under the law required by the Fourteenth Amendment. Nevertheless, they have neither the obligation nor the right to pursue their institutional goals by limiting the expression of contrary views by students or faculty, with the exception of the school-sponsored speech of K–12 teachers.

Deconstructing Huck

Inevitably, the current emphasis on racial equity in public education gives rise to disputes about the use of curricular materials that depict racist attitudes, language, or behavior. Such materials may be defended on the basis of historical accuracy or literary merit, but they may also be challenged on the ground that their use in public schools confers official sanction on content that demeans and embarrasses minority students. Unlike an open forum for public speech, in which government agents do not control what may be said by individual speakers, the construction of a K–12 curriculum requires public officials to make their own choices about which content should be included or excluded. Among other things, they must determine whether, how, and to what extent curricular materials should deal with racially sensitive issues, taking into account such matters as the age of the students, state standards, and conflicting constitutional arguments based on the First and Fourteenth Amendments.

The most obvious examples of curricular materials likely to be considered racist are stories by white authors that reflect the cultural standards of earlier periods. Well-known examples include Helen Bannerman's "The Story of Little Black Sambo," Mark Twain's *Adventures of Huckleberry Finn,* William Faulkner's "Dry September," Harriet Beecher Stowe's *Uncle Tom's Cabin,* and William Styron's *The Confessions of Nat Turner.* Ironically, sensitivity to racism may also conflict with efforts to diversify the curriculum because literature written by members of minority groups often grapples with hot-button racial issues and employs the language of racism. Works challenged on these grounds include Toni Cade Bambara's short stories, Richard Wright's *Black Boy*, Maya Angelou's *I Know Why the Caged Bird Sings*, and Carolivia Herron's *Nappy Hair*. To illustrate the arguments for and against including such works in the curriculum, it might be helpful to consider one representative controversy from each category: disagreements over the teaching of *Huckleberry Finn* in public secondary schools and a clash over the use of *Nappy Hair* in a Brooklyn elementary school.

As most Americans knew at one time but may have forgotten, Huckleberry Finn is a poor white boy who runs away from his abusive father and from two women who have undertaken to "sivilize" him. He teams up with Jim, a slave who seeks freedom when he learns of plans to sell him to a slave trader. Together, they drift down the Mississippi River on a raft, stopping off periodically for adventures in towns along the way. Although they are aiming for the free states of the North, a dense fog causes them to miss a fork in the river, and they sail deeper into slave territory. In the final section of the novel, Jim is imprisoned by the aunt of Huck's friend, Tom Sawyer. Tom joins them and spins elaborate plans for Jim's rescue, although he knows— as the others do not—that no rescue is necessary because Miss Watson set Jim free in her will and then passed away. These ending scenes are often criticized because Jim's behavior may be interpreted as gullible, submissive, and indicative of a sense of inferiority, whereas Tom exploits Jim for his own entertainment without regard for Jim's feelings and interests. Huck, though uncomfortable with Tom's behavior, does nothing to stop it. Additional sources of controversy include Jim's professions of ignorance and naïveté, the deference shown by an adult black male to two young white boys, and the pervasive assumption of white supremacy. Above all, opponents of teaching the novel in public schools note the repeated use of the word "nigger." Rejecting the claim that the term reflects the common practice of the time, they decry its use as "part of a strategy of enforcing African American subordination."[1]

Although the focus of the dispute has evolved over time, opposition to Twain's novel dates back to March 1885—two months after its publication —when the governing committee of the Concord Library made a great show of declining to shelve it. According to the *Boston Transcript*, "One member of the committee says that, while he does not want to call it immoral, he thinks it contains but little humor, and that of a very coarse type. He regards it as the veriest trash." The committee's objections failed to discredit the book. Calling them "a rattling tip-top puff," Twain gloated that the publicity would "sell 25,000 copies for us, sure."[2] Although this early controversy focused on vulgarity rather than racism, it introduced a theme that has continued unabated for more than a century: the fear that the novel's presence in such venues as libraries and schools may appear to confer official approbation on its content and style.

In recent years, *Huckleberry Finn* has been challenged in such diverse communities as Fairfax, Virginia; Shreveport, Louisiana; Upper Darby and State College, Pennsylvania; Newark and Milford, Delaware; Waukegan and Springfield, Illinois; Lincoln and Omaha, Nebraska; and Polk County, Florida. In the most widely publicized of these disputes, Richard Burton, president of the Pennsylvania state conference of the National Association for the Advancement of Colored People (NAACP), called on the officials of that state to ban the use of *Huckleberry Finn* in all its schools. "'We don't believe in censorship,' Burton said. 'But as far as curriculum is concerned, [*Huckleberry Finn*] should not be taught.'"[3] While accepting the book's continued availability in bookstores and public libraries, he objected to its presentation to underage students in a captive situation within state-sponsored schools. Similarly, the Pennsylvania NAACP argued that tax money "should not be used to perpetuate a stereotype that has psychologically damaging effects on the self-esteem of African-American children."[4] The organization was not, however, unanimous in its condemnation of *Huckleberry Finn*. Most notably, the president of the Philadelphia branch of the Pennsylvania NAACP, J. Whyatt Mondesire, proclaimed that the novel was "part of American folklore and history. . . . You're not going to learn anything by closing your eyes and not reading."[5] After a lively debate that ran from 1998 to 2000, Pennsylvania officials declined to institute a statewide ban on the use of Twain's novel in the public schools.

Another late 1990s challenge to *Huckleberry Finn* arose in Tempe, Arizona, when a fourteen-year-old high school freshman was assigned to read both Twain's novel and William Faulkner's short story "A Rose for Emily." Her mother, Kathy Monteiro, found the stories objectionable because they contain "repeated use of the profane, insulting, and racially derogatory term 'nigger.'"[6] In view of the rich variety of American literature, she suggested, there was no need to assign these particular works in secondary schools, where they caused psychological damage to black students and created a racially hostile educational environment. When school officials refused to withdraw the two works from the curriculum, Monteiro filed suit. A federal district court dismissed her complaint, finding no evidence of intentional racial discrimination on the part of school officials. The court also noted that her daughter was no longer in the freshman class in which those works were read. In asking the court to reconsider its decision, Monteiro alleged that racial harassment of black students had increased when *Huckleberry Finn* was taught and that school officials had ignored the resulting complaints. She also maintained that her claim of racial discrimination should be sufficient to cause the case to go to trial. When the district court once again ruled against her, she turned to the U.S. Court of Appeals for the Ninth Circuit, where she also lost.

According to the Ninth Circuit's decision, public-school officials cannot be constrained from including a particular literary work in the curriculum "on the ground that individuals or groups may find the contents injurious or offensive." While acknowledging the pain that some minority students might experience and their right to racial equity in the public schools, the court upheld the authority of school officials to determine what is appropriate for the students to learn. Indeed, it stated, "[A] student's First Amendment rights are infringed when books that have been determined by the school district to have legitimate educational value are removed from a mandatory reading list because of threats of damages, lawsuits, or other forms of retaliation." In the court's view, allowing such a threat to hang over school districts would promote curricular choices based not on educational merit but on concern about offending the "sensibilities of any number of persons or groups."[7] The court also denied that school boards necessarily engage in racial discrimination when they use curricular materials that some people deem to be racist.

As a matter of simple political reality, public-school officials, who are either elected or appointed by elected officials, cannot afford to ignore all (or most) of the people all (or most) of the time. Indeed, under the American system of public education, they are not meant to do so. Nevertheless, as this decision illustrates, they cannot be forced in any particular instance to bow to pressure either from the majority of the community or from vocal groups within it. To a limited extent, this element of public-school governance parallels the academic freedom of public universities as institutions, which provides legal protection against direct external coercion but is unable entirely to shield administrators from political or financial pressure.

Although the Ninth Circuit upheld the right of school officials to assign

Huckleberry Finn, by no means did it suggest that they are compelled to do so; the choice remains theirs. Accordingly, with the advent of each new dispute about this novel or similar works, participants on both sides present their arguments in the court of public opinion as a means of influencing the decisions of school officials. Such debates focus on two separate but related issues: whether *Huckleberry Finn* is racially demeaning and, if it is, whether its use in the schools is justified by such considerations as literary merit, historical accuracy, or the benefits of promoting open discussion of racism in America. Opponents of teaching the novel protest that nothing would justify the use of a racially demeaning book, while its supporters reply that even if it contains racist elements—which not all of them concede—their presence does not automatically trump every other consideration related to the book's literary, historical, and cultural value.

As the difference of opinion within the Pennsylvania NAACP suggests, the sides in this debate are not drawn up along strictly racial lines. This point is effectively illustrated in a collection of essays entitled *Satire or Evasion? Black Perspectives on Huckleberry Finn* (1992). Prominent among the anti-Twain contributors is John H. Wallace, who, as an administrative aide at—ironically—the Mark Twain Middle School in Fairfax, Virginia, led a drive to ban the novel. The opening of his essay is unequivocal: *Huckleberry Finn* is "the most grotesque example of racist trash ever written." The book depicts African Americans as stupid and dishonest, he asserted, and its classroom use undercuts the self-esteem of African American students, subjects them to demeaning material that would not be inflicted on members of any other race, compromises their opportunity for a good education, implicates the school in promoting racial stereotypes, and supports the theory of race-based intelligence. Wallace's essay is noteworthy for its emotional intensity; he wrote, for instance, that "*Huckleberry Finn* is an American classic for no other reason than that it ridicules blacks to a greater extent than any other book given our children to read" and that the "book and racism feed on each other and have withstood the test of time because many Americans insist on preserving our racist heritage."[8]

Among the African American scholars who differ from Wallace is Jocelyn Chadwick-Joshua, author of *The Jim Dilemma: Reading Race in Huckleberry Finn* (1998). In her view, Jim's failings are more than offset by his virtues, including honor, loyalty, communicative skill, duty, friendship, self-knowledge, wisdom, self-reliance, and courage. Far from denying the novel's negative elements, her central argument is that African Americans must not merely face the painful reality of their past but embrace it in order to become fully aware of themselves in the present: "We Americans, and particularly African Americans, need to find a clearer understanding of who we were, as wonderful and as painful as our history is, so that we can more successfully determine what we wish to become."[9] Protecting students from the prejudice that the novel reflects would, she maintained, undercut efforts to factor the truth of the past into present-day African American identity.

Looming over discussions of the classroom use of *Huckleberry Finn* is its reputation as one of the most important novels in American literature. Predictably, supporters maintain that a work of such prominence clearly belongs in the curriculum, whereas opponents deny that its reputation is based on genuine literary merit. This question of the book's standing in the literary community was addressed at length by Jonathan Arac, who asserted that it has been "hypercanonized." In his view, the novel has been misinterpreted as the story of an innocent young white American who arrives at the conclusion that racism is wrong, thus becoming a symbol of hope for the improvement of race relations in this country. It is for this reason, Arac suggested, that *Huckleberry Finn* has been unduly elevated into a feel-good symbol of racial enlightenment—an interpretation that acknowledges neither the racial stereotyping within the novel nor the reality of continued racism in present-day American society. "This covert politics of complacency," he wrote, "allows a little bit of fictional feeling to purify what is still unjust in the social and economic life of the United States."[10]

Arac challenged the assumption that African Americans who are offended by *Huckleberry Finn* must have misunderstood it. To the contrary, he charged, their objection to its use in the schools arises from their focus on racist scenes and language that contradict the claim that the novel is, as a whole, racially redemptive. He argued, for instance, that the word "nigger" was not socially acceptable in the mid-nineteenth century, as some critics have suggested, but was a conscious and deliberately provocative assertion of white supremacy. He also denied that Huck's support for Jim constitutes a condemnation of slavery.

Arac's comments, together with those of Wallace and Chadwick-Joshua, illustrate the major arguments on both sides of the debate over the use of *Huckleberry Finn*—and, by extension, other depictions of racist behavior and language. Defenders of the book maintain that properly taught, it demonstrates nobility in both Huck and Jim and offers a positive overall context for dealing with prejudice, racial stereotyping and language, and the need for racial equity. In their view, the book fully deserves its literary reputation, which in turn justifies its inclusion in the curriculum. Moreover, far from demeaning black students, its realistic depiction of the American past is essential to their understanding and appreciation of themselves in the present. Opponents of the novel retort that regardless of its author's intentions, its critical reputation, or its historical authenticity, it should not be taught in public schools because it embarrasses African American students, making them ashamed of their heritage and humiliating them before their classmates. More than anything else, these critics assert, the book's repeated use of the word "nigger" echoes in black ears in a way that even well-intentioned members of the majority race cannot fully appreciate.

The controversy surrounding Twain's use of the word "nigger" inevitably raises questions regarding the common use of that term within the black community. Chadwick-Joshua, for instance, asked how black students who use racist language themselves, and who hear it constantly in rap music and other venues, suddenly become unable to handle it in the context of a class discussion. To be sure, she acknowledged, the use of such language in the classroom might appear to legitimize it in a way that its appearance in popular culture does not, thus causing black students to "quietly seethe in frustration and real as well as perceived embarrassment."[11] Nonetheless, she suggested, the same words are likely to evoke quite a different reaction when they appear in literature written by black authors. The implication is that an important element in the students' response to class materials that include racist language is their perception of the author's intent, which is in turn influenced by the author's race.

Jim Knippling offered a different perspective, suggesting that far from enjoying carte blanche to use racist language at will, black authors are uniquely subject to the charge that they betray their race when they depict it in a way that invites the scorn of white readers and confirms negative racial stereotypes. To illustrate this point, he quoted Richard Wright, author of *Native Son,* who felt the presence of a "mental censor" within himself warning him to "beware the repulsion of respectable African American professionals who will consider themselves misrepresented and besmirched by [*Native Son's*] unflinching saturation in the sordid elements of Black American life." In the end, Wright determined to tell the truth as he saw it, "not only for others to read, but to free *myself* of this sense of shame and fear."[12] Nevertheless, despite the support of critics like Chadwick-Joshua, that approach is not without controversy. Even if African Americans use language among themselves that they resent when it comes from members of other races, that is not the same as accepting its presentation in public-school classrooms in association with the work of black authors. For one thing, as Knippling indicated, some African Americans do not agree that what they see as demeaning racial representations are acceptable if drawn by a member of their own race. Moreover, regardless of the author's identity or purposes, such materials may generate suspicion of racist intent when—and because—a white teacher chooses to introduce them.

A confluence of these conflicting views formed the basis of a controversy that took place in Brooklyn, New York, in 1998. It was inadvertently ignited by a first-year teacher, Ruth Sherman, who thought that the minority students in her third-grade class would enjoy *Nappy Hair,* a children's story by an African American author. The story, written by Carolivia Herron, features a little girl named Brenda, whose family, led by her Uncle Mordecai, celebrates the curliness of her hair and affirms the beauty of distinctively African features. As Herron has explained on numerous occasions, the character of Uncle Mordecai was based on her real-life Uncle Richard, who encouraged her to appreciate her own tightly curly hair. She wrote the story to counteract what she sees as the lamentable tendency of some African Americans to view their non-European features with shame and embarrassment. In her view, the word "nappy" would qualify as a racist insult only if there were something wrong with having that kind of hair. From this perspective, it is not the word itself but the discomfort it provokes that reeks of racism. Thus, one of her goals in writing the book was to reclaim that word and celebrate the physical characteristic that it describes as a positive affirmation of African identity.

Since *Nappy Hair* was not part of the third-grade curriculum in the New York public schools, Sherman photocopied pages for her students, who brought them home. Presented in stark black and white, the depiction of Brenda resembled Jim Crow–era stereotypes of African American children: spindly-legged, bushy-haired, and toothily grinning. More to the point, the story's title generated the kind of outrage associated with the word "nigger" in *Huckleberry Finn.* According to the news coverage of the controversy, Sherman first learned that she had a problem "when this parent came into my room and said she was surprised she didn't see a white hood on my desk." The protester, later identified as Cathy Wright, made additional copies of the book pages to distribute to her friends and neighbors. Shortly afterward, Sherman was summoned to the auditorium, where she found approximately fifty angry people, some of whom called her a "cracker" and told her that she had "better watch out."[13] When the district superintendent heard about threats of bodily harm, he summarily removed her from her classroom.

The Reverend Herbert Daughtry, pastor at a local Pentecostal church, acted as a spokesman for the protesting parents. In his view—which the school authorities later confirmed—Sherman should have sought administrative approval before using a noncurricular book, and she should have been given some guidance on how to present it. "'This is explosive stuff,' he said. 'Those in the black community know what I mean. Anything dealing with hair, skin color, features and all that stuff is a tinderbox of emotions. Did she have sensitivity while teaching it?'"[14] In an attempt to mediate the situation, Daughtry hosted a community meeting at which the book's author, Carolivia Herron, tried to persuade her listeners that the word "nappy" could be used in a constructive way. She failed. Among other things, audience members pointed out that Brenda herself never expresses joy at having nappy hair, and they doubted that such a story could possibly promote self-esteem in their children. Afterward, Herron explained that "'I love my nappy hair. I thought everybody loved their nappy hair. I thought we had gotten rid of this in the 60's. I should have known better. You can't get rid of a 200- or 300-year-old problem in 10 years. That was my mistake.'"[15] Her view was supported by Isoke T. Nia, an administrator at Teachers College, Columbia University, who said, "I would like to talk to the parents and ask them, 'What is it about your hair that you are offended by?'"[16]

In addition to objecting to the book itself, community members questioned whether a white teacher could understand its import from the perspective of African Americans. As one resident observed, "I'm suspicious of a white teacher teaching something so historically negative."[17] School officials, including Chancellor Rudy Crew, agreed. Crew, himself an African American, suggested that although *Nappy Hair* is not inherently a racist book, Sherman might have used it in a racially insensitive manner. In context, the term "racially insensitive" suggests that the person thus described did not set out to engage in racist behavior but acted unthinkingly on the basis of a majoritarian viewpoint that ignores or undervalues the concerns of minorities.[18] Jill Nelson, a well-known African American author, points out that "many African-Americans' enduring discomfort with some of the physical features of blackness" leads them to use "nappy" as an insult. Thus, Sherman's naïve use of that word "tapped into a well-guarded secret in a community that is often under attack and has much to defend against and be defensive about. I suspect that the negative reaction to "Nappy Hair" . . . springs from misinformation and embarrassment that this young white woman inadvertently exposed both the depth and absurdity of a race secret."[19] Even Herron, who continues to assert that her book is not racist, acknowledges problems with Sherman's use of it, including the distribution of black-and-white photocopies of book illustrations that looked like caricatures of African features. While praising Sherman for her good intentions, Herron told a reporter that the white teacher "doesn't know about that pain, that ache that preceded her into the room."[20]

Predictably, other commentators were less impressed by the seriousness of Sherman's alleged racial insensitivity. In an op-ed piece tellingly entitled "An Ignorant Cry of Racism Makes All Knees Jerk," Clyde Haberman reviled school officials for investigating Sherman while giving a free pass to the parents whose threats and insults necessitated her temporary removal from the classroom. In his view, the message sent to New Yorkers "was that a charge of racism, no matter how knee-jerk and baseless, will get you into hot water more readily than threatening someone with possible bodily harm." With respect to the accusation of racial insensitivity, he scoffed, "And in the touchy-feely twilight of this century, few sins will land you in purgatory faster than presumed insensitivity, especially on a matter of race, sex, religion, national origin or sexual orientation."[21] Similar criticisms arose when Chancellor Rudy Crew supported a principal who wanted to drop a book about the Revolutionary War from the curriculum because it used the word "nigger" once in a historical context. Crew attempted to straddle the fence by validating the principal's desire to head off another controversy while simultaneously urging white teachers not to avoid teaching multicultural materials for fear of giving offense.

Despite the charges of racial insensitivity, Sherman's only concrete violation of policy was to use a noncurricular book without administrative approval, and New York school officials viewed that lapse as a beginner's mistake rather than as insubordination. Consequently, no action was taken against her, and she was invited to return to her classroom. Unnerved by the threats, she requested a transfer and was sent to a school in Queens. Since then, she and Herron have appeared together to discuss the value of teaching *Nappy Hair,* and Herron's Web site includes an extensive discussion of the controversy.[22]

The Great Speech-Code Debate: Legal Arguments

At the university level, it is generally—though not invariably—assumed that adult students are capable of handling controversial material and defending their own opinions. Indeed, critical thinking and vigorous debate are widely considered to be indispensable elements of a college education. Even critics of the inclusion of books like *Huckleberry Finn* in K–12 curricula are less likely to argue that they are inappropriate for use in universities. This is not to say, however, that universities are free of disputes about racist speech. Public universities, as institutions, are entitled to shape and disseminate their own messages, and where race is concerned, those messages are clear and emphatic. Driven in part by intense governmental and social pressure to increase minority enrollment and to create a racially equitable educational climate, university administrations have forcefully opposed racial discrimination in word and action. Though entirely legal in itself, a university's commitment to that message raises First Amendment issues if it leads to adverse action against students or faculty for expressing views that conflict with those of the institution.

Not surprisingly, university officials cringe when students paint racist slogans on dormitory walls or stage blackface skits at fraternity parties. Apart from the negative effect of such antics on the recruitment and retention of minority students, administrators worry about lawsuits under state and federal civil rights legislation and about the Fourteenth Amendment's guarantees of due process and equal protection under the law. In an effort that peaked in the late 1980s and early 1990s, the administrations of some universities responded to these pressures by formulating speech codes. The intent of these codes was to punish gratuitous racist remarks without violating anyone's free-speech rights under the First Amendment and without compromising the faculty's academic freedom. Typically, speech codes also targeted offensive speech regarding such matters as gender, sexual orientation, ethnicity, national origin, and religion.

A brief discussion of three sample lawsuits involving university speech codes may serve to illustrate the content of such codes and their status under the First Amendment. The earliest of these was *Doe v. University of Michigan* (1989), which involved a speech code developed by the University of Michigan to counteract evidence of increasing racial intolerance on campus, such as a flyer that included the terms "saucer lips, porch monkeys, and jigaboos."[23] At a hearing before the Michigan State House of Representatives

Appropriations Subcommittee, forty-eight witnesses accused the university administration of indifference to growing racial problems. The subcommittee threatened to reduce the university's funding, and students threatened to sue, if action were not taken. In response, the acting president of the university instructed the director of its Affirmative Action Office to develop a policy to regulate discriminatory speech. Alluding to one of the recognized exceptions to the Free Speech Clause, the acting president declared that the provocative speech was similar to shouting "Fire" in a crowded theater. He also alleged that it had threatened material disruption to the university's educational mission. The policy went through twelve drafts, and a much-amended version was adopted by the Board of Regents.

The new policy created three zones on campus: university publications, which were exempt from the speech code; public areas such as lawns and sidewalks, in which nothing short of violence or property damage would lead to sanctions; and "educational and academic centers, such as classroom buildings, libraries, research laboratories, recreation, and study centers" in which "[a]ny behavior, verbal or physical, that stigmatizes or victimizes an individual on the basis of race, ethnicity, religion, sex, sexual orientation, creed, national origin, ancestry, age, marital status, handicap or Vietnam-era veteran status" was prohibited. In addition, the policy banned verbal or physical behavior that "[c]reates an intimidating, hostile, or demeaning environment for education pursuits, employment or participation in University sponsored extra-curricular activities."[24]

The penalties provided for students found guilty of violating the code included reprimand, community service, sensitivity classes, restitution, and eviction from university housing. Students who engaged in violent or dangerous behavior were subject to suspension or expulsion. A guide to the policy clarified that it pertained to such behaviors as distributing racist threats in residence halls, writing racist graffiti in study carrels, making disparaging remarks about women in class, and excluding homosexual students from a party to which all other students in a particular classification were invited. The guide also warned that people were not to be laughed at, joked about, or disparaged on the basis of the specified categories.

A graduate student in biopsychology filed a lawsuit seeking to have the policy declared unconstitutional. His academic field, he argued, includes "certain controversial theories positing biologically based differences between sexes and races [that] might be perceived as 'sexist' and 'racist' by some students, and he feared that any discussion of such theories might be sanctionable under the Policy." Despite the university's assertion that the speech code was not meant to preclude "classroom discussion of legitimate ideas," a federal district court found that it could indeed be invoked by students who objected, for instance, to a discussion of the theory that some races are less intelligent than others. In the court's view, the policy's profession of respect for academic freedom and freedom of speech represented little more than lip service; its real focus was on providing a recourse for students who felt offended. Rather than specifying what speech was or was not permitted, the code was designed to be triggered by the subjective response of any given listener. Moreover, the court noted, some students had been disciplined for offending people by discussing controversial ideas, which undercut the university's assertion that its policy did not apply to constitutionally protected speech. Indeed, the court declared, the policy was so vague that "it was simply impossible to discern any limitation on its scope or any conceptual distinction between protected and unprotected conduct." The key words "stigmatize" and "victimize" were not defined, and even if they had been, "the fact that a statement may victimize or stigmatize an individual does not, in and of itself, strip it of protection under the accepted First Amendment tests."[25]

In *Free Speech in the Campus Community* (1997), Robert M. O'Neil, former president of the University of Virginia and founding director of the Thomas Jefferson Center for the Protection of Free Expression, analyzed examples of student speech penalized under the Michigan speech code. He concluded "that the Michigan policy had been applied to speech which clearly would have been protected off campus."[26] In his view, no matter how laudable the goals, there is no justification for enacting special rules to limit controversial expression in a campus environment. Donald Alexander Downs, a political science professor at the University of Wisconsin-Madison, elaborated upon this idea: "Speech codes allow partisans, in effect, to 'criminalize' moral and political disagreement and feeling offended in a manner similar to the way in which the now discredited federal independent counsel law criminalized political and policy differences; rather than besting an opponent in the marketplace of ideas or in the political process, partisans who enjoy the support of authorities can take the coercive way out by turning the law against their foes."[27]

In 1988, shortly after the Michigan controversy had begun, the University of Wisconsin (UW) promulgated a speech code that avoided some of the problems associated with the Michigan policy but created new difficulties of its own. Like their Michigan counterparts, UW administrators were under pressure to address an increase in racial incidents, such as a fraternity party involving a mock slave auction and another featuring a caricature of a black Fiji Islander. With the help of Richard Delgado, a noted legal scholar, the university devised a code, "Policy and Guidelines on Racist and Discriminatory Conduct." Known more familiarly as the UW Rule, the policy proscribed "racist or discriminatory comments, epithets, or other expressive behavior directed at an individual," including remarks that "[d]emean the race, sex, religion, color, creed, disability, sexual orientation, national origin, ancestry or age of the individual or individuals" or "[c]reate an intimidating, hostile, or demeaning environment."[28]

Unlike the Michigan speech code, which applied with the greatest force to such academic venues as classrooms and libraries, the UW Rule pertained only to "non-academic matters."[29] Opinions expressed in class discussions were excluded from the policy's reach if they were not addressed to any individual and did not demonstrate the intent to create a hostile environment. Moreover, by specifying that it governed only student speech, the UW Rule avoided controversy regarding the academic freedom of faculty.[30] It also applied only to deliberately offensive speech, thus emphasizing the speaker's intent rather than the subjective response of the hearer. Examples of infractions of the UW Rule included name-calling, jokes, slurs, and the placing of hostile literature in a person's work or living space. Among the students sanctioned under it, two had called other students names—"Shakazulu" and "fat-ass nigger," respectively—and another had told an Asian American student that she did not belong in this country and that people like her were harmful to America's welfare.[31] Two years after the enactment of the UW Rule, the *UWM Post,* a student-run newspaper at the University of Wisconsin–Milwaukee, filed a federal lawsuit alleging that the restrictions were content-based and extended to speech that, no matter how distasteful and deplorable, was protected under the First Amendment.

The UW Rule's focus on speech directed toward individuals made the concept of "fighting words," defined by the Supreme Court in *Chaplinsky v. New Hampshire* (1942), particularly significant. Walter Chaplinsky was a Jehovah's Witness whose public preaching in Rochester, New Hampshire, was interrupted by irate residents of the neighborhood. As Chaplinsky was being escorted from the scene by police, the city marshal berated him and refused to arrest the people who had created the disturbance. Chaplinsky thereupon cried out, "'You are a God damned racketeer' and 'a damned Fascist and the

whole government of Rochester are Fascists or agents of Fascists.'" His out-
burst led to a conviction for violating a city ordinance that stated: "No person shall address any offensive, derisive or annoying word to any other person who is lawfully in any street or other public place, nor call him by any
offensive or derisive name, nor make any noise or exclamation in his presence and hearing with intent to deride, offend or annoy him, or to prevent
him from pursuing his lawful business or occupation." Despite the breadth
of the ordinance, the New Hampshire state courts interpreted it to exclude
only words that "have a direct tendency to cause acts of violence by the persons to whom, individually, the remark is addressed."[32] Using this standard,
the New Hampshire State Supreme Court upheld Chaplinsky's conviction.

When the case reached the U.S. Supreme Court, the point at issue was
whether the ordinance that criminalized Chaplinsky's remarks thereby violated his free-speech rights under the First Amendment. Pointing out that
the right to free speech is not absolute, the Court defined the following exceptions to it: "the lewd and obscene, the profane, the libelous, and the insulting or 'fighting' words—those which by their very utterance inflict injury
or tend to incite an immediate breach of the peace." According to the Court,
"It has been well observed that such utterances are no essential part of any
exposition of ideas, and are of such slight social value as a step to truth that
any benefit that may be derived from them is clearly outweighed by the social interest in order and morality." The Court also quoted a passage from
Cantwell v. Connecticut, another Jehovah's Witness case: "Resort to epithets
or personal abuse is not in any proper sense communication of information or opinion safeguarded by the Constitution, and its punishment as a
criminal act would raise no question under that instrument."[33] Noting that
the New Hampshire courts had interpreted the Rochester ordinance to apply
only to words whose utterance created an immediate threat of violence, the
Court upheld it.

Arguing before a federal district court in 1990, the University of Wisconsin's attorneys asserted that the UW Rule pertained only to speech that
violated the "fighting words" standard of *Chaplinsky* or at least had "minimum social value and . . . harmful effects."[34] In such circumstances, the attorneys maintained, the university was justified in balancing the speakers'
free-speech rights against the university's legitimate interest in promoting
racial equity and campus diversity. The court disagreed, finding that some
of the speech targeted by the UW Rule failed to meet the "fighting words"
standard and that the code itself omitted any mention of incitement to vio-

lence. While acknowledging that the original definition of "fighting words" had also covered speech whose very utterance inflicted injury, the court noted that that interpretation was no longer valid. Accordingly, the court declared that the UW Rule's proscription of intentionally offensive remarks intruded into the area of constitutionally protected speech. It also ruled that the ban on racist speech was content-based and prevented the advocacy of disfavored viewpoints or emotions. In addition to declaring the speech code overbroad because it prohibited expression protected under the First Amendment, the court found it vague because it did not specify, for instance, whether the mere intent to create a hostile environment was sufficient to constitute a violation of the policy.

Yet another variation on the regulation of racist speech was attempted by Stanford University, whose speech code was intended "to clarify the point at which free expression ends and prohibited discriminatory harassment begins." Prohibited under this policy were "discriminatory intimidation by threats of violence" and "personal vilification of students on the basis of their sex, race, color, handicap, religion, sexual orientation, or national and ethnic origin." For speech to be sanctionable under the policy, it had to be "intended to insult or stigmatize an individual or a small number of individuals" for any of the forbidden reasons. In a clear reference to *Chaplinsky*, the policy applied only to speech that was directly addressed to individuals and that used "insulting or 'fighting' words or non-verbal symbols" that "by their very utterance inflict injury or tend to incite to an immediate breach of the peace, and which are commonly understood to convey direct and visceral hatred or contempt for human beings."[35]

As a private institution, Stanford would ordinarily fall outside the scope of this book. It is, however, located in the state of California, whose law requires nonreligious private universities to follow the same rules as public universities with respect to the free speech of students. When students led by Robert J. Corry filed suit in 1994, the university's attorneys argued that the statute, known as the Leonard Law, was unconstitutional because it forced private institutions to tolerate speech they did not wish to tolerate. In the alternative, Stanford's attorneys maintained that even if the university were required to comply with the First Amendment, its speech code pertained only to "fighting words" that did not enjoy constitutional protection. They also defined the policy's target not as speech but as conduct— specifically, discriminatory harassment. The plaintiffs, who supported the Leonard Law, argued that Stanford's definition of "fighting words" was outdated because it encompassed not only incitement to violence but also language "that merely hurts the feelings of those who hear it."[36] In their view, the university's use of the term "discriminatory harassment" was merely an attempt to cloak its real intent, which was to ban the expression of certain ideas or emotions.

Stanford also pointed out that universities as institutions have a right to academic freedom. That principle would be violated, the university maintained, if Stanford were forced to provide a forum for speech inconsistent with its corporate message. According to this reasoning, the First Amendment protects Stanford's institutional free-speech rights from interference by the state but does not protect the students' free-speech rights from interference by Stanford. Corry and the other plaintiffs retorted that the speech code had no bearing on Stanford's ability to express its own institutional message. Rather, they maintained, it violated the Free Speech Clause by penalizing students for exercising their constitutional right to dissent from the corporate orthodoxy.

The case was heard before a California state court, which upheld the Leonard Law in a 1995 decision declaring that the state was entitled to regulate the behavior of private individuals and institutions. Indeed, the court noted, that is what almost all laws do. The court also rejected Stanford's argument that its code regulated conduct rather than speech, and it agreed with the plaintiffs that "fighting words" meant those that incite violence, not those that express hatred or otherwise give offense. In the court's view, the goal of the Stanford policy was to proscribe speech on the basis of racist, sexist, or other offensive content, which was exactly what the First Amendment and the Leonard Law were intended to prevent. Merely labeling such speech "discriminatory harassment" was not sufficient to transfer it to the category of conduct.

In response to Stanford's claim of institutional academic freedom, the court quoted Frankfurter's concurrence in *Sweezy v. New Hampshire* acknowledging a university's right "to determine for itself on academic grounds who may teach, what may be taught, how it shall be taught, and who may be admitted to study." As the court noted, this definition of institutional academic freedom had nothing to do with compelling individual speakers to conform to the institution's message. The court also disagreed with Stanford's claim that requiring it to tolerate discriminatory speech would muffle its own message of equity and diversity. "The Leonard Law does not chill the speech and expression of Defendants, who can ardently and effectively express their intolerance for intolerance through wholly constitutional means . . . the inability to punish a student under the Speech Code would not interfere with their ability to express their disapproval of any speech. Additionally, Defendants incorrectly suggest that 'academic freedom' provides them with carte blanche to do what they wish."[37]

Gerhard Casper, president of Stanford, issued an indignant statement in response to the decision and to the media coverage that followed it. He was particularly irked by press reports hailing the decision as a victory for academic freedom. "[A] ban on insulting fighting words based on group characteristics is not likely to have a chilling effect on almost all relevant speech," he maintained. "Academic freedom and free speech were quite safe at Stanford University before the decision."[38] Two words in that statement are particularly interesting: "almost" and "relevant." President Casper's use of the qualifying term "almost" is meaningless unless it concedes that *some* otherwise protected speech would, or at least might, be chilled by the application of the challenged policy. Taken in conjunction with Stanford's earlier assertion that, as a private institution, it was entitled to proscribe speech that the government could not prohibit, his remarks suggest that the need to foster equity and diversity outweighed the students' right to spew hate-inspired insults that lacked any serious intellectual or social value. If, as the word "almost" indicates, the policy occasionally chilled some other speech that he considered "relevant," that was an acceptable price to pay for admitting no exception to the university's rejection of bigotry. As the discussion of *Doe v. University of Michigan* indicates, a similar position was taken—equally unsuccessfully—by public-university administrators who argued that the rules of the street need not apply to university campuses, where all students are entitled to enjoy an equitable, nonhostile learning environment.

In context, President Casper's use of the word "relevant" appears to refer to remarks that are sufficiently well thought out to contribute to a meaningful discussion of controversial issues, as opposed to what he called "insulting fighting words based on group characteristics." On this basis, he continued to assert that even without judicial intervention, the Stanford administration could have been trusted to protect what it considered legitimate debate on any issue. As the decision pointed out, however, the First Amendment imposes no such qualitative limitations on freedom of speech. In any university to which the Free Speech Clause applies, officials are not empowered to pursue their own goals, however laudatory, by placing additional conditions—such as "relevance"—on the constitutionally protected speech of students.

The Great Speech-Code Debate:
Philosophical Underpinnings

Collectively, the three cases discussed in the previous section—*Doe v. University of Michigan, UWM Post v. Board of Regents of the University of Wisconsin System,* and *Corry v. Stanford*—offer some insight into the provisions of university speech codes as well as the legal arguments on both sides. Beyond that, or beneath it, lies the clash of philosophical beliefs and values that gave rise to the disputes in the first place. Stanley Fish, for instance, has suggested that speech codes are acceptable because the rules governing free speech are so eclectic and fact-driven as to be essentially meaningless. In the absence of a coherent understanding of what constitutes or should constitute protected free speech, he argued, each decision reflects a form of situation ethics rather than the consistent application of clearly defined rules. Accordingly, he defended speech codes: "I am persuaded that at the present moment, right now, the risk of not attending to hate speech is greater than the risk that by regulating it we will deprive ourselves of valuable voices and insights or slide down the slippery slope toward tyranny."[39] Like President Casper and other university administrators embroiled in speech-code lawsuits, Fish distinguished between "valuable" discourse and speech that is outweighed by the competing considerations against which it is balanced. More fundamentally, he assumed that the act of balancing these particular values against each other is justified because such balancing occurs all the time in a more or less ad hoc manner.

Some elements of Fish's position also appear in critical race theory, which provides an extensive philosophical justification for the use of speech codes. Critical race theory is based in part on the ideas of Herbert Marcuse, a Marxist philosopher whose academic career peaked in the 1950s and 1960s. Marcuse used the expression "repressive tolerance" to describe a majoritarian concept of free speech that perpetuates the subordination of minority groups. When everyone is nominally entitled to the same degree of free expression, he argued, dominant groups use their speech to marginalize and oppress the disadvantaged, while the free-speech rights of minorities do them no good because nothing they say has the power to affect public policy. By this reasoning, "free speech" is an Orwellian euphemism for ensuring that those already in control will remain there, since the nature of the status quo guarantees that those who suffer under it have no effective means of overturning it.

Marcuse also rejected the notion that freedom of speech means being tolerant of the expression of all views—an approach that indiscriminately protects the good and the bad, including words and deeds that militate against extending liberty to the entire culture. To be sure, he conceded, indiscriminate tolerance is justified in situations in which no important legal or political decisions are made; examples include personal conversations, academic discussions, and religious sermons. "But society cannot be indiscriminate where the pacification of existence, where freedom and happiness themselves are at stake: here, certain things cannot be said, certain ideas cannot be expressed, certain policies cannot be proposed, certain behavior cannot be permitted without making tolerance an instrument for the continuation of servitude." In Marcuse's view, the concept of free speech as it is commonly understood is unworkable in practice because it is based on the inaccurate assumption that each individual uses his or her own intellect to engage in open debate intended to seek objective truth. But in a society that unthinkingly holds common beliefs promulgated by those in power, he argued, "tolerance is administered to manipulated and indoctrinated individuals who parrot, as their own, the opinion of their masters, for whom heteronomy has become autonomy."[40]

Believing that people simply echo the ideas pounded into them by self-serving dominant groups, Marcuse maintained that the suppression of such parroted speech would violate no meaningful individual rights. Rather, such suppression is a necessary condition for social changes aimed at producing a just society. According to this argument, when this goal has been reached, the admittedly undemocratic means necessary to achieve it will no longer be needed. At that point, universal tolerance for the expression of all views may safely be reestablished because the promotion of "bad" ideas will no longer be able to cause damage. Those who adhere to what Marcuse defined as objectionable opinions will then be in the same position that, in his view, existing minorities presently occupy: that is, they will be free to speak, but their speech will make no difference. Thus, Marcuse's proposal would not fundamentally change the structure of society to equalize the balance of power between the in-group and the out-group. Rather, it would reconstitute the out-group to consist of those thinkers whose ideas conflict with Marcuse's concept of racial equity.

Drawing on Marcuse's arguments, among others, scholars working in the late twentieth and early twenty-first centuries have developed a school of thought known as critical race theory. It was introduced to general readers in 1993 in *Words That Wound: Critical Race Theory, Assaultive Speech, and the First Amendment,* cowritten by Mari J. Matsuda, Charles R. Lawrence III, Richard Delgado, and Kimberle Williams Crenshaw. In her section of the book, Matsuda expressed frustration with the belief that the elimination of racial discrimination, widely acknowledged to be a worthy goal, is to be sought only after free speech has been protected. She considered this qualification doubly ironic because, in her view, free speech is not a neutral value that serves everyone equally but a tool to perpetuate racial subordination. Accordingly, she described critical race theory as "a pragmatic response to the urgent needs of students of color and other victims of hate speech who are daily silenced, intimidated, and subjected to severe psychological and physical trauma by racist assailants who employ words and symbols as part of an integrated arsenal of weapons of oppression and subordination."[41]

While acknowledging the need for a robust free-speech principle that protects civil rights and other important values, Matsuda argued that it should not apply to speech that perpetuates racial subordination: "[R]acist speech is best treated as a sui generis category, presenting an idea so historically untenable, so dangerous, and so tied to the perpetuation of violence and degradation of the very classes of human beings who are least equipped to respond that it is properly treated as outside the realm of protected discourse." In her view, restraints on racist speech are particularly appropriate to the campus environment because of the youth and vulnerability of college students, many of whom are away from home for the first time. "Official tolerance of racist speech in this setting," she wrote, "is more harmful than generalized tolerance in the community at large."[42] Like Fish, she pointed out that free-speech rules are already inconsistent; for instance, free speech is not necessarily a defense against threats to such majoritarian values as property and reputation. Thus, she argued, lawmakers do not act on the basis of a fixed free-speech rule to which exceptions are never made. Rather, in defining those exceptions, they consider their own interests while ignoring those of minorities.

Like Matsuda, Charles Lawrence expressed outrage at the claim that the damage done by campus hate speech is not sufficiently important to justify the imposition of restrictions on the speakers. After providing numerous examples of students harmed by racially discriminatory speech, he asserted that official tolerance for such expression legitimizes both its content and its effects, including the intimidation of minority students. In his view, this prioritization of racist speech over social justice protects majoritarian interests at the cost of perpetuating the subordination of minority groups. "Whenever we decide that racist hate speech must be tolerated because of the importance of tolerating unpopular speech, we ask Blacks and other subordinated groups to bear a burden for the good of society—to pay the price for the societal benefit of creating more room for speech," he argued. "And we assign this burden to them without seeking their advice and consent. This amounts to white domination, pure and simple."[43]

Richard Delgado, the law professor who was instrumental in constructing the UW Rule, likened hate speech to assault and focused on its costs to the individual and to society as a whole. Those costs, he argued, not only justify but cry out for policies aimed specifically at protecting minority groups from the harm inflicted when such expression is officially tolerated. While conceding that existing remedies, such as penalties for defamation and for the intentional infliction of emotional harm, may be useful in some limited instances, he denied that they cover enough hate speech to be effective deterrents. In his view, their chief usefulness lies in the fact that by their very existence, they prove that exceptions to free speech are already made. The question is simply whether a competing value is sufficiently important to justify such measures.[44]

Prominent among scholars who have explicitly refuted critical race theory is Henry Louis Gates, Jr., director of the W. E. B. Du Bois Institute for African and African American Research at Harvard University. In his view, free-speech advocates do a poor job of explaining why speech codes are unacceptable when they merely "invoke the First Amendment like a mantra and seem to fall into a trance, so oblivious are they to further argumentation or evidence." Indeed, he observed, "[t]he strongest argument for regulating hate speech is the unreflective stupidity of most of the arguments you hear on the other side."[45] Like speech-code supporters, he ridiculed the notion that failure to tolerate hate speech, in particular, will somehow lead to unprecedented consequences that do not follow upon any of the existing restrictions on free speech. A more effective approach, he suggested, would be to confront the arguments of critical race theorists in order to demonstrate systematically where and why they fail to hold water.

Gates's refutation of critical race theory consists largely of the revelation of paradoxes and inconsistencies. Herewith a few examples:

- The central premise of critical race theory is that racist speech should be restricted because it helps to maintain "the larger structure of racism hegemonic in our society."[46] This claim implies that any specific instance of racist speech is not an isolated event, but a manifestation of ingrained racism in American society as a whole. But when white university administrators promulgate speech codes, the very act of taking such a step is a clear manifestation of antiracist conviction that undercuts the alleged justification for the code.

• In the act of representing the views of students harmed by hate speech, critical race theorists disprove their own assertion that racist expression silences those who suffer from it.

• Critical race theorists reject as inadequate statements that express a university's own opposition to racist speech without providing penalties for individual students who engage in it. In the absence of penalties to enforce civility, they protest, such policies are mere words. But so is hate speech. If words symbolizing the speaker's hatred or contempt for a particular race carry the power attributed to them, it is inconsistent to maintain that a university's words conveying the opposite message are without meaning or effect.

• One rationale supporting speech codes is the assertion that the current standards for determining what interests are sufficiently important to justify restrictions on speech are not racially neutral. Nevertheless, the same is true of the critical race theorists' attempts to define the forms of hate speech that should be subject to sanction. As an example, one suggested criterion for punishable speech is the promotion of belief in racial inferiority. But although that standard would protect some groups, including African Americans, it would not cover Jews and Asians, because hate speech directed toward them does not generally treat them as inferior but as evil. Thus, inferiority is too narrow a standard and would include too few groups. Conversely, if hate speech against any historically disadvantaged population could be penalized, the standard would become ridiculously broad because almost any group can show that it has been disadvantaged at one time or another.

After contradicting the philosophical arguments on which critical race theory rests, Gates turned to more pragmatic objections to speech codes. He noted, for instance, that more than twenty black students and no white students were called to account under the Michigan speech code. In the only full disciplinary procedure ever held under that policy, the defendant was a black student who had said in class that homosexuality is an illness. Similarly, he observed that although the Stanford code targeted in-your-face racial insults, it said nothing about patronizing attempts to "help" black students. Such actions, he suggested, are not only more damaging but also more likely to occur in the Stanford environment. Gates's discussion of this aspect of the Stanford code included the much-quoted "drunken undergraduate" standard: "It's safe to say that Stanford's faculty and administration, however benighted or enlightened they may be on racial matters, manage nicely without the face-to-face deployment of naughty epithets. In adopting the regulations, therefore, they sacrifice nothing but the occasional drunken undergraduate."[47]

Approaching the issue from a different perspective, Alan Charles Kors and Harvey A. Silverglate included speech codes in their broader condemnation of what they described as the failure of American universities to respect even an ordinary understanding of free speech, much less the more rigorous standard appropriate to higher education. In *The Shadow University: The Betrayal of Liberty on America's Campuses* (1998), they maintained that "[i]n a nation whose future depends upon an education in freedom, colleges and universities are teaching the values of censorship, self-censorship, and self-righteous abuse of power. Our institutions of higher education greet freshmen not as individuals on the threshold of adulthood, but as embodiments of group identity, largely defined in terms of blood and history, who are to be infantilized at every turn." With specific reference to critical race theory, they wrote, "It is intriguing that [Delgado, Lawrence, and Matsuda] dance so cautiously around the First Amendment, because, in reality, the three attack the underpinnings of modern First Amendment theory as fundamentally as did Marcuse's 'Repressive Tolerance.' Above all, the authors diverge from current First Amendment values by positing a goal or end result for free speech, when free speech, in constitutional theory, is a right in and of itself. As Matsuda put it, her 'confrontation [with] the contradiction between first amendment absolutism and the goals of liberty and equality' led to her current position. Lawrence, too, 'placed race at the center of his analysis.'"[48] For similar reasons, Kors and Silverglate took issue with the assertion that because of historic injustices, different standards should be applied to negative depictions of race and to the use of racial epithets depending upon the race of the speaker and that of the target.

Following the success of *The Shadow University*, Kors and Silverglate established the Foundation for Individual Rights in Education (FIRE), whose mission is "to defend and sustain individual rights at America's colleges and universities. These rights include freedom of speech, legal equality, due process, religious liberty, and sanctity of conscience—the essential qualities of individual liberty and dignity."[49] FIRE issues annual reports on university policies regulating student and faculty speech, and it offers a guide, "Correcting Common Mistakes in Campus Speech Policies," as well as numerous handbooks on student free-speech rights.[50]

Although FIRE and the AAUP differ significantly in many respects, they sometimes reach the same conclusions—including condemnation of campus speech codes. The basis of opposition to speech codes by the AAUP as an institution and by scholars associated with it is that regardless of the importance of the social goals that such codes are meant to serve, they conflict with the AAUP's fundamental understanding of a university's function. The organization's view on speech codes is summarized in *On Freedom of Expression and Campus Speech Codes* (1994), which states, "An institution of higher learning fails to fulfill its mission if it asserts the power to proscribe ideas—and racial or ethnic slurs, sexist epithets, or homophobic insults almost always express ideas, however repugnant. Indeed, by proscribing any ideas, a university sets an example that profoundly disserves its academic mission."[51]

Experts on the First Amendment who have held office in the AAUP have offered more extended discussions of speech codes in the context of the university's role in society. Among these is Walter P. Metzger, professor emeritus at Columbia University, who had been a member of the AAUP's Committee A on Academic Freedom and Tenure for almost forty years when it issued its statement on speech codes. In an essay entitled "A Stroll Along the New Frontiers of Academic Freedom," he challenged the assertion that restrictions on student speech are acceptable as long as they do not apply to professors. For one thing, he pointed out, policies like the Michigan code are written so broadly that even if purportedly aimed only at students, they could affect faculty speech. Moreover, although academic freedom as a professional standard pertains only to faculty, he maintained that speech codes set a poor example for students. The university should not, he argued, operate on the premise that it is wrong to say anything that offends anyone, nor should it suggest that the best way to deal with speech that we do not like is to prohibit it.

In *Free Speech in the College Community*, Robert M. O'Neil, who chaired the AAUP's Committee A on Academic Freedom and Tenure for seven years, challenged the assertion that by failing to regulate racist speech, universities give the impression that they approve of it. His argument rests on the distinction between the university's expression of its own views and the rules that it imposes on the private speech of its students. Student speech, he explained, expresses only the opinion of the speaker and says nothing, one way or the other, about the university's position. Conversely, universities that take it upon themselves to penalize the expression of views they find abhorrent face an insurmountable mountain of monitoring and regulation because whatever they do not restrict may be interpreted as carrying their approval.

The Kaiser, the Kremlin, and the Klan

As scholars on both sides acknowledge, the debate over speech codes is, at its heart, one element of a larger struggle to define the fundamental values of American higher education. It is by no means unique in this respect. During World War I and the Cold War, for instance, similar battles swirled around faculty and students who failed to toe a particular political line. In each instance, supporters of whatever restrictions were proposed at that time viewed them not as unwarranted impositions on the intellectual freedom of individuals but as necessary measures to preserve liberty and security. Nevertheless, like today's critics of speech codes, their opponents would not concede that such values as American involvement in World War I or the danger of Soviet communism justified permitting university administrations to pursue their institutional goals by constraining the free expression of students or faculty.

Cumulatively, the succession of "emergencies" that have allegedly justified the suppression of disfavored viewpoints serves, in itself, as a point in favor of the free expression of controversial ideas. In each instance, what is at issue is not the validity of a prevailing opinion—that America should enter World War I, fight communism, or seek social justice—but the assertion that those goals justify and indeed require the suppression of contrary ideas by students and faculty. To those who support speech bans of various kinds, an American university is not worthy of the name if it tolerates opposition to measures considered necessary to bring about the overthrow of tyranny—whether that of the kaiser, the Kremlin, or the Ku Klux Klan. But as Metzger, O'Neil, Gates, Kors, and other First Amendment scholars have eloquently argued, the specific role of universities in a free society is, perhaps paradoxically, to entertain even those ideas that might appear to threaten it. Far from being quixotic, this concept of a university is based on the realization that no majority, no matter how well established and self-confident, has a stranglehold on the whole truth. Conversely, if a view cannot be aired, neither can it be shown to be false. For that reason, no opinion expressed by a student or faculty member could conflict so thoroughly with the mission of a public university as would the suppression of that viewpoint.[52]

3

Price-Fixing in the Free Marketplace of Ideas

There is the greatest difference between presuming an opinion to be true, because, with every opportunity for contesting it, it has not been refuted, and assuming its truth for the purpose of not permitting its refutation.
—John Stuart Mill, *On Liberty*

IN *DOE V. UNIVERSITY OF MICHIGAN*, a biopsychology graduate student challenged a speech code that focused less on the intentions of the speaker than on the perceptions and feelings of the listeners. He questioned what would happen if, in his university courses, he brought up the theory of race-based intelligence, which states that people of African descent are statistically less intelligent than members of other races. Since the Michigan code forbade speech that demeans or stigmatizes people on the basis of race, Doe feared that any student offended by such a discussion might file a successful complaint. Despite the university's claim that the policy was not intended to chill classroom speech, the court found that a discussion of intellectual disparities based on race might well fall within its purview.

Because race-based intelligence is one of the most contentious areas of teaching and research at the university level, it provides an appropriate focus for a discussion of academic freedom as applied to the topic of race. At issue is the distinction between objective peer reviews of professors' teaching and scholarship, which are essential to maintaining the quality of academic work, and ideologically biased attempts to hamper the exploration and promulgation of ideas that conflict with a university's institutional message, political imperatives, or administrative goals.

An examination of three disputes involving the politically incendiary topic of race-based intelligence illustrates this point. The earliest of the three took place at City College of New York (CCNY), which has a long and colorful history of academic-freedom battles. Among the most notable was the denial of a faculty position to the prominent philosopher Bertrand Russell, whose allegedly immoral views impelled a state court to block his appointment to the CCNY Philosophy Department in 1940. Almost half a century later, that department found itself embroiled in another highly publicized dispute—this time because Professor Michael Levin wrote a letter to the *New York Times*.

Levin originally specialized in the philosophy of mathematics, but in mid-career, he turned his attention to biologically based differences between demographic groups. He began by asserting that the higher salaries earned by men are attributable to their genetic superiority in intelligence and competitiveness. Later, he drew upon the theory of race-based intelligence to explain the disproportionately high rate at which African Americans are convicted of crimes. He denied the moral necessity of affirmative action because, he maintained, African Americans have been accorded equal opportunity for decades, enjoy a better lifestyle than they would have had if their ancestors had remained in Africa, and impose a cost on society by committing crimes. According to an analysis of Levin's work by Richard Lynn, a British psychologist who endorses race-based intelligence, Levin explained the disproportionate representation of African Americans at lower socioeconomic levels as "a result of their lower average IQs and personality characteristics, not of discrimination against them by whites." These personality characteristics include "the traits of impulsiveness and the desire for immediate gratification which impair educational achievements and job performance."[1]

On December 28, 1986, the *New York Times* published an editorial deploring the practice of treating all black males as if they are likely to commit crimes. In particular, the editorial mentioned New York City retailers who would not permit black males to shop in their stores. While conceding that "blacks commit robbery at a rate 10 times that of whites," the editorial focused on "the vast, innocent majority of blacks" who were unjustly hampered as they went about their normal business. The editorial asserted that "John Rawls, the philosopher, suggests one widely respected answer: No one ought to endorse a social order that he could not accept if he were in the shoes of the most disadvantaged." On this basis, the editorial urged whites to "put themselves in the shoes of innocent blacks" in order to "keep fear in its place."[2]

In a letter to the editor published on January 11, 1987, Levin protested that the editorial would "illustrate the risk of misunderstanding philosophy, were it not so obviously an effort to bolster a proposition reached on nonphilosophical grounds." He stated that the editorial mistakenly used Rawls's work to suggest that whites should not take "even rational steps to avoid being victimized by black criminals." Rawls's proposition, Levin maintained, was not meant to apply "when specific information is available about the actual risks one faces." Moreover, he argued, the editorial interpreted Rawls one-sidedly because it did not urge blacks offended by exclusion from a shop to consider what risks they themselves would accept if they owned the shop. "Individual tastes in disaster may differ," he wrote, "but surely the innocent black turned away from a Madison Avenue boutique would not wish to change places with a boutique owner who has just been assaulted. It is unfortunate that innocent blacks must be inconvenienced because of the behavior of guilty blacks, but if we are to play the put-yourselves-in-his-shoes game, the innocent black who puts himself in the shoes of the vulnerable boutique owner should just as surely conclude that he would not let himself in under similar circumstances." Levin also attacked the newspaper's support for affirmative action, asking how "discrimination against innocent whites [could be] a tolerable price to pay for insuring jobs for blacks while discriminatory inconvenience for innocent blacks is too high a price to pay for reducing the risk of murder for white store owners?"[3]

Several small incidents followed the publication of Levin's *New York Times* letter, including the distribution of pamphlets outside his classroom and the burning of papers he had posted on his office door. Four months later, demonstrators protested outside his classroom and blocked the door. Chief Albert Dandridge of the CCNY campus police saw a student, Stephen Pearl, shove a police officer in what Dandridge interpreted as "an apparent effort to inflame the situation." Pearl and another student, Vardon Marshall, were reported to the dean of student affairs, George McDonald. Levin also found an anti-Semitic threat stuck to his office door: "We know where you live you Jewish bastard your time is going to come." He reported it to the university president, Bernard Harleston, who did not reply. In a further protest, dozens of students demonstrated outside his classroom, shouting and carrying banners proclaiming him a racist. The campus police subdued the protesters, and Levin again complained to President Harleston, who continued to take no action.

Pearl and Marshall were summoned to Dean McDonald's office to explain why they should not be sanctioned under a university policy forbidding demonstrations that disrupt classes or research. The letter sent to Pearl stated that he had blocked access to Levin's classroom and disrupted all the classes in that area; that when campus police had attempted to restrain him, "he cursed, continued to shout, scream, and behave in a disorderly manner"; and that "he pushed against security officers and exhorted other students to assault the security guards."[4] Instead of obeying the summons, Pearl and Marshall sent McDonald a letter signed by the International Committee Against Racism (INCAR), of which Pearl was president, accusing the college administration of racism. "[W]e will not even consider the charges being raised against Mr. Pearl and Mr. Marshall until the charges against Mr. Dandridge, [Dean McDonald], and the administration are resolved to our satisfaction," the letter stated. McDonald dropped the matter for fear of causing "chaos on campus."[5]

In September 1987, Levin once again complained that Pearl was distributing pamphlets outside his classes. In March 1989, Pearl led approximately twenty students into Levin's classroom, shouting and chanting through a bullhorn to demand his removal from CCNY. They also blocked his exit from the room. Levin wrote to Dean McDonald, who did not reply. A similar event occurred in March 1990, when approximately thirty-five demonstrators invaded his class. Levin had seen posters advertising the upcoming protest, and campus security officers were on hand. On their advice, he ended the class. A Faculty Senate resolution called upon the CCNY administration to enforce its policy against disruptions of classes, but no action was taken against the demonstrators, although the leaders' identities were known. Dean McDonald later testified that the rules were distributed to students for their information but were not strictly enforced because CCNY was "not a penal institution."[6]

New fuel was added to the fire in the winter of 1988, when Levin published a book review of E. D. Hirsch's *Cultural Literacy* and Allan Bloom's *The Closing of the American Mind*. In the review, which appeared in the Australian journal *Quadrant*, Levin criticized both authors for failing to address the evils of affirmative action. He argued that affirmative action wastes huge amounts of time, energy, and money for the sake of admitting college students whose probability of academic success is low. Challenging the belief that blacks would do as well as whites if tests were racially unbiased, he wrote, "[T]he average black is significantly less intelligent than the average white." As a result of affirmative action, he maintained, coursework is being dumbed down to accommodate unqualified black students. Furthermore, "if standards are going to be raised, cultural literacy reasserted and college education given its old depth and focus, the American polity will have to reconcile itself to an embarrassing failure rate for blacks."[7]

The CCNY Faculty Senate passed a resolution characterizing the book review as an expression of racial prejudice, but when President Harleston called for the establishment of a committee to investigate Levin, the senate did not respond. Levin's department chair and his dean asked him to withdraw from teaching his introductory philosophy course because of the risk of protests and because black students might prefer not to study with someone who held such a low opinion of their intelligence. Levin complied, although he later argued that the administration should have enforced its rule against demonstrations rather than validating them by silencing the speaker to whom the demonstrators objected.

Levin taught the introductory philosophy course the following semester without incident. He was scheduled to teach it again in the spring of 1990, but in January a letter he had written was published in the *American Philosophical Association Proceedings*. In it he suggested that the low number of blacks in philosophy departments is attributable not to racially biased tests or other actions on the part of whites but to the lower average IQ of blacks. According to his estimate, only 3 percent of blacks, compared to 14 percent of whites, have the IQ scores necessary for the study of philosophy. For this reason, he argued, predictions about the number of blacks expected to study philosophy should not be based on the total number of blacks in the population but on the number with the appropriate IQ. On this basis, the predicted proportion of black philosophers was 2 percent, which corresponded to the actual proportion. Levin concluded that whites should feel no need to do anything about the alleged underrepresentation of blacks in the field of philosophy.

The publication of this letter prompted Paul Sherwin, dean of humanities at CCNY, to write to the students in Levin's introductory philosophy course inviting them to switch to a newly established "shadow" section taught by another instructor. He informed the students about Levin's views, although as he later testified, most of them were freshmen and transfer students who would not otherwise have been aware of what the professor had written. He took this action over the objections of the new chair of the Philosophy Department, Charles Evans, who had refused to comply when Dean Sherwin had asked him to assign Levin's usual course to someone else. A similar shadow section was offered in the fall of 1990 despite Levin's objections and those of Evans and the Faculty Senate.

Sherwin's letter to the students in Levin's class stated that no one had complained about his treatment of his students, and no allegation had ever been made that he taught any form of racial discrimination. In a letter to Levin, the dean reaffirmed that "he had 'no reason to suppose [Professor Levin's teaching] is not being conducted in a highly professional way.'" Sherwin was, however, "concerned about the psychic damage your beliefs may inflict on those . . . who come to trust your authority."[8] Sherwin also stated that Levin's low opinion of his black students' ability would affect their academic performance. CCNY attorneys offered an additional defense of the shadow sections: "[T]hese particular controversial views, unlike views on, say, the justice of capitalism or the existence of God, go to the integrity of the teacher-student relationship itself, regardless of whether in Michael Levin's conscious mind they have any direct influence on how he treats any particular student that is willing to prove him wrong."[9]

CCNY had never before created shadow sections, and administrators denied any intention of doing so in response to other controversial views. Moreover, since several sections of the introductory philosophy course ran every semester, and since students who did not wish to study with Levin could simply have signed up for another professor's class, the fanfare attending the unnecessary identification of particular sections as "shadows" to Levin's courses clearly fulfilled a symbolic rather than a practical function. Sherwin defended this action by arguing that race is different from other contentious topics because it is not merely a matter of public debate but an element of personal identity. Like President Harleston, he considered it important to demonstrate the administration's solidarity with those who opposed Levin's views.

Levin protested that his spotless record with respect to his treatment of students reflected his understanding that a statistical difference between two groups has nothing to do with predicting the performance of an individual. Thus, Levin argued, it did not follow that because he believed that blacks as a race are less intelligent than whites, he therefore disparaged the ability of any individual black student. As a federal court later observed, "An irony of the Professor's position as a target of the President's Committee is that during his 22 years of classroom teaching, Professor Levin has taught more than 3,000 students and has never had a complaint that any has ever been treated unfairly on the basis of race."[10]

Administrative action against Levin intensified in the spring of 1990, when President Harleston pressed his demand that the Faculty Senate assign a committee to investigate charges of racism. The senate refused, and Harleston announced at a press conference that he himself would appoint a committee for that purpose. Noting that "[t]he process of removing a tenured professor is a complicated one," he declared that Levin's opinions offended "the basic values of human equality and decency and simply have no place here at City College." The committee that he appointed consisted of seven faculty members, none of whom was qualified in a relevant field, and three of whom had previously signed a petition questioning Levin's right to continue teaching. Harleston rejected a request from Levin's department chair to consider whether those three professors might be, or at least appear to be, biased in their judgment. His charge to the committee was "to review the question of when speech both in and outside the classroom may go beyond the protection of academic freedom or become conduct unbecoming a member of the faculty, or some other form of misconduct."[11] Since "conduct unbecoming a member of the faculty" constituted justification for firing a tenured professor, Levin protested that the investigation was intended to intimidate him into ceasing to express controversial racial views in his publications and public-speaking engagements.

The committee conducted no hearings and collected no data, nor did it speak with Levin. Without addressing the scholarly merit of Levin's work, the committee, like the university administration, focused on the alleged threat to racial equity. The committee chair later testified, "Really there is a clash between—there is an area of free speech which we hold sacred and civil rights which we hold sacred, too, and we discussed the interface between the two." Emphasizing "that there is no simple or totally satisfactory solution," the committee presented a mixed recommendation to Harleston. Though finding no grounds for disciplinary action based on the views Levin expressed outside the classroom, it urged university officials to continue offering shadow sections of his courses. Based on its assumption that Levin's writings would cause some unspecified proportion of his students to feel disparaged, the committee defined as its primary focus "the issue of speech that can have a direct impact on the process of education." Its chair testified that the committee believed that its view was supported by research in the social sciences, but he knew of no specific examples. Pressed, he could cite no evidence other than newspaper stories, his experiences with his own children, and his conviction that the harmful nature of Levin's views was self-evident. Moreover, the committee collected no data from students in Levin's courses or in the shadow sections and could not demonstrate how those particular students felt about his writings or what effect, if any, their feelings had had on their educational experience.

The committee's attempted compromise was inconsistent: it first stated that Levin could not be sanctioned for what he wrote and then declared that his writings justified the creation of shadow sections that stigmatized him. Similarly, although the committee recommended against pursuing disciplinary proceedings at that time, it suggested revising CCNY's harassment policies to allow students to challenge professors who belittled their intellectual ability, thus engaging in behavior that was "clearly unprofessional and inappropriate." The incompatibility of the committee's various recommendations led a federal district court to describe the report as "characteristically elliptical and, we must say, Orwellian double-speak."[12]

Although university officials acknowledged that Levin had ceased to publish or accept speaking invitations while the investigation was in progress, they denied having chilled his free speech. According to a CCNY attorney, "Michael Levin has, for whatever reasons, stopped talking, stopped writing, cut back a great deal. If he has done that because he fears some shadows on the wall, that is unfortunate, but it is not the fault of City College or of President Harleston or anybody else. . . . [T]here isn't anything for him to be afraid of and there never was."[13]

The American Civil Liberties Union (ACLU) offered to provide Levin with an attorney, but he felt that the ACLU regarded him as a crank whom it would defend as a display of its own adherence to principle. Instead, attorneys from the Center for Individual Rights, a conservative public-interest law firm in Washington, D.C., filed suit on his behalf.[14] Three points were at issue: whether the creation of the shadow sections violated his rights by stigmatizing him and limiting his contact with students because of the opinions he expressed; whether the university officials' failure to respond to disruptive demonstrations discriminated against him on the basis of his views; and whether the threat of disciplinary action hindered his ability to express controversial opinions. The federal district court ruled in favor of Levin on all three points. Noting CCNY's failure to demonstrate that his views had any effect on his students' ability to learn, the court found that "the shadow sections were established with the intent and consequence of stigmatizing Professor Levin solely because of his expression of ideas." Similarly, the administration had ignored its own policies by failing to discipline unruly demonstrators, although they knew "that these disruptions were intended to isolate and silence Professor Levin, and injure the learning environment of his students." Indeed, the administration had aided and abetted the demonstrators "by failing to affirm unequivocally Professor Levin's right to teach his classes unimpeded by the appalling behavior of the shouters, the intimidators and the bullies."[15]

In the court's view, Harleston's statements, including his charge to the investigative committee, indicated that Levin's dismissal was under consideration "solely on the basis of his statements on issues of public importance." The decision further states, "Academic tenure, if it is to have any meaning at all, must encompass the right to pursue scholarship wherever it may lead, the freedom to inquire, to study and to evaluate without the deadening limits of orthodoxy or the corrosive atmosphere of suspicion and distrust."[16] To be sure, the court acknowledged, universities as institutions enjoy academic freedom with respect to certain decisions, but they may not intimidate faculty members into ceasing to publish material that conflicts with any corporate viewpoint. The court ordered CCNY to cease offering shadow sections, to refrain from threatening action against Levin for the opinions he expressed, and to enforce its policy against class disruptions. With technical modifications, the U.S. Court of Appeals for the Second Circuit upheld this decision with respect to the shadow sections and the threat of disciplinary action. It vacated the part of the decision concerning demonstrations because it found that CCNY so rarely took action when classes were disrupted that Levin could not prove that he had been targeted because of his views.

As the Levin case was winding to a close, another CCNY professor, Leonard Jeffries, sued the university for violating his First Amendment rights. Although that controversy had nothing to do with race-based intelligence, it warrants discussion in the context of the Levin controversy. Jeffries, a scholar of black studies, was known for his anti-Semitic remarks; for instance, he once asked a job candidate, "Why does a Jew boy like you want to come to teach at this campus?"[17] He also spoke disparagingly of homosexuals and whites. Matters came to a head in the summer of 1991, when he gave a speech at a cultural festival in Albany. According to the U.S. Court of

Appeals for the Second Circuit, "Jeffries launched several ad hominem invectives at specific state and federal officials . . . calling one an 'ultimate, supreme, sophisticated, debonair racist,' and a 'sophisticated, Texas Jew.' Jeffries also told his audience that Jews had a history of oppressing blacks. He said that 'rich Jews' had financed the slave trade, and that Jews and Mafia figures in Hollywood had conspired to 'put together a system of destruction of black people' by portraying them negatively in films."[18]

Jeffries, who had served as chair of CCNY's Department of Black Studies for twenty years, had just been reappointed to another three-year term when he gave his speech. While acknowledging that the speech was protected by the First Amendment, President Harleston assigned university officials to determine whether Jeffries' ability to chair his department had been impaired by the controversy. When the officials reported that it had not, Harleston told them to keep investigating. They subsequently identified several reasons for terminating Jeffries' administrative appointment, including "a confrontation with another member of the faculty, delays in an important faculty search, deficiencies concerning the monitoring of grading, teaching of classes, and maintenance of records, failure to attend meetings, and other problems."[19] Despite a Faculty Senate protest, the trustees removed Jeffries from the position of department chair, and he sued.

Unlike Levin, Jeffries was seeking a financial award, and his case was decided by a jury. Judge Kenneth Conboy, who presided over the jury trial, had also heard the Levin case. When the jury found in favor of Jeffries, Judge Conboy wrote, "We observe that the defendants were put on notice by the *Levin v. Harleston* decision that retaliation against a faculty member for exercise of his or her free speech rights, in the absence of any actual interference in the functioning of the University, is prohibited by law. Despite this notice, the defendants proceeded to retaliate against Professor Jeffries for his speech outside the University."[20] The jury recommended awarding Jeffries $400,000 in punitive damages, but the judge reduced it to $360,000.

The U.S. Court of Appeals for the Second Circuit ordered a new trial with respect to the monetary award, but it upheld the rest of the decision. CCNY had violated Jeffries' First Amendment rights, the court declared, and he was entitled to be reinstated as department chair. Like the district court, the appeals court interpreted earlier Supreme Court decisions to mean that the university could not take action against Jeffries solely because of what it feared might happen as a result of his speech. Shortly afterward, the Supreme Court ruled in *Waters v. Churchill* (1994) that public employees—

in this case, a nurse in a public hospital—may be disciplined for statements that have the potential to cause disruption even if they do not actually do so. The Supreme Court thereupon vacated the judgment in the Jeffries case and sent it back to the Second Circuit for reconsideration in light of *Waters*.

The appeals court reversed its original decision and ruled in favor of CCNY. In response to Jeffries' argument that his speech as a professor enjoyed greater protection than the speech of a nurse, the court stated that his academic freedom was not compromised by his removal from an administrative post. No threat to his tenured faculty position existed, nor had any attempt been made to constrain either his public speech or his classroom instruction.

As the court's finding suggests, CCNY's behavior toward Jeffries differed significantly from its treatment of Levin. Levin later remarked, "There's been more of an effort to understand him, that he's giving voice to black resentment. . . . It doesn't matter if he's incoherent and he's got this bee in his bonnet about Jews. I don't recall anybody trying to understand me."[21] No shadow sections of Jeffries' courses were offered, although the administration, which found no fault with Levin's teaching, characterized Jeffries' classes as "a forum for bizarre, shallow, racist and incompetent pseudo-thinking and pseudo-teaching."[22] A reporter for *Time* magazine described one lesson: Jeffries arrived an hour late and explained that he had been trying to retrieve clothing from a laundry that had burned down. Jeffries drew on the chalkboard a "chart featuring 'the sun people' (i.e., people of color) at one corner of a triangle and 'the ice people' (i.e., not people of color) at another." Next to "ice people," Jeffries wrote "'individualist,' 'competitive,' 'exploitative.'" Attributing these characteristics to a lack of melanin, he stated that melanin allows blacks "to negotiate the vibrations of the universe and to deal with the ultraviolet rays of the sun."[23]

Despite Jeffries' long history of diatribes against Jews, whites, and homosexuals, his expression of such sentiments in class, and his repeated use of immoderate language, no threat existed to his continued employment at CCNY. Both he and Levin addressed fundamental elements of personal identity, but Jeffries' remarks were more readily recognized as protected speech, and his academic freedom was not balanced against the need for racial equity or civility. Harleston explained that the suggestion that blacks are less intelligent than whites tapped into a well of historical and social factors, which, in his view, justified measures that did not extend to speech about other elements of personal identity.[24]

O Pioneers

The belief that "race is different" also underlay a conflict over race-based intelligence that took place at my home institution, the University of Delaware (UD), beginning in October 1989. Although I was at the university at the time and am acquainted with most of the participants, I was not involved in the dispute. It was touched off by a university newsletter that announced faculty research grants, including a Pioneer Fund award to Linda Gottfredson, then an associate professor in the Department of Educational Studies. Gottfredson's original specialty was occupational psychology, but she later became interested in genetic theories of intelligence. Before arriving at UD, she had worked at the Johns Hopkins University on projects supported by the Pioneer Fund. As a faculty member at UD, she had received two previous grants from the Pioneer Fund, primarily to support conferences and the dissemination of research materials. The combined total of the three grants, including the one that started the controversy, was $174,000.

According to the Pioneer Fund Web site, the organization "is dedicated to furthering the scientific study of human ability and diversity." It also disseminates material, "no matter how upsetting those findings may be to any entrenched religious or political dogmas. We believe that ignorance, fear of knowledge, and suppression of academic freedom have never served humanity well, and that we should resist any encroachments on scholarship or the chilling effect of any form of political correctness or orthodoxy."[25] The references to "entrenched religious or political dogmas" and "political correctness or orthodoxy" describe opposition to the research the Pioneer Fund supports, which focuses heavily—though not exclusively—on studies of racial disparities in intelligence.

When Gottfredson's third grant was announced, a UD linguistics professor named William Frawley wrote to President E. Arthur Trabant expressing outrage at the award. As is true of most academic research grants, the funds were not given to Gottfredson as an individual but to the university on her behalf. Administered by the university's research office, faculty research grants cover such things as released time from teaching, secretarial support, research assistance, travel, equipment, books, photocopying, printing costs, and postage. Frawley protested that by administering money from the Pioneer Fund, the university was compromising its commitment to racial equity.

The evidence that Frawley presented to support his contention included the original Pioneer Fund charter, which declared that one purpose of the organization was to encourage the reproduction and advancement of people "descended predominantly from white persons who settled in the original thirteen states . . . or from related stocks."[26] Although that charter was no longer in use, Frawley argued that it remained an accurate representation of the Pioneer Fund's true purpose. He also cited numerous examples of what he described as racist work by previous grant recipients. Among the earliest and best known of these recipients was William Shockley, who won a Nobel Prize for his role in inventing the transistor. Turning to the study of eugenics, Shockley suggested that intelligence is hereditary and that the low intelligence and high birthrate of American blacks contributed significantly to increases in unemployment and crime. Another well-known Pioneer Fund scholar, Arthur Jensen, was professor emeritus in educational psychology at the University of California, Berkeley. He asserted that intelligence is inherited, that blacks are statistically lower in intelligence than other groups, and that these factors help to explain why so many blacks live in poverty.[27]

In a letter to President Trabant, Gottfredson protested that Frawley had misrepresented the Pioneer Fund, which she described as "a legitimate research foundation concerned with the study of heredity." She listed several prestigious institutions that had accepted grants from the Pioneer Fund, including Stanford University, the University of Pennsylvania, the Johns Hopkins University, and the University of California, Berkeley. While conceding that the original Pioneer Fund charter preferred whites, she pointed out that when it was drafted, UD did not admit black students. Just as the university had changed over time, she said, so had the Pioneer Fund, whose current charter contains no mention of racial bias. She also accused Frawley of sloppy scholarship for making excessive and uncritical use of articles by Barry Mehler, a humanities professor at Ferris State University whom she identified as an inveterate opponent of the Pioneer Fund. His work, she protested, was published largely in left-leaning popular newsletters and magazines, and Frawley's letter merely repeated unsubstantiated accusations based on political bias.

Pioneer Fund administrators entered the fray with a memorandum stating that Mehler's articles appeared in communist publications. Moreover, they stated, Mehler had never interviewed any of the Pioneer Fund trustees, and his methodology and motives were suspect. Asserting that Frawley lacked academic credentials in any relevant field, the memorandum accused him of parroting Mehler's claims in a letter "of an ideological and obsessive nature seemingly reflecting non-academic objectives." An attachment described the Pioneer Fund as an agency that makes grants "primarily for smaller 'niche' projects which have difficulty attracting funds from government sources or from the larger foundations." According to the attachment, the Pioneer Fund neither originates projects nor suggests results.

President Trabant asked the Faculty Senate Committee on Research to make a recommendation concerning the university's acceptance of future Pioneer Fund grants. It was generally agreed that the university could not penalize Gottfredson for the content of her work; the question was whether applying for research funding from a particular organization is a right protected by academic freedom or a privilege the university may curtail. Under AAUP standards of academic freedom, universities may refuse to accept research grants for neutral reasons: for instance, if a funding organization has a history of reneging on commitments, makes excessive financial demands on the university, or requires that some or all of the research results not be published. UD officials acknowledged that they could not limit Gottfredson's access to research funding solely because her research goals conflicted with the university's racial equity policies, but they maintained that they could decline to accept grants on behalf of faculty from organizations whose ideology they found unacceptable.

Despite repeated assurances that the research committee was not evaluating the content of Gottfredson's work, the committee chair requested copies of her applications to the Pioneer Fund as well as all the materials that she had distributed under its grants. The purpose, he explained, was to "have the fullest possible record of the relationship between the Pioneer Fund and the University of Delaware, and of the activities carried out as a result of that relationship." The committee also sought to ascertain "what actually went out from the University of Delaware in connect[ion] with your project." Although Gottfredson complied with the request, she questioned why that material was relevant if the target of the investigation was the Pioneer Fund and not the ideological content of her own work. As an arbitrator later agreed, her point was well taken. The committee's request for her applications and mailings inescapably suggested that its recommendation about whether to terminate access to Pioneer Fund grants would reflect not only the history and philosophy of the organization but also the content of her work. An example of the material the committee considered was an unsolicited mass mailing that Gottfredson had sent to the deans of medical schools, consisting largely of research by other scholars. The point of the mailing was to argue that discrepancies between the IQ scores of blacks and those of other races do not arise from social or educational disadvantages but from a real difference in intelligence. Accordingly, the mailing opposed affirmative-action admissions to medical schools on the ground that students thus admitted were genuinely less qualified than applicants who met the established criteria. This mailing, directed toward institutional policymakers rather than scholars, was a central issue in the committee's interview with the dean of the College of Education, Frank Murray.

Alluding to the medical-school mailing as well as to a conference held at UD with Pioneer Fund support, the committee asked Dean Murray whether Gottfredson's grant applications could be terminated without prejudice to academic freedom because she was not conducting original research but disseminating other people's work. The dean, who also held the H. Rodney Sharp Professorship of Education for his scholarly work on human intelligence, agreed that such activities are inferior to original research. He asserted that if he were in charge of awarding grants, he would not select projects of that kind. Nevertheless, he said, his opinion of the scholarly value of a particular project had nothing to do with Gottfredson's right to disseminate research findings, whether her own or someone else's, and to do so with grant support if she could obtain it. Although the quality of her scholarship was certainly reviewable in other contexts, his point was that her ability to secure funds to disseminate ideas could not be made contingent on an ad hoc assessment of her activities outside normal evaluation procedures.

Similar issues arose when the committee suggested that Gottfredson's grant proposals could be blocked on the ground that university employees may not involve the institution in political activities. The regulation to which the committee referred relates to political activism, such as supporting candidates for public office. Obviously, if that rule applied to all research that states an opinion on political questions or that has the potential to influence public policy, the publications of faculty in such fields as political science, international relations, urban affairs, and journalism would fall foul of it constantly—as would this book. The same is true of research in education, which, Dean Murray pointed out, often has political implications and is meant to influence public policy.

As these exchanges suggest, Murray persistently challenged the committee's assumption that the controversial nature of race-based intelligence justified the imposition of special rules. By repeatedly placing Gottfredson's activities in a larger context, such as other work on politics, intelligence, and race, he showed that the effort to block her grant proposals was not supported by any generally applicable policy. Instead of stopping there, however, he attempted to formulate rules to govern his own decisions about whether to sign off on grant applications from faculty in his college. The explosion that followed makes it easier to understand why other university administrators found the ad hoc approach so attractive.

Most of the opposition to Murray's plan focused on its stipulation that university officials could refuse to sign off on grant proposals that were not "consistent with the unit's mission and standards, broadly construed." The examples that he provided included proposals that were poorly conceived or irrelevant to the professor's discipline. Although Murray passionately denied any intention of rejecting proposals on the basis of their political orientation, the reference to being "consistent" with "mission" was criticized as a means of opening the door to ideological discrimination based on the university's goals or policies. Further controversy arose when Murray asked to see papers written by Gottfredson's students in order to investigate the allegation that students were being encouraged to echo her views on race. He argued that his request had nothing to do with academic freedom because he did not seek to constrain what she taught, but to exercise his right as dean to know what she was teaching. When the UD chapter of the AAUP disagreed, he did not pursue the matter.

In addition to raising questions about the academic merit of Gottfredson's Pioneer Fund work, the committee suggested that even if those activities qualified as scholarship—which it did not concede—a ban on Pioneer Fund grants would not violate her academic freedom because she would remain at liberty to pursue research in her field. Gottfredson protested that funding was essential to the specific projects she wished to undertake, such as organizing national conferences and producing and disseminating newsletters. She would also be at a disadvantage in doing her own research if she could not secure resources. Because of the political unpopularity of her views, she maintained, the Pioneer Fund was her only realistic source of support. The committee retorted that if no other organization would fund her work, it must lie too far outside the mainstream of her discipline to be academically credible.

The position articulated by the committee was not supported by generally applicable academic standards. Many successful scholars in the arts, humanities, and social sciences are fortunate if they can secure funding from even one agency. Moreover, the attractiveness of a project to potential funders, public or private, may have less to do with its academic merit than with its furtherance of the agency's mission or its congruence with the specific types of research the agency chooses to encourage. The committee's claim that if only one organization is interested in supporting a project, the work must be non-mainstream, which in turn automatically condemns it as academically inferior, is untenable on all points. Ideas that lie outside the mainstream of a particular field are not necessarily wrong. The need for scholars of varying views to fight it out and see whose evidence prevails in the long run is the whole point of academic freedom, which is not contingent on a scholar's ability to acquire external funding from even one source, let alone multiple sources. What was at issue in the Pioneer Fund debate was not whether race-based intelligence is controversial, or even whether it is accurate, but whether scholars who seek to demonstrate its accuracy are entitled to play by the same rules as everyone else.

In addition to suggesting that Gottfredson seek an alternative source of funding, UD officials denied that any action of theirs would cut her off from the Pioneer Fund. Without going through the university, she could solicit, accept, and administer any money awarded to her as an individual. The Pioneer Fund and Gottfredson quickly rejected that suggestion, not only as a matter of principle but also because of the tax implications. Moreover, UD's policies imposed burdensome conditions on the receipt of private research funding—notably, that work done under such grants would not fulfill the research requirement that makes up part of the faculty workload. Gottfredson would have had to maintain two separate research operations, one inside and one outside her university job, and nothing published with private grant support would have contributed to her merit raises or promotions. By adopting that model, she would have conceded, in effect, that her work on race-based intelligence was not scholarship but something more akin to a personal hobby.

After a six-month investigation, the committee issued a report which, to no one's surprise, recommended that the university cease processing applications for Pioneer Fund grants. Echoing speech-code advocates as well as the CCNY committee that had investigated Levin, the UD committee denied the existence of tension between academic freedom and the quest for racial equity. "The University's commitment to racial and cultural diversity is an essential part of, not a rival principle in conflict with, the University's commitment to the right of all people to participate in an environment of free and open inquiry," the report declared. As the committee defined it, intellectual freedom was not the right to promote controversial ideas but "access to free and open inquiry for all persons of whatever racial and cultural background"—a goal that would not be well served if UD "lends its prestige and credibility, and is made to appear to have supported the Pioneer Fund's activities." The committee emphasized that Gottfredson was not being instructed either to discontinue her research or to curtail the expression of her ideas, and she remained free to seek alternative funding.

In its report, the committee questioned the academic validity of the Pioneer Fund's procedures, which differed significantly from those of other agencies. Applications consisting of a single brief letter were submitted almost exclusively by recipients of previous grants or by other scholars whom they recommended, and proposals were not routinely evaluated by outside experts. Rather, decisions were made by a five-person board, often within a day or two. At the time the UD committee wrote its report, no one on the Pioneer Fund board had professional expertise in any relevant academic field: one was a banker, two were lawyers, and two were engineers. The UD committee viewed these procedures as evidence that projects were chosen not for their academic merit but for their promotion of the view that intelligence varies with race.

Consistent with the committee's ad hoc approach was its failure to address the acceptance of funds from other organizations that advocated viewpoints unacceptable to UD. The committee did not, for instance, recommend investigating whether applications to the National Organization for Women were expected to advance certain beliefs about gender equity or whether the university should decline funding from the U.S. Department of Defense, whose exclusion of openly homosexual men and women conflicted with the UD equity policy on sexual orientation. To justify its recommendation of a special Pioneer Fund rule, the committee provided a lengthy summary of a UD document proclaiming the institution's commitment to "equity for people of different backgrounds throughout all areas of University life." The committee viewed this affirmation as a "special commitment by the University" to an "effort to redress the results of generations of cultural, gender and especially racial discrimination." Indeed, the committee observed, the importance of racial equity was so unique that *"no general precedent applicable to other potentially controversial issues is established"* (emphasis added) by its recommendation to ban Pioneer Fund grants. At stake, the committee believed, was the university's ability to attract and retain minority students, as well as the quality of the educational experience for those who did attend. Like speech-code supporters and the CCNY administration, the UD committee concluded that either academic freedom should be redefined to focus on the right to a nonhostile learning environment, or if academic freedom inescapably clashed with racial equity, the latter must prevail.

The committee's justification for creating a special policy for Pioneer Fund grants was mired in inconsistency because its primary purpose, and that of the university administration, could not be achieved by means of a policy that applied to only one organization. The Pioneer Fund had been targeted because Professor Frawley happened to recognize its name, but a ban on its grants would not preclude applications to other agencies that already existed, or that might be established in the future, to support research on race-based intelligence or other inflammatory racial issues. Moreover, once UD established the precedent of rejecting grants because of ideological differences with the funding source, it could be assumed to accept the views of any agency from which it did take grants. The committee could have avoided this problem by recommending that UD develop a generally applicable policy for processing grant proposals, including straightforward language explaining the role of racial or other concerns. Perhaps recalling the incendiary response that had greeted Dean Murray's attempt to draft such a policy, the committee did not pursue this path. It declared instead, "We see no need for the establishment of any new form of research-funding oversight process designed to determine in advance whether outside funding sources to be solicited by the University are incompatible with the University's mission. We urge that University officials who review applications for external funding be reminded of their responsibility to consider the compatibility of applications and funding sources with the University mission."

Since the premise underlying the report was UD's "special commitment" to racial equity, the inescapable conclusion is that in the absence of any written policy that could be discussed and challenged, university officials serving at the pleasure of the administration should quietly weed out proposals deemed "incompatible with the University's mission." The suggestion that the applications themselves should be subject to this kind of review is significant because it implicates not only the reputation of the funding organization but also the content and viewpoint of the proposed research. If carried out, this procedure would make nonsense of the claim that Gottfredson and like-minded colleagues could apply for funding from alternative sources. Proposals to demonstrate the existence of race-based differences in intelligence would not be processed no matter what agency was involved.

The committee's proposed procedure for reviewing grant proposals is particularly ironic when juxtaposed with its scorn for the Pioneer Fund's application process. With the possible exception of department chairs, the university officials who sign off on grant proposals—particularly the professional staff employed in the research office—are unlikely to possess any more expertise in the relevant content fields than did the banker, the two lawyers, and the two engineers who made up the Pioneer Fund's review board. While castigating the Pioneer Fund for assigning nonexperts to *accept* proposals on the basis of their promotion of race-based intelligence, the committee recommended using UD's own nonexperts to *reject* proposals for exactly the same reason. Apparently, the relevant variable was neither the expertise of the reviewers nor the appropriateness of privileging one view over another but which view was to be privileged.

No such doubts appeared to trouble President Trabant, who wrote to the committee, "I note your statements that academic freedom does not require that the University approve and forward every application for external funding generated by members of the faculty. Furthermore, the University has a right to set its own priorities for support of scholarly activity." Shortly afterward, he announced a new policy: "The University of Delaware should neither seek nor accept any further financial support from the Pioneer Fund as long as the Fund remains committed to the intent of its original charter and to a pattern of activities incompatible with the University's mission." In response to a protest from the Pioneer Fund, the chairman of the board of trustees, which strongly supported the policy, wrote, "[O]ur Board has, as an important objective, that the University administration and faculty enhance the racial and cultural diversity of faculty, staff, and students." This aim conflicted with activities supported by the Pioneer Fund, which "either seek to demonstrate or start from the assumption that there are fundamental hereditary differences among people of different racial and cultural backgrounds." The letter further stated that even if the Pioneer Fund did not in fact endorse ideas inconsistent with UD's racial policy, the widespread perception that it did so might have a negative effect on the university's recruitment of minority students.

Two months after the ban went into effect, Gottfredson submitted a new application for a Pioneer Fund grant to support the preparation of a collection of essays based on a colloquium held at UD under an earlier grant. Jan Blits, then an associate professor in the Department of Educational Studies and her strongest supporter on the faculty, also submitted a Pioneer Fund application at that time. Blits had received a research stipend from the Pioneer Fund in the summer of 1988, and he and Gottfredson had cowritten two articles challenging the adjustment of IQ test scores to compensate for alleged unfairness to certain racial groups. Blits requested a Pioneer Fund grant to support a proposed study of campus policies that suppress research into racial issues.

When, inevitably, university officials refused to process either proposal, Blits and Gottfredson filed grievances with the UD chapter of the AAUP (AAUP-UD).[28] They charged that the new policy violated a provision of the university's "Statement on Academic Freedom": "The teacher is entitled to full freedom in research and in the publication of results, but research for pecuniary return should be based upon an understanding with the authorities of the University." UD officials replied that no restraints were being placed on teaching, choice of research topics, or ability to publish scholarly work. To Gottfredson and Blits, however, "full freedom in research" included an ideologically neutral opportunity to seek grant funding. The AAUP-UD agreed, as did the organization's national office. Jonathan Knight, longtime associate secretary of the national AAUP, said that he had never heard of a situation in which "two faculty members could not obtain monies from an outside foundation for their research, not because the foundation had a history of withholding funds or bad administration, but [because] the views and values of the source were called into question."[29]

Gottfredson's complaint, which was the more extensive of the two and encompassed the points made by Blits, stated that the ban on Pioneer Fund grants violated her professional academic freedom as well as her First Amendment rights. Describing applications for external grant funding as an inherent part of the scholarly process, she maintained that they could not be limited on ideological grounds. She denied the university's assertion that its policy was aimed solely at the Pioneer Fund, pointing out that her own activities had also been called into question.

Like Levin, Gottfredson proclaimed the right of scholars to pursue unpopular ideas so that the truth could emerge from an unhampered exchange of views among experts in the field. In a revised version of her complaint dated September 17, 1990, she wrote, "The Research Committee recommended banning Pioneer funds in large part because it found unacceptable that the Pioneer Fund might be supporting studies on genetic differences by race. The question of whether such differences exist is a matter to be settled, not by administrative fiat or political pressure, but by the scientific inquiry being conducted in various disciplines." By subjecting the Pioneer Fund and its grant recipients to disfavored treatment, the committee "has denied the legitimacy of seeking the truth on this question and has impugned the integrity of all scholars who entertain (or are thought to entertain) the question."

The dispute went into binding arbitration, and in August 1991, the arbitrator rejected the university's assertion that the ban on Pioneer Fund grants was based solely on the philosophy, or perceived philosophy, of that organization. The arbitrator found that the committee's recommendation was based in part on its explicit characterization of Gottfredson's work as incompatible with the university's mission. Taking issue with the letter written by the chairman of the board of trustees, the arbitrator declared that the ban could not be justified by the public's perception of the Pioneer Fund. "Academic freedom is a contractually conferred right, and public perceptions alone, no matter how volatile, cannot suffice to overcome that right," he declared in his report. "As the University noted, limitations on a faculty member's academic freedom must be fair, reasonable, and consistent. A University policy implemented in response to public perception alone, without regard to the factual underpinnings of that perception, cannot ensure a procedure that is fair, reasonable, and consistent."

Because of that flaw in the university's position, the arbitrator found it unnecessary to reach a decision about whether a ban on Pioneer Fund applications infringed upon academic freedom. Instead, he ruled in favor of Gottfredson and Blits on the ground that the university had violated its own policies and procedures when it "unfairly, thus wrongly, denied the grievants' funding requests by delving into the substantive nature of the grievants' work." Applications for grants from the Pioneer Fund would henceforth be processed like any others, and Gottfredson and Blits received a full year of research time to compensate for the disruption to their work caused by the dispute.

Theme and Variations

The outcomes of the CCNY and UD controversies rest on a distinction between a public university's right to take a stand on racial issues and the right of its faculty to express viewpoints that conflict, or are perceived as conflicting, with the institutional message. Stated in the converse, the university may not penalize faculty for the content of their speech, but nothing prevents the institution from expressing its own opinions. That premise came to the fore in a controversy that took place in 1996 at the University of New Orleans (UNO). Unlike the CCNY and UD disputes, this one did not involve a lawsuit or arbitration. Rather, it raised interesting points about what behavior is appropriate—as opposed to legal or constitutional—when a professor and a university administration find themselves at loggerheads over racial equity issues.

Like Levin, Edward Miller, Research Professor of Economics and Finance at UNO, came late to the study of eugenics. The dispute over his work began in July 1996, when he wrote a letter to the editor of a New Orleans newspaper, *Gambit*, stating that intelligence is related to the size of the brain and that whites have heavier brains than blacks. He expressed agreement with a statement by David Duke, former grand wizard of the Ku Klux Klan and founder of the National Association for the Advancement of White People, indicating that blacks are less intelligent than whites. Since Duke was widely regarded as the personification of racism in Louisiana, Miller's invocation of his name was provocative.

In his letter to the editor, Miller identified himself as a UNO professor but stated that the views he expressed were his own, not those of the university. Without taking action against Miller or attempting to silence his speech, the chancellor of UNO, Gregory O'Brien, wrote letters to all the major newspapers in the area expressing the university's strong disagreement with Miller's assertions. Among other things, the letter stated that although UNO respected freedom of speech, the institution placed an even higher value on its commitment to diversity. O'Brien's acknowledgment of Miller's First Amendment rights, tepid as it was, incensed Paul R. Valteau, Jr., sheriff of New Orleans Parish. In a letter to O'Brien, written on Sheriff's Department letterhead and signed with his official title, he said that race-based intelligence has been conclusively disproven. Offering no evidence to support that claim, he nonetheless used it to justify the assertion that racism is the only possible reason for anyone to promote race-based intelligence or to defend those who do so. "I believe it is incumbent on you to make a public and forceful statement denouncing Dr. Miller and his dangerous and racist assertions and let the courts protect his 1st Amendment rights," he declared. "Anything less would leave myself and the African American community questioning where the University of New Orleans really stands on matters of racism." He also remarked, "When I review your quest for a scientific research park for UNO, I now must view this in a different light. I must now question whether the research results which will come out of your park will be as specious as Dr. Miller's theory, which has apparently gained shelter and sustenance at your university."[30]

The sheriff's reference to the political support necessary to establish a new research park provides a good example of the external pressures that university administrators face when, no matter how correctly, they defend the right of faculty to engage in controversial speech. Although direct and specific threats are rarely published, the sheriff's underlying reasoning—that university administrations must penalize the expression of certain viewpoints if they do not wish to be identified with them—pervades the entire debate over racially offensive speech. Ironically, the sheriff's suggestion that the UNO administration should uphold racial equity and "let the courts protect [Miller's] 1st Amendment rights" recalls the rationale once used to justify the continuation of racial segregation after it had been declared unconstitutional: that segregationist school administrators should do what they believed right until the courts found a way to stop them.

Despite the anger engendered by Miller's remarks, the UNO administration took no action other than to wage a one-sided battle of words against him in campus publications. The campus newspaper, *Driftwood,* carried a long story criticizing Miller but allowed him only 300 words for a reply. Another campus publication, *UNO Notes,* adopted an editorial policy excluding information that conflicted with the university's commitment to diversity. Its columns were thenceforth closed to one side of the debate on race-based intelligence while material on the other side, some of it heated in tone, continued to appear. No one challenged UNO's right to control the content of its own publications; the question was whether its choices were fair and appropriate in the context of public higher education. At least in the campus newspaper, if not in the administration's own newsletter, it would seem more consistent with a public university's values and mission to encourage open debate on thorny questions than to use campus publications as a means of influencing popular opinion by the disproportionate allocation of ink.

Shortly after the publication of Miller's letter in *Gambit,* the provost of UNO sent him a scolding letter that, according to Miller, was placed in his personnel file. No further penalty was imposed or threatened, but the provost's filing of such a document certainly qualifies as adverse, if minimal, action. Without suggesting that Miller should cease to promote race-based intelligence, the provost accused him of violating a rule against the use of UNO letterhead for the expression of personal views outside a faculty member's area of expertise. Miller protested that he had used his personal stationery, and the record does not indicate how stringently the university generally enforced its letterhead regulations. The more significant issue, however, was the provost's implication that Miller's views on race-based intelligence were extraneous to his field of expertise.

Miller's academic appointment was in the Department of Economics and Finance. To the provost, race-based intelligence belonged in the Department of Psychology, whereas Miller saw it in terms of mathematical research and economic policy. As evidence of his competence as a researcher in the field of race-based intelligence, he listed his relevant publications and conference papers and argued that his background in mathematics and economics contributed to his opinions about the reasons for racially disparate poverty rates and the economic implications of ignoring race-based differences in ability. In his view, the provost's attempt to distance Miller's work on race-based intelligence from his UNO position stemmed not from any lack of professional competence on Miller's part but from "an opinion which is widespread (often called political correctness) that the only scientific research that should be done and disseminated is that designed to promote a particular view of the causes of inequality. . . . [T]he politically correct view is that poor black academic and economic problems are solely due to prejudice and actions by white people. This is an incorrect view, which encourages black hatred of white people . . . [and] leads to the imposition of quotas and discrimination against whites and Asians."[31]

Whereas Miller emphasized his competence to write and speak as an expert on race-based intelligence, the provost focused on Miller's field of expertise as a UNO professor: a different point, and one to which the normal standards of academia provide no universally applicable answers. On the one hand, if "field of expertise" is defined in terms of the subject matter taught in a particular department, then the university may choose to award merit pay and promotions only for work in that area no matter how much a professor may know about something else. On the other hand, it is not unusual for a professor's scholarly interests to evolve over the course of a long career, and many departments are more concerned with a project's quality and importance than with its content-area purity. Indeed, the ability to cross traditional disciplinary boundaries is increasingly valued as an asset in today's university departments. These parameters, which differ by discipline, are set by each university, usually at the department or college level.

In Miller's case, "his department had told him that he would be evaluated only on articles that he had published in mainstream economic journals."[32] If that was indeed the condition set by the department—not the viewpoint of the articles, but their appearance in journals deemed both meritorious and relevant to the discipline—it reflects a legitimate standard of scholarship. To be sure, Miller might claim that his research on race-based intelligence could not be published in mainstream journals because of the editors' ideological bias, but in the absence of evidence that other faculty in his department were permitted more latitude in deciding where to publish their work, any arguments he might make along those lines would have to be debated amid the ordinary rough-and-tumble of academic politics.

Most pertinent to the present discussion is whether work that lies outside the content-field parameters established by a professor's department is protected by academic freedom. According to the AAUP, the primary purpose of academic freedom is to allow experts in a field to pursue their research wherever it may lead, free from interference by university administrators or external forces. By this standard, Miller was correct in asserting that the decisive factor was his ability to understand race-based intelligence at a professional level and to contribute to the literature in the field. To be sure, universities are entitled to define the work for which they will provide merit raises and promotions, but the fine line drawn in Miller's case— whether an economist is working outside his field if he analyzes patterns of poverty in terms of race-based intelligence—illustrates the potential for mischief if it were that easy to deprive controversial ideas of the protection of academic freedom.

When a professor presents evidence to support a particular view, the ensuing debate should be based on the merit of his or her ideas, unfettered by any gerrymandering of the scope of academic freedom to fit content-area limitations that are, or should be, established on other grounds. Even if determined by the department faculty, not by the administration, the delineation of a content field with respect to merit pay and promotion should not be considered coextensive with the limits of academic freedom.[33]

The UNO dispute, like the controversies at CCNY and UD, was based on the same error that led to the formulation of speech codes. The root of the problem was that university administrators allowed themselves to be mouse-trapped into acting on the false premise that the university's treatment of scholars or students who promote unpopular racial views is a litmus test by which the institution's own commitment to racial equity may be measured. In reality, students have a constitutional right to speak freely as private individuals, and academic freedom is based on the understanding that faculty do not, and must not claim to, speak for the institution. When administrators yield to demands that they attempt to suppress unpopular speech by students and faculty, they weaken the university's ability to articulate its own message, and they expose the university to the perception that it is responsible for the content of speech that it cannot in fact control.

A Blanket on the Sidewalk

For the purpose of illustrating how conflicts over race-based intelligence fit into the larger picture of academic-freedom disputes, it might be useful to preview a later section of this book that deals with evolution, creationism, and intelligent design (ID). On the surface, students and faculty who believe that all living things are the product of either God or an unidentified intelligent designer appear to have far more justification for complaint than exponents of race-based intelligence do. Mainstream scientists exclude explanations based on creationism or ID from scientific research and instruction, scientific journals routinely reject articles supporting those explanations, grant agencies do not fund such proposals, and papers on those topics are generally not accepted for presentation at mainstream scientific conferences except as sociological curiosities. As a result, adherents of those views cannot demonstrate professional achievement in the currencies that university science departments value. They are, in fact, hindered at the very threshold of the academic world because in order to earn graduate degrees in such fields as paleontology and geology, they must submit coursework and dissertations containing information that they believe to be false. Indeed, some scientists would exclude them from those graduate programs altogether.

By contrast, the obstacles placed in the way of research into race-based intelligence may appear relatively minor. What matters, however, is not the severity of adverse action but the justification on which it rests. Proponents of creation-based or designer-based explanations for the origins of life have tried—and failed—to make their case for more than a century and a half. Indeed, even they concede that some of their ideas are not merely tangential but antithetical to science as it is presently defined. Accordingly, the basis for excluding such explanations from the discipline of science is that in an extended process of fact-based debate, their advocates have, by the normal standards of academia, been unsuccessful. Their claims rest largely on a sustained insistence on redefining "science" to accommodate assertions unsupported by the kinds of evidence that the discipline presently requires. Even if, for the sake of argument, we assume that explanations based on creationism and/or ID do indeed qualify as science and are being excluded solely because most scientists do not yet recognize that reality, the manner in which the debate is being conducted is consistent with the principles of academic freedom. The function of academic freedom is to define the process by which academic judgments are made, not to ensure either an outcome or a timetable.

By contrast, the controversies at CCNY, UD, and UNO arose from concerns about the probable social, psychological, and political consequences of demonstrating a link between race and intelligence. Statistically, the IQ test scores of people of African descent are lower than those of other groups; the question is why. And nowhere in the voluminous paperwork documenting these three disputes is evidence presented to substantiate any answer to that question. Almost as an act of faith or social virtue, those who rejected the concept of race-based intelligence assumed that racial disparities in IQ scores could not possibly reflect genuine differences. Although they made occasional references to unnamed studies that allegedly discredited race-based intelligence, they offered no data showing that differences in test scores arise from reversible environmental factors. The studies in question might well be compelling, but their credibility cannot be evaluated based on the mere assertion that they exist. Significantly, the omission of this material from the CCNY, UD, and UNO disputes suggests that critics of race-based intelligence did not consider the presentation of hard evidence essential to the point they were making. By substituting indignation and fervent rhetoric for a more scholarly approach, they implied that taking race-based intelligence seriously enough even to engage in that level of debate would betray the cause of racial equity.

Similar charges might be leveled against Professors Levin, Gottfredson, Blits, and Miller, who did not base their arguments on data supporting race-based intelligence. If the disputes at CCNY, UD, and UNO had been about which explanation of disparities in IQ scores is accurate, the result would have been zero–all. But the question at issue in each instance was not whether some races are statistically more intelligent than others. The question was whether professors who wished to demonstrate the truth of that proposition had a right to play by the same rules that applied to other professors, and the burden of proof rested squarely on the attackers. Professor Gottfredson, for instance, correctly maintained that her right to have her grant applications handled under generally applicable rules could not be made conditional on whether a committee of nonexperts carrying out an ad hoc review found her work persuasive. In that context, if she had based her argument on her data rather than on her academic-freedom rights, she would in effect have conceded the battle, particularly when no similar presentation of hard evidence was made by, or demanded of, her opponents. By contrast, critics of race-based intelligence at each institution were ethically and professionally obligated to demonstrate that such actions as establishing shadow sections of courses, initiating ad hoc investigations, refusing to process grant applications, and denying access to campus publications were based on something more than ideological disagreement. Even if they were correct in every assertion they made, they nonetheless deserved to lose the academic-freedom battle for failing to base academic decisions on a sustained process—or, indeed, any process—of fact-based debate.

In the ideal world of academic freedom, scholars marshal their evidence and ride merrily into battle with "QED" emblazoned on their shields. If casualties are carried from the field, such is the normal outcome of the process. But the actions taken against research on race-based intelligence smack more of prior restraint than of victory. To justify discrimination against faculty who promote certain ideas, it is essential to demonstrate, not that those ideas are offensive and may lead to adverse consequences, but that they are incorrect. Academic freedom would become meaningless if action could be taken against the proponents of a particular viewpoint, no matter how unpopular, on any basis other than generally applicable principles and procedures. No matter how ideologically or socially unacceptable a concept appears to its opponents, and no matter how numerous those opponents are, they may not apply discriminatory rules intended to obstruct research or hinder the dissemination of information or arguments that conflict with their own views. To do so is, in effect, to demand that theirs must be the only stall open for business in the free marketplace of ideas, while their opponents are reduced to peddling their wares from a blanket on the sidewalk.

4

Rainbow Before the Storm

But laws alone cannot secure freedom of expression; in order that every man may present his views without penalty there must be a spirit of tolerance in the entire population.

—Albert Einstein, *Out of My Later Years*

IN THE FOREGOING DISCUSSION OF DISPUTES about speech codes and race-based intelligence, the central issue was whether a public school or university may compel students and faculty to endorse an institutional message that is strongly influenced by constitutional requirements, by conditions placed on the acceptance of state and federal funding, and by social and political considerations. The present chapter expands the discussion by examining a controversial area of personal identity that is not explicitly referenced in the U.S. Constitution. By comparison with the treatment of race in public schools and universities, approaches to the topic of homosexuality are largely open to judgment calls by administrators who must determine what attitudes the institution will promote, how it will respond to dissenting views among students and faculty, and how it will deal with community pressure. Given this administrative latitude, public school and university officials do not speak with one voice about homosexuality to the extent that they do about race. Moreover, because sexual orientation has come to the fore as a social issue comparatively recently, the norms and expectations governing its treatment in public education are still under construction. To explore the relevance of these factors to the way American public education handles controversial topics, this chapter presents a series of case studies, first dealing with K–12 schools and then with universities, that illustrate different patterns of equity, tolerance, and rejection.

Diversity: Goal or Threat?

In June 1997 the public schools in the Los Angeles Unified School District (LAUSD) celebrated Gay and Lesbian Awareness Month as part of the district's "Educating for Diversity" initiative. A memorandum from the district office explained that the purpose was to emphasize the right of all students to participate fully in school activities and to be free from name-calling, physical violence, and other forms of discriminatory behavior. In addition to displaying posters provided by the district, administrators at Doris S. Leichman High School designated a bulletin board on which faculty and staff could post such items as an explanation of the pink triangle, a rainbow flag, and statistics on hate crimes.

Robert Downs, a teacher at Leichman High, disagreed with the school's message about homosexuality. On a bulletin board across the hall from his classroom, he posted such items as a copy of the Declaration of Independence, a statement that 60 percent of Americans disapprove of homosexuality, and information about anti-sodomy laws. He also posted a quotation from Leviticus: "Do not lie with a man as one lies with a woman; that is detestable. Do not have sexual relations with an animal and defile yourself with it. A woman must not present herself to an animal to have sexual relations with it; that is a perversion. Do not defile yourselves in any of these ways because this is how the nations that I am going to drive out before you become defiled." Another of his postings stated, "Obviously and without contention the simultaneous stimulation and mutual satisfaction which the complementary anatomical structures and functioning of the procreative organs of the man and woman produce indicate that they are purposefully intended for one another. Procreation and thereby the proliferation of the human species are further confirmation that such unions are appropriate and natural. Beyond this, the various organs of the digestive and excretory systems can and have been used for similar gratification, but obviously these acts are different and can be objectively evaluated as such."[1]

A similar sequence of events took place the following June, and two successive school principals either removed material from Downs's bulletin board or asked him to do so himself. The bulletin board, they declared, was not a free-speech zone for the expression of personal views that conflicted with the school district's message of inclusivity and its call for an end to anti-gay discrimination. Downs filed suit, alleging that he had a free-speech right to use the bulletin board to express his opinion. Among other things, he maintained that the principals and other education officials had an obligation to be viewpoint-neutral in regulating speech within the school. Where one opinion about homosexuality was expressed, he argued, competing opinions could not be suppressed.

Although the viewpoint-neutral standard would indeed apply in some contexts, the U.S. Court of Appeals for the Ninth Circuit ruled in *Downs v. Los Angeles Unified School District* (2000) that the situation at Leichman High was "a case of the government itself speaking, whether the government is characterized as Leichman High, LAUSD, or the school board." Accordingly, the court found, school officials had a right to limit the use of school bulletin boards to the presentation of the school's own message. "We do not face an example of the government opening up a forum for either unlimited or limited public discussion," the decision states. "Instead, we face an example of the government opening up its own mouth: LAUSD, by issuing Memorandum No. III, and Leichman High, by setting up the Gay and Lesbian Awareness bulletin boards. The bulletin boards served as an expressive vehicle for the school board's policy of 'Educating for Diversity.' . . . Because the bulletin boards were a manifestation of the school board's policy to promote tolerance, and because [the principal] had final authority over the content of the bulletin boards, all speech that occurred on the bulletin boards was the school board's and LAUSD's speech." The court further declared, "An arm of local government—such as a school board—may decide not only to talk about gay and lesbian awareness and tolerance in general, but also to advocate such tolerance if it so decides, and restrict the contrary speech of one of its representatives."[2]

Clearly, Downs's status as a public-school teacher whose speech could be regulated by school officials was central to the outcome of his case. Different standards applied to a controversy that erupted in New York City in the early 1990s in which the board's antagonists were not its own employees but vocal groups within the communities that elected the board members. Although the board retained the legal right to convey its own message, the political risk of doing so was significant, and the board exercised no control over the speech of the protesters.

At issue was a plan for first-grade instruction called the Children of the Rainbow Curriculum, which was developed in 1989 in response to an unusually high incidence of hate crimes. At the time, the sprawling New York City school system, which covers the Bronx, Brooklyn, Manhattan, Queens, and Staten Island, was divided into thirty-two districts. The residents of each district elected a local school board, and a central board oversaw the entire system. The president of each of the five boroughs appointed one member to the central board, and the mayor appointed two. The central board had the authority to hire, retain, or dismiss the chancellor, who served as chief executive officer of the school system.

To stem the wave of hate crimes, the central school board resolved to use the public schools as a vehicle for promoting tolerance for diversity. Accordingly, Chancellor Joseph Fernandez had his staff develop a multicultural curriculum divided into five theme-based units that integrated language arts, fine arts, health, social studies, and arithmetic. Intended to supplement rather than replace existing classroom instruction, the Rainbow Curriculum contained suggestions for multicultural activities and provided background information for teachers. It was accompanied by a lengthy reading list from which local school districts could choose material for classroom use. Since control of the public-school curriculum rested with the local boards, no specific activity or reading was mandatory. Districts that rejected any part of the Rainbow Curriculum were, however, required to explain how they planned to meet its diversity goals by other means.

Most of the 443-page curriculum dealt with race, ethnicity, and gender, and these sections stirred little controversy other than the complaint that more should be said about African Americans. Significant conflict arose, however, over the curriculum's extension of "tolerance for diversity" to include the promotion of nonjudgmental attitudes toward a variety of family structures, such as single-parent, adoptive, blended, and foster homes. Noting that nontraditional arrangements were well represented among New York City's teeming population, advocates of such instruction focused on the students' interests and feelings. In their view, the exclusive use of stories about children living in traditional nuclear families devalued other family structures. The school system should not marginalize children who do not live in two-parent homes, they contended, and classmates from traditional homes should learn to understand and accept other models.

Critics of this viewpoint emphasized the financial, medical, and academic advantages provided by two-parent homes. While agreeing that children should not be mocked or ostracized because of their living arrangements, opponents of the Rainbow Curriculum argued that public-school instruction should focus on the traditional nuclear family as the kind of household the children should aspire to establish later in life. From their perspective, the curriculum inaccurately and inappropriately suggested that the family structure on which this nation has long been based is nothing more than one lifestyle among many.

Although the entire family-structures concept was moderately controversial, three pages embedded within it generated a firestorm that engulfed all other concerns. Children from homes headed by homosexual couples, the curriculum explained, may have little experience of the traditional families on which most elementary-school books focus. Conversely, children from heterosexual homes may be ignorant or biased with respect to homosexuals. And regardless of the kind of home in which children lived, some were likely to identify themselves as homosexuals later in life, thus risking low self-esteem, social ostracism, violence, job and housing discrimination, and even rejection by their own families. Without suggesting any instruction in sexuality as such, the curriculum called for a nonjudgmental presentation of homosexual households "to help increase the tolerance and acceptance of the lesbian-gay community and to decrease the staggering number of hate crimes perpetrated against them." The curriculum continued, "Teachers of first graders have an opportunity to give children a healthy sense of identity at an early age. Classes should include references to lesbian-gay people in all curricular areas and should avoid exclusionary practices by presuming a person's sexual orientation, reinforcing stereotypes, or speaking of lesbians-gays as 'they' or 'other.'"[3]

The list of recommended readings appended to the Rainbow Curriculum included several books dealing with homosexuality. Two of these books were particularly controversial: *Heather Has Two Mommies,* written by Leslea Newman and illustrated by Diana Souza, and *Daddy's Roommate,* written and illustrated by Michael Willhoite. Neither story touches on the sexual practices of same-sex couples, although some controversy was generated by a description of artificial insemination in *Heather* and by some of the pictures of Daddy and his roommate.[4] Nevertheless, the real point of contention was the books' primary message: that homosexual households are normal and wholesome.

As author Leslea Newman later explained, she wrote *Heather* because of a remark made by a lesbian couple who had just adopted a little girl and could find no children's books depicting a family headed by two females. This chance encounter caused Newman to recall that as "a young Jewish girl with frizzy brown hair eating matzo ball soup with her *bubbe* on Friday night," she had never read stories about families like her own. She added, "As a grown woman who happens to be a Jewish lesbian, I am painfully aware of the lack of positive images or even any images of myself in the media."[5]

In the story that Newman wrote, a curly-haired little girl enjoys building a table with Mama Jane, a carpenter, and joining Mama Kate, a doctor, in listening to her heartbeat through a stethoscope. The three of them go to the park, bake cookies, and play with the cat and the dog. The story focuses on Heather's first day in a play group, where she discovers that other children have daddies. The woman overseeing the play group encourages each child to draw a picture of his or her family: a nuclear family, a single-parent home, a male homosexual household, and so forth. Having learned that the "most important thing about a family is that all the people in it love each other," Heather goes home hand in hand with her mommies.[6]

Daddy's Roommate differs from *Heather* in that the story is narrated by the child, a little boy whose parents are divorced and whose father shares a home with a roommate named Frank. The boy, who lives with his mother, spends his weekends boating, playing ball, and singing around the piano with Frank and Daddy. Despite the inclusion of drawings showing Frank and Daddy sharing a bed, shaving together, and engaging in intimate conversation, the book's most provocative elements are those that most closely resemble traditional depictions of nuclear families. The peanut butter and jelly sandwiches that Frank makes for the little boy and the bedtime stories he reads to him represent the real threat to the representation of homosexuality as unwholesome and "other." This normalization of the relationship between Daddy and Frank is underlined by the child's mind-bogglingly empathetic mother, who explains that the two men are gay, and that "[b]eing gay is just one more kind of love."[7]

Since Heather is cared for by two adults, her living arrangements parallel those of traditional families with respect to financial stability and parental care. Similarly, although the child in *Daddy's Roommate* lives in a single-parent home, he enjoys a comfortable middle-class lifestyle and receives a great deal of positive attention from adults. Accordingly, the contention that this particular type of nontraditional household should be discouraged did not rest on the claim that the child's education, health, and financial security were at risk. Rather, it was based squarely on the conviction that homosexuality itself is wrong. Critics of *Heather* and *Daddy's Roommate* feared that the presentation of such material in the schools would encourage children to regard homosexuality as an acceptable lifestyle and, perhaps, to engage in homosexual behavior. The conservative columnist George Will, for instance, suggested that teaching children to be indifferent to the moral implications of homosexuality might have the effect of "weakening social promptings toward heterosexuality."[8]

Supporters of the Rainbow Curriculum, who regarded homosexuality as biologically determined, scoffed at the belief that heterosexual children would "turn into" homosexuals if social strictures favoring heterosexuality were relaxed. At most, they claimed, young people who might have tried to deny or conceal their sexual orientation would instead embrace it. As Newman observed, "It seems to me that a disproportionate number of parents live in fear of their child's reading just one book with a gay character in it, for such exposure will, in these parents' minds, cause their child to grow up to be lesbian or gay. It is usually useless to point out that the vast majority of lesbians and gay men have been brought up by heterosexual parents and spent countless hours of their childhood reading hundreds of books about heterosexual characters. Fear is an irrational thing."[9]

People who considered homosexuality to be a reversible act of will protested that first-graders should not be taught that a wrong choice is just as normal as the right one. Indeed, they asserted, even if homosexuality does have a biological component, people who possess it need not flaunt it. Like the broader debate over family structures in general, the argument about homosexuality pitted concerns about ideological balance and the interests of children from nontraditional homes against the conviction that the public good is best served by promoting nuclear families as the norm and the desideratum of society. Further opposition came from representatives of various racial and ethnic groups, who argued that racial tolerance is not identical—or even comparable—to the belief that homosexuality is normal. As one candidate for a school-board seat explained in response to a questionnaire, "[S]exuality is not culture." Another candidate wrote, "In our multicultural society we need to teach multi-cultural ethnic subjects but not [a] multi-cultural behavioral life-style which does not fit in [a] school textbook."[10]

Not surprisingly, the Rainbow Curriculum's treatment of homosexuality was most fully embraced in diverse, progressive areas of Manhattan. Residents of more traditional neighborhoods, particularly in Brooklyn, Queens, and Staten Island, were appalled by it. In some instances, local school boards toned down that part of the curriculum or agreed to use some of it in the fifth or sixth grade rather than in the lower grades. Chancellor Fernandez accepted such compromises, reserving his fire for local boards whose outspoken refusal to define homosexual households as "families" had nothing to do with the students' grade level. Prominent among these was the board governing District 24 in Queens, which became so obstreperous that Fernandez suspended its operations and replaced it with three trustees. Reviled by George Will as "the sort of bureaucrat-bully who may yet shatter America's valuable but perishable support for public education,"[11] Fernandez was chided by the *Wall Street Journal* for what its editors considered his "extraordinary display of peremptory arrogance."[12] Less elegantly, the father of a little girl shouted during a demonstration, "I learned about [gay couples] on the street, and that's where she should, too."[13] Within days, the city school board reinstated the Queens board over the chancellor's objections.

Fernandez tried to ameliorate the situation by approving a few changes to the curriculum, such as replacing "lesbian-gay families" with "same-gender couples" and deleting the recommendation to include gay and lesbian references in all subject areas. His action was too little, too late. In the spring of 1993, the city's attention turned to an upcoming school-board election dominated by the controversy. Although only three of the curriculum's 443 pages dealt with homosexuality, the media's saturation coverage of that issue had caused the term "Rainbow Curriculum" to signify little more in the public mind than acceptance of homosexuality.

Candidates for seats on local school boards throughout the city were asked to fill out a voter-information questionnaire summarizing their views, and their responses offer a glimpse into the concerns expressed by both sides.[14] According to one candidate, the curriculum was "designed to support the social agenda of special interests, while at the same time [it] usurps parental and religious rights and family values." As this remark suggests, the election was widely viewed as a struggle between the forces of tradition and those of social change. A *Wall Street Journal* editorial, for instance, argued that class time should be devoted to basic instruction, not wasted on efforts to "inculcate whatever social goals that judges, advocacy groups and central-office bureaucracies deem as 'necessary.'"[15] Representatives of the Roman Catholic Archdiocese of New York and the Diocese of Brooklyn joined the fray, reviling the curriculum as "a fundamental challenge to traditional morality and family values by groups whose influence in government seems to have been growing at the Church's expense."[16]

School-board candidates who supported the Rainbow Curriculum shared their opponents' view that the campaign represented a struggle for the soul of New York, although they defined the battle quite differently. To them, the chief obstacle to ending anti-gay discrimination and violence was conservative resistance to a host of changes necessary to bring about equity and peace. "As an activist, I've been involved for years in fighting the right, from Anita Bryant to Pat Robertson," declared one candidate on her questionnaire. "We must take a stand against bigotry and intolerance." Another candidate wrote, "I'm a parent, a strong supporter of multicultural education, and want to prevent right wing elements from taking over the schools."

Late in the campaign, the Christian Coalition, a conservative religious organization headed by the television evangelist Pat Robertson, prepared voter guides purporting to describe the views of candidates for school-board seats. The guides were distributed in Catholic and conservative Protestant churches on the Sunday before the Tuesday election, prompting pro-curriculum groups, notably the American Civil Liberties Union and People for the American Way, to cry foul. In addition to accusing the churches of violating their tax-exempt status by participating in partisan politics, they protested that the voter guides were incorrect and misleading and that their late distribution prevented effective clarification. Representatives of the Christian Coalition and the Catholic Church responded that the guides merely provided information about the candidates. Nothing in the tax code, they declared, forbade distributing that material two days before the election to church congregations likely to oppose the curriculum.

By comparison with other school-board elections, the one that took place on May 4, 1993, attracted a high turnout: 12.5 percent of eligible voters as opposed to the usual single-digit percentages. Neutral tallies suggested that the two sides were more or less evenly matched with respect to wins and losses, and the media coverage focused on outcomes involving some element of the novel or unexpected. In the Bronx, for instance, support for school prayer and traditional values led to the victory of conservative Christian candidates despite their opposition to a multicultural curriculum that might have been expected to appeal to the diverse population of that borough. Another story involved an all-woman slate of candidates led by a lesbian, which captured six of the nine seats in a progressive Brooklyn district. The leader of that slate and a successful candidate in Manhattan became the city's first openly lesbian school-board members. Perhaps the most significant upset was the election of Chinese-born Louisa Chan in contentious

District 24 in Queens, whose board had been all-white, although the student population was 80 percent nonwhite. A supporter of the Rainbow Curriculum, Chan frequently tangled with other board members, leading the board president to revile her as "an evil, wicked woman."[17]

Ironically, the outcome of the election may have had little real effect on the fate of the Rainbow Curriculum. Before election day, the central school board chose one of Fernandez's staunchest opponents as its new president. Shortly afterward, it declined to renew Fernandez's contract for reasons that included but were not limited to the curriculum dispute. The new chancellor, Ramon Cortines, announced that his staff would try to develop a multicultural curriculum that would include sexual orientation while demonstrating sensitivity to the concerns of opposing parents. Little came of this attempt, and the same was true of a proposal by the new central-board president to revise the school system's diversity policy to cover only racial and ethnic groups. For all practical purposes, the Rainbow Curriculum controversy was over.

As this dispute illustrates, when grassroots outrage is augmented by the financing and expertise provided by national advocacy groups, the result can be an epic battle that pushes the boundaries of the original issue. In this instance, the stated reason for developing the Rainbow Curriculum was to stem hate crimes, and sexual orientation was included in order to protect gay and lesbian students from harassment. No one directly opposed this goal; the disagreement focused on the means necessary to achieve it. While deploring violence and injustice, opponents of the curriculum staunchly asserted their right to shape their children's views about homosexuality without having to deal with competing values promoted by the public schools. This position struck advocates for the homosexual community as a hopeless contradiction. In their view, homosexuals would be treated as equals only when they achieved full social acceptance, which would not happen as long as the negative attitudes taught in some homes went unchallenged. The result was a nonnegotiable tension between those who believed that the curriculum need not go beyond discouraging violence and those who saw no way to achieve that goal *except* by going beyond it.

To the extent that opposition to the values promoted in *Heather* and *Daddy's Roommate* was based on the parents' right to transmit their opinions about homosexuality to their children, it was weakened by widespread acknowledgment of the schools' authority to promote acceptance of various racial and ethnic groups regardless of the views expressed at home. Opponents of the curriculum's treatment of homosexuality attempted to reconcile the inconsistency by distinguishing between fostering respect for diverse racial and ethnic groups and promoting indifference to immorality. This position is tenable, however, only if homosexuality is a choice, whereas such characteristics as race and ethnicity are inborn. If homosexuality is biologically determined, then the only basis for treating it differently from other such traits would be the personal or religious conviction that it is immoral, which is no more objectively defensible than was the slavery-era belief that God created Africans to serve Europeans. Lacking incontrovertible evidence regarding the cause of homosexuality, critics of *Heather* and *Daddy's Roommate* raised no consistent, principled objection to using public education to counteract home-taught prejudice—which, arguably, was the purpose of the Rainbow Curriculum as a whole.

The curriculum's proponents were equally unable to prove conclusively that homosexuality is biologically based and thus in the same category as race and ethnicity. If it is not, public schools would still be obliged to discourage violence against individuals, but the basis for promoting acceptance of homosexuality as such would be far more open to debate. At a minimum, supporters of *Heather* and *Daddy's Roommate* would have to present a new rationale for including in the Rainbow Curriculum a topic that would have been shown to differ significantly from its other elements. Conducted without the benefit of scientific evidence that might decide the question, or at least refocus it, the dispute over the Rainbow Curriculum was far more political than academic.[18]

Just Tinkering

Under the circumstances that existed during the Rainbow Curriculum debate, the New York City school officials were clearly entitled to take popular opinion into account as they decided how to treat the topic of homosexuality within the curriculum. The same cannot be said of policies governing the speech of students as individuals. The American system of K–12 public education is deliberately structured to be responsive to community values and majority rule, but under current law, those factors apply more directly to the schools' own speech than to that of the students. Regardless of the beliefs about homosexuality endorsed by the majority of the community or by school officials, students are entitled to express their own opinions on the condition that they do not violate neutral rules, such as prohibitions against disrupting classes or attacking individuals. Accordingly, students may voice opposition to homosexuality despite a school's equity policy, or they may advocate for its acceptance even if school authorities disagree. Indeed, counterintuitive as it might appear, K–12 students enjoy more free-speech rights than do teachers because, unlike teachers, they are neither employees nor representatives of any government agency, but private individuals.

A few examples of relevant Supreme Court decisions may help to clarify the principles governing the right of K–12 students to express their personal opinions. Among the earliest and best known of these is *Tinker v. Des Moines Independent Community School District* (1969), which upheld the right of public-school students to wear black armbands to express opposition to the Vietnam War. The events leading up to the lawsuit began when Senator Robert F. Kennedy (D–New York) proposed a Christmas truce from December 15, 1965, until New Year's Day. To publicize this effort, he urged Americans who opposed the war to wear black armbands during that period. When school officials in Des Moines, Iowa, learned that antiwar residents had decided to join the protest, they promptly enacted a policy prohibiting students from wearing armbands in school. Mary Beth, Christopher, and John Tinker were among the students who ignored the ban. They were suspended from school and told that they could not return until they stopped displaying the armbands. The suspensions began on December 16, 1965, and lasted for approximately a week before the public schools closed for the holiday. By the time classes resumed in January 1966, the protest period had expired, and the Tinker children returned to school without their armbands.

The Tinker family sued the school district for preventing the students from expressing their opinion of the war in a nondisruptive manner. "Nondisruptive" was one of two key words in the case, since school officials argued that the threat of disruption justified the ban. The other crucial word was "threat." School officials maintained that the ban was justified because the general climate of public unrest surrounding the Vietnam War made any demonstration risky. The Tinkers retorted that on the day the students had worn the armbands before being suspended, no disruption of any kind had occurred. At issue in the lawsuit was whether, given the threat but not the reality of a disruption, the school officials' authority to maintain order outweighed the students' right to free expression.

A federal district court dismissed the complaint on the ground that the school officials had acted well within their authority. The U.S. Court of Appeals for the Eighth Circuit upheld that ruling on a tie vote, but the Supreme Court disagreed.[19] In one of its most frequently quoted passages, the Court declared, "It can hardly be argued that either students or teachers shed their constitutional rights to freedom of speech or expression at the schoolhouse gate."[20] Nevertheless, the Court also acknowledged a long history of precedents upholding the school officials' broad authority to establish policy, and much of the decision addresses the need to balance the students' right to free speech against the school officials' interest in maintaining discipline.

Among other things, the Court noted that the memorandum announcing the ban on armbands said nothing about a fear of disruption, focusing instead on a desire to avoid controversy. Moreover, the memorandum did not apply to other political symbols, such as political campaign buttons. Only armbands were excluded, and only after school officials had learned of plans to wear them to express a particular message. School officials also ignored the reality that when students did in fact wear the armbands, no disruption ensued.

While upholding the right of school officials to penalize students for actions that significantly interfered with the educational function of the schools, the Court noted that "in our system, undifferentiated fear or apprehension of disturbance is not enough to overcome the right to freedom of expression. Any departure from absolute regimentation may cause trouble. Any variation from the majority's opinion may inspire fear. Any word spoken, in class, in the lunchroom, or on the campus, that deviates from the views of another person may start an argument or cause a disturbance. But our Constitution says we must take this risk." The Court also set limits on the school officials' ability to regulate voluntary student speech: "[S]tate-operated schools may not be enclaves of totalitarianism. School officials do not possess absolute authority over their students. Students in school as well as out of school are 'persons' under our Constitution. They are possessed of fundamental rights which the State must respect. . . . Students may not be regarded as closed-circuit recipients of only that which the State chooses to communicate. They may not be confined to the expression of those sentiments that are officially approved."[21]

Although *Tinker* resoundingly championed the free-speech rights of students, a later Supreme Court decision, *Bethel School District No. 403 v. Fraser* (1986), appeared to roll back those rights to some extent. Matthew Fraser, a student at Bethel High School in the state of Washington, rose in a school assembly to nominate a friend for a student government office. Ignoring the advice of two teachers who urged him to moderate his proposed remarks, he delivered an address laced with sexual innuendoes. "I know a man who is firm—he's firm in his pants, he's firm in his shirt, his character is firm," he stated. Other examples included: "Jeff Kuhlman is a man who takes his point and pounds it in. . . . He doesn't attack things in spurts —he drives hard, pushing and pushing until finally—he succeeds." "Jeff is a man who will go to the very end—even the climax, for each and every one of you." Some students called out and made noises during this speech; others made physical gestures corresponding to the sexual references. The principal was not amused. Fraser was suspended for three days and removed from a slate of possible graduation speakers, although his classmates later elected him by means of write-in votes, and he spoke uneventfully at the 1983 graduation. To justify their actions, school officials cited a code of conduct that forbade disrupting school activities by "the use of obscene, profane language or gestures."[22]

The district court found the code of conduct impermissibly vague and noted that the possible sanctions it listed did not include the removal of one's name from a roster of proposed graduation speakers. Citing *Tinker* as a precedent, the U.S. Court of Appeals for the Ninth Circuit affirmed that decision. The Supreme Court reversed. In its view, making lewd remarks during a speech at a mandatory school assembly is not comparable to the private expression of a political viewpoint, such as opposition to the Vietnam War. To be sure, a speech nominating someone for a school office qualifies as political expression, and adults may use sexual references to emphasize their political views. Nevertheless, the Court found, "[i]t does not follow [that] the same latitude must be permitted to children in a public school." The decision also states that minors attending a school-sponsored event should not be forced to listen to "pervasive sexual innuendo . . . plainly offensive to both teachers and students" and "acutely insulting to teenage girl students." Pointing to laws that protect minors from exposure to vulgar and indecent material in radio and television programming, the Court found that public schools have no obligation to permit it.[23]

Two years later, another Supreme Court decision reinforced the distinction between rules that apply to purely individual student expression, such as wearing armbands to protest the Vietnam War, and rules governing student speech that forms part of a school-sponsored activity. *Hazelwood School District v. Kuhlmeier* (1988) involved a school newspaper at Hazelwood East

High School in St. Louis, Missouri, produced by students in a journalism class for which they received academic credit. The instructor of the course, who reported to the school principal, had the authority to approve or reject proposed stories. In the spring of 1983, a new teacher recently assigned to the class approved two stories that the principal later pulled from the paper. One included interviews with three pregnant students, and the other dealt with the effects of parental divorce on teenagers. In withdrawing the story about pregnant students from the paper before it went to press, the principal explained that he was concerned about the privacy of the students, their boyfriends, and their families. He also objected to the article's inclusion of material about birth control and sexual activity. The story about divorce raised similar privacy concerns, and the principal believed that a student's father mentioned in the piece had been treated unfairly.

Students on the newspaper staff sued the school, alleging that their First Amendment rights had been violated. The district court ruled in favor of the school, but the U.S. Court of Appeals for the Eighth Circuit reversed that decision on the ground that the newspaper was a public forum: that is, a venue whose purpose is to allow individuals to express their own viewpoints.[24] On this basis, the court ruled that school officials could not censor articles unless the school would have been legally liable for running them. The Supreme Court disagreed. Denying that a student newspaper produced in a journalism class constitutes a public forum, the Court ruled that the principal was entitled to exercise control because a reasonable observer would assume that the newspaper's content was sanctioned by the school. In distinguishing this case from *Tinker*, the Court noted, "The question whether the First Amendment requires a school to tolerate particular student speech—the question that we addressed in *Tinker*—is different from the question whether the First Amendment requires a school affirmatively to promote particular student speech. The former question addresses educators' ability to silence a student's personal expression that happens to occur on the school premises. The latter question concerns educators' authority over school-sponsored publications, theatrical productions, and other expressive activities that students, parents, and members of the public might reasonably believe to bear the imprimatur of the school."[25]

In addition to stipulating that school officials may regulate student expression that a reasonable observer would interpret as having been initiated or approved by the school, the Court imposed a second condition governing restrictions on student speech: "[E]ducators do not offend the First Amendment by exercising editorial control over the style and content of student speech in school-sponsored expressive activities as long as their actions are reasonably related to legitimate pedagogical concerns."[26] The combination of student speech that is or reasonably appears to be school-sanctioned and a "legitimate pedagogical concern" on the part of school officials constitutes what is known as the *Hazelwood* test.

Among the recent cases involving the *Hazelwood* test is *Morse v. Frederick* (2007), which arose when students in Juneau, Alaska, were excused from classes to watch the Olympic torch being carried toward the 2002 winter games in Salt Lake City. As the torch passed, an eighteen-year-old high school senior, Joseph Frederick, and unidentified friends held up a fourteen-foot banner saying "Bong Hits 4 Jesus." The principal, Deborah Morse, confiscated the banner and suspended Frederick for several days. He thereupon sued Morse and other school officials for violating his right to free speech.

Kenneth Starr, best known for his role as independent counsel in the Monica Lewinsky scandal during the Clinton administration, was among the attorneys who argued on behalf of the school officials. According to Starr and his associates, when Frederick unfurled his banner, he was attending the equivalent of a school-sponsored field trip. Students were released from class to attend the Olympic parade, in which the school band and cheerleaders participated. In those circumstances, the attorneys asserted, school officials had the authority to penalize speech that denigrated religion and promoted drug use. Frederick's attorneys responded that the parade was not school-sponsored but was organized by the Olympic Committee, took place in the public street, and was watched by people of all ages. They also argued that since Frederick's action did not pose any threat to the order or to the educational function of the school, he was entitled to express controversial views with which the principal disagreed. Even if the sign advocated marijuana use—which Frederick did not concede—proposals to decriminalize that substance had long been the subject of a perfectly legal political debate in Alaska.

The federal district court upheld the principal on the ground that the students' attendance at the Olympic parade was a school-sponsored activity, which meant that the standards articulated in *Hazelwood* applied. The U.S. Court of Appeals for the Ninth Circuit reversed this decision. Although it agreed that the students' attendance at the parade was school-sponsored, it found that *Tinker*, not *Hazelwood*, was the relevant precedent. In the court's view, Frederick had a right to display his banner as long as his action did not disrupt the school's educational function. In June 2007 the Supreme Court reversed that decision by a vote of 5–4. The Court declared that although the Olympic parade was not organized by the school and took place in a public street, the students' attendance could be considered school-sponsored because it occurred during normal school hours with the school's permission, and the students were supervised by school personnel. Noting that education officials have the right to restrict the promotion of drug use at school-sponsored events, the Court found that the principal did not act unreasonably either in interpreting "Bong Hits 4 Jesus" as an endorsement of marijuana use or in penalizing Frederick for it.

Perhaps the most provocative element of the decision was a concurrence by Justice Clarence Thomas, who stated that Frederick's free-speech rights could not have been violated because he had none. Arguing that *Tinker* should be overturned, Thomas asserted that the original intent of the First Amendment posed no obstacle to the authority of a public-school principal to regulate student speech. Interestingly, some conservative religious organizations that ordinarily share Thomas's opinions, such as the American Center for Law and Justice and the Christian Legal Society, differed with him on this one.[27] Those organizations have fought a long battle for recognition of the right of students to pray in public schools, and they continue to argue for an expanded view of contexts in which students may engage in religious expression. Accordingly, despite their abhorrence of drug use, they were not in favor of a Supreme Court decision that would endow school officials with almost unfettered authority to regulate student speech even when it does not pose any threat to the school's educational mission. Although Justice Thomas is unlikely to have intended any diminution in the students' right to religious speech, he appears to have been less concerned than the advocacy groups about the law of unintended consequences. If religious expression must be permitted whenever students are free to engage in the secular speech of their choice, as those organizations have long contended, then the converse is also true. If students' secular speech can be constrained, no guarantee exists that similar principles will not be applied to their religious speech. Despite the Court's attempt to draft a narrowly applicable decision in the "Bong Hits 4 Jesus" case, experience has shown that precedents, like waistlines, have a tendency to spread with age.[28]

Yes, They Can Talk About Homosexuality

The broad standards governing K–12 student expression were applied specifically to speech about homosexuality in a 2001 decision striking down a public-school policy that strongly resembled a university speech code. Enacted by the school board in State College, Pennsylvania, the challenged regulation prohibited "verbal or physical conduct based on [the victim's] actual or perceived race, religion, color, national origin, gender, sexual orientation, disability, or other personal characteristics, and which has the purpose or effect of substantially interfering with a student's educational performance or creating an intimidating, hostile or offensive environment."[29] Examples of proscribed behaviors included "unsolicited derogatory remarks, jokes, demeaning comments or behaviors, slurs, mimicking, name calling, graffiti, innuendo, gestures, physical contact, stalking, threatening, bullying, exhorting or the display or circulation of written material or pictures."[30]

David Saxe, legal guardian of two students in the State College schools, sued the school district on the grounds that he and his wards "openly and sincerely identify themselves as Christians. They believe, and their religion teaches, that homosexuality is a sin. Plaintiffs further believe that they have a right to speak out about the sinful nature and harmful effects of homosexuality." Under the policy, Saxe protested, students could be penalized "for speaking out about their religious beliefs, engaging in symbolic activities reflecting those beliefs, and distributing religious literature."[31]

The district court upheld the policy on the ground that the proscribed speech was not constitutionally protected, but that decision was reversed by the U.S. Court of Appeals for the Third Circuit. "There is," the appeals court declared, "no categorical 'harassment exception' to the First Amendment's free speech clause." The court found, among other things, that the challenged regulation permitted school officials to penalize students for speech that did not disrupt the school's operations but merely offended someone. "Although [the school district] correctly asserts that it has a compelling interest in promoting an educational environment that is safe and conducive to learning it fails to provide any particularized reason as to why it anticipates substantial disruption from the broad swath of student speech prohibited under the Policy," the court observed.[32]

Just as students have a right to oppose homosexuality despite the equity policies of their schools, they also have a right to support it even if school officials consider it immoral or unwholesome. Since the mid-1990s, students seeking to promote acceptance of homosexuality have formed extracurricular clubs for this purpose, relying on the federal Equal Access Act (EAA) of 1984 to shield them from hostile action by school administrators. The EAA, drafted by attorneys from the Christian Legal Society, was originally sponsored by members of Congress whose intent was to protect only student-led religious clubs. Unable to pass in that form, the legislation was broadened to include secular as well as religious student speech. Under the EAA, if a public secondary school that accepts federal funding has even one non-curriculum-related club, it may not discriminate against any student-initiated meeting held outside instructional time "on the basis of the religious, political, philosophical, or other content of the speech at such meetings." Public secondary schools are not required to have extracurricular programs at all, but if they choose to make noncurricular clubs available to students and wish to qualify for federal funding, they must follow the dictates of the EAA.

While giving secondary-school students broad latitude to form clubs of their choice, the EAA also sets limits. To be covered by the EAA, student meetings must not involve unlawful behavior, and they must not "materially and substantially interfere with the orderly conduct of educational activities within the school." Moreover, the EAA states, none of its provisions is meant "to limit the authority of the school, its agents or employees, to maintain order and discipline on school premises, to protect the well-being of students and faculty, and to assure that attendance of students at meetings is voluntary."[33] Although the purpose of the law is to protect the students' right to express ideas that may differ from those promoted by the school, some education officials have interpreted such phrases as "the orderly conduct of educational activities," "order and discipline," and "the well-being of students and faculty" as an invitation to exclude clubs that they consider controversial or unwholesome, such as those that promote acceptance of atheism or homosexuality.

Approximately a decade after the enactment of the EAA, a multifaceted test of its applicability to gay-friendly student clubs arose in Salt Lake City, Utah. The dispute began in 1995, when Kelli Peterson, a sophomore at East High School, came out as a lesbian. Shocked by the social ostracism and bullying she faced, the previously popular teenager joined two other homosexual students in seeking to form a club called the Gay-Straight Alliance, in which heterosexual and homosexual students would unite in an effort to promote social acceptance of homosexuality. Participants began by meeting privately in their homes and in school, but they soon sought to establish an official school club that could meet during in-school activity periods and post its notices on school bulletin boards. Shortly afterward, Peterson's sister, Holly, proposed to initiate a Gay-Straight Alliance at West High School, and similar attempts were made elsewhere.

In an interview for this book, the principal of East High School, Kay Peterson (no relation to Kelli and Holly), pointed out that the school's diverse population belied the popular conception of Salt Lake City as a homogeneous Mormon stronghold. The student body included Polynesians, Hispanics, and Native Americans in significant numbers, and as Peterson described them, the students ranged "from the governor's kids to kids who sleep in cars and kids who would be glad of a car to sleep in."[34] Illustrating this theme of diversity were the bright tropical shirt and the necklace of chestnuts he wore at the interview; as he explained, he was to play the role of a Polynesian tribal chieftain in a multicultural school assembly that afternoon.

Having identified himself as a devout Mormon who did not endorse homosexuality, Peterson set about clarifying why he had taken the seemingly inconsistent—or at least unexpected—action of approving the formation of a Gay-Straight Alliance in East High School. Apparently unaware of the passage of the EAA more than a decade earlier, principals in Salt Lake City exercised almost unlimited authority to shape the extracurricular programs of their schools, and his first impulse had been to refuse the students' request. Nevertheless, he had considered it his duty to hear what they had to say. Their main point was that openly homosexual students were being severely harassed, and students who sought to promote understanding and social acceptance wanted to meet once a week as an official school club.

After several lunch meetings with approximately fifteen students interested in forming the club, Peterson felt certain that the students' statement of purpose was sincere and that they were acting on their own behalf rather than as puppets of outside adult activists—a charge frequently leveled against the club when the controversy began. Although some faculty members feared that the club would be used to recruit homosexuals, Peterson believed that "the kids' concerns were harassment, an opportunity for sanctuary, a protected place to support each other and to try to solve some of the problems they felt." Perhaps the key factor in his decision to approve the club in December 1995 was his outrage at the harassment he witnessed when he made a point of circulating near the openly homosexual students outside class time. Particularly troubling, he recalled, was the fact that the tormentors were not deterred by his presence, apparently assuming that their actions would be acceptable to him.

With the principal's permission, the students drew up bylaws declaring that the Gay-Straight Alliance was intended to "increase awareness of diversity in high schools, to decrease prejudice, and to help students feel safe and welcome in their school environment." Among the club's other goals were education about gay-related issues, respect for all students regardless of their sexual orientation, and discouragement of "homophobia, anti-gay violence, bigotry and prejudice within the school community and in the city and state." The students sought permission to meet as a school club "to provide an opportunity for timely discussion of social and political issues of interest to them and to plan and perform community service projects."[35] All East High students, regardless of sexual orientation, were welcome to join.

Anticipating that the club would be controversial, Peterson sought advice from Douglas Bates, attorney to the state board of education. As Peterson recalled the conversation, Bates replied, "Yeah, I knew sooner or later this was going to happen to someone—so you're it." After Bates familiarized him with the provisions of the EAA, Peterson approached the Salt Lake City superintendent of schools, who took the question to the school board. Despite their lack of enthusiasm for the Gay-Straight Alliance, the board conceded that the EAA left little choice but to accept it. That view was not shared by some residents of Salt Lake City, who were horrified by the prospect of having a gay-friendly club in a public high school. Led by the Utah chapter of the Eagle Forum, which had a mailing list of 23,000 residents and an active telephone tree, protesters "wore out [the board members'] phones with calls."[36]

Although the Salt Lake City public schools were entitled to shape their own message about homosexuality, some members of the state and local school boards, as well as community residents, had difficulty in seeing a difference between the speech of the schools as institutions and that of the students as individuals. Recalling the Eagle Forum's earlier support of the EAA when the Forum viewed it as a vehicle for protecting student religious speech, an editorial in the *Salt Lake Tribune* pointed out, "It was a First Amendment issue then, and it is now; the only difference is that the Eagle Forum types don't like the content of this particular expression."[37] Less elegantly, the host of a local radio show, *Voice of Reason*, called opponents of the Gay-Straight Alliance "bird-brained Eagle Forumnistas" and remarked that the "very groups who fought for [the EAA] are the very groups having a cow over some students wanting to be treated the same as the students for whom the law was originally written."[38]

The *Deseret News,* owned by the Church of Jesus Christ of Latter-Day Saints, generally known as the Mormons, espoused the other side of the debate. Ignoring the difference between the schools' institutional message and the students' speech as individuals, the editors of the *News* maintained that accommodating the Gay-Straight Alliance in the public schools would create the appearance of sanctioning homosexuality, which, in their view, posed the threat of AIDS and other diseases, undercut the traditional nuclear family, and threatened the social and spiritual well-being of anyone drawn into it by such groups as the Gay-Straight Alliance. Similar opinions were expressed in letters to the editor of the *Deseret News.* For example, one local resident wrote, "As long as organizations are not infringing upon my own beliefs and rights, I will allow them to exist within the bounds of the law," but added that clubs whose views were opposed by conservative parents should not be allowed to meet in public schools.[39]

As the school board's attorney pointed out to Kay Peterson, a conflict of this type was inevitable. Indeed, it had been foreseen by members of Congress during the debates preceding the passage of the EAA, when opponents denied that the Act could be structured to protect only religious expression and those forms of secular student speech acceptable to its sponsors. In an exchange with Senator Slade Gorton (R-Washington), Senator Mark Hatfield (R-Oregon), the chief sponsor of the EAA, said, "When you throw the net out, you are going to garner in a few other things, but I do not think to the detriment or the efficiency of what you are seeking. It will not create a difficult problem." Gorton replied that Hatfield "has cast a huge net to catch an important, but modestly sized, fish and has pulled in an entire boatload of unintended consequences."[40]

When Gorton's "entire boatload of unintended consequences" washed up in Salt Lake City, the school board met on February 20, 1996, to consider options. In a raucous five-hour session at which approximately 100 of the 500 attendees spoke, the board considered three choices: render the EAA inapplicable by rejecting federal funding or by closing all noncurricular school clubs; recognize the Gay-Straight Alliance; or reject only that club and face a lawsuit, which, their attorney advised them, they would lose. Since the board could not afford either to decline federal funding or to risk costly litigation, it voted 4–3 to retain only curriculum-related clubs that would not bring the EAA into play. In so doing, the board emphasized that it regarded the shutdown of noncurricular clubs as a temporary measure to remain in effect only until state or federal lawmakers found a way to "bring back to the school board the ability to make decisions that won't force the board into one corner or the other."[41] More colorfully, a board member called on Congress "to get their nose and their camel out of our tent and reinstate this board of education to the top of the totem pole."[42]

The Utah Eagle Forum congratulated the school board for its decision, observing that "[h]omosexuals can't reproduce, so they recruit. And they are not going to use Utah high school and junior high campuses to recruit."[43] By contrast, the executive director of the Utah ACLU declared, "One day we will look back on this as one of the most shameful episodes in Utah history —but then, I say that once a month."[44] As a result of the school board's action, forty-two clubs were disestablished, although not all high schools had offered all of them. Among the disbanded organizations were the Polynesian, Latino Pride, Native American, Human Rights, Bible, Chinese Checkers, Beef, Meat, Funk Dance, and Star Wars Clubs; the Salt Lake Lawn Chair Rewebbing Association; the Ultimate Frisbee Organization; the Young Democrats and the Young Republicans; the Hat Club for Men and Women; and Students Against Drunk Driving. Each school retained twenty-eight to thirty-eight clubs, including the Art, French, German, Drama, Dance, Science, and Cheerleading and Pep Clubs; the Future Business Leaders of America and the Future Homemakers of America; the Student Government; and sports teams. In addition, the excluded groups were given the option of paying six dollars an hour to rent classroom space after school hours to meet as private entities. Among the groups that took advantage of this opportunity was the Gay-Straight Alliance.

Students who objected to the ban demonstrated outside the state capitol to urge the reinstatement of the extracurricular program. Reflecting the division of opinion among their elders, some students blamed the Gay-Straight Alliance for creating the problem, while others held its opponents responsible. Another demonstration took place outside East High School when 700 students walked out of their classes. They returned after Kay Peterson, armed with a bullhorn, pointed out that if they remained outside much longer, they would have to make up the missed school day. (He was amused by a photograph of himself with the bullhorn that appeared on the front page of the *New York Times*, which prompted a friend to ask, "Don't you have *any* sense?") Some opponents of the Gay-Straight Alliance continued their protest by asking approval to form an Anti-Homosexual League; others proposed establishing a club called SAFE: Students Against Faggots Everywhere.

Unfortunately for any school-board members who thought that the vote would end the controversy, one point on which the Gay-Straight Alliance and its foes agreed—though for different reasons—was that the board's action was unacceptable. The result was a federal lawsuit, *East High Gay/ Straight Alliance v. Board of Education of Salt Lake City School District*, in which attorneys provided by the Utah ACLU and the Lambda Legal Defense and Education Fund represented the student leaders of the Gay-Straight Alliance. The Utah Attorney General's Office, aided by attorneys affiliated with the Rutherford Institute, defended the district.[45] According to the students' complaint, "Rather than grant permission to [the Gay-Straight Alliance], the Board and members of the public disfavored the content of the speech and viewpoints of that group and opposed allowing any group of students interested in discussing gay, lesbian, and bisexual issues to meet on school premises."[46] To be sure, no law required the Salt Lake City school board to offer an extracurricular program. The question was whether, having chosen to establish such a program, the board had impermissibly terminated it for unacceptable reasons.

The students also challenged the school board's contention that all the clubs that retained official school recognition were curriculum-related. In their view, Future Business Leaders of America, Future Homemakers of America, Improvement Council of East [High School] (ICE), the National Honor Society, and the Odyssey of the Mind were noncurricular. By recognizing these clubs, the students argued, school officials had triggered the EAA and were thus required to recognize the Gay-Straight Alliance as well. The school officials replied that they had not closed down the extracurricular program because of opposition to homosexuality. Rather, they asserted, their goal was to avoid the financial liability that might arise if students used their rights under the EAA to form groups like a Demolition Derby Club, which some students had asked to establish. They also maintained that the challenged clubs were reasonably related to the curriculum.

When the case reached the federal district court in 1999, Judge Bruce S. Jenkins instructed the plaintiffs to refrain from basing their arguments on the personal motives of school officials. "Courts find a much surer footing in first addressing the *effect* of a legislative enactment and in measuring whether it has a discriminatory effect on a particular group or viewpoint," he wrote.[47] Accordingly, the central question in the lawsuit was not whether the school board had acted out of anti-homosexual bias but whether any of the remaining clubs were noncurriculum-related. If the court found that the school had retained even one noncurricular club, it would have to close that club or recognize the Gay-Straight Alliance.

The key legal precedent used in deciding the case was *Board of Education of the Westside Community Schools v. Mergens* (1990), in which the Supreme Court defined a noncurricular club as "any student group that does not *directly* relate to the body of courses offered by the school. In our view, a student group directly relates to a school's curriculum if the subject matter of the group is actually taught, or will soon be taught, in a regularly offered course; if the subject matter of the group concerns the body of courses as a whole; if participation in the group is required for a particular course; or if participation in the group results in academic credit."[48] On this basis, the federal district court found that only ICE was a noncurriculum-related club. As the court noted, the school officials themselves seemed to concede this point when, in the fall of 1998, they terminated ICE as an independent entity and folded it into the student government. Accordingly, the court found that the rights of the Gay-Straight Alliance had been violated by its exclusion during the 1997–98 school year, when ICE was a recognized school club. Other than that, the court found that all the challenged clubs were curriculum-related, which left the Gay-Straight Alliance no basis for demanding recognition after the fall of 1998. The case was thereupon dismissed.[49]

Two years after the federal district court issued its ruling in *East High Gay/ Straight Alliance v. Board of Education of Salt Lake City School District* (1999), another group of homosexual students proposed to form the East High School PRISM (People Recognizing Important Social Movements) Club. Unlike the Gay-Straight Alliance, which conceded that it was noncurricular, PRISM claimed curricular status. According to the students' application, their club would "expand and enhance our study and understanding of American history and government, law and social institutions" by acting "as a prism through which historical and current events, institutions and culture can be viewed in terms of the impact, experience and contributions of gays and lesbians." The students explained, "We want to talk about democracy, civil rights, equality, discrimination and diversity."[50] Cynthia Seidel, assistant superintendent of the Salt Lake City school district, rejected the application. In her letter to the students, she defined "the organizing subject matter of the club" in terms of a focus on homosexuality, which was "not taught in the courses you cite."[51] The students thereupon filed suit, alleging that her decision reflected ideologically based hostility to the viewpoint they proposed to apply to material that was, in itself, undeniably curriculum-related.

Citing the school district's standards for history instruction, including critical thinking and an appreciation for diversity and freedom, the court declared that "the subject matter of the PRISM club is 'actually taught . . . in a regular course,' as required for approval."[52] Accordingly, the court issued an injunction ordering the school district to recognize PRISM as a school club.

PRISM's victory, like the Gay-Straight Alliance's loss, was soon swallowed up in a political process generated by public dissatisfaction with the Salt Lake City policy. On September 5, 2000, the school board voted 6-1 to reinstate noncurricular clubs—not to promote homosexuality, its members hastened to explain, but to revitalize the schools and to provide opportunities that would enhance students' college applications. The Gay-Straight Alliance was among the newly recognized school clubs.[53]

The controversy over the Gay-Straight Alliance illustrates two common misperceptions about student speech in K–12 schools, particularly at the secondary level. The first unfounded belief is that the school does not have to recognize, or even tolerate, student speech that opposes the school's own message or the majority values of the community. The second is that student speech can be considered "disruptive" because it is unpopular. It is already clear that students may, as individuals, express disagreement with the school's policies and messages, but the second point merits some discussion. To be sure, school officials enjoy broad authority to decide what is necessary to maintain order, and the free-speech rights of students are not coextensive with those of adults. Nevertheless, this use of the heckler's veto violates the fundamental purpose of the EAA.[54] If school officials could ban any activity that caused or might cause a backlash, then the applicability of the EAA to any particular idea would depend on its popularity or on the school officials' perception of its popularity. Philosophically, this approach conflicts with the EAA's emphasis on the right of students to express their views outside instructional time. The potential practical difficulties are also obvious. If, for instance, a strong religious majority prevailed in a particular community, its members could enjoy their own religious activities while raising a fuss about the meetings of minority religionists or nonbelievers, which would permit school officials to exclude minority clubs on the ground that they caused disruption. Thus, even at the K–12 level, students are entitled to a reasonable degree of latitude in expressing their views as individuals.

Whose Money, Whose Mouth?

Although the right of university students to express their opinions in non-curricular clubs is well established, public universities face their own battles when those opinions involve homosexuality. In some instances, university administrations balk at recognizing or supporting gay-friendly clubs; in others, they pursue an equity policy with respect to homosexuality that conflicts with the beliefs and practices of some other student groups. Lawsuits involving universities that balked at recognizing gay-friendly clubs include the following examples:

- *Gay Alliance of Students v. Matthews* (1976). The U.S. Court of Appeals for the Fourth Circuit struck down a Virginia Commonwealth University policy that excluded homosexual student organizations on the ground that membership might be detrimental to some students.
- *Gay and Lesbian Students Association v. Gohn* (1988). When the Gay and Lesbian Students Association was denied funding at the University of Arkansas, the U.S. Court of Appeals for the Eighth Circuit declared that having decided to provide financial support to student organizations, the university could not discriminate on the basis of viewpoint.
- *Gay Lesbian Bisexual Alliance v. Pryor* (1997). The attorney general of Alabama instructed the University of South Alabama to deny funding to the Gay Lesbian Bisexual Alliance because, under university policy, no organization that "fosters or promotes a lifestyle or actions prohibited by the sodomy and sexual misconduct laws of [the Alabama code]" could be supported.[55] The U.S. Court of Appeals for the Eleventh Circuit ruled that the university could not discriminate against the club on the basis of the viewpoints expressed by its members, including advocacy of changes in the sodomy and sexual misconduct laws.

More common, in recent years, are differences of opinion between university administrations that support gay-friendly student clubs and students who oppose them. Like the protesters who objected to Gay and Lesbian Awareness Month, the Rainbow Curriculum, and the Gay-Straight Alliance, some university students view clubs that promote acceptance of homosexuality as contributors to a broader attack on traditional values. In *Board of Regents of the University of Wisconsin System v. Southworth* (2000), for instance, students and alumni challenged an entire set of funding criteria that their attorney described as "skewed to the left."[56] The University of Wisconsin required students to pay an activity fee in addition to tuition; when the lawsuit was filed in 1996, the fee was $331.50 per year. Approximately 80 percent of the activity fee was used to support such general student services as the student union, student health facilities, and intramural sports. The other 20 percent was available for distribution among the university's 623 registered student organizations (RSOs), some of which promoted political or ideological viewpoints. Decisions about allocating funds to the various RSOs were made by the student government or, more rarely, by student referendum.

From the university's perspective, the extracurricular program contributed to the students' educational experience by "'stimulating advocacy and debate on diverse points of view,' enabling 'participation in activities,' 'promoting student participation in campus administrative activity,' and providing 'opportunities to develop social skills,' all consistent with the University's mission."[57] The university's broad view of its extracurricular program was not shared by students and alumni who protested that students should not have to pay activity fees to support RSOs with whose viewpoint they disagreed. Led by a conservative Christian law student named Scott Southworth, they demanded that the university allow them to withhold their contributions from such groups as the UW Greens (an environmentalist group), the Campus Women's Center, and the Lesbian, Gay, Bisexual and Transgender Campus Center. By refusing to provide that option, they maintained, the university was violating their constitutional rights to free speech, free association, and freedom of religion.

The students and the alumni won the first round when the federal district court ruled that mandatory student activity fees could not be used to fund any groups that engaged in ideological or political speech. The U.S. Court of Appeals for the Seventh Circuit, finding that the extracurricular program was not part of the university's central mission, agreed that the students' right to free speech was violated by the enforced financial support of RSOs that promoted ideas they found objectionable. The Supreme Court disagreed. Adopting the university's broad view of the goals of its extracurricular program, the Court found that a public university's mission may include "facilitating the free and open exchange of ideas by, and among, its students" as long as support is offered in a viewpoint-neutral manner.[58]

"It is inevitable," the Court declared, "that the government will adopt and pursue programs and policies within its constitutional powers but which nevertheless are contrary to the profound beliefs and sincere convictions of some of its citizens. The government, as a general rule, may support valid programs and policies by taxes and other exactions binding on protesting parties." The Court further stated, "The University may determine that its mission is well served if students have the means to engage in dynamic discussions of philosophical, religious, scientific, social, and political subjects in their extracurricular campus life outside the lecture hall. If the University reaches this conclusion, it is entitled to impose a mandatory fee to sustain an open dialogue to these ends."[59]

The one respect in which the Court declined to uphold the university's policy pertained to the allocation of funds to RSOs through the student government and student referendums. Although both parties had stipulated that those procedures were viewpoint-neutral, the Court expressed reservations about the use of a majority vote to determine which organizations were to be funded. "The whole theory of viewpoint neutrality is that minority views are treated with the same respect as are majority views," it stated. "Access to a public forum, for instance, does not depend upon majoritarian consent."[60] Accordingly, the case was remanded to the lower courts for further consideration of the university's method of distributing student activity fees with respect to its implications for viewpoint neutrality. The resulting changes were so substantial that although the protesting students had failed to prevent their activity fees from being used to support groups with which they disagreed, a court later found that they had prevailed to the extent of bringing about "access to funding by groups with viewpoints that are different or contrary to groups that have been funded in the past."[61]

Another group of conservative Christian students prevailed unequivocally in a lawsuit against the Southern Illinois University (SIU) School of Law. The plaintiffs belonged to a student chapter of the Christian Legal Society (CLS), whose members were required to endorse a statement of faith outlining basic Christian principles. Although the statement did not explicitly mention homosexuality, CLS interpreted it to include acceptance of "the Bible's prohibition of sexual contact between persons of the same sex. A person who engages in homosexual conduct or adheres to the viewpoint that homosexual conduct is not sinful would not be permitted to serve as a CLS chapter officer or member."[62] The organization emphasized that its meetings were open to all students, and people who had repented of past homosexual acts were eligible for full membership.

The SIU School of Law recognized the CLS chapter until March 2005, when its status as a registered student organization was withdrawn. Acting in response to a student's complaint, the dean concluded that CLS's regulations violated two SIU policies. One of them guaranteed that the institution would provide equal educational opportunities to all its students regardless of, among other things, sexual orientation. The other denied recognition to any student group that failed to adhere to federal or state nondiscrimination laws. Although CLS remained free to meet in the law school's classrooms as a private organization, its members regarded the dean's action as a violation of their constitutional rights to free association, free speech, and free exercise of religion. The practical consequences included loss of access to the school's Listserv, bulletin boards, storage facilities, private meeting space, and funding, as well as the removal of CLS from the published list of student organizations.

The federal district court declined to order the university to reinstate CLS pending a trial, but the U.S. Court of Appeals for the Seventh Circuit reversed this decision. In *Christian Legal Society v. Walker* (2006), the appeals court found that the university was unlikely to be able to show that CLS was in conflict with either of the stated policies. SIU attorneys failed to identify any specific state or federal law that CLS was violating, and no affirmative-action or equal-opportunity regulation appeared likely to apply to a student group. As the Supreme Court has observed in several cases, including *Southworth*, extracurricular student organizations represent the views of the students as individuals rather than the official speech of the university, and that remains true even when student clubs are recognized and funded by the institution. Thus, a policy preventing the university itself from discriminating on the basis of sexual orientation did not apply to student clubs.[63]

Following this early victory, CLS lost two similar cases in 2009. In *Christian Legal Society Chapter of the University of California, Hastings College of the Law v. Kane*, the U.S. Court of Appeals for the Ninth Circuit upheld a district court decision in favor of the law school. At issue was a policy requiring officially registered student clubs to be fully open to all students regardless of, among other things, sexual orientation. Noting that CLS was free to meet on campus as a private organization, admitting whomever it liked, the Ninth

Circuit found the policy to be a reasonable and viewpoint-neutral condition for official recognition of student organizations. As the district court observed, "CLS may be motivated by its religious beliefs to exclude students based on their religion or sexual orientation, but that does not convert the reason for Hastings' policy prohibiting the discrimination to be one that is religiously-based."[64] The district court also found that the law school's requirements were not intended to, and indeed did not, interfere materially with CLS's freedom of expression. Citing *Kane*, a federal district court upheld a similar policy in *Christian Legal Society v. Eck* (2009) filed by the CLS chapter at the University of Montana School of Law. In December 2009, the Supreme Court agreed to hear the California case, entitled *Christian Legal Society Chapter of the University of California, Hastings College of the Law v. Martinez* now that Leo P. Martinez had replaced Mary Kay Kane as chancellor and dean. At the time of this writing, the oral argument is pending.

Clearly, struggles over the treatment of homosexuality in public schools and universities are rooted in a broader public debate regarding the origin of homosexuality, its morality, and its role in the spread of AIDS. Homosexuality thus constitutes an effective example of a controversial topic whose treatment in public education is influenced by public opinion—a particularly important factor in the absence of the constitutional constraints that apply to race. Moreover, although everyone involved in these controversies claims to be carrying the banner of liberty, the practical application of that term varies. The inclusion of gay-friendly material in the public schools may, for instance, be presented as suppression of traditional moral values or as justice to a long-ignored segment of the population. Conversely, the exclusion of homosexual themes may be attacked as state-sponsored promotion of majoritarian bias, or it may be defended as appropriate deference to the parents' right to shape their children's moral values.

Like differences of opinion about race, disagreements about the acceptability of homosexuality are complicated by the failure of some administrators to distinguish between the institutional message of a public school or university and the free speech of the students as individuals. Once that difficulty has been resolved, however, the lack of hard evidence concerning the cause of homosexuality renders the debate itself largely a matter of personal opinion. Proponents of gay-friendly instructional materials and student clubs act as if homosexuality has been shown to be genetically based, while opponents proceed on the assumption that it is a choice.

Underlying each side of the debate is a subtext in which a particular attitude toward homosexuality functions as an element, and in some instances as a symbol, of a comprehensive world-view. Evidence of this subtext appears, for instance, in statements made by participants in the dispute over the Rainbow Curriculum. Supporters spoke of celebrating choice, focusing on the feelings and interests of individuals rather than on one-size-fits-all norms and expectations, and preventing the public schools from becoming conduits for religious-based conservative doctrine. Opponents were determined to uphold absolute rather than situational standards of morality, to preserve the dominance of the nuclear family, and to prevent the public schools from promoting liberal, permissive attitudes. As these larger contexts suggest, what is at stake in disputes over homosexuality is not only a bulletin-board display, an elementary-school reading list, a student club, or the allocation of an activity fee. Not far beneath conflicting attitudes toward homosexuality lies a struggle between differing visions of the future of America.

Competing beliefs about homosexuality are not unique in serving as indicators of social and ideological world-views. Among other prominent examples is the tension between evolutionists and antievolutionists. Although critics of modernism and liberalism use many of the same arguments to attack both homosexuality and evolution, they must also take account of one significant difference: whereas the basis of homosexuality has not been scientifically demonstrated, evolution has been the subject of more than a century and a half of empirical testing. The resulting disputes transcend arguments about what should be taught in a particular instance and delve into the nature of knowledge itself: not only *what* we know but *how* we know it. As an example of the treatment of controversial material in public schools and universities, this conflict pushes the boundaries of the discussion beyond the choice of one view, one constituency, or one set of facts over another. To grapple with the issues raised by disputes over the teaching of evolution is to hold politics in one hand and epistemology in the other.

5

Here Comes Darwin

It is clear from a churchman who has been elevated to a very eminent position that the Holy Spirit's intention is to teach us how to go to Heaven, and not how the heavens go.
> —Galileo Galilei, "Letter to Madame Christine of Lorraine, Grand Duchess of Tuscany," referencing Caesar Cardinal Baronius

DISPUTES CONCERNING THE TREATMENT of race and homosexuality in public schools and universities are, in our present state of knowledge, differences of opinion in which each view is defended by examples and argument rather than by reference to hard data. Accordingly, lawsuits involving controversial speech on these topics set out to determine not which side is factually correct but which constituency prevails under constitutional law or under professional standards of academic freedom. But because disputes over the teaching of evolution pertain to an academic discipline whose very definition limits it to ideas that are empirically testable, the discussion is complicated by the potential for, and the necessity of, factual accuracy. It is clear, for instance, that K–12 school boards have the authority to govern teachers' in-class speech, but does that authority extend to ordering teachers to convey factual misinformation to their students? What are the rights of K–12 and university students whose personal beliefs conflict with what they are required to learn in class? In public universities, at what point does a professor's academic-freedom right to promote unconventional views cross the line to become incompetence in the field? The list goes on.

Bacon vs. the *Beagle*

The current debate over the teaching of evolution in public schools and universities is a direct outgrowth of the uproar that surrounded the publication of Charles Darwin's *On the Origin of Species* in 1859. Indeed, despite advances in scientific knowledge and changes in political and legal tactics, the underlying terms of the conflict have remained constant for more than a century and a half. For that reason, disputes that have taken place in the late twentieth and early twenty-first centuries can be fully appreciated only if viewed as the most recent stage of an ongoing story. Divorced from their historical context, their larger significance is obscured.

Identifying the appearance of *On the Origin of Species* as the starting point of the current controversy over the teaching of evolution is not meant to suggest that evolution itself was a new idea in 1859. In one form or another, it had been discussed from the eighteenth century on by such scientists as Georges-Louis Leclerc (Comte de Buffon), Jean-Baptiste Lamarck, and Darwin's grandfather, Erasmus Darwin. Indeed, references to the general concept may be found in much earlier works. Empedocles suggested, among other things, that the universe is gradually changing and that species can become extinct; and Darwin himself mentioned Aristotle's suggestion that sharp teeth for biting and flat ones for chewing developed in accord with their respective functions. Nevertheless, although the idea that living things might have evolved into their present forms had aroused controversy long before Darwin came on the scene, his theory of natural selection quickly became the antievolutionists' primary target.

In brief, natural selection means that if a slight genetic variation produces a beneficial trait, such as an adaptation that aids in reaching food, then individuals born with that trait enjoy an improved chance of surviving and reproducing. Offspring that inherit it will outperform and eventually replace individuals that lack it, and if the process of change continues, the eventual result may be a new species. Conversely, a variation that does not aid in the competition for survival is likely to die out.[1]

Scientists who followed Darwin did not hesitate to disagree with his interpretations of the data that he had collected on the 1831–36 voyage of the H.M.S. *Beagle* and elsewhere, and indeed some of his findings have been generally discredited. Nevertheless, the primary reason for the storm of controversy surrounding the theory of natural selection is not the science behind it but the fact that it makes belief in God optional. To be sure, divine action may be identified as the ultimate cause of the changes that result from natural selection. It may be said, for instance, that God willed a particular finch's beak to be a particular shape or programmed primitive forms of life to evolve in preordained ways. Nevertheless, the theory of natural selection provides an explanation for survival and change that neither requires divine intervention nor serves as evidence that it has occurred. For centuries, religious believers had pointed to the wonders of creation to prove the existence of God. The natural explanations offered by Darwin reduced belief in divine creation to a mere matter of opinion, and therein lies the heart of the controversy.

A related source of the outrage generated by Darwin's work was its deviation from the system of classification and induction named for the Renaissance sage Sir Francis Bacon; elements of it had been use for centuries before Bacon's time. Practitioners of the Baconian method sought to acquire knowledge about living things by collecting them, classifying them according to their similarities and differences, and eliminating specimens whose apparent similarity to the rest of the group was based on accident. By studying the individuals within each classification, Baconian scientists would infer truths about the categories themselves and about the relationship of one category to another. Their methodology included induction, logical argument, and analogy, and they relied heavily on authoritative texts.

The Baconian method was based on three assumptions: that each species is fixed in its final form, that the number of species is small enough to allow scientists to encompass all of them, and that the sorting of specimens into categories can be accomplished with total or near-total accuracy. Most significantly, adherents of the Baconian approach believed that the final outcome of scientific inquiry could and should be absolute, unchanging truth. Darwin denied not only the conclusions reached through the use of that scientific method but the method itself and, beyond that, the world-view on which it stood.

Darwin did not, of course, single-handedly replace the Baconian approach to science with what is now known as the modern scientific method. The concepts underlying the modern scientific method were employed in some form by such early thinkers as Copernicus, Galileo, and Sir Isaac Newton, as well as by other scientists of Darwin's day. Nevertheless, it is fair to say that the widespread acceptance of Darwin's theories by the mainstream scientific community sounded the death knell of the Baconian approach. In brief, the scientific method that Darwin employed is based on empirically testable hypotheses that offer the most probable natural explanations for all the facts known at a given time. These explanations are subject to being verified, modified, or refuted by further experimentation or observation. To use William Van Alstyne's phrase, each of them is a "proxy of truth" that stands only until a better approximation is demonstrated.[2] Modern science views the natural world as being in a constant state of flux and as offering too much variety to be encompassed by a closed classification system. This contest between the Baconian and Darwinian methodologies, far from being of mere historical interest, lies at the heart of current debates over science instruction in K–12 schools and universities. Creation-based material may have a claim to be considered science under the Baconian approach of classification and argument, but it cannot qualify if the threshold question is whether it is subject to empirical testing.

The Bishop vs. the Bulldog

The earliest public debate on Darwinism took place at a meeting of the British Association for the Advancement of Science less than a year after *On the Origin of Species* was published. It pitted the Reverend Samuel Wilberforce, bishop of Oxford, against the naturalist Thomas Henry Huxley, whose persistent and impassioned defense of natural selection earned him the sobriquet "Darwin's Bulldog." In their most frequently quoted exchange, Wilberforce taunted Huxley by asking whether his ape ancestor was on his grandfather's side or on his grandmother's. As Huxley recalled, "If then, said I, the question is put to me would I rather have a miserable ape for a grandfather or a man highly endowed by nature and possessed of great means of influence & yet who employs these faculties & that influence for the mere purpose of introducing ridicule into a grave scientific discussion, I unhesitatingly affirm my preference for the ape."[3]

An extended debate about Darwin's ideas was carried on between two Harvard professors, the paleontologist Louis Agassiz and the botanist Asa Gray. Agassiz's arguments, essentially unchanged, form the basis of one side of the current debate about science instruction in K–12 schools and universities. Describing Darwin's ideas as "mere guesses," he reviled natural selection as "a scientific mistake, untrue in its facts, unscientific in its methods, and mischievous in its tendency."[4] By "unscientific," he meant, of course, non-Baconian. In accord with the Baconian system of classification, he maintained that evolution could not be considered valid unless Darwin could show an almost unbroken series of fossil remains marking the gradual transition from one species to another.

Essential to Agassiz's world-view was the premise that all living things owe their existence to the personal, deliberate handiwork of an omniscient and benevolent Creator. He embraced the concept of natural theology posited by an eighteenth-century Anglican clergyman and philosopher, William Paley, who maintained that nothing but intelligent design could account for the existence of characteristics that allow living organisms to accomplish vital tasks. As Paley observed, "The marks of design are too strong to be gotten over. Design must have a designer. That designer must have been a person. That person is God."[5]

Interestingly, Agassiz's rival, Asa Gray, also believed that all living things had been intelligently designed by God. Indeed, both of them could be identified with the current intelligent-design movement with respect to the use of that phrase. Unlike Agassiz, however, Gray was a proponent of what is now known as theistic evolution: that is, the belief that God set in motion the forces that eventually led to the present state of the universe. To him, religion and science occupied separate spheres of knowledge. His religious faith persuaded him that God was the ultimate cause of all natural processes, and Darwin's work helped to explain how those natural processes worked.

Gray pointed out that long before Darwin came on the scene, geologists and physicists had found natural causes for phenomena that had previously been considered the result of direct supernatural intervention. Evolution, as he saw it, was simply one more discovery of natural processes; it did not, in itself, either prove or disprove that the ultimate cause of those processes was God. "Darwinian evolution (whatever may be said of other kinds) is neither theistical nor nontheistical," he wrote. "Its relations to the question of design belong to the natural theologian or, in the larger sense, to the philosopher."[6] Darwin later described Gray as the person who best understood *Origin*, and he supported Gray's assertion that any belief about the ultimate cause of life must lie outside the scope of science.

Darwin addressed these issues more fully in his *Autobiography*, published almost thirty years after *Origin*. According to his own account, he entered adulthood an orthodox Christian who regarded the Bible as the source of morality and truth. In the course of his scientific education, he came to realize that some of the Bible's historical narratives were factually inaccurate, and he began to interpret the text metaphorically rather than literally. Later, his advancing knowledge of science led him to deny the existence of miracles, and thence he "gradually came to disbelieve in Christianity as a divine revelation." When he wrote *Origin,* he was still a theist in the sense that he believed that the First Cause had to be something "having an intelligent mind in some degree analogous to that of a man."[7] Since then, however, that conviction had weakened in him, and he identified himself as an agnostic.

In passages echoed by many of his twenty-first-century supporters, Darwin asserted that religious belief, or the lack thereof, is irrelevant to assessing the validity of scientific theories. Just as the theory of light is accepted even though it does not explain the ultimate source of light, and the theory of gravity is accepted without explaining the origin of gravity, so the theory of evolution should be judged solely in terms of the evidence it provides to explain how living things developed after they had come into existence. He also refuted the charge that his work undercut morality by defining human beings not as the children of an omniscient God but as the products of mechanistic, materialistic, deterministic forces. Moral behavior, he asserted, need not be based on the belief that one must conform to God's laws. It can arise from personal experiences and from anticipation of what will happen as a consequence of pursuing one line of action rather than another.

Darwin's claim that evolution is compatible with morality was challenged by W. S. Lilly in an article published the same year as the *Autobiography.* Just as Agassiz furnished the scientific basis for current opposition to evolution, arguments resembling those offered by Lilly are still used today to support the contention that natural selection gives rise to immorality. The title of his article is "Materialism and Morality," but it might more appropriately be called "Materialism *versus* Morality" or "Materialism *or* Morality." He posited two competing forces: spiritualism, which supports belief in absolute morals, and materialism, which generates moral relativism. Although he conceded that people brought up in traditional morality might continue to act in accord with those principles even if they later became materialists, he suggested that future generations raised in materialism would operate on a basis of "enlightened selfishness" rather than "duty for its own sake."[8]

Underlying Lilly's specific accusations against evolutionists was his overarching belief that they denied, or at least ignored, the existence of anything that could not be empirically verified. Thomas Huxley, "Darwin's Bulldog," stepped forward to refute this charge in terms that continue to be heard in today's debates. He himself, he affirmed, was aware of many phenomena that lie outside physical science and that cannot be tested in a laboratory. By asserting that empirical evidence is essential in science, he explained, he did not mean to imply that nonmaterial truth cannot exist. Rather, his point was that such inquiries belong to disciplines other than science. He also noted that doubts about the existence of God, free will, and immortality had been in existence far longer than the scientific theories to which Lilly attributed them. Even if modern science were entirely obliterated, Huxley said, such doubts would remain because they have nothing to do with science.

Like Huxley, Joseph LeConte, the first professor of geology at the University of California, Berkeley, denied that evolution must be associated with a materialist perspective. "Evolution is one thing and materialism quite another," he wrote. "The one is an established law of Nature, the other an unwarranted and hasty inference from that law."[9] James McCosh, president of the College of New Jersey (later Princeton University), agreed that there is no necessary dichotomy between evolution and religion: "We give to science the things that belong to science, and to God the things that are God's."[10]

A natural outgrowth of the debate over Darwin's ideas was an attempt to reconcile science and religion by demonstrating, through the use of Baconian methods and scientific terminology, that Genesis is factually correct. In several articles published in the *Popular Science Monthly* in the mid-1880s, William Gladstone, who served four terms as prime minister of England, presented an account of evolution in which the various kinds of living things —beasts of the water, birds of the air, and so forth—appeared in the order listed in Genesis. To support his thesis, he referenced the work of long-dead scientists and, it was later shown, misrepresented the findings of the one contemporary writer whom he cited. As he himself conceded, he, like Bishop Wilberforce, had no scientific credentials. That lack of expertise was not an obstacle to engaging in the reasoning and argumentation characteristic of the Baconian approach, but in the new world of Darwinian science, his use of Bible-based reasoning rather than empirical methodology led to his being savaged by Darwin's Bulldog, among others.

Although Huxley provided copious scientific evidence to refute Gladstone's account of evolution, the two men were actually in agreement about the underlying premise of Gladstone's work: that there is no necessary conflict between religion and evolution. Gladstone, however, attempted to reconcile evolution with specific dogma—a literal reading of Genesis— whereas Huxley focused more broadly on belief in God. Like Asa Gray, Huxley asserted that religion and evolution deal with different issues and thus need not conflict as long as neither strays onto the other's ground. This point was echoed by W. D. Le Sueur, another contributor to the *Popular Science Monthly* debate. Le Sueur argued that science could not be tied to "theological cannon-balls" in the form of religious texts that dictated to the scientist "what he must incorporate into his system of thought, or what venerable doctrines he must bow to in passing."[11] In his view, an ethical scientist must follow empirical evidence wherever it leads while deferring to religion in such matters as sin, redemption, and one's relationship with God.

Almost forty years after the publication of *Origin,* Andrew Dickson White, cofounder and former president of Cornell University, stepped back from the specifics of the debate over science and religion to analyze its overall shape. He identified three phases of religious opposition to science: "the general use of scriptural texts and statements against the new scientific doctrine," "the pitting against science of some great doctrine in theology," and "attempts at compromise by means of far-fetched reconciliations of [religious] textual statements with ascertained fact."[12] Among examples of the third stage, he mentioned Gladstone's effort to reconcile evolution with Genesis. Each such attempt, he wrote, "mixes up more or less of science with more or less of Scripture, and produces a result more or less absurd."[13] Joseph LeConte, who defined evolution in terms of a divine plan put into motion at the beginning of the universe, made a similar point. "[A]fter every struggle between theology and science, there has been a readjustment of some beliefs, a giving up of some notions which really had nothing to do with religion in a proper sense, but which had become so *associated* with religious belief as to be confounded with the latter—a giving up of some line of defense which ought never to have been held, because not within the rightful domain of theology at all."[14]

Darrow for Darwin vs. Bryan for the Bible

By the end of World War I, the Darwinian theory of evolution was firmly established within the scientific community, but it remained controversial in the arena of popular opinion. This was particularly true in the United States, where a fundamentalist religious revival led to calls for a return to traditional values and practices. Evolution was reviled not only in its own right but also as a symbol of the entire materialist, secularist, modern world-view. Surrounded by cultural unrest that manifested itself in such forms as social and political revolutions, the stirrings of labor unions, and even new music and hairstyles, antievolutionists sought to turn back the clock. Not surprisingly, they preferred the Baconian approach, with its openness to Bible-based reasoning and its promise of absolute certainty, to a scientific method that, they felt, used an unnecessarily bewildering abracadabra of complexity and constant change to undermine Genesis.

Over the course of this debate, the actual content of the theory of evolution was obscured by misrepresentations and caricatures that impeded serious discussion. Scientists attempted to set the record straight, but their erudite refutations of their opponents' misstatements, often delivered in an irritated manner, backfired. Evolution, cried their foes, was the brainchild of elitist, leftist, secularist intellectuals whose criticism of ordinary people made a mockery of democracy and common sense. Above all, antievolutionists deplored the social and moral implications arising, they believed, from the notion that far from being the lovingly created children of God, humans are nothing more than animals who owe their existence to blind chance and brutality.

When antievolutionists turned their attention to public schools and universities, as inevitably they did, their arguments brought a new dimension to the evolution-creationism controversy. The tension between religion and science remained a constant factor, but its introduction into the context of public education raised additional questions concerning the assignment of authority to determine what American youth are to be taught. On what basis should such decisions be made, and above all, what constituencies should participate in the decisionmaking?

Consistent with the controversy as a whole, the emerging struggle over the teaching of evolution in public schools and universities pitted popularism and majoritarianism against content-area expertise. The authority of school boards to determine curriculum was widely accepted in principle, but advocates on both sides argued that it could not be invoked to justify the teaching of falsehood. Creationists contended that school officials could not legitimately encourage students to value a series of guesses and half-truths over the Word of God, and their opponents retorted that mainstream scientific thought could not be subordinated to religious prejudice. Further complicating the situation was the lack of unity within the ranks of religious believers. The frequently repeated claim that evolution and its supporters were inherently godless was challenged by theistic evolutionists who, following the lead of such thinkers as Asa Gray, Thomas Huxley, and Joseph LeConte, saw no conflict between religious faith and evolution. In their view, the question of a dichotomy between science and religion arose not from belief in God but from a literal reading of Genesis.

The first legal battle over the teaching of evolution, and perhaps still the most famous, was the Scopes "monkey trial" that took place in July 1925.[15] Earlier that year, Tennessee had enacted a law making it "unlawful for any teacher in any of the universities, normals and all other public schools of the state, which are supported in whole or in part by the public school funds of the state, to teach any theory that denies the story of the Divine creation of man as taught in the Bible, and to teach instead that man has descended from a lower order of animals."[16] The penalty for noncompliance was a fine of $100 to $500 per offense. (The price of a Model T Ford in 1925 was approximately $300.) In response, the newly formed American Civil Liberties Union offered free legal representation to any Tennessee teacher who would agree to violate the law and thus create a test case.

Led by a chemical engineer named George Rappleyea, a group of businessmen and professionals in Dayton, Tennessee, seized upon the ACLU's offer as an opportunity to bring publicity and outside money to the city. They persuaded John Scopes, a mathematics teacher and football coach who was filling in for the regular biology teacher, to offer himself as a plaintiff. Scopes taught from a textbook entitled *Civic Biology*, by George W. Hunter, which contained brief references to the gradual development of beneficial adaptations. These were considered sufficient to fall under the proscription of the law, and a justice of the peace swore out a warrant. Amid blisteringly negative publicity about embarrassing the South by creating a lowbrow media circus, the officials of Dayton called a grand jury into special session to indict Scopes, thus fending off an attempt to move the test case to Chattanooga.

Almost immediately, star performers entered the case on both sides. Acting as a counterweight to the ACLU, the World's Christian Fundamentals Association (WCFA) arranged for the former secretary of state and presidential candidate William Jennings Bryan, one of the best-known orators of his time, to serve on the prosecution team. Bryan had not practiced law for more than thirty years, and the prosecutor, A. Thomas Stewart, handled most of the case with the assistance of two other attorneys, Ben McKenzie and William Jennings Bryan, Jr. Nevertheless, the senior Bryan was a prestigious and passionate critic of evolution, and his presence guaranteed that the case would not be limited to such purely legal issues as the state's authority to determine curriculum.

Shortly after Bryan joined the prosecution team, Clarence Darrow, a well-known liberal attorney, offered his services to the defense. To the dismay of the ACLU, which considered Darrow a publicity hound whose outspoken antagonism toward religion would make it easier to characterize the case as a clash between religion and irreligion, Scopes accepted Darrow's representation. "'It was going to be a down-in-the-mud fight,' he recalled, 'and I felt that situation demanded an Indian fighter rather than someone who graduated from the proper military academy.'"[17] Accordingly, Darrow joined Dudley Field Malone and Arthur Garfield Hays, the attorneys provided by the ACLU, in defending Scopes.

From the time the lawsuit was announced, the prevalence of fundamentalist Christians in Rhea County, where Dayton was located, raised questions about the court's bias toward religious values. The noted—and highly irreverent—journalist H. L. Mencken commented in one of his columns, "There are, in fact, only two downright infidels in all Rhea county, and one of them is charitably assumed to be a bit balmy."[18] Later, he wrote, "I have hitherto hinted that an Episcopalian down here in the coca-cola belt is regarded as an atheist. It sounds like one of the lies that journalists tell, but it is really an understatement of the facts. Even a Methodist, by Rhea county standards, is one a bit debauched by pride of intellect. It is the four Methodists on the jury who are expected to hold out for giving Scopes Christian burial after he is hanged."[19] As for Clarence Darrow, the crowd was "glaring at him as if they expected him to go off with a sulphurous bang every time he mopped his bald head."[20]

The image of Dayton as a hotbed of fundamentalism was strengthened by accounts of such events as nightly tent revivals and preaching on the courthouse lawn. According to L. Sprague de Camp, a preacher named Joe Leffew declared, "I ain't got no learnin' and never had none. Glory be to the Lamb! Some folks work their hands off up to the elbows to give their young-uns education, and all they do is send their young-uns to Hell. . . . I ain't let no newspaper into my cabin for nigh unto a year since the Lord bathed me in His blood. . . . I never sinned enough to look in one of these here almanacs . . . I've eight young-uns in the cabin and three in glory, and I know they're in glory because I never learned 'em nothin'."[21]

The defense's concern about religious bias was exacerbated when the trial opened with a prayer by a fundamentalist minister, after which Judge John Raulston read the first thirty-one verses of Genesis aloud. He explained that under the state's new antievolution law, the court's business was to determine whether Scopes's biology instruction conflicted with the verses he had just read. The law itself, he admonished, was not on trial. When fundamentalist ministers continued to offer lengthy prayers at the beginning of each court session, the defense lawyers objected, as they did to the prominent display of a large banner saying "READ YOUR BIBLE." The judge refused to discontinue the prayers, but after several days, he had the banner removed over McKenzie's anguished protest that if a man could not be told to read his Bible, "then is time for us to tear up all of the Bibles, throw them in the fire and let the country go to hell." The chief prosecutor continued the religious theme. While denying that the antievolution law was "sponsored by a lot of religious bigots," he proclaimed that "when science treads upon holy ground, then science should invade no further." The people of Tennessee had "the right to bar the door to science when it comes within the four walls of God's church upon this earth."[22]

It might seem that such overt promotion of a literal interpretation of the Bible should have been found unconstitutional on the spot, but the First Amendment applied only to federal action, not to state action, when the Scopes trial took place in 1925. Evidence that the court—or the state antievolution law—promoted a particular religion was not necessarily determinative, as it would be today. Thus, to frame the issue of religious bias in a manner that would hold up on appeal, the defense attorneys turned not to the U.S. Constitution but to the Tennessee state constitution, which banned "any religious establishment or mode of worship."[23] According to the defense attorneys, that provision made it unlawful to privilege the biblical account of creation over the claims of science.

Amid all this discussion of religion, witnesses representing the scientific community were conspicuous by their absence. During the preparation period, the prosecutors spoke with a few potential expert witnesses, including a self-taught geologist named George McCready Price. Among other things, Price asserted that all fossils are the same age and originated with Noah's Flood. He declined to testify because his work carried no weight outside creationist circles, but Bryan later named him as an example of a reputable scientist. Darrow retorted, "You only mentioned Price because he is the only human being in the world so far as you know that signs his name as a geologist and believes like you do." Bryan mentioned another example, identified only as "Wright," whom Darrow denounced as "a man that every scientist in this country knows is a montebank and a pretender and not a geologist at all."[24] In the end, the prosecution decided to call no expert scientific witnesses. Instead, they argued that the lawyers, not scientists, should explain what evolution meant in the context of this case.

The defense had its own problems with respect to expert witnesses, since prominent scientists who were invited to testify declined to associate themselves with the case. Eight scientists of moderate reputation did go to Dayton, but only one of them was allowed to testify, and only in the absence of the jury. Despite Darrow's impassioned argument that the jury could not determine whether evolution conflicted with Genesis without knowing what evolution was, the prosecutors persuaded the judge otherwise. Their chief argument was that since the law asserted that a conflict exists between evolution and Genesis, and the law itself was not on trial, there was no point in debating whether what it said was true. The best Darrow could do was to get the testimony of Maynard M. Metcalf, a zoologist at the Johns Hopkins University, into the record. Among other things, Metcalf stated that all the "zoologists, botanists and geologists" of his acquaintance believed "that evolution is a fact, but I doubt very much if any two of them agree as to the exact method by which evolution has been brought about, but I think there is— I know there is not a single one among them who has the least doubt of the fact of evolution."[25]

The two threads of religion and science came together most memorably during the famous climax of the trial, when Darrow questioned Bryan directly about his views on evolution. Bryan was eager to uphold the Bible against Darrow's disbelief, but the other prosecutors, who thought that turning Darrow loose on Bryan was a recipe for disaster, fought hard to prevent it. Scopes later wrote that the trial transcript was necessarily incomplete on this point because the court reporter could not record "what six or seven screaming individuals are saying simultaneously."[26]

Darrow began his examination by asking Bryan a series of questions about biblical stories that contradict science. As an example, when Bryan affirmed his belief that the sun stood still for Joshua, Darrow pointed out that the earth moves around the sun, not vice versa, and that if either body stood still, the planet would be incinerated. Bryan replied that that had no bearing on his belief. In response to questions about such matters as the age of the earth and the development of language, he stated that he neither knew nor cared what secular disciplines might say to contravene the biblical account. He repeatedly affirmed that his goal was to uphold the inerrancy of the Bible, and to his ears any argument against it was simply more evidence of hostility toward religion.

As the ACLU had feared, Bryan frequently pointed to Darrow's agnosticism as evidence that the trial represented a struggle for the soul of America. As the ACLU had also feared, Darrow was stung into heated retorts, such as, "We have the purpose of preventing bigots and ignoramuses from controlling the education of the United States, and you know it, and that is all." His most frequently quoted remark to Bryan was an assertion that biblical literalism does not represent the whole of religion: "I am examining you on your fool ideas that no intelligent Christian on earth believes."[27] At that point, Judge Raulston deemed it expedient to adjourn. Since both sides agreed to forgo closing arguments, that was, for all practical purposes, the end of the trial.

Predictably, Scopes was found guilty, and the judge fined him $100. On appeal, the Supreme Court of Tennessee overturned the decision on a technicality: Tennessee law empowered the jury, not the judge, to determine the fine. The appeals court also discussed the central issues in the case and suggested, among other things, that the trial had focused excessively on Genesis. According to the court, the goal of the antievolution law was to prevent the public schools from teaching that humans evolved from lower animals. The observation that such teaching would contradict Genesis was merely an illustration, not the main thrust of the law. The court also denied that the religion clause of the state constitution was relevant. Since no religion teaches evolution as a matter of faith, the court found, banning it from the public schools had nothing to do with religion. Finally, the court touched on the third central issue of the Scopes case: who should control the curriculum. Not surprisingly, in view of the rest of its decision, the court came down in favor of the state and school authorities. Scopes was free to express his views about evolution on his own time, but as a public-school employee, he was required to teach as the state bade him to do. The input of the scientific community was not considered at all except for references to theistic evolution in a concurring opinion.

The widely shared assumption that control of science instruction belonged to state officials and not to the scientific community was forcefully expressed by Bryan both before and during the trial. To Bryan, whose dedication to populism earned him the nickname "the Great Commoner," the collective will of the people was paramount and beyond question. Throughout the trial, he contrasted himself with Darrow, whom he accused of insulting the jury's intelligence. He also suggested, in the peroration of a closing argument that he wrote but never delivered, that public response was the most important factor the jury should consider. "If the law is nullified, there will be rejoicing wherever God is repudiated, the Savior scoffed at and the

Bible ridiculed," he wrote. "If, on the other hand, the law is upheld and the religion of the school children protected, millions of Christians will call you blessed and, with hearts full of gratitude to God, will sing again that grand old song of triumph: 'Faith of our fathers.'"[28]

Bryan was particularly scathing in his treatment of the scientific community, which accused him of scientific illiteracy when he said, for instance, that if traits were indeed inherited, then the prodigal son would have been more similar to his brother. He also suggested that the theory of gravity was acceptable because it can be proven by dropping rocks, whereas no comparable evidence exists for evolution. Brushing aside any explanation offered by mainstream scientists, he portrayed them as elitist, antidemocratic snobs who should be brought to heel by the will of the majority. In an early example of attempts to vilify intellectualism and modernism by associating them with communism, he wrote, "A scientific soviet is attempting to dictate what shall be taught in our schools and, in so doing, is attempting to mould the religion of the nation. It is the smallest, the most impudent, and the most tyrannical oligarchy that ever attempted to exercise arbitrary power."[29]

Among the scientists who responded to Bryan was Edward L. Rice, a biology professor at Ohio Wesleyan University who had long supported Darwinism. In an article published in *Science* in the same year as the Scopes trial, he remarked that as a scientist, he could ignore Bryan. As a teacher, however, he felt it necessary to protest that state legislatures were not equipped to decide what constitutes good science. By contrast with Bryan, who spoke in political terms about the censorship of religious views and the power of state legislatures, Rice maintained that the main point was the factual accuracy of the information taught in the schools. Like many other scientists, he protested that Bryan demanded impossible proofs, interpreted evolution in terms of a Baconian approach that had been superseded by the modern scientific method, and confused scientific disputes about the specific details of evolution with disagreement about the validity of the theory itself. Although absolute certainty is not part of modern science, Rice maintained, there is such a thing as "practical certainty." "In the almost unanimous judgment of biologists," he wrote, "the evolutionary theory has reached this status." He also complained that "Mr. Bryan advances no new evidence; the data collected by scientists he ignores or denies. To the biologists, the evidence seems conclusive for evolution; to Mr. Bryan, it has no significance. In large part, doubtless, this difference is due to Mr. Bryan's simple ignorance of the facts."[30]

Incorporation's Children

Three years after the *Scopes* decision, the state of Arkansas adopted an antievolution law similar to the one in Tennessee except that it did not mention Genesis. Under the Arkansas statute, it was "unlawful for any teacher or other instructor in any University, College, Normal, Public School, or other institution of the State, which is supported in whole or in part from public funds derived by State and local taxation to teach the theory or doctrine that mankind ascended or descended from a lower order of animals and also it shall be unlawful for any teacher, textbook commission, or other authority exercising the power to select textbooks for above mentioned educational institutions to adopt or use in any such institution a textbook that teaches [that theory]."[31] Noncompliance was punishable by a fine and the loss of teaching credentials.

The effort to pass this legislation was led by Ben M. Bogard, a Baptist preacher and the founding president of the American Anti-Evolution Association, which "was open to everyone except 'Negros, and persons of African decent, Atheists, Infidels, Agnostics, such persons as hold to the theory of Evolution, habitual drunkards, gamblers, profane swearers, despoilers of the domestic life of others, desecrators of the Lord's Day, and those who would depreciate feminine virtue by vulgarly discussing relationships.'"[32] (The spellings appear as they do in the original.) The bill failed in the state senate, but it was enacted by means of a successful popular initiative in the election of 1928.

For decades, attempts to repeal, weaken, or challenge the antievolution law were fruitless. In the mid-1960s, however, the Supreme Court declared state-sponsored school prayer unconstitutional, and critics of the Arkansas statute saw an opportunity. By then, the Supreme Court had issued a series of opinions reinterpreting the First Amendment to apply to the states as well as to the federal government. Called incorporation theory because it was based on incorporating the First and Fourteenth Amendments, this interpretation of the U.S. Constitution meant that state law, like federal law, had to conform to the Establishment Clause of the First Amendment: "Congress shall make no law respecting the establishment of religion." For the first time, state laws that advanced or inhibited religious views could be challenged in federal court.

Shortly after the Supreme Court applied incorporation theory to state-sponsored school prayer, the Arkansas Education Association (AEA), the Arkansas School Board Association, the Arkansas Parent Teacher Association, and the American Association of University Women undertook a concerted campaign to overturn the 1928 antievolution law as a violation of the Establishment Clause. Among their opponents was Governor Orval Faubus, best known for having called out the Arkansas National Guard to prevent the racial desegregation of Little Rock's Central High School—where, by coincidence, the lawsuit against the antievolution law began. Echoing sentiments expressed by William Jennings Bryan four decades earlier, Faubus said that he "supported the antievolution law 'as a safeguard to keep way-out teachers in line.'"[33]

When the AEA and its allies were unable to repeal the law by political means, Susan Epperson, a second-year biology teacher at Central High, agreed to serve as plaintiff in a lawsuit filed in the Chancery Court of Arkansas. An Arkansas native, she held a degree from a religious college and identified herself as a born-again Christian. Nevertheless, she later explained, "I'm a science teacher and if you've studied some science, and the more you study, you understand that evolution is a very unifying principle in the understanding of all kinds of biology. To leave it out, to not be able to say anything about it, is really shortchanging your students, not giving them the full picture."[34] In the academic year 1965–66, when Epperson filed her suit, Central High School had just purchased new biology textbooks that suggested a common ancestry for humans and apes. Epperson claimed that she would be guilty of violating the antievolution law if she used the new textbook and of insubordination if she did not.

Like Judge Raulston in the Scopes trial, the Chancery Court judge who heard Epperson's case excluded scientific evidence about the validity of evolution, and the trial took only two hours. He found the law unconstitutional, in part because it was so vaguely worded that teachers would be hard pressed to know exactly what was forbidden. On appeal, the Arkansas Supreme Court issued a two-sentence ruling upholding the law as a reasonable exercise of the state's authority to determine curriculum. Nevertheless, the ruling appeared to support the contention that the law was vague by observing that it did not specify whether teachers were forbidden to promote evolution as truth or to mention it at all.

When the case reached the U.S. Supreme Court, Epperson's attorney, Eugene Warren, had to show either that the antievolution law was unconstitutionally vague, as the lower courts had suggested, or that it violated the Establishment Clause, or both. He was aided in this endeavor by an unlikely source: his opponent. Assistant attorney general Don Langston, who was clearly unenthusiastic about defending the antievolution statute, interpreted it to mean that teachers could not even mention evolution. Moreover, he asserted, this restriction applied to colleges and universities as well as to K–12 schools. Since the Arkansas Supreme Court had declined to interpret the law, the reading supplied by the state's attorney was authoritative, and it all but invited the Court to strike down the statute. As the legal scholar Randall Bezanson observed, "Langston, in effect, has handed Eugene Warren the case on a silver platter."[35]

In the end, Langston's statement that the law forbade any mention of evolution, not just the promotion of evolution as objective truth, turned out to be irrelevant. Under either interpretation, the Court decided, the law would violate the Establishment Clause because it "selects from the body of knowledge a particular segment which it proscribes for the sole reason that it is deemed to conflict with a particular religious doctrine; that is with a particular interpretation of the Book of Genesis by a particular religious group." While acknowledging that curricular decisions ordinarily belong to state and local authorities and not to the federal judiciary, the Court declared the antievolution law to be an exception: "There is and can be no doubt that the First Amendment does not permit the State to require that teaching and learning must be tailored to the principles or prohibitions of any religious sect or dogma." Moreover, the Court observed, "In the present case, there can be no doubt that Arkansas has sought to prevent its teachers from discussing the theory of evolution because it is contrary to the belief of some that the Book of Genesis must be the exclusive source of doctrine as to the origin of man."[36]

No longer able to exclude evolution from science instruction, antievolutionists set about finding a way to include creation-based ideas. Following the example set by William Gladstone decades earlier, they began to focus on developing scientific proofs of the Genesis account of creation, an approach they called creation science. Their efforts were advanced by a Yale law student, Wendell Bird, who suggested that as a matter of religious neutrality, schools that taught either creation science or evolution had to present the other view as well. Bird's approach sidestepped the issue of scientific validity by defining creation science and evolution as competing belief systems that had to be given equal time because the government could not support one over the other.

Building on model legislation developed by Henry Morris of the Institute for Creation Research (ICR), Bird produced a bill that described creation science and evolution as equally scientific and equally religious. While conceding that teaching only creationism might violate the Establishment Clause, the bill stated that the same was true of excluding the scientific proofs of divine creation while presenting ideas consistent with secular humanism, defined as a belief system that contradicts a literal interpretation of the Bible and thus constitutes a competing faith. Since the bill's supporters listed evolution among the tenets of secular humanism—along with such concepts as globalism, feminism, pacifism, and materialism—they believed that the teaching of evolution, in and of itself, promoted the religion of secular humanism. Under this formulation, religious neutrality was impossible, because anything inconsistent with biblical literalism was, by the definitions embodied in the bill, to be considered part of a competing faith system. This duality underlies the argument that the only way for the government to avoid favoring one religion over another is to include Bible-based material whenever secular information is presented.

Supporters of this approach, which they called "balanced treatment," claimed that their goal was to protect academic freedom. Their use of that term was idiosyncratic because they neither distinguished between K–12 and university education nor referred to the choices of faculty or students, individually or collectively, at any level. To advocates of balanced treatment, academic freedom signified the right to have one's views taught in the public schools—in this instance, by including creation science in science classes. Only thus, they claimed, could believers in a literal interpretation of Genesis have academic freedom. The alternative was described as religiously motivated censorship of ideas that conflicted with secular humanism.

In 1980 a creationist activist named Paul Ellwanger produced model legislation, the Balanced Treatment for Creation-Science and Evolution-Science Act, based on the work of Morris and Bird. This bill, later enacted into law in Arkansas, provided that if either evolution or creation science was taught in K–12 public schools, then both had to be represented in courses, textbooks, and school-library collections. The purposes of the legislation included "protecting academic freedom for students' differing values and beliefs; ensuring neutrality toward students' diverse religious convictions; ensuring freedom of religious exercise for students and their parents; guaranteeing freedom of belief and speech for students; preventing establishment of Theologically Liberal, Humanist, Nontheist, or Atheist religions; preventing discrimination against students on the basis of their personal beliefs concerning creation and evolution; and assisting students in their search for truth." As enacted in Arkansas, it included the disclaimer, "This Legislature does not have the purpose of causing instruction in religious concepts or making an establishment of religion."[37]

In defining creation science, the Balanced Treatment Act focused on "the scientific evidence (and the scientific inferences from that evidence) indicating (1) 'the sudden creation of the universe, energy, and light from nothing'; (2) 'the insufficiency of mutation and natural selection in bringing about development of living kinds from a single organism'; (3) that changes occur only within fixed limits of the original kinds of plants and animals; (4) separate ancestry for man and apes; (5) explanation of the earth's geology by catastrophism, including the occurrence of a world-wide flood; and (6) the 'relatively recent' inception of the earth and biological 'kinds.'"[38] These concepts were simply asserted rather than demonstrated. Among the proofs offered for the simultaneous creation of all living things, for example, was the unsupported claim that dinosaur footprints had been discovered in Texas superimposed over human footprints, thus showing that humans and dinosaurs had coexisted.

When a mathematics teacher in Little Rock failed to persuade his local school board to adopt a balanced-treatment policy, a local clergyman, the Reverend W. A. Blount, led a lobbying campaign to have the Balanced Treatment Act enacted into law in Arkansas. At his urging, a member of his congregation, state senator James Holsted, sponsored the bill. In later testimony, Holsted acknowledged that he knew little about creation science, but he introduced the legislation because he believed that divine creation should be taught in public schools. Without seeking input from scientists, science teachers, the state board of education, or the attorney general's office, the Arkansas Senate passed the bill by a vote of 22 to 2 after fifteen minutes of debate. Within a week, the Arkansas General Assembly passed it without discussion, and Governor Frank D. White signed it. As all this suggests, the Balanced Treatment Act enjoyed enormous public support; indeed, the governor later said, "This is a terrible bill, but it's worded so cleverly that none of us can vote against it if we want to come back up here."[39]

Despite its popularity, the Balanced Treatment Act was not without powerful opposition. The Reverend Bill McLean, a Presbyterian minister serving as the principal officer of the Presbyterian Church in Arkansas, volunteered to serve as the lead plaintiff in a lawsuit funded by the Little Rock chapter of the ACLU. Among the other twenty-two plaintiffs in *McLean v. Arkansas*

were two more Presbyterian ministers, a Methodist bishop and two Methodist ministers, an Episcopal bishop, a Catholic bishop, an African Methodist
Episcopal bishop, and a Southern Baptist minister. The plaintiffs also included organizations such as the AEA, the National Association of Biology
Teachers, the American Jewish Congress, and the American Jewish Committee.

The defendants were state education officials who were being sued to
constrain them from enforcing the new law. Despite serious reservations
about the law, Arkansas attorney general Steve Clark undertook to defend
it on the grounds of fairness, tolerance, and academic freedom. To the dismay of creationists, he rejected an offer of assistance by Wendell Bird, now
an attorney, who had, as a law student, developed the balanced-treatment
concept.

In response to claims based on the Establishment Clause, supporters
of the Balanced Treatment Act denied that the concepts of creation and a
creator are inherently religious. In their view, the same could not be said
of evolution, which they saw as an important element of the religion of
secular humanism. Accordingly, they argued that if public schools taught
only evolution, such instruction would impermissibly favor secular humanism over Christianity. Far from violating the Establishment Clause,
the Balanced Treatment Act would bring science instruction into compliance with it.

Although proponents of the legislation mentioned the academic freedom of science teachers, their purpose was not to empower those teachers
to make independent decisions either individually or collectively. Rather,
they suggested that the teachers' academic freedom required the state authorities to establish and enforce policies that mandated balanced treatment even if individual teachers (and, in this case, the Arkansas Education
Association) disagreed with it. An important element of academic freedom
as a professional standard in public universities—the right of experts in a
field to define its standards—was subordinated to the legislature's authority and to the need to ensure that the views of biblical literalists were not excluded from science classes. Moreover, the statute's populist approach
placed the views of the public above those of science teachers by asserting
that if enough people believe in something, then the suppression of that
viewpoint is the antithesis of academic freedom no matter what the teachers think.

The primary assumption underlying the balanced-treatment movement was that evolution and creationism represent people's personal convictions, and those of one group are as valid as those of the other. Indeed, advocates of creation science considered that belief to be superior to evolution because it comported with the inerrant authority of the Bible, whereas they viewed evolution as a series of guesses based on human reason. As Henry Morris explained, "[I]t is precisely because Biblical revelation is absolutely authoritative and perspicuous that the scientific facts, rightly interpreted, will give the same testimony as that of Scripture. There is not the slightest possibility that the *facts* of science can contradict the Bible."[40]

Not surprisingly, opponents of the Balanced Treatment Act denied that it promoted academic freedom, which, they pointed out, has nothing to do with how many people believe in a certain idea or with the notion that people have a right to hear their views presented in class. The determinative factor, they maintained, was whether, despite its newly acquired name, creation science met the standards for science established by experts in the field. If it did not, then academic freedom would preclude, not require, its inclusion in the science curriculum.

To opponents of the bill, creation science did not come close to meriting attention in science classes. They challenged the creation-science understanding of what constitutes evidence—for instance, the claim that because the occurrence of a great flood can be verified, all of Genesis is worthy of consideration as science. More fundamentally, they noted that the core element of creation science—the role of God as creator—is, by its nature, impossible to prove or disprove by natural means. Consequently, they argued, creation science failed to meet the threshold requirement for being considered science. There remained no justification for forcing teachers either to state falsely that creationism is science or to forgo teaching evolution.

During a two-week trial in federal district court presided over by Judge William R. Overton, expert witnesses on both sides discussed three major questions: whether creation science is science, whether creation science is religion, and whether the teaching of evolution advances a secular-humanist view that qualifies as a religion.[41] The court's responses were no, yes, and no. In the court's view, the history of the law showed it to be an attempt to teach religion as science, as did letters written by Paul Ellwanger, the principal author of the Act. In those letters, Ellwanger acknowledged that creation science was not science and urged Arkansas legislators to conceal their religious purpose. He thus "show[ed] an awareness that [the Balanced Treatment Act] is a religious crusade, coupled with a desire to conceal this fact." In attributing a similar purpose to the bill's sponsor and other legislative advocates, the court pointed to the haste with which the bill was rushed through without participation by important constituencies, such as state education officials, scientists, and the attorney general. "The State failed to produce any evidence which would warrant an inference or conclusion that at any point in the process anyone considered the legitimate educational value of the Act," the decision states. "It was simply and purely an effort to introduce the Biblical version of creation into the public school curricula."[42]

Moving from the legislation's origins to its content, the court observed that like the antievolution law at issue in *Epperson*, the Balanced Treatment Act reflected the fundamentalist assumption "that there are only two positions with respect to the origins of the earth and life." In keeping with this belief, the Act's supporters used Genesis as the basis for defining creation science and then identified evolution as its opposite. This approach misrepresented evolution, but perhaps more significantly, it opened the door to the argument that if evolution can be discredited, then creation science must be true no matter how little scientific evidence can be shown to support it. As Judge Overton observed, the alleged scientific support for the literal truth of Genesis "consisted almost entirely of efforts to discredit the theory of evolution through a rehash of data and theories which have been before the scientific community for decades. The arguments asserted by creationists are not based upon new scientific evidence or laboratory data which has been ignored by the scientific community."[43]

Under the Balanced Treatment Act's dualistic approach, creationism offers one account of the origin of life, whereas evolution offers another. As the expert testimony indicated, however, the theory of evolution begins with the premise that life exists. Because it makes no attempt to identify the ultimate source of life, it is not directly parallel to creationism. Some evolutionists believe, as individuals, that that source is God; others deny it. The point is that those are personal views that fall outside the scope of science.

Having found that creation science is religion and not science, the court turned to the issue of academic freedom. While noting that K–12 teachers do not have the academic freedom to teach whatever they wish, the court rejected the argument that what they say in class should be based on the purported right of the public to have its views presented in the public schools. "The application and content of First Amendment principles are not determined by public opinion polls or by a majority vote," the decision states. "Whether the proponents of [the Act] constitute the majority or the minority is quite irrelevant under a constitutional system of government. No group, no matter how large or how small, may use the organs of government, of which the public schools are the most conspicuous and influential, to foist its religious beliefs on others."[44]

Advocates of balanced treatment, notably Wendell Bird, successfully urged Arkansas officials not to appeal the *McLean* decision. Believing that the attorney general was neither motivated nor prepared to handle it well, they preferred to turn their attention to a new case in Louisiana. Unlike the Arkansas statute, the Louisiana version of the Balanced Treatment Act did not explicitly mention God. It also omitted examples from the biblical account of creation, although it was later amended to permit teachers to mention the Bible in science classes. Its main point was that academic freedom, as defined by proponents of balanced treatment, required the development of constitutionally acceptable materials for teaching creation science as a counterbalance to the theory of evolution. If the liberals who controlled public education were permitted to continue to teach only evolution, they maintained, then students would be deprived of the opportunity to learn the whole truth. The Balanced Treatment Act would thus serve the cause of academic freedom by "providing more scientific information and ending exclusive instruction in just one scientific viewpoint."[45]

The Louisiana Balanced Treatment Act established panels of creation scientists to develop curricular materials in that area. School officials were forbidden to discriminate against anyone who professed creationism or who chose to teach creation science, although no comparable protection was provided for evolution. Like the Arkansas statute, the Louisiana bill did not require that either evolution or creation science be taught, but neither could be presented without the other. The sponsor of the Act, state senator Bill Keith, expressed the view that "[e]volution is no more than a fairy tale about a frog that turns into a prince, but this is what we are teaching our schoolchildren today."[46] Another legislative supporter demonstrated the common misunderstanding that if something is true, it must by definition qualify as science. "If there is a God, and he exists, that will be a fact, will it not, a scientific fact?" he asked. "If he does not, that would seem to be a scientific fact as well."[47] Still another raised the long-standing argument that evolution is detrimental to morality. "I think that if you teach children that they are evolved from apes . . . then they will start acting like apes."[48] A state senator who opposed the bill protested: "What [Keith] is doing is to have something taught by force of law that can't win on its own merits. The legislature is not the proper place to make scientific judgments."[49]

The bill, which passed by a vote of 26–12 in the Louisiana State Senate and 71–19 in the Louisiana House of Representatives, was signed into law in July 1981. Shortly afterward, Don Aguillard, a biology teacher from Lafayette, Louisiana, and other plaintiffs challenged the law in court. The original lead defendant was Governor David Treen, later replaced by Edwin Edwards, who won the governorship in 1983. The plaintiffs' attorney, provided by the ACLU, was Jay Topkis, who had successfully challenged the U.S. Postal Service's refusal to deliver copies of D. H. Lawrence's novel *Lady Chatterley's Lover* on the ground that it was obscene. On the defense side, Wendell Bird and other creationist attorneys, having been appointed special attorneys general (in Bird's case, of Georgia), finally had their opportunity to run the case as they saw fit.

In 1985, a federal district court granted summary judgment in favor of the plaintiffs. "If the state cannot prohibit the teaching of evolution, manifestly it cannot provide that evolution can be taught only if the evolution curriculum is 'balanced' with a curriculum involving tenets of a particular religious sect," the court stated.[50] Affirming this decision later the same year, the U.S. Court of Appeals for the Fifth Circuit pointed to the history of the creation science movement: "Indeed, the Act continues the battle William Jennings Bryan carried to his grave. The Act's intended effect is to discredit evolution by counterbalancing its teaching at every turn with the teaching of creationism, a religious belief."[51] Moreover, the appeals court found that if creation science had been "a genuine academic interest," the state would have required it to be taught in its own right. Defining it solely as a counterbalance to evolution, whose place in the curriculum was secured by scientific credibility that creation science lacked, revealed that the intent of the law was political rather than pedagogical.

Turning to the Act's avowed secular purpose—the advancement of academic freedom—the Fifth Circuit declared, "Although states may prescribe public school curriculum concerning science instruction under ordinary circumstances, the compulsion inherent in the Balanced Treatment Act is, on its face, inconsistent with the idea of academic freedom as it is universally understood. In reaching this conclusion we reject the state's argument that compelled instruction in creation-science is necessary to promote academic freedom because public school teachers believe it illegal to teach creation-science. No court of which we are aware has prohibited voluntary instruction concerning purely scientific evidence that happens, incidentally, to be consistent with a religious doctrine or tenet."[52]

When the Supreme Court agreed in 1986 to decide *Edwards v. Aguillard*, the American Association of University Professors and the American Council on Education filed an amicus curiae brief. The AAUP, representing faculty, and the ACE, representing university administrations, argued that although the Balanced Treatment Act applied only to K–12 schools, it would affect academic freedom as it pertains to university professors. Standing by the principle that "the traditional function of the community of scholars, in the exercise of their academic freedom, is to determine what is or is not authentic to their disciplines," the authors of the brief stated that the "judgment that a particular body of thought is 'scientific' is not for the state to make, if academic freedom is to be preserved." Asserting that the locus of control in defining what constitutes science rests not with state legislatures but with scientists, the AAUP and ACE challenged the "assumed prerogative of the legislature to single out a particular doctrine as worthy of acceptance on a scientific basis, and to command that it be treated as such, when the overwhelming opinion of the scientific community is that the doctrine is not science at all. The legislative usurpation of the academic prerogative to determine what constitutes science infringes protected academic freedom interests." The brief added, "If those who know most about a subject sometimes decide wrongly, matters are not likely to be mended by putting the decision into the hands of those who know less."[53]

In another amicus curiae brief, the American Federation of Teachers (AFT) used the term "academic freedom" to refer to the exercise of professional discretion by K–12 teachers. According to the AFT, "[A]cademic freedom is the teacher's freedom to determine the form and content of instruction and teaching materials consistent with professional and curricular standards. . . . Teachers should, and do, have the freedom to teach scientific theory, whether or not it happens to coincide with a particular religious doctrine. . . . But teachers do not have the freedom to disregard the First Amendment by teaching religious doctrine, even if couched in scientific terminology."[54]

Lest there be any doubt about the mainstream scientific community's opinion of creation science, a brief filed by the prestigious National Academy of Sciences (NAS) stated categorically, "'Creation-science' is not science. It cannot meet any of the criteria of science. Indeed, it fails to display the most basic characteristic of science: reliance upon naturalistic explanations." Among other things, the NAS stated that creation science focused almost exclusively on attacking evolution in the false belief that it is possible to prove one theory by discrediting another. Moreover, according to the NAS, even creation science's attacks on evolution rested on nonscientific bases. For instance, in an attempt to counter evidence that the earth is older than a literal reading of Genesis would suggest, creation scientists claimed "that the Creator recently created the earth and the universe with the *appearance* of great age." As the NAS observed, "This kind of ad hoc reliance upon supernatural power to deal with the empirical falsification of a 'creation-science' postulate permits 'creation-science' to account for anything, but explain nothing, and disqualifies it from consideration as science."[55]

The NAS also agreed with the AAUP, the ACE, and the AFT that the definition of science should rest firmly in the collective hands of the mainstream scientific community. "Academic freedom is badly served by an Act which compels science teachers to teach, and science students to learn, material that has been found by the scientific and academic communities to be without value as science or which, alternatively, persuades them to abandon the teaching of the best theoretical framework science currently has to offer," the brief stated.[56]

Supporting this position was a brief filed by seventy-two Nobel Prize winners, who urged the Court to consider the potential impact of the Balanced Treatment Act on science education and, thence, on America's place in the world. "Scientific education should accurately portray the current state of substantive scientific knowledge," they declared. "Even more importantly, scientific education should accurately portray the premises and processes of science. Teaching religious ideas mislabeled as science is detrimental to scientific education: It sets up a false conflict between science and religion, misleads our youth about the nature of scientific inquiry, and thereby compromises our ability to respond to the problems of an increasingly technological world."[57]

Supporters of the Balanced Treatment Act presented a different perspective on academic freedom. Conservative Jewish, Catholic, and Protestant groups joined three members of the U.S. House of Representatives in a brief prepared by Rutherford Institute attorneys. Comparing themselves with John Scopes, they stated that they were "arguing against dogmatism and in favor of freedom of thought."[58] On this basis, they denied that the community of scientific experts had the right to define the discipline. Framing the debate as a matter of one opinion against another, they maintained that a legal issue such as freedom of speech cannot "depend, in the final analysis, upon the outcome of the scientific dispute." More fundamentally, they challenged the entire structure of modern empirical science and asserted a counterclaim in favor of Baconian reasoning. To them, the case rested not on demonstrating "whether creation-science is empirically legitimate, but in showing that the legitimacy of creation-science does not depend upon empirical claims. Yet the definition of what counts as empirical cannot come from science; it is, rather, an epistemological matter."[59]

When *Edwards v. Aguillard* was argued before the Supreme Court, the plaintiffs' attorney, Jay Topkis, made a point of observing that the Balanced Treatment Act did not serve the cause of academic freedom, which is "not a term; it's an incantation, as [Bird] uses it." In his view, the Act forced teachers to "give balanced treatment, regardless of whether the evidence is balanced," and to teach pseudoscience as the price of teaching science.[60] Topkis was interrupted by Justices Thurgood Marshall and Lewis Powell, whose questions were based on the understanding that the term "academic freedom" applies to universities and university professors. When they asked whether Topkis thought that K–12 teachers have academic freedom, he reminded the Court that it was not he, but his opponents, who had made academic freedom an issue by identifying it as the primary secular purpose of the Balanced Treatment Act. Agreeing that K–12 teachers are subject to state authority with respect to curriculum, he said that his point was that the Balanced Treatment Act failed to promote academic freedom in any sense. "Oh, sure, Your Honor. Academic freedom. We got to give God equal time. That's their idea of academic freedom," he scoffed.[61] Balanced treatment would be a reasonable approach, he concluded, only if it were true that evolution is religion or that creationism is science. Otherwise, no justification existed for a law whose real purpose was to balance religion against science.

Although Bird had omitted academic freedom from his initial presentation to the Court, he was forced to address it in his rebuttal. Suppose, a justice asked him, students were permitted to study German only if they also studied French because the authorities "didn't particularly like Germans and they do like French." Would that represent academic freedom? Bird replied that it would. "[A] legislature may not use the term 'academic freedom' in the correct legal sense," he explained. "They might have in mind, instead, a basic concept of fairness; teaching all of the evidence."[62] His point appeared to be that academic freedom is always served by bringing in additional material, since he did not otherwise explain how teaching two languages, of all those in current use, would promote fairness or constitute "teaching all of the evidence."

In its decision striking down the Balanced Treatment Act, the Court observed that academic freedom is often understood as "enhancing the freedom of teachers to teach what they will." From that perspective, it was not germane to this case because K–12 teachers may be told what courses to teach and what materials to use. As the decision noted, however, academic freedom appears in the Act as a secular justification for including creation science as well as evolution in the science curriculum. "Even if 'academic freedom' is read to mean 'teaching all of the evidence' with respect to the origin of human beings, the Act does not further this purpose," the Court stated. "The goal of providing a more comprehensive science curriculum is not furthered either by outlawing the teaching of evolution or by requiring the teaching of creation science." Because teachers were already at liberty to teach all scientific evidence relating to the development of life, the Court found that "[t]he Act actually serves to diminish academic freedom by removing the flexibility to teach evolution without also teaching creation science, even if teachers determine that such curriculum results in less effective and comprehensive science instruction."[63] Moreover, in addition to narrowing the discussion of the development of life to only two approaches, the Act increased the probability that the subject would not be presented at all.

Based on the invalidity of the Balanced Treatment Act's stated secular purpose and on the history of attempts to promote creationism through public education, the Court found that the statute was religiously motivated. "Out of many possible science subjects taught in the public schools, the legislature chose to affect the teaching of the one scientific theory that historically has been opposed by certain religious sects."[64] The Act thus violated the Establishment Clause in two ways: by encouraging the teaching of religious dogma in public schools and by hampering the teaching of a scientific theory because it conflicts with that dogma.

Although a few organizations continue to promote creation science, *Edwards v. Aguillard* (1987) motivated most antievolutionists to develop a new approach. Creation science itself emerged after *Epperson v. Arkansas* (1968) ended attempts to ban evolution instruction, and after *Edwards,* antievolutionists sought to develop a credible scientific theory that could be taught in public schools as a counterbalance to evolution. In pursuit of this goal, they omitted the specifics of Genesis, but they continued to focus more on discrediting evolution than on generating empirical evidence to support an alternative approach. Accordingly, they continued to define academic freedom as inclusion for its own sake without regard for academic merit.

6

And Yet It Moves

Eppur si muove.

—Attributed to Galileo Galilei, probably apocryphal

AS THE ANTIEVOLUTION MOVEMENT regrouped after its defeat in *Edwards v. Aguillard* (1987), a new organizational leader emerged: the Discovery Institute, founded in 1991. Through its Center for Science and Culture, the institute promotes the development and teaching of intelligent design (ID): the contention that only the acts of an intelligent designer could account for the diversity and complex structure of living things. Earlier proponents of ID, such as William Paley and Louis Agassiz, openly professed their belief in God as the intelligent designer. Most of today's advocates, maintaining that ID is science and not religion, describe religious faith as a personal viewpoint and not an inherent element of ID. Far from promoting a religious view, they maintain, ID demonstrates the existence of an intelligent designer who, if not God, could have been a space alien or a time-traveling cell biologist.

Underlying the modern ID movement are terminology and arguments dating back to Darwin's time, such as examples presented in the 1870s by the zoologist St. George Jackson Mivart to demonstrate the fallacy of natural selection. Mivart's central argument was that in its early stages, a variation caused by natural selection—for instance, a longer neck on a giraffe —would not yet be sufficiently developed to serve any useful purpose. Thus, there would be no reason for that variation to persist and to develop further, because it would not provide a competitive edge to the organism that possessed it. In the case of the giraffe, a slightly longer neck would create the need for a heavier body to support it, and thus the need for more food, without providing enough extra reach to make much difference in food acquisition. As an additional example, Mivart pointed to sea urchins, which have pincers on the ends of flexible stems. In their early stages, Mivart said, pincers without the stems would not have been useful and thus would not have persisted. In Mivart's view, such evidence demonstrated that natural selection did not occur; rather, the giraffe has always had the long neck, and the sea urchins the pincers, with which the intelligent designer endowed them.

Darwin's reply to Mivart anticipated the responses of scientists to the current ID movement. First, he addressed the specifics of Mivart's claim. He suggested that even a slightly longer neck would help a giraffe to reach some food too high for most of its competitors, and the heavier body would help to repel predators. He also demonstrated that some living species of sea urchins display pincers without stems, which negates the assertion that pincers and stems must have appeared simultaneously. More broadly, he challenged Mivart's use of a Baconian approach that involves examining specimens and reasoning from the evidence thus presented rather than conducting controlled empirical studies. In particular, he criticized Mivart for claiming that his arguments had never been refuted when, in Darwin's opinion, Mivart simply ignored any evidence that contradicted his views.

In the current ID movement, a concept similar to Mivart's is known as irreducible complexity and is associated primarily with Michael Behe, a biochemistry professor at Lehigh University. The structure most often used to illustrate this point is not the giraffe's neck but the bacterial flagellum, a tiny projection at the back end of a bacterium that aids in the organism's movement. Behe and other ID supporters argue that removing even one of the dozens of essential proteins that make up the flagellum would render it useless as a propeller, which means that it could not have evolved one part at a time but must have originated in its present form.[1] Their opponents reply that although earlier stages of the flagellum might not have acted as the present structure does, evidence shows that it did fulfill a secretory function. Like Mivart, Behe and his associates assert that no proof exists to discredit their arguments. Like Darwin, their critics retort that the clear empirical refutation of irreducible complexity will not go away merely because ID advocates choose to ignore it.

Background Story

The unmistakable echoes of the Darwin-Mivart exchange were heard in a lawsuit filed against the school board in Dover, Pennsylvania, in 2004. Indeed, any of the antagonists in the nineteenth-century debates over Darwin's ideas would have felt right at home. The dispute that led to the lawsuit began in 2002, when Alan Bonsell and William Buckingham joined the Dover school board. In a board retreat held that winter, Bonsell mentioned the teaching of creationism as one of his goals for the district. He later defined creationism as meaning that the earth is only a few thousand years old, that no common ancestors exist between one species and another, and that all living things appeared suddenly in their present forms. He also said that science should be redefined to include supernatural explanations. Buckingham shared Bonsell's convictions and joined him in leading a shaky 5–4 antievolution majority on the board.

Within a year, Bonsell was head of the school board's curriculum committee, after which he became board president. Buckingham succeeded him in each of those offices. Both men continued to press for what they called a balance between evolution and creationism. Assistant superintendent Michael Baksa, in charge of curriculum for the district, had the thankless task of trying to work out an agreement between them and the highly resistant science teachers at Dover High School. Those negotiations put Baksa into what the author Edward Humes called the "classic role of nice guy caught in the middle."[2] In view of all that has been said about the extensive authority of school boards to determine curriculum, it might seem odd that the board sought the teachers' cooperation rather than simply issuing orders. No doubt the constitutional thin ice associated with creationism was a factor, but it was not the only one.

Former Speaker of the House Tip O'Neill (D-Massachusetts) once remarked, "All politics is local," and something similar might be said of the application of constitutional law in public schools. Dover is a small town, and the science teachers were well-known figures in the community; the head of the Science Department had been teaching at Dover High School for more than forty years. As the story unfolds in the court documents, it becomes evident that the district officials were trying to pacify board members and voters who held creationist views without precipitating an open rift with the science teachers. The teachers, for their part, sought to uphold their professional responsibilities without being insubordinate. If a quiet, behind-the-scenes compromise had been reached, the lawsuit would probably not have taken place. But Bonsell and Buckingham would settle for nothing less than the presentation of divine creation as an alternative to evolution in science classes, and the teachers would not comply. Although the teachers were not plaintiffs in the lawsuit, their refusal to teach creationism as science formed the core of the community resistance that arose when the board started flexing its muscles.

For more than a year, Buckingham and Bonsell supplied the science teachers with creationist material, and the teachers repeatedly explained why it was scientifically inaccurate. The underlying problem, the teachers said, was that evolution did not mean what the board members thought it meant. Evolution traces the development of life forms already in existence; it does not attempt to identify the ultimate cause of life. For this reason, the teachers, who described themselves as religious believers, saw no conflict between evolution and their personal faith in God as creator. They also tried to explain the concept of natural selection, but with little success. The veteran department head, Bertha Spahr, testified at the trial, "He had asked us more than once if we teach man comes from a monkey. In response to that in utter frustration I looked at Mr. Buckingham and I said, 'If you say man and monkey one more time in the same sentence, I'm going to scream.' He did not do that, and I didn't have to."[3]

Matters came to a head in the spring of 2004, when the teachers, who had been asking for new biology textbooks for at least a year, renewed their request. The book they had chosen was *Biology: The Living Science*, by Kenneth Miller and Joseph Levine (Prentice Hall, 2002, 2004). At a school-board meeting on June 7, 2004, Buckingham protested that the book was "laced with Darwinism." In his view, "It is inexcusable to have a book that says man descended from apes and nothing to counterbalance it." He also objected to a mention of Charles Darwin on a timeline illustrating the history of biology. "This country wasn't founded on Muslim beliefs or evolution," he added. "This country was founded on Christianity and our students should be taught as such." At another meeting a week later, he confronted the audience directly: "I challenge you to trace your roots to the monkey you came from"; and "2,000 years ago someone died on a cross. Can't someone take a stand for him?"[4] He and Bonsell held out for textbooks that would pair evolution with creationism. The science teachers and some community members mentioned the possibility of legal action against the teaching of creationism in public schools, and a representative of Americans United for

Separation of Church and State (AU) indicated that that organization was prepared to pursue a lawsuit if necessary.[5]

After consulting with the Discovery Institute, Buckingham called Richard Thompson, president and chief counsel of the Thomas More Law Center (TMLC). According to its Web site, TMLC's purpose "is to be the sword and shield for people of faith, providing legal representation without charge to defend and protect Christians and their religious beliefs in the public square." To TMLC, "What is science, and what is not science, is merely a convention."[6] Thompson offered to represent the board free of charge if its opponents carried out their threat of legal action.

From that point on, Buckingham, Bonsell, and their allies spoke only of ID, not of creationism. They steadfastly declined to define the term except to say that it was not the same as creationism and it was not religious. Buckingham later testified, "I don't know everything about intelligent design. I just know that it's another scientific theory that we thought would be good to have presented to the students."[7] Similarly, Baksa and his boss, Superintendent Richard Nilsen, said nothing more than that they sought to add balance to the curriculum by presenting an alternative to evolution. Nevertheless, the science teachers and their supporters continued to protest that ID and creationism are essentially the same thing, as did the school district's attorney, Stephen Russell. In an e-mail to Superintendent Nilsen, Russell said that he had spoken with Thompson and that "[t]hey refer to the creationism issue as 'intelligent design.'"[8] Russell also pointed out that if the school district lost the lawsuit, which he considered probable, it might be liable for the costs and the attorneys' fees of the winning side. TMLC, which had agreed not to charge for its own services, was not prepared to assume that liability. Buckingham later testified that when the school district's financial risk was explained to him, he said, "'My response to that is what price is freedom. Sometimes you have to take a stand."[9]

At a board meeting on August 27, 2004, Buckingham presented an ID textbook, *Of Pandas and People: The Central Question of Biological Origins*, by Percival Davis and Dean H. Kenyon. Published in 1989 and updated in 1993, it is intended for use in colleges as well as high schools. Its central premise is that living things were designed by an intelligent entity in more or less their present forms. There is no mention of God or of a creator, and some statements are qualified by such phrases as "It may be assumed" and "Even if it is true that." As a whole, the book combines empirical science with the Baconian method, including assumptions and arguments based on what the authors deem probable. The authors imply, for instance, that the designer must be benign as well as intelligent because every organism possesses the appropriate traits, even if humans do not always understand the reasons for them. The text also presents the standard arguments against natural selection. In a twist on Mivart's reference to the giraffe's neck, for instance, the authors suggest that the special circulatory system required by the structure of the giraffe's body would have to have developed at the same time as everything else or it could not have developed at all.

Buckingham offered a simple deal: if the teachers wanted new biology books, they would also have to use *Pandas*. Since four of the other board members had agreed to vote with him, he went into the meeting with a 5–4 majority. But one board member changed her mind, and the final count was 5–4 in favor of authorizing funds to purchase *Biology* but not *Pandas*. Buckingham subsequently solicited donations from the congregation of his church to purchase sixty copies of *Pandas*, which were donated to the school district through Bonsell's father. When direct questions arose at the next board meeting, neither Bonsell nor Buckingham disclosed the source of the funds.

Although the two men wanted *Pandas* to be used as a course text, district officials persuaded them to agree that copies would be kept in the science classrooms for reference but would not be part of the curriculum. That arrangement ended on October 7, when the school board curriculum committee, headed by Bonsell, approved an addition to the district's science curriculum: "Students will be made aware of gaps/problems in Darwin's theory and of other theories of evolution including, but not limited to, intelligent design." This policy was to be operationalized by using *Pandas*. Ordinarily, such a proposal would have been passed along to a broader curriculum committee that included teachers and community members, but Buckingham, who was by then president of the board, skipped that step. Baksa gave the broader curriculum committee and the science teachers a few days' notice that this curriculum change was to be brought up for a vote by the board, and the teachers developed a plan that provided for discussion of problems in evolutionary theory without mentioning ID or *Pandas*. Baksa prepared a third version of the policy to combine the Bonsell language with the teachers' proposal.

At the board meeting on October 18, the science teachers mounted spirited opposition to the proposed curricular change, saying that it was certainly unscientific and probably illegal. Among other things, they pointed out that a brochure that accompanied *Pandas* listed the book as a resource for creation science. Moreover, they protested, it dealt largely with the ultimate origin of life, which lies outside the scope of science. In the end, the board passed Bonsell's proposal, although a press release later stated that Baksa had written it. The board added to the proposal the sentence "Origins of life will not be taught." The teachers protested that *Pandas* does teach the origin of life, whereas evolution does not. Buckingham later testified that he thought the "no origins" language would prevent the teachers from saying that one species evolved from another.

Although the science teachers had no constitutional right to academic freedom, their standing in the community as experts in their fields meant that their involvement, or perceived involvement, in academic decision-making lent credibility to the results. Accordingly, the district issued a press release indicating that the policy had been developed "[i]n coordination with the science department teachers, the district solicitor, and the school board."[10] Nilsen later testified that he was taken aback by the teachers' furious response, prompting the plaintiffs' attorney to remark, "Dr. Nilsen, there is no way anybody could reach that interpretation about the teachers' position from what the teachers said at that October 18th meeting."[11]

Shortly after enacting the new policy, the board developed a statement that teachers were to read to their ninth-grade biology classes before beginning instruction on evolution:

> The Pennsylvania Academic Standards require students to learn about Darwin's Theory of Evolution and eventually to take a standardized test of which evolution is a part.
>
> Because Darwin's Theory is a theory, it continues to be tested as new evidence is discovered. The Theory is not a fact. Gaps in the Theory exist for which there is no evidence. A theory is defined as a well-tested explanation that unifies a broad range of observations.
>
> Intelligent Design is an explanation of the origin of life that differs from Darwin's view. The reference book, *Of Pandas and People,* is available for students who might be interested in gaining an understanding of what Intelligent Design actually involves.
>
> With respect to any theory, students are encouraged to keep an open mind. The school leaves the discussion of the Origins of Life to individual students and their families. As a Standards-driven district, class instruction focuses upon preparing students to achieve proficiency on Standards-based assessments.[12]

Nilsen instructed the science teachers to read the ID statement aloud without saying anything about it. He also told them to respond to student questions by saying, "[T]hat is a good question, we appreciate your interest, please research that on your own behalf or talk to your parents about it."[13] Since the statement was part of the board-mandated curriculum and not an out-of-left-field issue raised by a student, the instruction that teachers were to avoid discussing it was, at best, unusual. The teachers protested that the statement not only was misleading in its vague and comprehensive criticism of evolution but also failed to express similar reservations about ID— a point they were not allowed to mention to the students.

Nilsen's implication that the ID statement was somehow *in* the curriculum but not *of* the curriculum was compounded by his trial testimony, in which he attempted to rebut the plaintiffs' claim that the students were being taught ID. Although students were supposed to learn something from hearing the statement, he said, the act of reading it to them did not constitute teaching them anything. To an educator such as himself, he explained, "teaching" meant lesson plans, objectives, outcomes, materials, and assessment. The plaintiffs' attorney took apparent delight in propounding progressively more absurd hypotheticals, asking Nilsen, for instance, whether it would be "teaching" to tell students that William the Conqueror invaded England in 1066, that Thomas Jefferson wrote the Declaration of Independence, that John Wilkes Booth shot Abraham Lincoln, or that William Jennings Bryan upheld creationism in *Scopes*. "It's learning without question," Nilsen said in response to one such barrage. "But as I've defined it, teaching? No."[14]

Whether reading the ID statement aloud was teaching or not, it certainly did not involve teachers. With the backing of their union, the science faculty endorsed a letter written to Nilsen by the senior biology teacher, Jennifer Miller. In accordance with previous Supreme Court rulings, Miller did not assert that K–12 teachers have academic freedom to make final decisions about what to teach. Rather, her position was that the board's authority had to be exercised within certain parameters, which the board in this instance had exceeded. Allying themselves with the definition of academic freedom propounded by the AAUP and the National Academy of Sciences, she and the other science teachers asserted that the scientific community, not the Dover school board, had the authority to define science.

Miller's letter stated: "INTELLIGENT DESIGN IS NOT SCIENCE. INTELLIGENT DESIGN IS NOT BIOLOGY. INTELLIGENT DESIGN IS NOT AN ACCEPTED SCIEN-

TIFIC THEORY." Reading the statement to the students would suggest that ID should be accepted "as a valid scientific theory, perhaps on par with the theory of evolution. That is not true. To refer the students to 'Of Pandas and People' as if it is a scientific resource breaches my ethical obligation to provide them with scientific knowledge that is supported by recognized scientific proof or theory."[15] The school officials had already said that no student would be forced to listen to the statement, and they decided to extend the opt-out opportunity to the faculty as well. Accordingly, it was Nilsen and Baksa, not the science teachers, who read the statement to the biology classes.

At that point, proevolution parents represented by attorneys provided by AU and the ACLU filed suit in federal district court, as they had been threatening to do for months. TMLC attorneys represented the school officials. Since the first-named plaintiff was Tammy Kitzmiller, mother of two students at the high school, the case was entitled *Kitzmiller v. Dover Area School District*.

As was true of earlier cases involving the teaching of creation science, the outcome of *Kitzmiller* hinged on whether the school board had violated the Establishment Clause of the First Amendment by promoting a religious view. To make that determination, the court had to decide whether ID is in fact science. If it is, the board's authority to determine the content of instruction would have a good chance of prevailing. If, however, ID is not science, then the board would be hard pressed to show either a legitimate secular reason for including it in the science curriculum or a secular benefit resulting from doing so. Absent a convincing secular purpose and effect, the board's action would not pass muster with the Establishment Clause.

Since the Dover school board said that ID is science, and the scientific community maintains that it is not, a key question in *Kitzmiller* was locus of control.[16] K–12 school boards have the authority to decide what should be taught within each discipline, but do they have the right to define the discipline in terms unacceptable to the community of experts in the relevant field? Thus, although academic freedom did not give the teachers at Dover High School the right to decide what to teach, it did come into play with respect to the right of the scientific community, rather than the school board, to define what constitutes science. Since that aspect of academic freedom is intended to further the growth of knowledge by placing such matters in the hands of content-area experts rather than turning them over to political officeholders or majoritarian voters, the question raised in *Kitzmiller* was how much of a voice, if any, content-area experts should have with respect to the presentation of their discipline in K–12 public schools.

No one suggested that AAUP policies, in and of themselves, are binding on K–12 authorities. Rather, the question was whether the same reasoning that underlies academic freedom in universities—the belief that judgments about a discipline are best made by those who know the most about it— should extend to other contexts. When the case came to trial, Judge John E. Jones III permitted both sides to call expert witnesses to their hearts' content in an effort to sort out whether ID is in fact science and what bearing, if any, the views of experts in the field have or should have on K–12 curricular decisionmaking.

Underlying all the topics addressed by the expert witnesses in *Kitzmiller* were two key questions. First, can ideas that are presented as logical, intuitive, inductive, or persuasive be described as scientific in the absence of empirical evidence to support them? Second, does a search for the ultimate cause of life fall under the aegis of science? Based on their answers to these questions, the expert witnesses went on to argue either that ID is science or that it is not. Finally, the expert witnesses either supported or denied the contention that ID is, as one witness put it, "creationism lite"—that is, essentially religious. A few representative examples of the testimony of the expert witnesses on each side may help to negotiate the thicket of their voluminous testimony on each of these points with some degree of brevity and clarity.[17]

What Constitutes Scientific Evidence?

Representing the mainstream scientific community, the National Academy of Sciences defines science is "a particular way of knowing about the world. In science, explanations are restricted to those that can be inferred from confirmable data—the results obtained through observations and experiments that can be substantiated by other scientists. Anything that can be observed or measured is amenable to scientific investigation. Explanations that cannot be based on empirical evidence are not a part of science."[18] Accordingly, NAS defines a scientific theory as "a well-substantiated explanation of some aspect of the natural world that can incorporate facts, laws, inferences, and tested hypotheses."[19] By this standard, reasoning and analogies may be persuasive, logical, and even true, but they are not science unless backed up with hard evidence.

An alternative definition of scientific theories was offered by the chief pro-ID expert witness, Professor Michael Behe. In Behe's revision, a scientific theory is "a proposed explanation which focuses or points to physical, observable data and logical inferences."[20] The substitution of "proposed" for NAS's "well-substantiated" confers the status of a scientific theory— comparable to evolution—on ideas that mainstream science would consider hypotheses at best. Behe thus removes the NAS requirement that an idea must withstand rigorous empirical testing before it can be considered a theory. Similarly, his formulation replaces empirical testing with observable data, such as the complexity of life, and the inferences drawn from such data. These changes signal a return to the Baconian methodology that preceded Darwinism, which permits armchair scientists to construct what they consider well-reasoned or persuasive ideas without subjecting them to testing or even ensuring that they are testable. An example of such reasoning appears in Behe's book *Darwin's Black Box* (1996): "[A]t some point a supernatural designer must get into the picture. I myself find this line of reasoning persuasive. In my estimation, although possible in a broadly permissive sense, it is not plausible that the original intelligent agent is a natural entity."[21]

In addition to inductive or intuitive reasoning, ID relies on analogies to support its arguments. The most popular of these was propounded in the eighteenth century by William Paley, who suggested that just as the complex structure of a watch could have come about only through the actions of a watchmaker, so the universe must have been designed and brought into existence by an intelligent being. Modern variations on Paley's analogy of the watch include mousetraps, cellphones, and computers. Scott Minnich, associate professor of microbiology at the University of Idaho, pointed out that such complex machines are unquestionably the products of design, not of evolution. The same is true of complex living organisms, he testified, and added, "Tell me why it isn't."[22] Kevin Padian, professor of paleontology and evolutionary biology at the University of California, Berkeley, replied that the flaw in that particular analogy is that we can infer that mechanical or electronic devices must have been designed because they have no potential to develop in any other way. The same is not true of living things, which grow, change, reproduce, and mutate. Thus, what we infer from the mousetrap cannot be inferred from the mouse. More broadly, Padian rejected inductive reasoning and analogy as sources of scientific evidence. Like Darwin and Huxley, he protested that ID proponents, most of whom are not scientists, use scientific jargon and "invoke a smoke-and-mirrors pantomime of scientific logic" as a substitute for substantive results.[23]

The contrast between the mainstream scientific community's concept of evidence and that of ID supporters was illustrated by conflicting testimony about irreducible complexity. Behe asserted that in a complex living system like a bacterial flagellum, "the removal of any one of the parts causes the system to effectively cease functioning."[24] Echoing the arguments of Mivart and Agassiz, he reasoned that the entire complex structure must have come into being all at once because, without all the parts, the system would not work. Scott Minnich made a similar point: "If [the complex structure] is the summation of all the parts that provide function, and the loss of a single component renders the machine useless (much like the 'invented' machines we make) *then natural selection has nothing upon which to select.*"[25]

Although Behe and Minnich conceded that they had done little, if any, testing, they maintained that irreducible complexity is scientific because it is subject to being tested. Moreover, referencing the analogies involving mousetraps and computers, Behe described irreducible complexity as "well-tested from the inductive argument. We can, from our inductive understanding of whenever we see something that has a large number of parts, we have always found that to be design. And so, an inductive argument relies on the validity of the previous instances of what you're inducing. So I would say that, that is tested."[26]

Unlike proponents of irreducible complexity, one of its opponents, Kevin Padian, did conduct research on it. His work demonstrated transitional stages between the phases of development of the bacterial flagellum, and it showed that even without key proteins needed for its propeller function, the flagellum serves other purposes that would have been sufficient to sustain it through the evolutionary process. Kenneth Miller, professor of biology at Brown University and coauthor of the textbook used at Dover High School, wrote in his expert report, "The great irony of the flagellum's increasing acceptance as an icon of anti-evolution is the fact that research had demolished its status as an example of irreducible complexity almost at the very moment it was first proclaimed."[27] Behe himself conceded that irreducible complexity is logically flawed because removing a part from an existing organism is not a way to prove whether it could have evolved over millennia. He also acknowledged that an intelligent designer could have programmed a complex structure to evolve gradually into its present form. Nevertheless, without directly responding to the data offered to refute irreducible complexity, he continued to maintain that it not only constitutes convincing proof against evolution but is in fact science.

A striking example of the differences between mainstream science and ID with respect to the nature of evidence occurred when the plaintiffs' lawyer questioned Behe about a statement in *Darwin's Black Box:* "We can look high or we can look low, in books or in journals, but the result is the same. The scientific literature has no answers to the question of the origin of the immune system." The attorney surrounded Behe with fifty-eight books and articles dated 1971 to 2006, all of which presented scientific evidence of the evolution of the human immune system. Behe replied, "Well, these books do seem to have the titles that you said, and I'm sure they have the chapters in them that you mentioned as well, but again I am quite skeptical, although I haven't read them, that in fact they present detailed rigorous models for the evolution of the immune system by random mutation and natural selection."[28] Similarly, Minnich stated categorically that there is no proof of intermediate stages in evolution from one species to another, and when the plaintiffs' attorney cited data to the contrary in several scientific publications, he replied without explanation that the evidence was insufficient. Padian reflected the views expressed by several contemporary evolutionists when he wrote, "Nothing would make IDC [intelligent design creationists] reject their propositions; they are matters of faith, not science."[29]

Underlying these arguments about irreducible complexity and other challenges to evolution was an assumption on the part of ID advocates that discrediting evolution would validate ID because those are the only two possible explanations for the origin of life. Behe claimed, for instance, that the biology textbook cowritten by Miller supports ID because it describes the research in some areas of evolution as "incomplete and unfinished." "This is a telling admission," Behe wrote. "If evolutionary theory is 'incomplete and unfinished,' if it has not explained speciation and the origin of life, if it has uncertainties, then those areas remain open, and possible answers to those questions cannot be artificially restricted to the ones that Kenneth Miller or other Darwinists would prefer."[30] More forcefully, Minnich testified, "If [evolution is] disproven, then you can infer an intelligence."[31] This framing of the debate represents a fundamental point of contention between the two sides. For one thing, mainstream science does not produce the kind of certainty contemplated by the Baconian model. Rather, science generates hypotheses and subjects them to rigorous testing in a never-ending cycle in which existing information is supported, modified, or superseded. Thus, the plaintiffs' experts argued, to say that research on evolutionary theory is "incomplete and unfinished" is simply to say that it is science. More fundamentally, they denied that evolution and ID are in one-on-one competition with each other. In their view, the theory of evolution says nothing about the ultimate cause of life, and no scientific theory can be proven by discrediting a competitor.

Can Science Demonstrate the Existence of God?

According to the NAS, "Religions and science answer different questions about the world. . . . No one way of knowing can provide all of the answers to the questions that humans ask."[32] Consistent with this distinction was the testimony of Kenneth Miller, who identified himself as a Catholic who believes that God created the universe. He testified that science begins with the premise that life exists and deals with what happened after that point. It does not attempt to identify the ultimate cause of life. This is not to suggest, he cautioned, that whatever lies outside the realm of science is unimportant or that it cannot be true; it means only that some answers must be sought through religion or philosophy rather than through science. As a result, science can neither confirm nor deny the existence of anything outside its sphere, including an intelligent designer. In an op-ed piece that appeared in the *New York Times,* Michael Behe seemed to agree that perhaps "the ultimate explanation for life is beyond scientific explanation." Nevertheless, he went on, "I don't want the best scientific explanation for the origins of life; I want the correct explanation."[33] Accordingly, he told the *Kitzmiller* court that presenting students with materialistic, naturalistic evolutionary theory in the absence of any suggestion about the ultimate source of life leads them to a false sense of how living things developed. Scott Minnich added that since ID does not state that the intelligent designer is supernatural, it cannot be excluded on the ground that science does not encompass supernatural explanations. Similarly, the school board's attorney stated in his closing argument that the "possibility of causation, which some might classify as supernatural, at least in light of current knowledge, does not place intelligent theory beyond the bounds of science."[34]

Is Intelligent Design Science?

Among the few points on which the expert witnesses on both sides agreed were these: at least 90 percent of the evidence offered in support of ID is aimed at discrediting evolution rather than demonstrating the accuracy of ID; the vast majority of the mainstream scientific community stands solidly behind evolution and in opposition to ID; and ID has no hope of being accepted as science under the norms of mainstream science. Supporting these conclusions is the fact that only a handful of ID proponents are university-level scientists, and most of them are not in fields directly related to evolution. Indeed, one pro-ID expert witness conceded on cross-examination that "really the entire scientific community rejects the idea that intelligent design is science."[35] Another testified, "And although I do think that intelligent design is well substantiated, I think there's not—I can't point to external— an external community that would agree that it was well substantiated."[36]

Faced with this reality, the pro-ID witnesses in *Kitzmiller* had no choice but to argue that mainstream scientists have neither the legal nor the moral right to define the discipline. Rejecting mainstream science's reliance on empirical verifiability, they decried it as evidence of a materialistic and even atheistic bias. In their view, explanations based on analogies and plausibility should be admissible as science because the alternative is to lose any truth that falls outside the limits of modern science. By referring to empirical research as "methodological naturalism," they suggested that the exclusion of an intelligent designer from science is attributable not to "the" scientific method but to an ideologically motivated "ism." The opinion of the mainstream scientific community, they argued, is just that: the mere opinion of partisans on one side of a debate whose other side is at least equally meritorious. Proevolution witnesses countered that their opponents' assertions were motivated by a desire to identify a predetermined conclusion as science. "Science cannot be defined differently for Dover students than it is defined in the scientific community as an affirmative action program for a view that has been unable to gain a foothold within the scientific establishment," the plaintiffs' attorneys argued.[37]

Because the specific ID material at issue in *Kitzmiller* was *Of Pandas and People*, its scientific merit was directly relevant to the case. Unfortunately for the board, not only the plaintiffs' witnesses but even the chief defense witness pointed out major factual errors in the text. For example, *Pandas* states one of the central tenets of ID: "[V]arious forms of life began abruptly through an intelligent agency with their distinctive features already intact: Fish with fins and scales, birds with feathers, beaks, and wings."[38] Among the copious evidence offered to refute this claim was Miller's discussion of fish fossils that "lacked many of the characteristics possessed by fish today, including jaws, paired limbs and bony internal skeletons."[39] *Pandas* also states that no fossils showing intermediate forms between land mammals and whales have been discovered, but another expert witness, the paleontologist Kevin Padian, showed that such fossils had been found even before *Pandas* was published, and several additional examples have come to light since then. "[I]f you rest your case on a lack of evidence," he remarked, "and then evidence emerges, not only does your case against the science collapse, but your case for an alternative becomes weaker."[40]

Among Padian's targets was a description in *Pandas* of the first amphibians as labyrinthodonts, whereas a labyrinthodont "is a type of tooth, not a type of animal."[41] The book also identifies the *Ichthyostega* as the oldest amphibian, but according to Padian, it is not an amphibian at all. Padian concluded that what he called "Intelligent Design Creationism" is "an ideologically motivated, sociopolitical movement with no science content." In response to the question, "Is it your understanding that intelligent design refutes the claim that life has changed over time?" He replied, "I don't think intelligent design refutes anything in science that I'm aware of."[42]

Unlikely as it might seem, some of the evidence against *Pandas* came not from the antievolution side but from the chief defense expert, Michael Behe. As one of the few ID supporters to hold advanced degrees in a biology-related field, he confirmed that different species share common ancestors. Faced on cross-examination with excerpts from *Pandas* that contradicted his version of ID and brought it closer to creationism, he reiterated his support for teaching ID as science even as he disassociated himself from some of the statements in *Pandas*. Among other things, he acknowledged that the textbook's description of what the theory of evolution says was riddled with error.[43]

Is Intelligent Design Religion?

Following days of testimony demonstrating factual inaccuracies in *Pandas,* the final blow to its status as a legitimate scientific text was struck not by a scientist but by a philosopher. Testifying for the plaintiffs, Barbara Forrest, professor of philosophy at Southeastern Louisiana University, argued that ID "is virtually identical [to creationism] in argument form, content, and purpose. Intelligent design is, in other words, just the next chapter in the anti-evolution movement by religious fundamentalists that began even before *Scopes* and evolved in response to what Professor Behe might call the 'selective pressures' of the *Epperson, McLean,* and *Edwards* decisions."[44]

Most significantly, Forrest compared pre-publication drafts of *Pandas* with the final version of the book.[45] The term "creation" and its cognates are used pervasively throughout the drafts, and Forrest pointed to numerous passages in the published book that are identical to the corresponding material in the drafts except for the substitution of "ID" for "creation." This demonstration was particularly telling because no matter what Behe, Minnich, and other witnesses said about ID, the specific text recommended in the Dover policy was *Pandas*. If the court found *Pandas* to be a creationist text, it would be difficult to argue convincingly that the policy was secular.

As the plaintiffs' expert witnesses hammered home their message that ID is religion and not science, the *Kitzmiller* defendants protested that ID did not mention the Bible or identify the designer as God, nor even as a supernatural being. They also attempted to turn the tables by arguing that if ID is religious, so is evolution. As Behe explained in his expert report, "Darwin's theory of evolution is utterly different from, say, the theory of gravity or electromagnetic theory because of the philosophical, theological, and other non-scientific claims that have been made on its behalf. No one today claims that, say, electromagnetic theory allows a person to be an 'intellectually fulfilled atheist,' but that claim has been made for Darwin's theory."[46] Underlying Behe's outrage were atheistic affirmations made by some scientists, notably Richard Dawkins, Stephen Jay Gould, and George Gaylord Simpson.[47] The specific quotation referenced in Behe's report appears in Dawkins's *The Blind Watchmaker*: "[A]lthough atheism might have been *logically* tenable before Darwin, Darwin made it possible to be an intellectually fulfilled atheist."[48] This was by no means a new idea; Darwin himself had observed that the theory of evolution, without explicitly denying the existence of God, posits a natural mechanism that accounts for the complexity of life without reference to the supernatural. Nevertheless, like Darwin's contemporary opponents, Behe and other ID supporters were vexed by the denial of what had been one of the central proofs of God's existence. The triumphalist tone of Dawkins's diatribe did nothing to mitigate their resentment. While acknowledging that abrasive rhetoric can indeed be annoying, proevolution expert witnesses averred that regardless of the terms in which such sentiments are couched, the personal beliefs of scientists—whether Dawkins's atheism or Miller's Catholicism—are irrelevant. Despite ID claims to the contrary, the work of mainstream scientists is accepted or rejected based not on ideological grounds but on the use of rigorous empirical methodology to demonstrate scientifically sound, verifiable results.

By contrast, Behe affirmed a more direct connection between theology and science, thus deviating in yet another respect from the majority of ID advocates. In an article quoted by the attorney who cross-examined him, Behe had written, "The ID argument is less plausible for those for whom God's existence is in question, and is much less plausible for those who deny God's existence." Asked in court whether ID is "a God-friendly theory," Behe responded not by denying that ID is ideologically based but by implying that the same is true of evolution. Everyone, he suggested, interprets evidence "based not only on the science itself, but what they perceive as other ramifications of the theory."[49] The plaintiffs' expert witnesses rejected this explanation. In their view, the claim of a theory to be considered scientific rests entirely on its content and on the quality of the empirical evidence supporting it. By that standard, ID is, as Barbara Forrest expressed it, "in essence, a religious belief. It is not a scientific belief with a religious component attached to it."[50]

Judgment Day and Its Aftermath

Having heard twenty-one days of this sort of testimony, Judge Jones ruled in favor of the plaintiffs. He wrote, "Although proponents of the IDM [intelligent design movement] occasionally suggest that the designer could be a space alien or a time-traveling cell biologist, no serious alternative to God as the designer has been proposed by members of the IDM, including Defendants' expert witnesses."[51] The court also rejected the argument that ID is secular because it does not mention God: "ID's religious nature is evident because it involves a supernatural designer. The courts in *Edwards* and *McLean* expressly found that this characteristic removed creationism from the realm of science and made it a religious proposition."[52] In particular, the court cited Forrest's testimony regarding the substitution of ID for creationism in the otherwise unchanged text of *Pandas*. "This word substitution is telling, significant, and reveals that a purposeful change of *words* was effected without any corresponding change in *content*."[53] Further, based on evidence regarding both ID in general and the board's actions in particular, the decision declared, "The disclaimer's plain language, the legislative history, and the historical context in which the ID policy arose, all inevitably lead to the conclusion that Defendants consciously chose to change Dover's biology curriculum to advance religion."[54] In the court's view, Bonsell, Buckingham, and their allies on the board "knew that ID is considered a form of creationism" and embraced it for that reason.[55] On these grounds, the court struck down the ID policy as an unconstitutional promotion of religion.

Because state and local school officials are empowered to determine K–12 curriculum, courts usually defer to that authority even when they openly disagree with the decisions of school officials. If the *Kitzmiller* court had not found that ID is religious, the policy might have stood, no matter what the Dover High School teachers or the mainstream scientific community said. Consequently, the only reason the question of academic freedom entered this case was that the Dover school officials, like the defendants in *McLean* and *Edwards,* cited academic freedom as a secular justification for the policy. Dismissing that argument, Judge Jones wrote, "This tactic is at best disingenuous, and at worst a canard. The goal of the IDM is not to encourage critical thought, but to foment a revolution which would supplant evolutionary theory with ID."[56]

Although the decision hinged on the advancement of religion and not on academic freedom, the AAUP viewpoint triumphed to the extent that the court relied upon the mainstream scientific community as the definitive authority on what constitutes science. On that basis, the court dismissed Behe's inductive and analogical reasoning as "bare assertion" and faulted him for failing to "directly rebut the creationist history of *Pandas* or other evidence presented by Plaintiffs showing the commonality between creationism and ID."[57] In effect, the court held the ID expert witnesses to the standards of modern science as defined by the mainstream scientific community, including the production of hard data and the refutation of evidence presented in opposition to one's claims. Thus, the decision states, "ID is at bottom premised upon a false dichotomy, namely, that to the extent evolutionary theory is discredited, ID is confirmed." It concludes that "[W]hile ID arguments may be true, a proposition on which the Court takes no position, ID is not science."[58]

Turning from the nature of ID to the actions of the Dover school board, the court once again raised the question of content-area expertise. Having mentioned the school officials' professions of ignorance regarding the content of ID, Judge Jones remarked, "Despite this collective failure to understand the concept of ID, which six Board members nonetheless felt was appropriate to add to the ninth grade biology class to improve science education, the Board never heard from any person or organization with scientific expertise about the curriculum changes, save for consistent but unwelcome advices from the District's science teachers who uniformly opposed the change."[59] In context, this statement did not imply that the teachers or other content-area experts had a constitutional right to participate in determining the curriculum. Rather, it acknowledged that they were the most credible source of information about the discipline. Although the board had no legal obligation to consult them, its failure to do so exposed it to the charge of pursuing a predetermined agenda. If its true goal had been to improve science instruction, Judge Jones suggested, it would not have ignored the judgment of experts in the field.

In addition to questioning how the board could have been so determined to promote ID without knowing what it is, the judge took issue with some of the testimony offered by Bonsell and Buckingham. Before the trial began, the plaintiffs' attorneys conducted interviews, known as depositions, in an attempt to gather information to persuade the court to halt the reading of the ID statement pending trial. They were unsuccessful, in part because they could not identify the source of the private donations used to purchase *Pandas*. Both Bonsell and Buckingham swore under oath that they did not know where the books had come from. Even at trial, Bonsell testified, "They just sort of came on our doorstep."[60] When the truth later emerged, Buckingham explained that he knew where the money had been collected but not who had given how much. If the plaintiffs' attorney had asked whether he had collected the money at his church, he said, he would have answered in the affirmative, but no one asked him the right question. This lack of candor backfired. "[T]he inescapable truth," the decision states, "is that both Bonsell and Buckingham lied at their January 3, 2005 depositions about their knowledge of the donation for *Pandas*. . . . This mendacity was a clear and deliberate attempt to hide the source of the donations by the Board President and the Chair of the Curriculum Committee to further ensure that Dover students received a creationist alternative to Darwin's theory of evolution. We are accordingly presented with further compelling evidence that Bonsell and Buckingham sought to conceal the blatantly religious purpose behind the ID policy."[61]

Judge Jones, a Pennsylvania Republican who owed his judgeship to President George W. Bush, ended his decision by noting that he would probably be branded a judicial activist. He was right. The term "judicial activism" denotes a judge whose rulings effectively change the law rather than interpreting it, but advocacy groups routinely apply that label to any judge with whose decisions they disagree.[62] Phyllis Schlafly, founder and president of the Eagle Forum, pointed out that conservative Christian voters had helped

President Bush to gain the White House. "[T]his federal judge, who owes his position entirely to those voters and the Bush who appointed him, stuck the knife in the backs of those who brought him to the dance in *Kitzmiller v. Dover Area School District,*" she wrote.[63] In response to numerous criticisms of this kind, Jones remarked, "The implication was that I should throw one for the home team. . . ."[64]

Education by Disclaimer

Kitzmiller was not by any means the only lawsuit to address the use of a disclaimer to counteract the teaching of evolution. Prominent among other examples are *Freiler v. Tangipahoa Parish Board of Education* (1997) and *Selman v. Cobb County School District* (2005).[65] Although these cases raise no new academic-freedom issues, they are worth mentioning to clarify the context of *Kitzmiller* and other antievolution controversies.

The events leading up to *Freiler* began in 1993, when the school board in Tangipahoa Parish, Louisiana, considered a policy to permit the teaching of creation science, defined as "the theory that the universe, including all forms of life, was created literally in the manner described in the Bible by a higher Being, or, as alternately described, the theory of intelligent design or creation by a Divine Creator."[66] That proposal was rejected, but the next year, the board passed a policy requiring teachers to read the following statement to their students before teaching evolution: "It is hereby recognized by the Tangipahoa Board of Education, that the lesson to be presented, regarding the origin of life and matter, is known as the Scientific Theory of Evolution and should be presented to inform students of the scientific concept and not intended to influence or dissuade the Biblical version of Creation or any other concept. It is further recognized by the Board of Education that it is the basic right and privilege of each student to form his/her own opinion or maintain beliefs taught by parents on this very important matter of the origin of life and matter. Students are urged to exercise critical thinking and gather all information possible and closely examine each alternative toward forming an opinion."[67]

When the proposal's sponsor was asked about accounts of creation other than that of the Bible, he replied, "We can talk about Hindu, we can talk about Mohammed, we can talk about all this other stuff, but there are two basic concepts out there." Echoing the concerns of nineteenth-century critics who believed that Darwin's ideas would promote materialism and devalue life, he explained, "[S]omebody comes and tells [students] that they are mere accident," and "If it was an accident, life is not important, because, you see, it's just an accident. Human lives are not important, that means that this thing of abortion is—gives more validity to that, because life is not important, and—and the fact that the crime record—crime rate is sweeping our nation, sweeping our state, you see, it gives credibility there because life is not important because we are just here by accident."[68] No alternatives to evolution other than creationism were considered, and the stated goal of the policy was to avoid conflict with the views taught in many homes.

A federal district court struck down the policy on the ground that its only purpose was "to convey a message of endorsement of religion." According to the court, "In mandating this disclaimer, the School Board is endorsing religion by disclaiming the teaching of evolution in such a manner as to convey the message that evolution is a religious viewpoint that runs counter to the religious belief of the Biblical theory of Creation, or other religious views." The court admonished the board: "While encouraging students to maintain their belief in the Bible, or in God, may be a noble aim, it cannot be one in which the public schools participate, no matter how important this goal may be to its supporters."[69] The U.S. Court of Appeals for the Fifth Circuit noted that antievolution disclaimers are not necessarily unconstitutional, and that respecting the beliefs of parents is a valid secular purpose even if the parents' beliefs are religious. Nevertheless, the court struck down the Tangipahoa policy because its primary effect was "to protect and maintain a particular religious viewpoint."[70] The court noted, for instance, that the only alternative to evolution mentioned in the policy was religious.

Selman v. Cobb County School District (2005) arose when a textbook committee sought to change an antievolution policy. Among other things, the policy limited evolution instruction to senior high school, excluded it from courses required for graduation, and ordered that any elective in which it appeared should be clearly identified to students and parents. The policy also provided that class instruction and library collections that touched on human origin "shall include, but not be limited to, the creation theory."[71]

The textbook committee set out to strengthen evolution instruction in order to comply with the Georgia state standards. In particular, it recommended that the biology course required for graduation should use *Biology: The Living Science,* the same Miller-Levine textbook that the teachers in Dover, Pennsylvania, wanted to use. The school board replied that the old policy could be superseded only if the following disclaimer were inserted into the textbooks: "This textbook contains material on evolution. Evolution is a theory, not a fact, regarding the origin of living things. The material should be approached with an open mind, studied carefully, and critically considered." The stated purpose of the disclaimer was "to foster critical thinking among students, to allow academic freedom consistent with legal requirements, to promote tolerance and acceptance of diversity of opinion, and to ensure a posture of neutrality toward religion."[72]

The board's use of the term "academic freedom" to mean the inclusion of antievolution information dates back to *Scopes,* but its specific wording—"to allow academic freedom consistent with legal requirements"—is intriguingly ambiguous. The most common antievolution definition of academic freedom is that science instruction should include the views of people who oppose evolution, and this phrasing may imply nothing more than a claim that the law requires "academic freedom" in this sense. More interestingly, it could represent an acknowledgement that some of the views in question are religious and that the policy can accommodate them only as far as the law allows. The latter interpretation, perhaps intended to make the policy constitutional, would also render it pointless from the perspective of its supporters. Despite claims to the contrary, existing law does not permit public schools to recognize supernatural explanations as science.

In response to criticism of the disclaimer, the board, like the proponents of the Balanced Treatment Act in *McLean* and *Edwards,* argued that the omission of references to God, the Bible, or creation was sufficient to render the policy religiously neutral. They also maintained that the disclaimer merely informed parents and students of the book's content and promoted open discussion of the debate over evolution. Opponents of the disclaimer retorted that religious opposition to evolution was the only reason for implying that it was uniquely in need of "critical thinking," which was apparently not required in the study of any other scientific theory. Moreover, they asserted, the statement that evolution is "theory" and not "fact" revealed a creationist orientation. In mainstream science, facts are what theories explain, not what good theories grow up to be. They also protested that the disclaimer, which was adopted without input from the scientific community, falsely implied that the debate about the validity of evolution is scientific in nature. The board subsequently added an admonition to teachers to focus on science and to remain religiously neutral. Teachers were also to suggest that science and religion are not mutually exclusive and that science does not explain everything.

The district court found that the promotion of critical thinking and respect for the views of parents who do not believe in evolution were legitimate secular purposes. Nevertheless, the decision stated, the effect of the disclaimer was to advance religion. Among other things, the misuse of the terms "theory" and "fact" promoted the inaccurate belief "that evolution is a problematic theory lacking adequate foundation."[73] The U.S. Court of Appeals for the Eleventh Circuit declined to decide the merits of the case because the district court had conflated several different standards for determining whether a state action unconstitutionally advances religion. In addition, key documents were missing from the materials sent to the appeals court. The case was returned to the district court, and in December 2006, the parties reached a settlement. While maintaining that the disclaimer was constitutional, the Cobb County board agreed to stop using it and to forbid the practice of tearing out the pages of biology textbooks that mention evolution.

Science as a Team Sport

Unlike the policies discussed so far, one widely discussed battle over evolution instruction focuses on guidelines that do not require anyone to do anything. It arose in Kansas, whose state board of education publishes curriculum standards to which no local district is compelled to adhere. There is, however, a catch: the state's high-stakes tests are based on the board's standards, and the scores on those tests affect the schools' funding as well as the students' future prospects. This sharing of control makes it possible to argue either of two positions. According to the antievolutionist side, the state school board has no affirmative duty to include any particular topic, including evolution, in the state standards. Moreover, the omission of evolution violates no constitutional right because nothing prevents the districts from continuing to teach it. Their opponents condemn this assertion as disingenuous. In their view, the primary—and clearly intended—effect of eliminating evolution from the high-stakes state tests is to arm creationists with an allegedly secular club with which to beat school districts into omitting anything on which the students will not be tested.

This dispute began in 1997, when, as a matter of routine, the state board of education appointed a curriculum committee of twenty-seven scientists, science teachers, and parents to update science standards enacted in 1993. Basing its work on model standards provided by national science organizations, the committee defined evolution as a major organizing principle of science. An antievolutionist member of the state board of education, Steve Abrams, sought advice from the Creation Science Association for Mid-America.[74] He subsequently proposed reducing the coverage of evolution and adding ID to the standards and to the state tests.

After splitting 5–5 on Abrams' proposal, the board asked the curriculum committee to reconsider its treatment of evolution. When the committee refused, Abrams and two other board members formed an ad hoc subcommittee to rewrite the standards with help from two creationist groups. The subcommittee's proposed standards did not treat evolution as an organizing principle of science, and references to the emergence of one species from another were omitted. Evolution remained in the standards, but only with respect to small changes within species. In addition, the subcommittee deleted or substantially revised references to the age of the earth and to the big-bang theory of the origin of the universe.

The most significant proposed change in the standards related to the definition of science itself. Adopting the wording favored by the NAS, the curriculum committee had described science as "a well-substantiated explanation of some aspect of the natural world that can incorporate facts, laws, inferences, and tested hypotheses (e.g., atomic theory, evolutionary theory)." The subcommittee deleted "well-substantiated" and changed "natural explanations" to "logical explanations," thus opening the door to Baconian science and to nonverifiable explanations.[75] It also admonished teachers to be respectful of non-mainstream scientific perspectives.

On August 11, 1999, the school board considered both the science committee's final draft and the standards proposed by the Abrams subcommittee. Ignoring the state's education agencies, its governor, and the presidents of its public universities, all of whom endorsed the committee's standards, the board voted 6–4 in favor of the Abrams version. Supporters maintained that these standards did not fall foul of *Epperson, McLean,* or *Edwards,* because they neither banned the teaching of evolution nor required the inclusion of creation science or ID. The board also stated that the secular reason for its action was the improvement of science instruction. Predictably, this claim galvanized the science establishment into a full-throated protest similar to the one it later staged in *Kitzmiller.* Unlike the Dover school officials, however, the Kansas board has never had to face that onslaught in a lawsuit. The board's battles have been fought in the court of public opinion, where wins and losses are measured not by judicial decisions but by election results.

This political element was particularly prominent because the new Kansas standards were adopted during the run-up to the 2000 presidential election. Governor Bill Graves, a Republican, accused the school board of deliberately using the evolution issue to "make a rhetorical splash at the behest of the conservative wing of the state Republican Party."[76] Moreover, half of the board's ten members were up for reelection in 2000, including three of the six antievolutionists. With the help of the governor, proevolution Republican moderates knocked those incumbents off the ticket in the Republican primary. Since all of the Democratic candidates opposed the new standards, the 2000 election would significantly change the makeup of the board.

Largely because of the furor generated by the Kansas state standards, the battle between creationism and evolution became such a hot topic that even the presidential candidates were asked about it. As expected, the Republican nominee, George W. Bush, advocated teaching creationism as well as evolution. The Democratic nominee, Albert Gore, made a bigger news splash by saying that although he preferred evolution, schools should be able to teach both approaches if they wished to do so. Since Gore had long positioned himself as something of a scientific guru with respect to such matters as the Internet and global warming, his comment was a jawdropper. Eugenie Scott, executive director of the National Center for Science Education, exclaimed, "My God, that's appalling! I understand politicians like to compromise and that faced with one group who say that two plus two equal four and another group that says two plus two equals six, will tend to arrive at a position that says two plus two equals five. Unfortunately, sometimes the answer has to be four, and this is one of those times."[77] Gore's spokeswoman later clarified that he had meant that creationism could be taught as religion or culture, not as science. Steve Kraske of the Kansas City Star summarized the situation in these terms: "On the second day, the media created a new campaign issue—evolution vs. creationism. And the presidential candidates said, 'This is not good.'"[78]

As expected, when the new board took office after the 2000 election, its members voted 7–3 to adopt the standards developed by the science curriculum committee. Evolution was once again the organizing principle of biology, and science was defined in terms of natural rather than logical explanations. But the ballot box giveth, and the ballot box taketh away. In the election of 2004, antievolutionists once again attained a 6–4 majority on the school board. This time, they proposed not only to change the treatment of evolution but also to promote the teaching of ID. To support this initiative, they held three days of public hearings on the scientific evidence favoring ID.

Mainstream scientists, who boycotted the hearings, ridiculed the accusation that they were afraid to face tough questioning by the Kansas board. Rather, they described the hearings as a show trial designed to justify a predetermined outcome. The board sought their participation, they charged, not to foster a sound, data-driven discussion of scientific theory, but to bolster the false assertion that ID is the subject of serious scholarly debate. One scientist, asked by a reporter whether he ought not to take this opportunity to present the truth, said that he had given up because no matter how clearly scientists demonstrated that ID is scientifically groundless, its proponents ignored the data and continued to make the same unsubstantiated and discredited claims.

The proposed 2005 science standards were based on a variation of the balanced-treatment concept which, in this instance, took the form of framing instruction on the origin of species as a debate between evolution and ID. This teach-the-debate approach enjoys broad public support because of its apparent neutrality, fairness, and inclusivity. Reversing the traditional model of *Scopes* and *Epperson,* it puts mainstream scientists, not creationists, in the position of trying to exclude other people's ideas from the curriculum. Thus, opposition to teach-the-debate may easily be vilified as censorship and elitism. To scientists, teach-the-debate is simply another pretext for shoehorning religion into science classes. In their view, the only scientific debates over evolution concern specific details of the theory, not its fundamental validity. Since no existing policy prevents teachers from discussing genuinely scientific disagreements with respect to how evolution works, mainstream scientists see ID-focused teach-the-debate policies as vehicles for misrepresenting ID as a legitimate scientific alternative. In their view, the mass of data produced since Darwin's time demonstrates convincingly that the only debate to be taught is religious or cultural, not scientific. There is, they repeatedly affirm, no scientific debate between evolution and ID, because ID is not science.

Despite the opposition of the science community, the ID-friendly Kansas science standards were adopted in November 2005. There was some discussion of a possible lawsuit, but most opponents focused their attention on the upcoming 2006 campaign. Five of the board's ten seats were up for reelection, and four of them were held by ID supporters. Once again, the real decision point was not the election in November but the Republican primary in August. One of the four antievolutionist incumbents retired from the board and was replaced on the ticket by a proevolution Republican, and another was defeated in the primary by a moderate Republican challenger. Thus, two ID supporters were still in the running, and two held seats that were not up for reelection. Since all of the Democratic candidates were proevolution, it appeared that no matter what happened in the election, the board would have at least a 6–4 majority in favor of evolution.

Six to four it was. On Valentine's Day, 2007, the board voted by that margin to restore the standards developed by the science curriculum committee. Evolution was once again described as an organizing principle of science, which once again required natural explanations. If we include the standards that were in place before all this started, this was the fifth set of standards in nine years. The proevolution standards survived the 2008 election, but the definition of science will be up for reelection again in 2010.

Inevitably, both sides continue to take every opportunity to wave the banner of academic freedom, used here to signify that the curriculum should include all material that is objectively accurate and relevant without regard for ideological interests. That explanation fits both sides equally well: the difference between them lies not in how they define, or, arguably, misdefine, academic freedom but in what they consider to be objectively accurate and relevant scientific content. As is often the case, each side's understanding of what is necessary to uphold its own freedom necessarily involves frustrating the choices of the other side.

The most interesting academic-freedom issue raised by the Kansas evolution controversy relates to the role of content-area experts in defining their discipline for purposes of K–12 state standards. Although no law requires school boards to consider the views of content-area experts, refusal to do so carries political risk for a reason that parallels the AAUP's justification for academic freedom: the difficulty of explaining how K–12 education is improved by privileging the preferences of nonexperts over up-to-date expert information about the field. To be sure, William Jennings Bryan and other populists have argued for decades that the locus of control in K–12 education rests with elected or politically appointed school boards because of a long-established conviction that public education should reflect the will of the people exercised through their representatives. As suggested by the outcomes of recent Republican primaries in Kansas, however, the perception of a necessary conflict between the will of the people and the principles of ac-

ademic freedom may be erroneous or, at best, reflective of only certain segments of the population. Like university scholarship and teaching, K–12 instruction must depend to some extent on expert definitions of academic disciplines and of what constitutes high-quality work within them.

Intelligent Design at the University Level

From *Scopes* through *Kitzmiller,* antievolutionists have found it difficult
to identify credible scientific experts willing to support ID as science. Even
scientists like Kenneth Miller, who define themselves as believers in a divine creator, see no conflict between their personal faith and their scientific
commitment to evolution, because evolution explains how life has developed since it came into being, not how it originated. As a biochemist,
Michael Behe is perhaps the most directly qualified antievolution expert,
but as he readily acknowledges, he is not a specialist on the fossil record. Indeed, paleontologists and geologists have long boasted that although experts
in those fields are divided with respect to the details, mechanisms, and
timetables of evolution, none of them has denied the theory itself.

The claim that no university-level paleontologist or geologist has embraced creationism has been challenged by recent news stories about creationists who have earned graduate degrees in those fields. In the academic
year 2006–7, for instance, the University of Rhode Island awarded a Ph.D.
in geosciences to a creationist named Marcus R. Ross. Although Ross continues to assert that the earth is no more than 10,000 years old, his faculty
advisor stated that his doctoral dissertation, which deals with fossil evidence
from the Cretaceous period, conforms to the expectations and timetable of
mainstream paleontology.

In an interview with the *New York Times,* Ross explained this apparent
contradiction by asserting that the Bible is one way of understanding the
history of the earth, paleontology another. "People hold all sorts of opinions
different from the department in which they graduate. What's that to anyone else? . . . I was working within a particular paradigm of earth history. I
accepted that philosophy of science for the purpose of working with the people" at Rhode Island. By saying in the dissertation that certain events occurred far earlier than 10,000 years ago, "I did not imply or deny any endorsement of the dates."[79]

Ross's remarks raise some new points with respect to the distinction between a scientist's personal opinions and what he or she presents as science.

The conventional view, expressed by Kenneth Miller and other proevolution expert witnesses in *Kitzmiller,* is that because scientists base their professional conclusions on empirical data, their private beliefs about religion are irrelevant. Ross's implication that he considers at least some of what he wrote in his dissertation to be incorrect distinguishes him from theistic evolutionists like Miller, who fully accept whatever science demonstrates and define their personal belief in a divine creator as lying outside science. Although this double vision may be defended on the ground that it is the only effective way to get around the ideological bias of mainstream scientists, the credibility of antievolutionist explanations of the development of life is likely to suffer if proponents of those views say whatever is necessary to earn science degrees while simultaneously denying the truth of what they are saying.

Eugenie Scott of the National Center for Science Education argued that refusing to accept the results of the scientific method because of religious beliefs is, in itself, a form of closed-mindedness that is inconsistent with science. She also expressed concern about how Ross and other creationists who have recently earned mainstream science Ph.D.s would use their new credentials—a point that other mainstream scientists have declared to be none of the university's business. As a graduate student, Ross appeared on a DVD promoting ID, and his identification as a Ph.D. candidate in geosciences appeared to suggest that his continued belief in a literal interpretation of Genesis demonstrated the superiority of religious faith over science. He is presently an assistant professor of geology and assistant director of the Center for Creation Studies at Liberty University, a Baptist institution founded by the Reverend Jerry Falwell. It remains to be seen whether he and other creationist scientists will suggest, as Behe did in *Kitzmiller,* that beliefs based on religious faith acquire scientific credibility when bona fide scientists declare them to be superior to mainstream science.

Behe himself provides a good example of another issue: the academic-freedom rights of professors whose understanding of the discipline differs from that of their peers. The extent to which he differs may be inferred from his department's Web site. Under the heading "Department Position on Evolution and 'Intelligent Design,'" his colleagues affirm their commitment to the "recognition that the validity of any scientific model comes only as a result of rational hypothesis testing, sound experimentation, and findings that can be replicated by others." Having affirmed its "unequivocal" support for evolution, the department states, "The sole dissenter from this position, Prof. Michael Behe, is a well-known proponent of 'intelligent design.' While we respect Prof. Behe's right to express his views, they are his alone and are in no way endorsed by the department. It is our collective position that intelligent design has no basis in science, has not been tested experimentally, and should not be regarded as scientific."[80]

In view of Behe's publications and his testimony in *Kitzmiller*, his department's disclaimer of his work raises an interesting question about the definition of academic freedom. If, as his department's statement affirms, work in ID "has no basis in science . . . and should not be regarded as scientific," does academic freedom protect the advancement of that view as science by a professor in a biology department? To clarify that point, consider the more extreme example of a hypothetical geography professor who claims that the earth is flat and denies the existence of such evidence as photographs from spacecraft. Would academic freedom protect the publication and teaching of those ideas under the aegis of the university?

One purpose of academic freedom is to protect deviations from the status quo of a given discipline, and the more unpopular those views are, the more important it is to protect them in order to ensure intellectual freedom and the growth of knowledge. Inherent in this proposition is a recognition of the inevitability of error—what might be called the oops factor. A new approach may supplant the old, or a traditional view may withstand challenge, but either way, academic freedom must ensure that the contest takes place in the free marketplace of ideas. But even if the full range of opinion and interpretation is protected regardless of probability, let alone popularity, can there ever be a point at which refusal to acknowledge empirically verifiable reality crosses the line from academic freedom to professional incompetence?

When I have raised this question with academic audiences, participants have generally concluded that such a line does exist, particularly with respect to scientific data and historical facts as opposed to interpretations and opinions. Acknowledging the existence of the line is not, however, the same as determining what is to happen if someone crosses it. Robert M. O'Neil, commenting on Arthur Butz's denial of the Holocaust, suggested that a more serious question of competence would arise if Butz were, not an engineering professor, but a specialist in modern European history. Nevertheless, O'Neil sounded a note of caution: "At some point, an institutional concern about competence would challenge the presumption of protection which academic freedom affords even the most extreme or provocative of professorial speech."[81]

Using creationist biologists as an example, Ronald Dworkin suggested that when university officials decide whom to hire, they are entitled to favor mainstream scientists "whose work strikes other academics as promising." The same standard does not apply, however, to the dismissal of a professor who begins non-mainstream work after earning tenure. In Dworkin's view, tenured professors should operate under the principle of ethical individualism, which confers on them "a paradigmatic duty to discover and teach what they find important and true, and this duty is not . . . subject to any qualification about the best interests of those to whom they speak. It is an undiluted responsibility to the truth, and it is, in that way, the closest a professional responsibility can come to the fundamental ethical responsibility each of us has, according to the ideals of ethical individualism, to live our lives in accordance with our own felt convictions."[82] Dworkin's understanding of academic freedom differs from that of the AAUP because for him the locus of control rests unreservedly with the individual professor, and collective faculty authority over a field is limited to gatekeeping.

Clearly, the essential values to be upheld are intellectual liberty, the free marketplace of ideas, and humanity's continued growth in knowledge and wisdom. Although I cannot go so far along the individualist path as Dworkin, I would protect the academic-freedom rights of professors whose pursuit of truth takes them far outside the accepted boundaries of their disciplines, because I see no better way to further the goals of academic freedom. No bright line separates the cutting edge from the lunatic fringe, and less harm is likely to result from tolerating an occasional outlier than from dismissing faculty on the basis of the ideas they are trying to prove.

7

The Mote and the Beam

Academic freedom is not the freedom to speak or to teach just as one wishes.
It is the freedom to pursue the scholarly profession, inside and outside the
classroom, according to the norms and standards of that profession.
— Matthew W. Finkin and Robert C. Post, *For the Common Good*

CONSISTENT WITH THE GOVERNANCE structure of K–12 public education, disputes involving the treatment of controversial material in elementary and
secondary schools focus on reconciling the well-established principle of public control with the need for a curriculum that is up-to-date, accurate, and intellectually competitive in the world market. At the K–12 level, popular control is assured; what is up for debate is the role of content-area experts. The
converse is true in public universities. In an environment in which academic
decisionmaking is dominated by professors, some critics seek to increase
the influence of populist or majoritarian values. In particular, they advocate
giving students, alumni, legislators, and administrators a greater voice in
such matters as course content, hiring policies, and professors' out-of-class
expression of political views. The stated goal of this proposed shift in locus
of control is the pursuit of intellectual diversity in universities deemed to
be so infused with liberalism that conservative faculty cannot thrive and conservative students feel like outsiders.

In pursuit of these aims, some critics of public universities declare that
academic freedom applies not only to faculty but also to students, whose
rights may be violated if faculty express certain viewpoints in or out of class.
They also invoke academic freedom on behalf of the public as represented

by state legislators, whom they urge either to regulate faculty speech or to encourage university administrators to do so. Implicit in such proposals is the assumption that administrators, more than faculty, are likely to be influenced by financial and political pressures brought to bear by state officials answerable to the public. No matter how framed, these proposals rely, as indeed they must, on reconceptualizing *what* academic freedom is by redefining *whose* it is.

One of the best-known articulations of the desire to dilute the decision-making authority of the professoriate is the Academic Bill of Rights (ABR), a legislative proposal written and promoted by David Horowitz, a former liberal student activist turned antiliberal crusader.[1] By no means does the ABR encompass the entire movement to increase the conservative voice on university campuses; some scholars and advocacy groups pursue that goal independently of the ABR and its chief sponsors. Nevertheless, the ABR's focus on two of the primary themes of this book—locus of control and the scope of academic freedom—makes it useful as a case study. In particular, the extensive debate surrounding the ABR goes beyond the proposal itself to address long-standing issues underlying the perennial dispute over ideology on American campuses.

Prof Slam

The ABR was first mentioned in 2002, when Horowitz initiated the Campaign for Fairness and Inclusion in Higher Education to publicize what he saw as leftist political discrimination in the hiring and retention of faculty, the selection of campus speakers, and classroom instruction. The following year, he promoted the ABR at a conference of the American Legislative Exchange Council, a conservative organization of Republican state legislators. Although versions of the ABR have since been introduced in the U.S. House of Representatives and discussed at a U.S. Senate committee hearing, most of the political action regarding this proposal has taken place in state legislatures.[2] Echoing the arguments presented by William Jennings Bryan in his antievolution crusade, proponents of state-level ABR legislation argue that the taxpayers' representatives have a duty to ensure that publicly funded educational institutions take the majority's views into account in determining curriculum. So far, versions of the ABR have been introduced in the legislatures of approximately thirty states, but no such proposal has yet passed into law.[3]

Not surprisingly, the ABR has been the subject of heated debate among academics. The most vocal of Horowitz's critics include Michael Bérubé, Paterno Professor in English Literature and Science, Technology, and Society at the Pennsylvania State University; John K. Wilson, a freelance writer and blogger; and Graham Larkin, formerly professor of art and art history at Stanford University, now curator of European and American art at the National Gallery of Canada.[4] Among advocacy groups, the chief supporters of the ABR include Students for Academic Freedom (SAF) and the David Horowitz Freedom Center (previously the Center for the Study of Popular Culture), both founded by Horowitz and dedicated to promoting the ABR and the arguments underlying it, and the American Council of Trustees and Alumni (ACTA).[5] Chief among the organizational opponents of the bill are the American Association of University Professors and Free Exchange on Campus, a coalition made up of such groups as the AAUP, the American Civil Liberties Union, People for the American Way, and the AFL-CIO.

At first reading, many of the provisions of the ABR appear to be so wholly unobjectionable that it is hard to understand how the bill could possibly generate debate—and therein, paradoxically, lies one source of the controversy surrounding it. The ABR states, for instance, that faculty should be hired and evaluated on the basis of their professional competence, not their political views, that students' grades should reflect their knowledge of the content field and not their political or religious affiliations, and that faculty should not turn their instruction into political, religious, or antireligious indoctrination. By claiming that new legislation is needed to compel universities to comply with these aims, the ABR asserts as truth that which is in fact the subject of debate: that such basic values as free speech, diversity of thought, political independence, and fair grading of student work are not presently enforced in American higher education. Supporters of the legislation declare that outrages occur frequently, that they are grossly underreported, and that existing university policies are inadequate to protect student and faculty rights. Opponents challenge the credibility, accuracy, and relevance of many of the alleged offenses against the rights of conservative faculty and students. Moreover, they maintain, the claim that current university policies are insufficient to address any violations that may occur is based at least in part on the conservative activists' strategy of bringing a one-sided version of complaints straight to trustees, legislators, or the media without giving university officials a chance to act. Critics of the bill also take issue with some of the premises on which it rests, such as the conflation of academic freedom with broad First Amendment protections of one person's opinion against another's.

As supporters take pains to point out, the language of the ABR is very broad. It is facially neutral with respect to political orientation, and it neither requires nor prohibits any specific action. Far from reassuring the bill's opponents, however, that vagueness is seen as both misleading and dangerous. It is misleading, they say, because the ABR, as portrayed in speeches and publications by conservative activists, is anything but politically neutral and nondeterminative. Moreover, they protest, the absence of clear legislative definitions or parameters would give enforcers of the ABR broad latitude in regulating campus speech, and faculty would have no way of knowing what, specifically, was forbidden. In effect, opponents of the legislation accuse its advocates of playing a double game. On the one hand, the bill is couched in legislative language so bland and outwardly unobjectionable that anyone who opposes it appears to be an enemy of free speech, intellectual diversity, and basic fairness. On the other hand, its supporters assure conservative legislators and advocacy groups that the legislation will have a significant pro-conservative impact not only on curriculum, faculty hiring, and promotion and tenure decisions but also on the behavior of professors with respect to the organizations they join, the courses they teach, the texts they assign, the research conclusions they share with students, and even the cartoons they post on their office doors. To opponents of the legislation, the disparity between what it says and what it will allegedly accomplish raises disingenuousness to the level of unconstitutionality.

A Blast from the Past

The debate over the ABR and the claims on which it rests recall a well-known early defense of conservatism on campus: William Buckley's *God and Man at Yale: The Superstitions of "Academic Freedom,"* published a year after the author's graduation from Yale in 1950. Unlike the more circumspect proponents of the ABR, Buckley did not hesitate to trumpet the conservative aims of his proposal. As his subtitle suggests, he viewed professors' claims of academic freedom as a shield for the promulgation of ideas that, in his view, had no place in a Yale University classroom. Accordingly, his purpose in writing the book was "to expose what I regard as an extraordinarily irresponsible educational attitude that, under the protective label 'academic freedom,' has produced one of the most extraordinary incongruities of our time: the institution that derives its moral and financial support from Christian individualists and then addresses itself to the task of persuading the sons of those supporters to be atheistic socialists."[6] In response to the assertion that academic freedom furthers the pursuit of new knowledge through research, he retorted that it was inappropriately applied to classroom teaching. Indeed, he suggested, perhaps professors should not be assigned to do research at all. Instead, research could be funded by privately endowed institutes through which individual donors could finance any type of investigation they chose to support.

Despite the differences between *God and Man at Yale* and the ABR, they agree on two important points: that the people who finance and run institutions of higher education are entitled to determine what is taught therein and that the majority of such people support the promulgation of conservative views. Because the ABR is aimed primarily at public universities, its supporters take a populist stance, urging the promotion of conservative opinions on the ground that these are consistent with the wishes of the majority of taxpayers.[7] Buckley, focusing specifically on a private Ivy League institution, was unabashedly elitist in his deference to Yale alumni and trustees. Nevertheless, the underlying view regarding locus of control is the same in both instances: professors are employees whose professional discretion is rightfully limited by the will of those who pay them. For example, compare Buckley's statement that "[i]t is of the essence of freedom that citizens not be made to pay for what the majority does not want" with Horowitz's call for "accountability on the part of those institutions to the wider community that supports them and underwrites the affluence to which their principals have become accustomed."[8]

To support the contention that the academic judgment of faculty should be subordinated to that of the university governors, Buckley argued that "the faculty at Yale is morally and constitutionally responsible to the trustees of Yale, who are in turn responsible to the alumni and thus duty bound to transmit to their students the wisdom, insight, and value judgments which in the trustees' opinion will enable the American citizen to make the optimum adjustment to the community and to the world."[9] Having cited several examples of Yale professors who, in his opinion, were attempting to subvert Christianity and individualism by making those beliefs appear incompatible with modern scholarship, he called upon his fellow alumni to protest what he saw as "Yale's intellectual drive toward agnosticism and collectivism."[10] If such writers as Karl Marx, Thomas Huxley, and John Dewey were to be studied, he wished to ensure that professors would do all in their power to persuade students of the fallacy of those authors' arguments. As he explained, "The educational overseer—the father who sends his son to school, or the trustee who directs the policy of the school—is violating no freedom I know of if he insists, let us say, that individualism instead of collectivism be inculcated in the school. Rather, he is asserting his own freedom."[11]

Underlying Buckley's position was the assumption that the views of the university president and those of the majority of trustees, parents, and alumni—whom he described as the "elite among our citizenry"—coincided with his own.[12] On this basis, he argued that compelling professor-employees to advance those ideas was an appropriate means of enforcing the relevant majority's rights. Moreover, he maintained, professors should not merely teach certain viewpoints as a matter of duty but should promote them with the wholehearted zeal of true conviction. As he explained, "I believe . . . that the attitude of the teacher ought to reveal itself, and that, assuming that the overseers of the university in question have embraced democracy, individualism, and religion, the attitudes of the faculty ought to conform to the university's."[13] In his view, the establishment of such an orthodoxy would not abridge the rights of faculty, since anyone who held a different opinion would be free to teach elsewhere. "Freedom is in no way violated," he concluded, "by an educational overseer's insistence that the teacher he employs hold a given set of values."[14]

The extent to which Buckley's views are reflected in the arguments supporting the ABR is a matter of intense debate, particularly with respect to two points: whether the blandly worded legislation is intended to promote conservatism on campus and whether it is intended to threaten, or would in fact threaten, the free speech of professors whose views are incompatible with those of ABR advocates. To convey the overall sense of this convoluted and fast-moving debate, it may be useful to summarize what both sides say about a few key issues: the necessity for the ABR, the purposes and interests it serves, and the extent to which the beliefs of students, legislators, and university administrators should influence what is taught in university classrooms.

Despite the claims of ABR supporters that the legislation is politically neutral, it is unquestionably fueled by the conviction that universities are dominated by liberal faculty whose professional standards for hiring, tenure, promotion, publication, and admission to graduate programs embody a liberal viewpoint. Among the proponents of this position is Ben Shapiro, who, like

William Buckley, wrote his book shortly after graduating from college—in Shapiro's case, from the University of California, Los Angeles. In *Brainwashed: How Universities Indoctrinate America's Youth* (2004), Shapiro argues that "[f]rom race to the environment, from religion to sex, from the War on Terror to the Arab-Israeli conflict, universities push a never-ending line of liberal claptrap. The higher education system indoctrinates America's youth."[15] According to the author of the ABR, David Horowitz, this liberal bias is attributable to hiring policies that amount "to an illegal political patronage operation, which provides huge advantages to the Democratic Party and to the political left." The result, he maintains, is the funneling of academic energy into such causes as racial equity, opposition to capital punishment, and promotion of campaign finance reform. The last pursuit is particularly hypocritical, he suggests, because liberal academics and those whose ideas they promote "enjoy the benefits of a system in which students are taxed to provide funds almost exclusively to one side of the political debate."[16]

To support the accusation of political bias in university hiring and instruction, ABR advocates cite surveys showing the political party membership of professors in selected disciplines. Among the most widely discussed is a 2002 study published by the American Enterprise Institute for Public Policy Research, which employed student volunteers to check voter registration records.[17] Faculty in the Democratic, Green, or Working Families Party were coded *L*, for "Left." Republicans and Libertarians were coded *R*, for "Right." With the single exception of the Division of Engineering at Brown University, the study was limited to faculty in the humanities and social sciences, particularly in such fields as English, political science, sociology, African American studies, and women's studies. The American Enterprise Institute justified the exclusion of departments generally believed to be conservative, such as business and law, by asserting a need to focus on "major, uncontroversial, and socially significant fields of study."[18] The results bore out the institute's claim of political disparity: at Cornell, for instance, 166 professors from the selected units were coded *L* and only 6 were coded *R*. At Harvard, the results were 50 to 2, and at Stanford, 151 to 17. (The differences in the sizes of the samples reflect a variation in the number of departments or programs that the student investigators at each institution chose to cover.) No college or university included in the study had a majority of *R* professors or equivalent numbers of *L* and *R*.

Based solely on the political affiliations of professors in the targeted departments, the authors of the survey concluded that "colleges are now hostile environments for economic and cultural conservatives. . . . If you stray from the liberal consensus you will soon find yourself without allies, without tenure, and eventually without a position." Similarly, they described American universities as "virtual one-party states, ideological monopolies, badly unbalanced ecosystems. They are utterly flightless birds with only one wing to flap. They do not, when it comes to political and cultural ideas, look like America."[19] The use of such phrases as "look like America," which are associated with appeals for racial and gender equity, places the call for parity in political party membership on the same plane. By the repeated use of civil-rights logic, language, and rhetoric, ABR supporters imply by analogy something that would otherwise require extended debate: that membership in conservative political parties is a protected category, relevant to academic appointments and decisionmaking, and deserving of attention if it is underrepresented.

A similar report was produced in 2003 by the Center for the Study of Popular Culture (CSPC), which was renamed the David Horowitz Freedom Center in 2006. The CSPC used voter registration records to determine the political party affiliations of humanities and social sciences professors in thirty-two schools, including Ivy League institutions, liberal arts colleges, and public universities. To justify limiting the study to certain fields, the authors cited the need to ascertain the political leanings of professors who "teach courses focusing on issues affecting the society at large." They did not address the claim that the same may be said of professors in such departments as business, medicine, and law. Voter registration records were deemed the least subjective means of drawing definitive conclusions about the "assumptions, views and values that affect the outlooks of Americans who finance, attend, administer and teach at these educational institutions."[20]

The CSPC study showed that in the departments and programs selected for inclusion, 1,397 faculty were registered as Democrats, and only 134 as Republicans. Based on the assumption that the ratio of Democrats to Republicans in the general population is approximately equal, the authors protested that "not a single department at a single one of the 32 schools managed to achieve a reasonable parity between the two." According to the report, the faculty party-membership ratios, which "are impossible to understand in the absence of political bias in the training and hiring of college instructors," create "a hostile learning environment for conservative students contemplating an academic career." The authors concluded that the preponderance of registered Democrats in certain departments, in and of itself, demonstrates that conservative students cannot express their views without fear of retribution and that a student interested in such areas as "Austrian school economics, traditionalist literary criticism, conservative historiography or religious poetry will have a difficult time finding a professor who wants to take her on."[21] They also claimed that the presence of such a high proportion of Democrats shows that conservative faculty are at risk of being fired even if their academic records meet the standards for retention. Accordingly, the authors urged passage of the ABR as a means of remedying what the study presented as the proven prejudicial treatment of conservatives throughout higher education.

Not surprisingly, studies that rely on the political party affiliations of faculty in departments believed to be the most liberal reach different results than do studies based on in-depth questionnaires sent to faculty across a range of disciplines. An example of the latter may be found in *Closed Minds? Politics and Ideology in American Universities* (2008), by Bruce L. R. Smith, Jeremy D. Mayer, and A. Lee Fritschler. Declaring themselves to be "more concerned with diagnosis than with remedies," the authors set out to "present a reasoned analysis of what the actual problems are with the universities as they seek to deal with complex social, political, and cultural trends."[22] Central to the book is a 2007 survey designed by the authors and conducted by the University of Virginia's Center for Survey Research. The study found that of every five faculty members, three described themselves as liberal, one as moderate, and one as conservative. Although liberals remained dominant, the ratio was a far cry from the results of the pro-ABR surveys.[23] Indeed, as Martin Plissner, political analyst and former director of CBS News, observed, "[Y]ou don't have to be conservative and paranoid to expect that a show of hands between liberals and conservatives among the nation's academics doesn't figure to be close. In politics, college towns are not generally found to be bastions of the right."[24] He went on to note that these results are even more predictable—and grossly exaggerated—when a study systematically ignores all departments in which an examination of faculty political affiliations might yield different results. In a similar vein, a prominent critic of the ABR, Michael Bérubé, derided the methodology of the ABR studies as "Cherry-Picking 101." "When it comes to cooking data," he remarked, "Horowitz is the Iron Chef."[25]

Beyond the data lies the question of their significance. If indeed a particular department is dominated by Democrats, what conclusions may be drawn from that fact? To ABR advocates, it demonstrates not only that hiring, promotion, and tenure are politically biased but also that conservative students and faculty cannot be treated fairly. In their view, this conclusion need not rest on specific examples of ill treatment suffered by conservative students and faculty because the prevalence of liberal professors, and thus of liberal thought, is an injustice in itself and inevitably leads to the oppression of the conservative minority. Naturally, their opponents deny that all Democrats think alike or that liberals systematically oppress conservatives. Bérubé asserts, for instance, that "there are many important intellectual issues for which one's political party affiliation is simply irrelevant."[26] At a legislative hearing in Pennsylvania, Robert Moore, an assistant professor of sociology at Saint Joseph's University in Philadelphia, made a similar point: "The assumption that political affiliation, either on the left or the right, automatically leads to the suppression of thought in the classroom, is offensive to professors across the board. Merely establishing political party affiliation, donations, and self-described political labels does nothing more than establish political party affiliation, donations, and self-described political labels. As a question of proof of advocacy or activism, or suppression of alternative viewpoints on campus, merely asserting something repeatedly does not make it so. To assume that a professor is unable to separate political views from professional responsibilities is an insult to all professors, right or left, in the academy."[27]

Moving from defense to offense, ABR opponents charge that in attempting to demonstrate the prejudices of university professors, pro-ABR studies betray their own bias by zeroing in on such areas as women's studies, African American studies, ethnic studies, history, and English while systematically ignoring departments presumed to be more conservative. Far from seeking to foster political neutrality, critics of the surveys assert, such studies reflect an intense resentment of the presence, let alone the dominance, of liberal views in any academic discipline or, indeed, in any area of public life. Among other things, they offer no proof that the prevalence of Democrats or liberals in any field is, in itself, sufficient to show that individuals are being treated unfairly on the basis of their conservative views.

A Study in Differential Ox-Goring

In disputes over campus speech codes, critical race theorists have asserted that the simple fact of being in the minority all but guarantees biased treatment if decisions are governed by majority rule. This contention rests in part on the premise that when policies reflect the assumptions and interests of the majority, then a call for specific examples of injustices done to individual members of the minority misses the point. The minority is not equal within that culture even if generally applicable rules—determined by the majority on the basis of its beliefs and goals—are implemented evenhandedly. Although conservative scholars generally oppose critical race theory, they employ similar reasoning to justify the need for the ABR. Identifying conservatives as the minority in certain academic disciplines, they reference the philosophy and rhetoric of civil rights movements to bolster the assertion that conservatives' rights cannot be adequately protected when they themselves are underrepresented among the decisionmakers. Conversely, as members of the majority, liberal defenders of the status quo (paradoxical as that concept may appear) echo the position taken earlier by conservatives with respect to such issues as Protestant and white hegemony: we are dominant because we earned it fair and square, and to challenge our position, it is necessary to show that we are wrong either in our ideas or in specific instances of our treatment of students, colleagues, or applicants.

Although Smith, Mayer, and Fritschler found neither that American higher education demonstrates a pervasive left-wing bias nor that it is seriously threatened by an impending right-wing power grab, their research did support the premise that any dominant viewpoint within an institution will inevitably influence decisionmaking to some extent. An example may be found in their nuanced consideration of the academic hiring process. To begin with, they took issue with the belief that public universities enjoyed a halcyon period of fair and equitable hiring prior to the advent of "political correctness." The old paternalistic system, they pointed out, tended to perpetuate bias with respect to racial, gender, ethnic, social, and institutional background along with a form of ideological orthodoxy designed to avoid rocking the departmental boat. By contrast, the current process of faculty hiring, which requires broad consensus in favor of a particular candidate, tends "to produce common-denominator hires" in which "even a handful of holdouts can scuttle an appointment."[28] Such a system, the authors concluded, may indeed militate against the hiring of candidates, including conservatives, whose approach to the field is marginal or antithetical to that of the departmental majority—as was also true in the past, when similar results arose from a different process and favored a different set of views.

Some conservative critics of higher education, believing that the influence of an unacknowledged orthodoxy hampers the pursuit of truth, suggest that only by embracing a wider view will liberals be able to enhance their own academic integrity while deepening and broadening their respective disciplines. Among these critics is Mark Bauerlein, professor of English at Emory University and a regular contributor to the *Chronicle of Higher Education*. Bauerlein has testified at state legislative hearings pertaining to the adoption of the ABR, and he has appeared with Horowitz on several occasions; in 2008, for instance, they served on a panel at the Modern Language Association convention. Nevertheless, some of his essays suggest not a legislative solution but a need to change academia from within, relying on persuasion rather than on external intervention. An example of this aspect of his work may be found in an essay published in the *Chronicle of Higher Education* in 2004, in which he maintained that certain disciplines, such as the social sciences and education, are based on premises that "discourage non-leftists from pursuing academic careers." Such premises include constructivist theories of education, Marxist economics, support for affirmative action in African American studies programs, and the marginalization of the traditional nuclear family in women's studies programs. This leftist orientation is so ingrained, wrote Bauerlein, that the exclusion of conservatives is not recognized as the blackballing of a particular viewpoint. Among other things, he stated that mentors will not direct theses with a conservative bent, professional conferences revolve around liberal perspectives, and available academic positions do not match conservative research interests. In his view, "Political orientation has been embedded into the disciplines . . . so what is indeed a political judgment may be expressed in disciplinary terms." Nevertheless, he concluded that "we can't open the university to conservative ideas and persons by outside command. That would poison the atmosphere and jeopardize the ideals of free inquiry. Leftist bias evolved within the protocols of academic practice (though not without intimidation), and conservative challenges should evolve in the same way."[29]

By contrast with Bauerlein, some ABR supporters have chosen a riskier route. To support their call for a change in the locus of control in academic decisionmaking, they recount stories of injustices deliberately imposed upon individual students, faculty members, and job applicants solely because of their conservative views. That approach is attractive because it is simple to explain to nonacademic audiences, carries a strong emotional impact, and lends itself to clear-cut recommendations for policy changes. If the overt oppression of conservatives as individuals could be shown to be widespread and not effectively addressed by existing university policies, then the case for reform would be irresistible. Moreover, the policies of the AAUP, arguably the single most outspoken foe of the ABR, explicitly forbid the suppression of dissenting views, the use of class time to promote ideologies unrelated to the subject matter of the course, and the evaluation of students or colleagues on ideological rather than academic grounds.[30] Despite significant disagreement about what constitutes a violation of each of those principles, it is clear that the university community as a whole would not defend the ideologically motivated abuse of students or faculty. The drawback is that the evidence presented by ABR supporters falls far short of bearing out their claims, and by going that route, they abandon a more textured and potentially more fruitful discussion of endemic majoritarian bias in exchange for spectacular accusations that they are ultimately unable to support.

A representative sampling of such accusations may be found in promotional materials for the ABR and in its supporters' testimony before legislative committees. Horowitz's essay "The Campus Blacklist," for instance, includes an account of a conservative history professor who accused his department of having declined to hire the best-qualified candidate for a position in Asian history because, during a lunch conversation, the candidate expressed opposition to school vouchers. Based solely on this professor's unsupported accusation that the search committee, of which he was not a member, had based its decision on that lunch conversation, Horowitz wrote, "In other words, if one has a politically incorrect view on K–12 school vouchers, one must be politically incorrect on the Ming Dynasty too. This is almost a dictionary description of the totalitarian mentality. But there is more than dogmatism at work in this calculation. This attitude also reflects the priorities of an entrenched oligarchy, which fears to include those it cannot count on to maintain its control."[31]

Since no evidence exists either to confirm or to contradict the story of the rejected job applicant, and the anonymity accorded to the participants precludes investigation, this account cannot be clearly identified as a falsification or an exaggeration. For those very reasons, however, anecdotes such as this—undocumented and unverified as they are—cannot be accepted uncritically as proof of wrongdoing, nor can they be generalized into broader indictments of particular institutions or of higher education as a whole. Even when participants' names and other details of an alleged incident are provided, the result is likely to be a "he said, she said" stalemate that is of little probative value. For example, one professor denied Horowitz's allegation that she had called him a racist and further denied that she had later apologized for it. In some instances, professors targeted by ABR supporters have been able to demonstrate that the charges leveled against them were, at best, ill-informed and misleading. One such professor was accused of offering his students extra credit for attending out-of-class liberal events. The truth —documented by the syllabus—was that the extra credit could be earned by attending any campus event relevant to the course, including a lecture by Horowitz. In another instance, a statement attributed to the author of an article was shown to be a summary of someone else's work.

Perhaps the best illustration of the inefficacy of this approach is the failed attempt to enact a version of the ABR in Pennsylvania, where the insufficiency of the proof offered to support the claims of ABR supporters led to the rejection of the bill after exhaustive hearings and a great deal of political wrangling. The chair of the investigative committee was a conservative Republican who expressed little sympathy for faculty liberals, noting that they had called the investigation a witch hunt and had tried to derail it. Nevertheless, in his report on behalf of the committee, he concluded that none of the many anecdotes offered by ABR supporters provided convincing evidence of discrimination against conservative faculty or students. The same was true of the contention that existing university policies were ignored or were insufficient to deal with any problems that might arise.[32]

When confronted with evidence of misleading, incomplete, or inaccurate assertions, Horowitz has repeatedly replied that he does not have the staff to investigate every claim and that it is not his job to scour the country for students who can prove that they were harmed by liberal bias. As one reporter wrote, "Horowitz acknowledges his small staff can't confirm every incident it receives, and his fact-checkers can be 'very loose with the truth.' But he mostly dismisses the criticisms as inconsequential. 'I will stake my life that there are professors all over this country in classrooms who are . . . venting their prejudices in classes where it has no place.'"[33] This response recalls the first chapter of Ken Kesey's *One Flew Over the Cuckoo's Nest*, in which the narrator, Chief Bromden, asserts that everything he says "is the truth even if it didn't happen."[34] What matters, Bromden suggests, is not the factual accuracy of the events he recounts but the extent to which his narrative provides insights into larger social and political truths. Similarly, Horowitz and his supporters appear to be less concerned with fairness to individual professors than with promulgating their unswerving belief that such abuses are happening, and indeed must be happening, because of the prevalence of liberal faculty in some departments.

In essence, the case in favor of the ABR, as it has been discussed so far, resolves itself into three levels. The first is the claim that the majority of faculty in certain departments and programs hold liberal views, which is generally accepted. The second is the assertion that the cultures of some disciplines are so imbued with liberalism that academic standards have become conflated with ideological beliefs. This complex question is matter for discussion later in this chapter. The third is the accusation that conservatives in academia are frequently subjected to egregious injustice. The evidence offered to support this allegation includes the political affiliations of faculty in targeted departments, unsubstantiated or discredited anecdotes, and an unwavering insistence that widespread abuse is taking place but is poorly documented because universities do not take it seriously and because conservatives are afraid to speak up for fear of retaliation. This position will remain untenable unless it can be supported by significantly better evidence than has yet been offered.

The Humpty Dumpty Factor

Humpty Dumpty, a character in Lewis Carroll's *Through the Looking-Glass*, defines "glory" as "a nice knock-down argument" and declares, "When *I* use the word . . . it means just what I choose it to mean—neither more nor less."[35] Similarly, in Douglas Adams's *Hitchhiker's Guide to the Galaxy*, the hapless space traveler Arthur Dent is told that he is "safe" when he is in fact an unwelcome stowaway in a Vogon spaceship piloted by monstrous green super-bureaucrats who write the worst poetry in the universe. He responds, "Ah, . . . this is obviously some strange usage of the word *safe* that I wasn't previously aware of."[36] Much the same spirit appears to animate the ABR controversy, in which "defenders of academic freedom" means "us," and "people who would force a discredited orthodoxy down everyone else's throat" means "them." An examination of each side's definition of three key concepts—indoctrination, academic freedom, and balance—may help to illustrate this element of the debate.

On its face, the ABR's provision that "[f]aculty will not use their courses for the purpose of political, ideological, religious or anti-religious indoctrination" does not appear to be particularly controversial.[37] Indeed, the AAUP, opposed as it is to the ABR, seeks to hold public universities to a similar standard. The point of dispute is not whether indoctrination is acceptable in principle but what constitutes indoctrination in practice. To ABR supporters, the term "indoctrination" may be used to characterize any faculty expression of liberal opinion, oral or written, in or out of class, because in their view such statements have a coercive effect. ABR opponents deny that professors indoctrinate when they make brief references to political or religious topics, assign certain texts, express opinions about the course content, publish material that reflects their interpretation of their research, or teach courses in such areas as women's studies and African American studies.

An example of this difference of opinion about what constitutes indoctrination involves the posting of political cartoons on office doors. Testifying before the Pennsylvania legislative committee, Horowitz criticized university administrators for failing to require faculty to remove signs saying "Elect John Kerry" and "God Is Not a Republican" during the election of 2004. Because those signs represented the majority view of faculty in the department, he argued, posting them on office doors coerced students into accepting or appearing to accept a liberal viewpoint. It also suggested that political views affected the grading of student papers and the hiring and promotion of faculty. Horowitz has stated repeatedly that the same is true when liberal faculty lead campus demonstrations or urge universities to take positions on political or social issues. Predictably, ABR opponents deny that the simple statement of a political opinion constitutes indoctrination, coercion, or abuse. Whether liberal or conservative, such communications are, in their view, a legitimate exercise of the faculty's right to free expression. They also suggest that if posting political signs and cartoons, leading protests, and lobbying the university administration are offered as examples of objectionable faculty behavior that illustrates the need for the ABR, then it is inconsistent to assert, as ABR advocates often do, that the bill is not designed to suppress or penalize faculty speech. Moreover, they point out, any limits placed on the free expression of faculty in public universities would apply to everyone regardless of viewpoint.

In addition to objecting to professors' out-of-class activities, ABR supporters identify in-class speech as a source of indoctrination. The AAUP's 1940 *Statement of Principles on Academic Freedom and Tenure* states, "Teachers are entitled to freedom in the classroom in discussing their subject, but they should be careful not to introduce into their teaching controversial matter which has no relation to their subject."[38] This passage is often quoted to suggest that the AAUP's opposition to the ABR is inconsistent with its own acknowledgment that faculty should not introduce political or religious topics into their instruction. Here, too, the disagreement lies not in the words themselves but in how they are interpreted. To ABR supporters, any comment, no matter how brief, that suggests a liberal viewpoint constitutes deviation from the subject matter of the course for the purpose of indoctrination. Students for Academic Freedom (SAF), for instance, has suggested that only in a course on the American presidency would it be appropriate for a professor to mention President George W. Bush at all. ABR opponents, including the AAUP, protest that forbidding all casual conversation and every passing remark would be too restrictive. In a footnote to its 1940 *Statement*, the AAUP clarifies that the intent of the passage quoted above "is not to discourage what is 'controversial.' Controversy is at the heart of the free academic inquiry which the entire statement is designed to foster. The passage serves to underscore the need for teachers to avoid *persistently* intruding material which has no relation to their subject" (emphasis added).[39] Accordingly, the AAUP proscribes only the misuse of substantial amounts of class time for any kind of tangent, ideological or otherwise. Indeed, according to the AAUP, the occasional introduction of current-event topics into a class in any discipline is a valid pedagogical technique that facilitates the use of analogies to clarify the course material and to help students relate it to their own lives and times.

In addition to objecting to extraneous remarks, ABR supporters maintain that even if classroom speech is clearly relevant to the topic of the course, it may nonetheless constitute indoctrination. In testimony before the Pennsylvania legislative committee, for instance, Horowitz quoted the academic-freedom policy at the Pennsylvania State University, which closely resembles the AAUP's 1940 *Statement*. As evidence that this policy was not sufficiently enforced, he spoke of a women's studies course in which students presented a group project on abortion, and the professor argued in favor of abortion rights. No details of the course were provided, and it was not clear how much the professor had said or whether she had attempted to coerce students to express agreement with her views. Although a discussion of abortion is by no means an obvious deviation from the content field of women's studies, Horowitz has stated in his publications and in his testimony before legislative committees that any professorial expression of liberal opinion constitutes indoctrination. His rationale is that conservative students, who are in a minority, cannot possibly feel free to disagree and are not sufficiently mature to note the fallacies in the professor's statements. Indeed, he and other

ABR supporters consider the very existence of certain departments or programs, such as women's studies and African American studies, to be a violation of ideological neutrality. To them, those disciplines are, by their very nature, little more than the systematized indoctrination of a particular ideology. From that perspective, the relevance of abortion to a course in women's studies makes no difference.

In response to accusations such as these, ABR opponents argue that professors do not indoctrinate when they require students to be aware of relevant information, such as the theory of evolution, even if it contradicts the students' personal beliefs; when they assign controversial texts; or when they state opinions they have formed as a result of their research. "Instructors indoctrinate when they teach particular propositions as *dogmatically* true," the AAUP emphasizes in a 2007 statement. "It is not indoctrination when, as a result of their research and study, instructors assert to their students that in their view certain propositions are true, even if those propositions are controversial within a discipline. . . . [I]f an instructor has formed an opinion on a controversial question in adherence to scholarly standards of professional care, it is as much an exercise of academic freedom to test those opinions before students as it is to present them to the public at large."[40]

Inherent in the broad definition of indoctrination favored by ABR supporters is the implication that the rights of conservative students are in some manner violated by the expression of professorial opinions with which they disagree or, more broadly, by the existence of an academic community in which their own views are not widely shared. According to ABR supporters, students' rights fall under the heading of academic freedom, which, as they describe it, is indistinguishable from general First Amendment free-speech rights. Under this understanding of academic freedom, a professor's opinion is no more valid than a student's, particularly with respect to humanities and social sciences disciplines whose conclusions are not necessarily based on empirical experimentation.

As we have seen, the AAUP's use of the term "academic freedom" is based on the premise that decisions about the interpretation of research and the appropriate content and methodology of college courses should be made not by legislators or university administrators—or students—but by people with advanced degrees and research competence in the relevant fields. It is distinct from the general free-speech rights protected by the First Amendment, which are predicated on something other than the extent of the knowledge underlying a speaker's opinions. For example, students or university administrators who believe in creationism are entitled to express that belief, but under AAUP standards, the content of a biology course on the development of species is to be determined by the biology faculty, as are the nature and standards of their research and the conclusions to be drawn from it. Neither students nor administrators could justly claim that their right to free speech confers an equal say in designing a biology course, shaping the research of biology professors, or interpreting the results of that research. In a discussion of Hillary Clinton's performance as secretary of state, the students, the biology faculty, and the administrators would stand on level ground. With respect to judgments based on the professors' expertise, however, only the faculty would be able to exercise academic freedom as such.

According to the definition that appears in the ABR, "[a]cademic freedom consists in protecting the intellectual independence of professors, researchers *and students* in the pursuit of knowledge and the expression of ideas from interference by legislators or authorities within the institution itself" (emphasis added).[41] This understanding of academic freedom replaces content-field expertise with a standard of "intellectual independence" that applies to students and faculty alike. As the ABR supporters' view of indoctrination suggests, they consider the students' intellectual independence to be violated if professors express opinions with which the students disagree or require them to learn material that they find offensive.

To be sure, the assertion that professors should not impose an orthodoxy —for instance, by ridiculing students' beliefs or assigning grades on the basis of ideology—meets with no opposition in principle. In *Freedom in the Classroom* (2007), the AAUP affirms, "It is a breach of professional ethics for an instructor to hold a student up to obloquy or ridicule in class for advancing an idea grounded in religion, whether it is creationism or the geocentric theory of the solar system," and the same is true of a student's political views. "But," the statement continues, "the current application of the idea of a 'hostile learning environment' to the pedagogical context of higher education presupposes much more than blatant disrespect or harassment. It assumes that students have a right not to have their most cherished beliefs challenged. . . . It is neither harassment nor discriminatory treatment of a student to hold up to close criticism an idea or viewpoint that the student has posited or advanced. Ideas that are germane to a subject under discussion cannot be censored because a student with particular religious or political beliefs might be offended."[42] As both the content and the tone of this statement suggest, the AAUP has little patience with the claim that the students' right to hold and express opinions is violated if they are required to listen to ideas with which they disagree, learn academic content that contradicts their personal beliefs, or respond to professorial challenges to their opinions. Michael Bérubé tapped into the source of this concern when he wrote that some students "distrust . . . intellectual debate itself." He continued, "There is, I believe, all the difference in the world between students who relish a good give-and-take, either with their peers or with their professors, and those who simply want never to encounter a serious liberal argument in their four years."[43]

On the other side of the debate, ABR supporters protest that organizations like the AAUP and scholars like Bérubé misrepresent the goal of the proposed legislation. Far from inhibiting debate, they say, their intent is to replace what they regard as ideologically biased instruction with a balanced presentation of varied views. According to the ABR, "Curricula and reading lists *in the humanities and social sciences* should reflect the uncertainty and unsettled character of all human knowledge in these areas by providing students with dissenting sources and viewpoints where appropriate. While teachers are and should be free to pursue their own findings and perspectives in presenting their views, they should consider and make their students aware of other viewpoints. Academic disciplines should welcome a diversity of approaches to unsettled questions" (emphasis added).[44]

Like the surveys of professors' political affiliations, this provision of the ABR singles out humanities and social science disciplines while ignoring other fields that use qualitative methodologies to explore "unsettled questions" relating to political, social, and ethical concerns. Even more troubling to opponents is the ABR's use of the phrase "where appropriate." This qualification adds to the legislation's ambiguity by suggesting that in some instances, the presentation of varied views may *not* be appropriate. The most benign interpretation is that a discussion of genocide, for instance, need not attempt to enumerate its social benefits. Nevertheless, all the examples of alleged professorial imbalance that the ABR would purportedly remedy relate to the expression of liberal views, and the only disciplines covered by this provision are those whose faculties are widely viewed as being particularly liberal. Accordingly, some critics of the ABR question whether the term "where appropriate" might be interpreted to allow a conservative scholar to laud George W. Bush's presidency, for instance, without giving respectful consideration to the dissenting view that he should be tried as a war criminal. They also suggest that the ABR invokes such values as balance, intellectual diversity, and respect for the free-speech rights of individuals as a means of diluting higher education with discredited or insufficiently documented ideas that do not merit consideration under normal academic standards. As ABR supporters concede, instruction would become incoherent if every possible opinion were presented in every course, which means that judgment calls will always have to be made. The question is by whom, on what basis, and under what stated or implied compulsion.

Since conservative views are unlikely to prevail in any discipline unless a significant proportion of the faculty adheres to them, the ABR's call for diversity in course content is complemented by the statement that "[a]ll faculty shall be hired, fired, promoted and granted tenure on the basis of their competence and appropriate knowledge in the field of their expertise and, *in the humanities, the social sciences, and the arts*, with a view toward fostering a plurality of methodologies and perspectives" (emphasis added).[45] As the pro-ABR political surveys indicate, ABR supporters attribute what they regard as an ideological bias in these particular departments to the prevalence of Democrats on the faculty. In light of those surveys and the resulting rhetoric from ABR supporters, it is difficult to escape the conclusion that the provision for hiring faculty "with a view toward fostering a plurality of methodologies and perspectives" amounts to affirmative action for members of conservative political parties. To ABR supporters, no contradiction exists between this goal and the call for ideological neutrality, because in their view, leftist political bias is the only reason for the relative shortage of conservative scholars in the targeted fields. Predictably, ABR opponents protest that this call for "balance" is in fact a back-door strategy whereby conservative scholars unable to meet the normal standards for academic success are to be shoehorned into universities by legislative or populist fiat.

How Free Is the Marketplace?

In any rational assessment of the alleged lack of balance in academic decisionmaking, ideological bias must be distinguished from legitimate academic standards. As several commentators have observed, that distinction becomes complicated if an ideological viewpoint has been infused into norms and expectations that are perceived, or misperceived, as neutral standards of scholarly excellence. An important difference exists, however, between making such an accusation and providing convincing evidence to back it up. A few case studies, hypothetical and actual, may serve to outline the parameters of this issue.

The best example of a situation in which the charge of ideological bias cannot be supported is the battle between advocates of intelligent design (ID) and the mainstream scientific community. ABR supporters vigorously deny that their calls for balance and for the inclusion of diverse views are meant to apply to ID. Indeed, they accuse their opponents of bringing ID into the discussion in an ideologically motivated attempt to discredit and ridicule the ABR movement. Nevertheless, the language of the proposed legislation and its underlying logic do in fact correspond with ID claims. Like the ABR supporters, ID advocates maintain that certain viewpoints are excluded from instruction on the basis of ostensibly neutral standards that are, in fact, tailored to fit the ideology of the majority of faculty in a particular field. Similarly, both ABR and ID advocates argue that when almost all of the scholars in a discipline exclude a competing viewpoint from the classroom, they violate the dissenters' free-speech rights as well as the students' right to an unbiased education. Far from justifying the exclusion of alternative views, the very fact that the majority rejects them makes it all the more important to present them in the name of intellectual diversity and balance. In this regard, the ABR's reference to the "uncertainty and unsettled character of all human knowledge" and its call for "a diversity of approaches to unsettled questions" perfectly describe the ID advocates' view of science instruction.[46]

The demand that ID be included in scientific literature and instruction rests, at its most basic level, on a misplaced application of the notion that one person's opinion is as good as another's. This notion leads to the conclusion that the refusal to include ID represents ideological bias on the part of the evolutionary scientists who control the field. Consequently, despite the impassioned disclaimers of ABR supporters, ID is the example that ABR opponents most often present to support their contention that, in the words of the AAUP, "[a]ttempts to legislate 'balance' in classrooms could require that opinions be given equal weight with facts, and imply that all theories about a given topic have equal legitimacy, regardless of expert consensus within a discipline."[47]

Underlying the rejection of ID as a scientific theory is the evidence that emerges from empirical studies in such fields as paleontology and geology. By contrast, the humanities, arts, and social sciences—as well as some disciplines ignored by the ABR—employ qualitative approaches to topics that are, at least to some extent, matters of opinion. Nevertheless, such disciplines are not bereft of legitimate academic standards that may be used to discriminate between viable and nonviable lines of argument. Consider the following hypothetical example. A student in an American literature class, convinced that the history of racial inequity in America has been grossly exaggerated in order to justify affirmative-action policies, selects a handful of out-of-context and partial quotations from Frederick Douglass's autobiography. He uses these quotations in a paper to support the demonstrably inaccurate assertion that Douglass did not depict slavery as having been particularly oppressive. When the student loses points for this use of Douglass's work, he complains that the professor, whose liberal views on affirmative action are well known, has unfairly penalized him for expressing ideas that are unappealing to the professor. In this example, the student's right to express his personal opinion about racial inequity does not take precedence over the legitimate standards of literary analysis. Among other things, these standards require consideration of the text as a whole and attention to the specific point at issue: Douglass's perception of slavery rather than the student's. The student is entitled to take issue with what Douglass said—for example, by presenting evidence to show that his depiction of slavery was exaggerated or idiosyncratic—but the student has falsified the text rather than engaging with it. A low grade on such a paper cannot be dismissed as the result of political bias or as an attempt to create a hostile learning environment for conservative students, the professor's political party affiliation and choice of cartoons for the office door notwithstanding.

Even in matters that are subject to differing interpretations or views, such as arguments over the fundamental fairness of affirmative action, there is a significant difference between the students' right to disagree with the professor and the far more controversial assertion that professors should employ some standard other than their own academic judgment to determine the readings they assign, the material they teach, and the views they express. Robert M. O'Neil testified to this point during the ABR hearings in Pennsylvania: "[T]o say that students may not be penalized for holding views different from those of the professor is a far cry from saying that students should not be exposed to, and required to study, even highly uncongenial and offensive views as part of the learning process."[48]

The reference to the ID dispute and the hypothetical account of a student's misinterpretation of Douglass's autobiography provide examples of unfounded accusations of ideological bias in instruction and grading. It would, however, fly in the face of reason to assert that the ideological convictions of the majority of professors in a particular field are never conflated with legitimate professional standards. Indeed, all of the disputes discussed throughout this book feature people so immersed in their own world-view that what others would identify as partisanship appears to them to be nothing more than a reflection of reality. There is no basis for assuming that university personnel are immune to this facet of human psychology. Indeed, one of the many ironies of the ABR movement is that its use of unsubstantiated, inflated, and misleading claims to support sweeping generalizations creates a rhetorical situation in which genuine problems may be obscured by the surrounding clutter.

A highly publicized case in point arose at my own institution, the University of Delaware (UD), with respect to a program called the Curricular Approach to Residence Life, launched in 2004. In August 2007 the consultant Shakti Butler was brought in to offer a two-day training session for resident assistants (RAs)—UD students who were to run most of the activities in the yearlong Residence Life program. A handout for this session, entitled "Diversity Facilitation Training," defines "race" as an unwarranted system of classification initiated by whites to assert their superiority and to sustain their power in society.[49] According to the document, all whites in America are racists, and nonwhites cannot be racists because even if they are prejudiced, they lack the power to enforce their beliefs. No such thing as a white nonracist exists in America; rather, the illusion of white nonracism allows whites to evade responsibility for the oppression of minorities. These ideas are reinforced in the document by a history of Europe and the United States that emphasizes white exploitation of other races. Additional text suggests that concepts of racial categories were foisted on the poor by the rich, in part for the purpose of preventing racial intermarriage lest it lead to the genetic elimination of whites.

Each of UD's eight dormitory complexes had its own Curricular Approach to Residence Life program, and not all were implemented in the same way. Common to all were one-on-one sessions with RAs and RA-led group sessions involving all the residents of a particular floor, known as floor meetings. Both types of sessions were to take place at intervals throughout the year. UD training materials for RAs included one-on-one questions that they were to ask about each student's personal beliefs and experiences relating to race, sexual identity, and oppression, among other things. The RAs took notes during the one-on-one sessions and forwarded them to their superiors with an assessment of which had been the best and the worst conversations. Although the university maintained that those designations pertained to the RAs' performance, not to the views expressed by the dormitory residents, critics protested that "best" and "worst" were linked to the extent to which the student had expressed the desired views.

In the floor meetings, RAs were to encourage students to explore self-identity, stereotypes about other groups, and diversity-related actions. Some activities called for students to move to one side of the room or the other to indicate whether they agreed or disagreed with a given proposition, such as gay marriage. According to the training materials provided to RAs, each floor meeting was to have a theme related to stereotypes: for instance, students were to consider the stereotypes they held and how those affected other people, and they were to understand that every member of society is in some way affected by marginalization based on stereotypes. Mimicking the planning model more appropriately associated with classroom instruction, in which the instructor determines the goals of a course and defines the knowledge or competencies that students are expected to acquire, UD Residence Life established such goals as understanding one's social identity and recognizing the evil nature of systemic social oppression in America. The learning outcomes or competencies to be acquired in conjunction with these goals were defined, as instructional outcomes are, in terms of what every student was expected to do—for instance, "Understand your congruence with citizenship values."[50] Consistent with this approach, the questionnaire designed to measure the effectiveness of the program asked students such questions as whether they had become more aware of their own use of stereotypes and whether they had gained understanding of the oppression faced by minorities in our society.

On October 30, 2007, the Foundation for Individual Rights in Education (FIRE) issued a press release protesting the Curricular Approach to Residence Life program. Materials that FIRE had acquired, such as the "Diversity Facilitation Training" handout, UD instructions to RAs, the questionnaire used to determine whether the program had been effective, and materials from the Residence Life Web site, were posted on the FIRE Web site. Describing the UD program as "Orwellian," FIRE called for its immediate termination. The FIRE president, Greg Lukianoff, who condemned the program as "a grave intrusion into students' private beliefs," said, "The university has decided that it is not enough to expose its students to the values it considers important; instead, it must coerce its students into accepting those values as their own. At a public university like Delaware, this is both unconscionable and unconstitutional."[51] FIRE representatives later stated that the Curricular Approach to Residence Life had been brought to their attention first by a student's father and shortly afterward by Professors Jan Blits and Linda Gottfredson, who, more than a decade earlier, had submitted applications for Pioneer Fund grants to study racial issues.

FIRE sent a letter to Patrick Harker, UD's new president, only a day before the press release was issued on October 30, thus forcing the incoming administration to play catch-up in the midst of a media controversy. On November 1, President Harker shut down the Curricular Approach to Residence Life program. "While I believe that recent press accounts misrepresent the purpose of the residential life program at the University of Delaware," he wrote, "there are questions about its practices that must be addressed and there are reasons for concern that the actual purpose is not being fulfilled." He promised a "full and broad-based review" undertaken in conjunction with the Faculty Senate.[52] Accordingly, the Faculty Senate, at its meeting on November 5, instructed its Student Life Committee to investigate what had led to the controversy and to oversee the planning for a new program, which was to include substantial faculty participation.

The Student Life Committee's report, submitted on February 22, 2008, noted that the stated goal of the Residence Life program was for each participant to "[b]ecome an engaged and active citizen by understanding how your thoughts, values, beliefs, and actions affect the people with whom you live and recognize your responsibility to contribute to a sustainable society at a local, national, and global level." The word "sustainable," most commonly associated with environmental responsibility, was used in this context to cover broader issues, such as social justice. The learning outcomes associated with this goal included, among other things, understanding the effects of social identities and "how differences in equity impact our society." In the committee's view, the underlying problem was that the program, based on a curricular model better suited to classroom instruction, had been implemented in large part by RAs—that is, undergraduate students. "[S]ome of the topics that were addressed in the curriculum were worthy of discussion," the committee stated in its report, "but it would have been appropriate for the discussions on those topics to be led by qualified professionals and faculty" rather than RAs. The committee was particularly critical of the use of such words as "curriculum" and "educational," since that language "implies academic content" that

has "withstood rigorous review by faculty members and academic departments." Instead, the committee suggested, terms such as "residence life
program" should be employed, and the program itself should emphasize
"community development and social activities" rather than "attempt to
replicate learning models that occur in the classroom." "[A]lthough the intent of the curriculum was to engage students in discussion and debate
about important topics related to citizenship," the committee observed,
"on several occasions stated learning outcomes and activities suggested a
particular view was correct over another rather than encouraging students
to have an open and honest discussion." To remedy this problem, the committee noted that the proposed new Residence Life program would include
such formulations as "Learn to articulate their point of view while re-
spectfully engaging in dialogues about different ideas."[53] The committee
recommended faculty participation in planning and implementing the program, and it urged Residence Life staff to work with the Office of Educational Assessment to design an appropriate questionnaire to assess the
program's success.

UD officials initially stated that the Residence Life sessions were voluntary, and critics of the program did not suggest that the university had imposed any penalty on dormitory residents who failed to attend. Nevertheless, the university acknowledged that student attendance at those sessions
was a factor in the evaluation of RAs, and the training materials for RAs
stated, "All students are expected to be at their floor meetings. This ensures
that lesson plans are delivered to each student."[54] The FIRE Web site, to
which the committee briefly alluded in its report, includes samples of e-
mails which, FIRE states, were sent to dormitory residents by RAs indicating that the sessions were mandatory. The Faculty Senate committee found
that, at a minimum, if university policy made Residence Life meetings optional, that message had not been conveyed to the students. "It is imperative," the committee emphasized, "that students clearly understand that participation in Residence Life programming is voluntary rather than having an
impression that it is mandatory. Respecting the moral autonomy and intellectual integrity of students should be a primary goal of all Residence Life
programs."[55]

On May 5, shortly before the Faculty Senate meeting at which a revised
Residence Life program was to be discussed, Adam Kissel, director of the Individual Rights Defense Program at FIRE, urged the UD faculty not to approve or lend their credibility to the proposed plan. "On the basis of exten-

sive evidence, I strongly believe that ResLife is attempting to use the faculty to restore its highly politicized and unabashedly coercive 'sustainability' curriculum," he wrote. "This educational programming plainly goes far, far beyond the environmental initiatives supported at the highest levels of the university. It is intended to be indoctrination into an ideology. The proposal offers only meager, halting respect for the private conscience of UD students." Noting that the same Residence Life staff who had run the Curricular Approach program were still in place, he predicted that they would take every opportunity to indoctrinate students. "And do not let yourself be fooled into thinking the damage will be minimal if students can opt out," he told the faculty. "ResLife has so thoroughly integrated its agenda into the essential information about getting to know the university that for a student to opt out of the educational programming, the student would have to opt out of floor meetings, roommate agreements, hall governance, even parties. It is not appropriate to ask a student to opt out of his or her entire residential experience because of the desire to avoid pressure to conform to ResLife's views."[56]

Much of the discussion at the May 5 senate meeting addressed the repeated use of the term "sustainability" in the proposed Residence Life materials. According to a May 2 article by Kissel, "[F]or ResLife, sustainability is not just about the environment. Documents written or promoted by Residence Life officials demonstrate that sustainability is a highly politicized, comprehensive agenda outlining 'acceptable' positions on controversial topics such as affirmative action, gay marriage, abortion, corporations and worldwide redistribution of wealth."[57] Similarly, a UD professor quoted in the student newspaper remarked, "I think we need a very clear, written definition of sustainability so that we can see that it is turning off the showers and that it's not a code word for the kind of political agenda that Residence Life is pushing throughout the fall."[58]

Having adjourned without a vote on May 5, the senate reconvened the following week to consider a proposal in which "sustainability" had been replaced by "environmental sustainability." An attempt to change that term to "conservation" failed. After all the senators who wished to speak had done so, the floor was opened to general discussion. With respect to the question of coercion, Michael Gilbert, vice president for student life, confirmed that the number of students who attended Residence Life sessions would no longer be considered in the evaluations of RAs. He also confirmed that RAs would work on "social and recreational events," while "[p]ersonal develop-

ment and program content will be done by faculty and professional staff."[59]
The proposal passed by a vote of 45–7.

In February 2009 the Faculty Senate received a report assessing the new
Residence Life program as it had been implemented in the fall of 2008. On
a questionnaire designed by the Office of Educational Assessment, 92 percent of respondents agreed or strongly agreed that they had known that attendance was voluntary. Asked whether they felt that their opinions were
respected, 63 percent agreed or strongly agreed, and 35 percent had no opinion. On an item pertaining to the respect shown by Residence Life staff for
the students' privacy and opinions, 81 percent agreed or strongly agreed,
and 17 percent had no opinion. Other items asked whether students had
learned about environmental sustainability, had profited from social gath-
erings, had been made to feel welcome, felt supported in their academic endeavors, and so forth.

Among the justifications offered for the Curricular Approach to Residence
Life program were the need to address racial incidents and the difficulty in
recruiting and retaining minority students. Similar factors had motivated
the development of the university speech codes discussed earlier, and regardless of intentions, the same core academic-freedom problem arose in
both instances. Like the authors of speech codes, the designers of the Residence Life program failed to distinguish between the speech of the university and that of the students. It is one thing for the university to promulgate
institutional messages and ensure that all students are aware of them. It is
quite another thing to establish "learning objectives" for students such that
their agreement with the institutional view constitutes success, and their
disagreement constitutes failure, in determining whether the program has
met its goals. Moreover, as the debate over the word "sustainability" suggests, it is not altogether clear whether the University of Delaware as an institution endorsed all the views promoted on its behalf in the program.

The Curricular Approach to Residence Life program also impinged on academic freedom by confusing the roles of faculty and staff with respect to
curriculum development. In the wake of the controversy, administrators as
well as the Faculty Senate suggested that the situation might not have become so extreme had the planning involved people more familiar with such
concepts as instructional goals, learning outcomes, and what Residence Life
documents called "lesson plans" for floor meetings. The Student Life Committee's recommendation that the Residence Life staff consult the Office of
Educational Assessment about evaluation questionnaires suggests the same

reasoning. Even without knowledge of the program's details, the title Curricular Approach should have raised a red flag when applied to activities designed and implemented by Residence Life staff and RAs. In this respect, academic freedom as it relates to the faculty's collective responsibility for instruction would have been strained regardless of the specific content of the program.

Since the controversy at the University of Delaware involved a Residence Life program not directed by faculty, an example involving faculty behavior may be useful in rounding out the discussion. A well-documented incident of this kind arose at Missouri State University when an undergraduate student, Emily Brooker, took a required course taught by Frank Kauffman, an assistant professor in the School of Social Work. One of the course assignments required students to write a letter to the state legislature urging the passage of a bill permitting homosexuals to adopt children. Brooker refused to comply on the ground that homosexual adoptions were inconsistent with her personal and religious beliefs. There was general agreement that the legitimate, objective standards of the social work profession include unbiased treatment of individual clients and advocacy for their needs. The question was whether Brooker's refusal to engage in this particular form of advocacy on this particular matter represented a failure to meet those standards. After another faculty member interceded, Kauffman permitted students to choose their own advocacy projects, and Brooker did hers on Missouri's Head Start program.

At the end of the semester, Kauffman filed an academic complaint against Brooker for violating the School of Social Work's Standards of Essential Functioning in Social Work Education. He cited what he perceived to be her lack of respect for diversity, poor interpersonal skills, and unprofessional behavior. An investigating board looked into the matter, and Brooker later complained that the board raised what she considered inappropriate questions about her religious beliefs in relation to her ability to serve homosexual clients. As a condition of being permitted to graduate with her class in May 2006, she was required to sign a letter agreeing to abide by the code of ethics of the National Association of Social Workers (NASW). Among other things, the code requires social workers to be "sensitive to cultural and ethnic diversity and strive to end discrimination, oppression, poverty, and other forms of social injustice. These activities may be in the form of direct practice, community organizing, supervision, consultation, administration, advocacy, social and political action, policy development and implementation, education, and research and evaluation." The code of ethics further states, "Social workers should act to prevent and eliminate domination of, exploitation of, and discrimination against any person, group, or class on the basis of race, ethnicity, national origin, color, sex, sexual orientation, gender identity or expression, age, marital status, political belief, religion, immigration status, or mental or physical disability."[60]

If the code's inclusion of sexual orientation and gender identity or expression represents the infusion of liberal bias into the ostensibly neutral standards of the social-work profession, then the investigating board had no principled basis for questioning whether Brooker's attitude toward homosexual clients would compromise her competence as a social worker. Indeed, raising that question might be seen as a violation of the code with respect to religious discrimination. The converse is also true, however. The sense of the standard that mentions sexual orientation is that social workers must work to end whatever discrimination their clients suffer individually or as a class. The only reason to suggest, by omission, that it is acceptable to ignore discrimination against homosexuals would be the belief that the social worker's personal views on this matter—unlike her views on race, ethnicity, age, and the rest—trump the client's right to protection. As a practical matter, however, it would be impossible for any individual social worker to do all the things listed in the code all the time for every group. Clearly, the assessment of whether Brooker failed to meet these standards either by holding the religious view that homosexuality is wrong or by refusing to lobby for a particular piece of legislation depends on the narrowness with which the code is interpreted. That question became central later in the controversy, when the university commissioned an external review of the School of Social Work.

After graduation, Brooker filed a highly publicized lawsuit against Missouri State University. Through the Alliance Defense Fund, whose Web site describes it as a conservative Christian organization dedicated to religious freedom, right-to-life policies, and family values, she secured the services of attorney David French, who later became president of FIRE. Missouri State president Michael T. Nietzel protested that Brooker's situation had not been brought to the attention of the administration, which had had no opportunity to evaluate the actions of Kauffman and the investigating board in the context of university policy. Rather, he said, the lawsuit was filed and the media notified as if university policy were insufficient to protect Brooker's rights, when in fact that question had not been tested. The lawsuit ended in an out-of-court settlement that cleared Brooker's record and provided a modest financial award. Neitzel commissioned both an external review of the School of Social Work and an internal review of the university's free-speech policies and grievance procedures, and Kauffman was required to receive extensive counseling from the associate provost.

The external review of the School of Social Work proved to be scathing. Among other things, the reviewers recommended eliminating the school's Standards of Essential Functioning and revising admission procedures and promotion and tenure policies that were described as excessively subjective and open to ideological bias. The reviewers observed in their report that "[m]any students and faculty stated a fear of voicing differing opinions from the instructor or colleague. This was particularly true regarding spiritual and religious matters; however, students voiced fears about questioning faculty regarding assignments or expectations. In fact 'bullying' was used by both students and faculty to characterize specific faculty. It appears that faculty have no history of intellectual discussion/debate. Rather, differing opinions are taken personally and often result in inappropriate discourse." In particular, the external review committee found that the NASW code of ethics was inaccurately represented to students and inappropriately "used in order to coerce students into certain belief systems regarding social work practice and the social work profession. This represents a distorted use of the Social Work Code of Ethics in that the Code of Ethics articulates that social workers should respect the values and beliefs of others."[61]

Because the case did not go to trial, neither Brooker's complaint nor Neitzel's denial of some of her allegations was ever tested in court. Accordingly, the external review provides the best evidence describing how the School of Social Work operated at that time. Based on this report, there can be no doubt about the infusion of ideology into professional norms and standards. In particular, broad professional duties such as advocating for improved treatment of individuals and groups were interpreted to mean that all of the individual social workers in a particular situation—in this instance, a university course—could be coerced into endorsing precisely the same measure for meeting precisely the same social aim. Perhaps most damning was the inconsistency inherent in the suggestion that mere personal disagreement with the beliefs, identity, or lifestyle of some clients might be sufficient to disqualify a social worker. If that were so, then adherents of the views prevalent in the School of Social Work at that time would have had to disqualify themselves from serving conservative religious clients.[62]

Following the settlement of Brooker's lawsuit, disagreement remained about the need for the Missouri state legislature to initiate more sweeping reforms. President Nietzel protested that the university administration would have intervened much sooner if Brooker had employed internal procedures rather than going straight to an advocacy group, the media, and the courts. While supporting increased publicity for university policies and procedures, he denied the need for the state legislature to become involved in a massive overhaul of the university's treatment of free speech and student grievances. Similarly, the AAUP argued in a letter to the legislature that the outcome of the Brooker incident demonstrated that Missouri State's internal safeguards were sufficient to address any violations of student rights that might occur. To some critics of higher education, however, the fact that the Brooker case had arisen at all suggested, at the very least, that the university administration was insufficiently attentive to an academic unit that the external review report later described as not only ideologically oppressive but in massive disarray. These critics regarded legislative intervention and the empowerment of conservative students as essential means of ensuring that violations would be less likely to occur in the future. Critics also expressed doubt that the university administration would have acted against even the most egregious manifestations of liberal bias unless galvanized into doing so by the lawsuit and the accompanying publicity and legislative attention.

The Brooker incident became a catalyst for attempts to bring about broader changes in the locus of control not only at Missouri State, but throughout the state's system of higher education. In April 2007, the Missouri House of Representatives passed the Emily Brooker Intellectual Diversity Act, which later died in the state senate. The bill attempted to use the publicity surrounding the Brooker case to jump-start sweeping proposals, some of which had no demonstrated basis in fact and were only tangentially related to the issues raised by the treatment of Emily Brooker. In effect, the discovery of a single instance of genuine abuse was treated as proof of the accuracy of any and all claims about liberal bias and ineffective protection for student rights in public universities. Similarly, the bill reflected the premise that any proposed regulation of universities was justified by the fact that a violation was known to have occurred.

The Brooker Act focused on having institutions of higher education issue regular reports on their promotion of intellectual diversity through their selection of campus speakers and their policies on such matters as admission,

scholarships, hiring, promotion and tenure, curriculum, and course evaluations. The most controversial aspect of the bill was an amendment providing protection for student belief in the inerrancy of the Bible, which led
to protests that in the name of "intellectual diversity," professors would be
pressured to accept the premises of creationism or intelligent design as valid
responses in science classes. More broadly, the bill's critics decried it as an
attempt to place subjective preferences on the same level as academically
sound information. A revised version of the bill, introduced in 2008 as the
Emily Brooker Higher Education Sunshine Act, omitted some of the most
controversial elements, including the reference to biblical inerrancy. Like
the ABR, it was framed in apparently neutral language that nonetheless generated skepticism about the intended outcome of calls for "ideological balance" in hiring and promotion and for the inclusion of "alternative claims
of truth" in university courses.[63]

The 2008 version of the Brooker Act generated no more interest than its
predecessor did, and the same appears to be true of a version introduced in
2010. Of greater significance is the broader question of whether or how the
locus of control in academic decisionmaking should be shifted in response
to demonstrable abuses. Ironically, the ABR movement, which ostensibly
seeks to address such injustices, is in fact an obstacle or at least a distraction.
Its fundamental flaw is that under the guise of such buzzwords as "balance"
and "diversity," it would advance conservative interests on the basis of un-
proven assertions, overgeneralizations, and inaccurate information. Owing
in part to the attention diverted to this movement and the defensiveness and
anger that it generates, too little focus has been placed on more credible discussions of possible infusions of ideology, whether liberal or conservative,
into the norms of disciplines ranging from humanities and social sciences
to business and law. As a result, the extent of the real problem—as opposed
to manufactured hysteria—is too uncertain to serve as the basis for any proposed policy change other than the need for further and, as far as possible,
dispassionate exploration of this issue and its implications for the policies
and practices of American higher education.

With respect to the principles to be applied in such an exploration, the
AAUP *Declaration* rings as true today as it did in 1915:

> The university teacher, in giving instruction upon controversial matters,
> while he is under no obligation to hide his own opinion under a mountain
> of equivocal verbiage, should, if he is fit for his position, be a person of a
> fair and judicial mind; he should, in dealing with such subjects, set forth

justly, without suppression or innuendo, the divergent opinions of other investigators; he should cause his students to become familiar with the best published expressions of the great historic types of doctrine upon the questions at issue; and he should, above all, remember that his business is not to provide his students with ready-made conclusions, but to train them to think for themselves, and to provide them access to those materials which they need if they are to think intelligently.

8

All Roads Lead to *Garcetti*

Public opinion is at once the chief safeguard of a democracy, and the chief menace to the real liberty of the individual.
—American Association of University Professors, *Declaration of Principles on Academic Freedom and Academic Tenure*

ACADEMIC FREEDOM ENJOYED NO LEGAL protection when, in 1915, the fledgling American Association of University Professors began a campaign to persuade universities to adopt it as a professional standard. Beginning in the mid-twentieth century, courts—including the Supreme Court—repeatedly mentioned academic freedom, but the constitutional basis on which it rested was not clearly defined. Courts routinely used tests derived from general public-employee law to decide cases involving the free-speech rights of professors, and the issue was further complicated by decisions that treated academic freedom as an attribute of the university as an institution, not of the faculty. Nevertheless, by the end of the twentieth century, a widespread belief existed among professors in public universities that their academic-freedom rights were securely protected by the First Amendment. That belief, ill founded in the first place, was seriously challenged by a Supreme Court decision, *Garcetti v. Ceballos* (2006), and subsequent lower-court decisions.[1]

To lay the groundwork for a discussion of *Garcetti* and its aftermath, it is essential to consider what academic freedom means as a professional standard and what it means as a matter of constitutional law. As a professional standard voluntarily adopted by most American universities, public and private, academic freedom reflects the premise that "He who pays the piper calls the tune" does not apply to university education. In the words of the AAUP's 1915 *Declaration of Principles on Academic Freedom and Academic Tenure*, "The lay public is under no compulsion to accept or to act upon the opinions of the scientific experts whom, through the universities, it employs. But it is highly needful, in the interest of society at large, that what purport to be the conclusions of men trained for, and dedicated to, the quest for truth, shall in fact be the conclusions of such men, and not echoes of the opinions of the lay public, or of the individuals who endow or manage universities."[2]

Far from being merely a matter of faculty privilege, freedom from populist or authoritarian constraint is an essential element of any system of higher education worthy of the name. Without it, universities cannot carry out their educational function and fulfill their role in society. As the *Declaration* explains, "To the degree that professional scholars, in the formation and promulgation of their opinions, are, or by the character of their tenure appear to be, subject to any motive other than their own scientific conscience and a desire for the respect of their fellow experts, to that degree the university teaching profession is corrupted; its proper influence upon public opinion is diminished and vitiated; and society at large fails to get from its scholars, in an unadulterated form, the peculiar and necessary service which it is the office of the professional scholar to furnish."

In so writing, the authors of the *Declaration* were responding to what they perceived to be a major threat to the very fabric of American higher education. Unlike the German institutions with which they are often compared, America's early colleges and universities were run by lay boards that viewed faculty as mere employees subject to any orthodoxy the board might choose to impose. This master-servant view of faculty status persisted through the nineteenth century as the lay overseers, lacking expertise in the professors' fields of study, sought to apply ideological, theological, or populist considerations to the pursuit and dissemination of knowledge. Several of these early disputes are discussed in *The Development of Academic Freedom in the United States* (1955), a seminal work by Richard Hofstadter and Walter P. Metzger.[3] More immediate to the establishment of the AAUP were controversies that arose during the early years of the twentieth century, when university professors were summarily fired for their views on such matters as America's entry into World War I, the rise of labor unions, and immigration policy.

To the AAUP's founders, it was clear that the American system of higher education could not take its place as a world leader unless experts in each field were free to advance knowledge, promote critical and creative thinking, and support or challenge orthodox thought. This goal could never be achieved, they felt, if faculty were viewed as mere employees in a master-servant model, subject to sanctions based not on their professional competence but on their conformity to an orthodoxy imposed by trustees. Accordingly, they deplored situations "in which the relation of trustees to professors is apparently still conceived to be analogous to that of a private employer to his employees; in which, therefore, trustees are not regarded as debarred by any moral restrictions, beyond their own sense of expediency, from imposing their personal opinions upon the teaching of the institution, or even from employing the power of dismissal to gratify their private antipathies or resentments." Asserting that a professor's ultimate responsibility is not to the university administration but "primarily to the public itself, and to the judgment of his own profession," the *Declaration* describes faculty as

> the appointees, but not in any proper sense the employees, of the [trustees]. For, once appointed, the scholar has professional functions to perform in which the appointing authorities have neither competency nor moral right to intervene. . . . So far as the university teacher's independence of thought and utterance is concerned—though not in other regards—the relationship of professor to trustees may be compared to that between judges of the federal courts and the executive who appoints them. University teachers should be understood to be, with respect to the conclusions reached and expressed by them, no more subject to the control of the trustees, than are judges subject to the control of the president, with respect to their decisions.

In stating that faculty should determine the content and academic quality of teaching and scholarship, the authors of the 1915 *Declaration* did not place ultimate control in the hands of individual professors. Rather, they asserted that the faculty as a whole, within the institution and in each area of expertise, should be charged with judging the quality of academic work and with defining and upholding appropriate professional standards. Accordingly, the *Declaration* defined a university as "a great and indispensable organ of the higher life of a civilized community, in the work of which the trustees hold an essential and highly honorable place, but in which the faculties hold an independent place, with quite equal responsibilities—and in relation to purely scientific and educational questions, the primary responsibility."

While maintaining that academic freedom serves the public interest, the authors of the *Declaration* acknowledged that some segments of the public would undoubtedly resist any approach that diminished the power of the majority or its representatives to regulate the speech of professors. To be sure, the authority to dismiss or otherwise penalize professors rests with trustees, but such actions may be motivated by popular sentiment that the trustees share or fear. When professors engage in controversial teaching, scholarship, or public activism, either the majority of taxpayers or a highly vocal group is likely to protest that work paid for by the public should be shaped to the public's specifications. Michael Bérubé, among others, has responded to this argument by noting that public universities have multiple sources of income, and in some instances the state's contribution has become so small that it is no longer accurate to say that professors in those institutions owe their compensation to the state. More to the point, however, is the underlying question: If taxpayers support public higher education, to what extent are their representatives entitled to shape or control its academic content? To the authors of the *Declaration,* the answer was clear. What the public buys for its money is a venue within which certain highly important public goals are pursued, none of which is compatible with a locus of control external to the content fields within which the teaching or research is done. It is thus illogical to claim that the public is not getting its money's worth when faculty operate independently of political or institutional control, since that is the only circumstance under which the institution can fulfill the public service that the funding was intended to facilitate. As the *Declaration* explains,

> This brings us to the most serious difficulty of this problem; namely, the dangers connected with the existence in a democracy of an overwhelming and concentrated public opinion. The tendency of modern democracy is for men to think alike, to feel alike, and to speak alike. Any departure from the conventional standards is apt to be regarded with suspicion. . . . An inviolable refuge from such tyranny should be found in the university. It should be an intellectual experiment station, where new ideas may germinate and where their fruit, though still distasteful to the community as a whole, may be allowed to ripen until finally, perchance, it may become a part of the accepted intellectual food of the nation or of the world. Not less is it a distinctive duty of the university to be the conservator of all genuine elements of value in the past thought and life of mankind which are not in the fashion of the moment.

Commenting on this issue in *For the Common Good* (2009), Matthew C. Finkin and Robert W. Post wrote, "The 1915 *Declaration* identified a structural paradox: in a democracy, all institutions of higher education must ultimately depend on popular support, yet faculty cannot pursue new knowledge or instill independence of mind if they are bound by the pieties of public opinion." Financial and political considerations may lead administrators to call for "restraint," "responsible behavior," and "respect for the opinions of others," and such goals are not necessarily incompatible with academic freedom. "[A]cademic responsibility and restraint are indeed required by academic freedom, because academic freedom is the right to pursue a scholar's profession according to the norms of that profession, and faculty can accordingly be held accountable for compliance with these norms." Nevertheless, they suggested, "there is a fundamental distinction between holding faculty accountable to professional norms and holding them accountable to public opinion."[4]

As Finkin and Post also observed, university administrators are subject to pressure not only from state legislators but also from the individuals and groups that control other sources of university funding, such as government grants, corporate donations, and private contributions. Although academic freedom, as defined by the courts, protects public universities as institutions, that protection pertains only to their legal rights. It does not insulate administrators from pressures associated with the possible financial or political consequences of displeasing certain constituencies. By contrast, policies protecting the academic freedom of the faculty from interference by university officials provide a counterweight to external pressure. Although nothing prevents a public, corporate, or private donor from withholding support for any reason, the academic freedom of the faculty changes the rhetoric of the debate because no form of support can be made directly contingent on the administration's adoption of certain measures if those measures lie outside the scope of its authority.

Getting It Off the Drawing Board

The 1915 *Declaration*, written by a small and elite group of faculty, did not represent the general practice at that time and was, at first, not widely adopted. Perhaps the most striking illustration of that point was the passage, in 1925, of a Tennessee law that criminalized the teaching of evolution not only in K–12 schools but also in public universities. The antievolution law epitomized two then-prevailing notions that the AAUP sought to overcome. The first was the master-servant model of university governance under which faculty are subject in every respect to the will of those who fund and run the university. The second was the idea that professors in public universities have a duty to promulgate whatever beliefs the majority holds sacred. But support for academic freedom was gaining ground even in 1925, as evidenced by the AAUP's entry that year into what would turn out to be prolonged discussions with the Association of American Colleges (now the Association of American Colleges and Universities), a national organization representing university administrations. In 1940 the two organizations issued a joint *Statement of Principles on Academic Freedom and Tenure,* which has since been revised to include interpretive comments (1970) and updated language (1990). Endorsed by university administrators as well as faculty, this statement has become central to the conceptualization of academic freedom in modern American universities.

Like the 1915 *Declaration,* the more concise 1940 *Statement* affirms that the purpose of academic freedom is not to privilege faculty but to serve society. It states: "Institutions of higher education are conducted for the common good and not to further the interest of either the individual teacher or the institution as a whole. The common good depends upon the free search for truth and its free exposition. Academic freedom is essential to these purposes and applies to both teaching and research. Freedom in research is fundamental to the advancement of truth. Academic freedom in its teaching aspect is fundamental for the protection of the rights of the teacher in teaching and of the student to freedom in learning."[5]

The very act of jointly formulating this statement embodied the principle of shared governance between faculty and administration. It marked the relationship between university administrators and professors as something other than that of master and servant, or employer and "mere" employee, although the ideal language to express that relationship remained elusive. The 1915 *Declaration* refers to faculty as "appointees" rather than "employees" of the trustees and assigns them primary responsibility for academic decisions, and the 1940 *Statement* calls them "officers of an educational institution." Both documents suggest that shared governance is a necessary condition for the implementation of academic freedom with respect to teaching and scholarship, and a report issued by an AAUP committee in 1920 maintained that unless faculty were able to influence institutional policy, they could not be expected to take the risks necessary to make real progress in scholarship and creativity.

The relationship between public-university administrations and faculties was more fully explored in several subsequent AAUP documents, notably the 1966 *Statement on Government of Colleges and Universities,* issued jointly with the American Council on Education and the Association of Governing Boards of Universities and Colleges. This document, endorsed by organizations representing faculty, university administrators, and trustees, issues "a call to mutual understanding," integration, and joint effort. In defining the respective duties of trustees, administrators, faculty, and students, it emphasizes that even when the authority to make a particular decision rests with one of these entities, there should be consultation, clear avenues of communication, and the right to dissent. To the faculty, it allocates "primary responsibility for such fundamental areas as curriculum, subject matter and methods of instruction, research, faculty status, and those aspects of student life which relate to the educational process. On these matters the power of review or final decision lodged in the governing board or delegated by it to the president should be exercised adversely only in exceptional circumstances, and for reasons communicated to the faculty."[6]

Among the specific areas in which the *Statement on Government* recommends deference to faculty judgment are the hiring, retention, and promotion of faculty. As the authors explain, "[S]cholars in a particular field or activity have the chief competence for judging the work of their colleagues; in such competence it is implicit that responsibility exists for both adverse and favorable judgments. Likewise, there is the more general competence of experienced faculty personnel committees having a broader charge. . . . The governing board and president should, on questions of faculty status, as in other matters where the faculty has primary responsibility, concur with the faculty judgment except in rare instances and for compelling reasons which should be stated in detail."

Reflecting on this statement, Finkin and Post noted that the process by which it was developed as well as the recommendations it contains do not resemble anything likely to be seen in the corporate world: a difference whose roots lie in the fundamental purposes of universities. "Ordinary business organizations serve private economic interests. These interests can be arbitrary or personal," they wrote. To further such interests, the management is empowered to silence dissent within the organization. "Principles of academic freedom, by contrast, presuppose that institutions of higher education serve the public interest and that they promote the common good. The common good is not to be determined by the arbitrary, private, or personal decree of any single individual; nor is it to be determined by the technocratic calculation of rational and predictable profit incentives."[7] Rather, Finkin and Post suggested, the achievement of the public goals to which higher education is dedicated requires open debate and serious attention to the input of faculty who bring to the table high-level expertise in their content areas along with pedagogical and institutional knowledge. An AAUP report written in 2009 by a subcommittee of which Finkin was a member extended this reasoning to criticisms of the administration: "It would be inconceivable for a corporate subordinate to challenge a superior's authority to override the subordinate's decision without facing the prospect of sanction. It is not inconceivable for a faculty to challenge the right of the administration or of a governing board to disregard the faculty's judgment."[8]

A final AAUP document that relates to this discussion is the 1994 *Statement on the Relationship of Faculty Governance to Academic Freedom*. "[A] sound system of institutional governance is a necessary condition for the protection of faculty rights and thereby for the most productive exercise of essential faculty freedoms," the *Statement* declares. "Correspondingly, the protection of the academic freedom of faculty members in addressing issues of institutional governance is a prerequisite for the practice of governance unhampered by fear of retribution."[9] Referring to the categories of decisionmakers identified in the *Statement on Government*—trustees, administrators, faculty—the *Statement on the Relationship of Faculty Governance to Academic Freedom* suggests that the amount of control exercised over any specific matter should be proportionate to the degree of responsibility that each constituency bears for that aspect of the university's mission. In teaching and research, the voice of the faculty should be paramount—not as a privilege but as the best means of achieving educational goals.

According to the *Statement on the Relationship of Faculty Governance to Academic Freedom*, it is essential for faculty to exercise authority over the admission, grading, and instruction of students as well as the hiring, retention, promotion, and dismissal of faculty in order to advance both academic freedom and the quality of teaching and scholarship within an institution. "Protecting academic freedom on campus requires ensuring that a particular instance of faculty speech will be subject to discipline only where that speech violates some central principle of academic morality, as, for example, where it is found to be fraudulent. . . . Protecting academic freedom also requires ensuring that faculty status turns on a faculty member's views only where the holding of those views clearly supports a judgment of competence or incompetence." Such judgments can be made only by faculty, since it is they "who have the expertise to form judgments on faculty competence or incompetence."[10] Overall, faculty should be able to express their ideas about teaching, research, and the governance of the institution without fear of reprisal.

Of course, not all public universities abide by all of these standards all the time. Based on investigations conducted by its Committee A on Academic Freedom and Tenure, the AAUP maintains a list of censured administrations that have signally failed to do so. Nevertheless, these are the exception rather than the rule, and even those administrations that are censured for specific actions or policies may honor academic freedom in other respects. The conviction that certain decisions should be made by content-area experts has so permeated the academic culture that a university's comprehensive failure to comply with that principle would undercut any claim to intellectual leadership or even credibility. Allowing for variations among institutions with respect to details and degrees of implementation, it is fair to say that academic freedom is well established as a professional standard. Far less settled is its status as a constitutionally protected right.

A Special Concern of the First Amendment

In lawsuits involving academic freedom, courts are likely to find that the university as an institution, rather than the faculty, enjoys constitutional protection. This conceptualization of academic freedom makes no practical difference when the faculty and the administration unite to repel an external challenge, such as an intrusive state statute or an action by a disgruntled student. It does come into play, however, when the dispute is between the administration and the faculty, since courts tend to view the academic freedom of the institution as empowering the administration rather than the faculty. Exacerbating this problem is the courts' practice of applying one-size-fits-all standards to all public employees, including professors, without regard for fundamental differences in workplace expectations. The tests applied to controversial speech, in particular, derive from cases whose circumstances are far removed from the purposes and cultures of universities.

This was true even before 2006, when the Supreme Court's decision in *Garcetti* provided additional cause for concern.

Several of the earliest Supreme Court decisions that mention academic freedom involved attempts by state legislatures to impose loyalty oaths and other anticommunist measures on public employees, including teachers in public schools and universities. An example is *Wieman v. Updegraff* (1952), which dealt with an Oklahoma statute under which all public employees in the state, including faculty in public schools and universities, had to sign a loyalty oath. More than a full page in length, the oath required public employees to declare their fidelity to the United States and their willingness to take up arms in its defense. In taking the oath, they stated that they did not advocate, or belong to any organization that advocated, the unlawful overthrow of the government. They also affirmed that they were not members of the Communist Party or of any Communist front or subversive organization, had not been members of any such group within the previous five years, and would not join any such group. Several faculty and staff members at the Oklahoma Agricultural and Mechanical College refused to take the oath and challenged it in court. The Supreme Court struck down the law on the ground that mere membership in an organization was insufficient cause to dismiss someone from public employment, since membership might be innocent.

The language pertaining to the free-speech rights of teachers appears in a concurrence written by Justice Felix Frankfurter. Although the decision applies to public employees in general, the concurrence suggests that it is particularly important for teachers at all levels of public education. "It is the special task of teachers to foster those habits of open-mindedness and critical inquiry which alone make for responsible citizens, who, in turn, make possible an enlightened and effective public opinion," Frankfurter wrote. "Teachers must fulfill their function by precept and practice, by the very atmosphere which they generate; they must be exemplars of open-mindedness and free inquiry. They cannot carry out their noble task if the conditions for the practice of a responsible and critical mind are denied to them." In his view, teachers "must have the freedom of responsible inquiry, by thought and action, into the meaning of social and economic ideas, into the checkered history of social and economic dogma. They must be free to sift evanescent doctrine, qualified by time and circumstance, from that restless, enduring process of extending the bounds of understanding and wisdom, to assure which the freedoms of thought, of speech, of inquiry, of

worship are guaranteed by the Constitution of the United States against in-
fraction by National or State government."[11] In contrasting "evanescent
doctrine" with the "enduring process" associated with the growth of knowledge, Frankfurter echoed a view expressed in the 1915 *Declaration:* that holding teachers and researchers hostage to the passing fancies of public opinion, far from promoting or embodying democracy, poses an overwhelming
threat to it.

Five years later, Frankfurter wrote a concurrence in *Sweezy v. New Hampshire* that focused on university-level academic freedom. Unlike his language in *Wieman,* his remarks in *Sweezy,* through (mis)applications in later
decisions, have weakened the right to free expression by individual faculty
members. *Sweezy* arose when the attorney general of New Hampshire,
under the authority of the state's Subversive Activities Act, questioned Paul
Sweezy about his social and economic views and his alleged involvement
with the Communist and Progressive Parties. Sweezy, a Marxist economist
and a former instructor at Harvard University, had given guest lectures in a
humanities class at the University of New Hampshire (UNH), and the attorney general asked about those as well. Although Sweezy answered most
of the attorney general's questions, he balked at those he considered irrelevant to the investigation, including inquiries about his remarks at UNH.
Pleading not the Fifth Amendment but the First, he refused to say whether
he had advocated socialism or Marxism in those lectures. He remained ob-
durate even when questioned by a judge, whereupon he was jailed for contempt of court. The Supreme Court found numerous flaws in the attorney
general's investigation and the underlying state law, including uncertainty
about the extent to which the attorney general's inquiries were relevant to the
stated goal of national security. The Court also questioned the nature of the
information the legislature wished to acquire and its authority to compel responses.

Although Sweezy was not a member of the UNH faculty, the Court took
the opportunity to discourse upon the principle of free inquiry in American
universities. The decision states, "The essentiality of freedom in the community of American universities is almost self-evident. No one should un-
derestimate the vital role in a democracy that is played by those who guide
and train our youth. To impose any strait jacket upon the intellectual leaders in our colleges and universities would imperil the future of our Nation.
No field of education is so thoroughly comprehended by man that new dis-
coveries cannot yet be made."[12]

By far the most significant reference to academic freedom in *Sweezy* appears in Frankfurter's concurrence, in which he quoted a statement by scholars at a conference in South Africa: "It is the business of a university to provide that atmosphere which is most conducive to speculation, experiment and creation. It is an atmosphere in which there prevail 'the four essential freedoms' of a university—to determine for itself on academic grounds who may teach, what may be taught, how it shall be taught, and who may be admitted to study."[13] This quotation has been used repeatedly to uphold not only the university's freedom from outside interference but also the authority of the administration to make decisions in these four areas and to determine how much input, if any, the faculty is to have. In a recent article in the *Georgetown Law Review,* Judith Areen took issue with this interpretation of the statement from the South African conference. In its original context, she argued, it referred to the whole university, faculty as well as administrators.[14] Nevertheless, no matter what the authors of the statement—or Frankfurter—might have had in mind, the effect of this quotation, as interpreted by the courts, has been to uphold the authority of trustees and administrators in conflicts with faculty.

By contrast with the "four freedoms" passage in *Sweezy,* a much-quoted reference to academic freedom in *Keyishian v. Board of Regents of the University of the State of New York* (1967), written by Justice William Brennan, pertains specifically to the free speech of teachers. At issue in this lawsuit was New York's Feinberg Law, enacted in 1939 and extended to public universities in 1953. The relevant provision required teachers and professors in public institutions to sign a certificate indicating that they were not presently Communists and had disclosed any previous membership in the Communist Party. Other employees of such institutions were subject to a loyalty oath. At the State University of New York at Buffalo, four faculty members refused to sign the certificate, and a library worker refused to take the oath.

In a 1952 decision, *Adler v. Board of Education of the City of New York,* the Supreme Court had upheld a provision of the Feinberg Law that excluded from state employment anyone who belonged to an organization that advocated the violent overthrow of the government. In the intervening years, the Court had issued decisions such as *Wieman,* which rejected the notion that simply belonging to a group was sufficient to justify termination of employment. Moreover, the Feinberg Law required the dismissal of any teacher guilty of sedition, but it did not define the term. As a result, the Court found, "[t]he teacher cannot know the extent, if any, to which a 'seditious' utterance must transcend mere statement about abstract doctrine, the extent to which it must be intended to and tend to indoctrinate or incite to action in furtherance of the defined doctrine. The crucial consideration is that no teacher can know just where the line is drawn between 'seditious' and nonseditious utterances and acts." To illustrate this point, the Court expressed uncertainty about whether assigning texts describing Marxist theory and discussing them in class would constitute advocating Marxism under the Feinberg Law. "The very intricacy of the plan and the uncertainty as to the scope of its proscriptions make it a highly efficient *in terrorem* mechanism. It would be a bold teacher who would not stay as far as possible from utterances or acts which might jeopardize his living by enmeshing him in this intricate machinery. . . . The result must be to stifle 'that free play of the spirit which all teachers ought especially to cultivate and practice.'"[15]

The Court's discussion of the unconstitutional vagueness of the Feinberg Law included an often-quoted passage: "Our Nation is deeply committed to safeguarding academic freedom, which is of transcendent value to all of us and not merely to the teachers concerned. That freedom is therefore a special concern of the First Amendment, which does not tolerate laws that cast a pall of orthodoxy over the classroom." Unlike the courts' interpretation of the "four freedoms" quotation in *Sweezy,* this passage explicitly links the larger social purposes of education to the ability of teachers to make judgments about what to teach—a point that also arises in the Court's earlier reference to the need for a "free play of the spirit" in classroom instruction. In this instance, by threatening teachers with dismissal for seditious utterances without clarifying what "sedition" means, the Feinberg Law would intimidate them into suppressing even constitutionally protected speech. "The danger of that chilling effect upon the exercise of vital First Amendment rights must be guarded against by sensitive tools which clearly inform teachers what is being proscribed," the Court stated.[16]

Despite the Supreme Court's ringing endorsement of academic freedom in *Wieman, Sweezy,* and *Keyishian,* these cases turned on the constitutionality of statutes that applied to all public employees, not just to teachers. To the extent that they affected academic freedom, they strengthened the right of a public university as an institution to be free from external interference, but they did not address the balance of power between the faculty and the administration. The same is true of lawsuits in which disgruntled students or faculty sue universities over decisions made jointly by faculty and administration or made by one entity and endorsed by the other. When the faculty and the administration agree, the academic freedom of the institution serves both groups.

An example of such a lawsuit may be found in *Regents of the University of Michigan v. Ewing* (1985), which began when the faculty of a combined undergraduate and medical program dismissed a student, Scott Ewing. Although he had been struggling all along, the immediate cause of Ewing's dismissal was his performance on an important qualifying examination, on which he received the lowest score ever recorded. In upholding the dismissal, the Supreme Court relied heavily on the fact that the decision had been made by faculty experts in the field: "The record unmistakably demonstrates . . . that the faculty's decision was made conscientiously and with careful deliberation, based on an evaluation of the entirety of Ewing's academic career. When judges are asked to review the substance of a genuinely academic decision, such as this one, they should show great respect for the faculty's professional judgment. Plainly, they may not override it unless it is such a substantial departure from accepted academic norms as to demonstrate that the person or committee responsible did not actually exercise professional judgment."[17]

In reinforcing the view that courts should defer to faculty judgment on academic matters, the Court suggested that the same applies to university administrations with respect to the "multitude of academic decisions that are made daily by faculty members of public educational institutions—decisions that require 'an expert evaluation of cumulative information and [are] not readily adapted to the procedural tools of judicial or *administrative* decisionmaking'" (emphasis added). Elsewhere in this passage, however, the Court fell back on the language of institutional academic freedom. For example, it indicated its "reluctance to trench on *the prerogatives of state and local educational institutions* and our responsibility to safeguard *their* academic freedom" (emphasis added). A footnote reinforced this point: "Academic freedom thrives not only on the independent and uninhibited exchange of ideas among teachers and students . . . but also, and somewhat inconsistently, on autonomous decisionmaking by the academy itself. . . . Discretion to determine, on academic grounds, who may be admitted to study, has been described as one of 'the four essential freedoms' of a university."[18] To be sure, the word "academy" could denote an assembly of scholars, but in this context, its autonomous decisionmaking is clearly distinct from the "independent and uninhibited exchange of ideas among teachers and students." When disagreements arise between faculty and administration, the courts' use of precedents regarding the academic freedom of the "academy" or the "university" generally comes down in favor of the administration. It is only when faculty and administration are in agreement that institutional academic freedom is likely to protect the faculty.

Another example of this type of case is *Grutter v. Bollinger* (2003), in which the Supreme Court upheld an admissions policy at the University of Michigan Law School (UMLS). The policy was initiated by a faculty committee, approved unanimously by the entire faculty, and implemented by the administration. Among other things, it stated that the need for a racially diverse student body should be considered during the admissions process. It did not establish quotas, but it did set a goal of admitting an undefined "critical mass" of previously underrepresented groups. According to the testimony of UMLS witnesses, including both faculty and administrators, the policy's primary intent was to enhance class discussion and improve the educational experience for all students by increasing the variety of perspectives represented in UMLS education. Barbara Grutter, an unsuccessful white applicant, sued on the ground that the denial of admission was based on her race. The Court ruled that the policy, which did not include quotas and served a legitimate pedagogical purpose, was constitutional.

With respect to academic freedom, the decision states,

> We have long recognized that, given the important purpose of public education and the expansive freedoms of speech and thought associated with the university environment, universities occupy a special niche in our constitutional tradition. In announcing the principle of student body diversity as a compelling state interest [in *Regents of the University of California v. Bakke,* 1978], Justice Powell invoked our cases recognizing a constitutional dimension, grounded in the First Amendment, of educational autonomy: "The freedom of a university to make its own judgments as to education includes the selection of its student body." From this premise, Justice Powell reasoned that by claiming "the right to select those students who will contribute the most to the 'robust exchange of ideas,'" a university "seeks to achieve a goal that is of paramount importance in the fulfillment of its mission."[19]

As noted in the decision, faculty played a major role in formulating and approving the admissions policy, and the decision seems to suggest that their participation validated the academic nature of the policy. Nevertheless, in the context of this case, the references to the university's "educational autonomy" cannot be read as upholding the academic-freedom rights of the faculty rather than, or separate from, those exercised by the administration.

Test Anxiety

Inevitably, in the course of the energetic and sometimes splenetic exchanges of ideas that characterize university culture, situations arise in which administrations are accused of violating the academic-freedom rights of the faculty as a whole or those of individual professors. When courts are asked to adjudicate such complaints, they are likely to do so on the basis of generic public-employee law. Thus, when locus of control in university decisionmaking becomes a matter of constitutional law, faculty academic freedom is determined, not by the considerations that govern it as a professional standard, but by the rules that define the free-speech rights of public employees in very different workplaces.

To explore the distinction between academic freedom as a constitutional right and academic freedom as a professional standard, I propose to compare a few representative court decisions with the way the same disputes would have been handled if they had been decided under professional standards of academic freedom. The first of these cases, *Parate v. Isibor* (1989), began when Natthu Parate, an untenured associate professor of civil engineering at Tennessee State University, had a dispute with his dean over a student's grade. Based on a system that Parate had established at the beginning of the semester, the student's score fell in the middle of the B range. He refused to change the grade to an A because, among other things, the student had presented fraudulent medical excuses and had cheated on an examination. The student appealed to the dean, Edward Isibor, who ordered Parate to raise the student's grade and to change his grading scale so that, in the future, any student who earned the number of points the complaining student had received would have an A for the course. Parate signed off on the grade change but appended a note saying that he was doing so on orders from the dean. Isibor demanded that Parate sign the document without annotation, and under threat of hostile job action, Parate did so.

Following these events, Parate was ordered to make further changes to his grades and grading criteria. The court later noted that many of the complaining students whose interests were represented by Isibor were Nigerians, as was Isibor, whereas Parate was an Indian. Parate was also denied travel funds, given low performance evaluations, publicly insulted, and subjected to a hostile classroom visit from Isibor and the department chair, Michael Samuchin. The court summarized the visit:

> After Parate began to call the roll, he was immediately interrupted. Isibor shouted from the back of the room: 'Stop the roll call, don't waste time; cir-

culate the paper for a roll call.' Adhering to Isibor's directive, Parate began to teach his class, but was again interrupted by Isibor's shouts. Isibor next ordered Parate to complete one of the problems from the textbook. After Parate began to work out the problem on the blackboard and explain it to the students, Isibor again interrupted him. Isibor demanded that Parate complete the problem on the blackboard without addressing the students; that the students complete the problem on paper; and that Samuchin copy Parate's work from the board. Isibor soon approached the blackboard himself and began to work on the same problem that Parate and the students were completing. After severely criticizing Parate's teaching skills in front of his students, Isibor collected the students' papers and left the classroom.[20]

Isibor subsequently removed Parate as the instructor of the course and ordered him to attend it as a student. Parate did so until he was told to desist.

When Parate's contract as a tenure-track but as yet untenured associate professor expired, he was informed that it would not be renewed. He thereupon sued the university. The U.S. Court of Appeals for the Sixth Circuit, having acknowledged the "problems inherent in resolving clashes between the academy and individual academics when both parties claim a constitutional right to academic freedom," proceeded to resolve those problems in favor of the academy, which the court saw as synonymous with the administration. The court identified only one small matter in which Parate had rights of any kind: although Isibor had the authority to change Parate's grades, he should not have forced the professor to sign the change-of-grade form himself. The decision states, "Arguing from their First Amendment right to academic freedom, the defendants assert an interest in supervising and reviewing the grading policies of their nontenured professors. If they deemed Parate's grade assignments improper, however, the defendants could have achieved their goals by administratively changing Student 'Y's' grade. We conclude that by forcing Parate to change, against his professional judgment, Student 'Y's' grade, the defendants unconstitutionally compelled Parate's speech and chose a means to accomplish their supervisory goals that was unduly burdensome and constitutionally infirm."[21] Even this minor victory for Parate was based not on academic freedom, which is mentioned here only with respect to the administration, but on his generic right not to be compelled to speak.

In explaining the decision, the appeals court cited Justice Frankfurter's reference to the four essential freedoms of the university as well as *Ewing's* reference to the "autonomous decisionmaking [of] . . . the academy itself."

The court concluded that deference to the administration was appropriate because "while the Supreme Court has often expressed a reluctance to intervene in the prerogatives of state and local educational *institutions,* it has remained committed to the protection of *their* academic freedom, 'a special concern of the First Amendment'" (emphasis added). The court did not meaningfully weigh the academic freedom of professors against that of the administration; it merely asserted that "[a]lthough defendants' behavior was unprofessional, their actions [in Parate's class] did not violate Parate's First Amendment right to academic freedom."[22] Without denying that faculty have such a right, the court did not reference it except in the negative. As Michael A. Olivas remarked in the *Stanford Law Review,* "Considering the extraordinary facts underlying *Parate,* it is unlikely that any administrative interference with a professor's teaching methodology will ever be found to violate the First Amendment."[23]

Without doubt, the norms and procedures that would be used to evaluate Parate's situation under the professional standard of academic freedom would differ materially from those employed by the Sixth Circuit in determining whether his First Amendment rights had been violated. Under AAUP standards, one of the central premises of academic freedom is that assessments of the competence of faculty as teachers and scholars are to be made by their peers, and administrators should give great weight to that peer evaluation. This principle holds true even if the administrators are or were teachers or researchers in the relevant field. By contrast, in determining whether Parate's First Amendment rights had been violated, the appeals court said nothing about the absence of faculty input into the assessment of his teaching, nor did it address the academic freedom of the faculty as a whole. The court took the position—quite rightly—that it is not the business of the judiciary to assess the quality of a professor's teaching, but from there it proceeded to the conclusion that whatever Isibor and Samuchin had said about Parate's work had to be considered determinative.

A review based on professional standards of academic freedom would focus on an element that the court did not consider: the hard evidence demonstrating Parate's level of competence as a teacher. To make this determination, Parate's peers might have done such things as examining his syllabi, assessing his students' success as compared with that of students in other sections of a multisection course, comparing the student evaluations of his courses with those of his peers, and sitting in on his classes. As a professional matter, teaching, like scholarship, should be assessed according to generally accepted standards in a particular field and not in a haphazard or arbitrary fashion. The circumstances of the administrators' visit to Parate's class raises doubts in this respect because, at the very least, it is not clear what standards they applied or whether there was any possibility that they might have found his teaching satisfactory. Based on the court's description of the visit, it is not even clear whether its purpose was to evaluate Parate or to harass him. From this perspective, the court's statement that "[t]he university may constitutionally choose not to renew the contract of a non-tenured professor whose pedagogical attitude and teaching methods do not conform to institutional standards" rings hollow because "institutional standards," in this case, may be synonymous not with best practices in Parate's field but with conformity to the dean's wishes.[24]

Because of the lack of information about the quality of Parate's teaching, it is impossible to say whether a peer assessment would have supported the renewal of his contract. There is, however, no doubt that the outcome of a professional review would have been based on different questions from those that occupied the court. To the court, upholding academic freedom meant deferring to the administrators' actions, no matter how bizarre, rather than subjecting them to judicial second-guessing. If the matter is cast in that light, then ruling in favor of Parate would have placed the court in opposition to "the university" in determining who is fit to teach. If, however, the matter is viewed in the context of professional academic freedom, then the tension is not between the court and the university, or even between the administration and Parate, but between the validity of academic decisions that include a faculty voice and the validity of those that do not. For this reason, the court's statement that "[t]he First Amendment concept of academic freedom does not require that a nontenured professor be made a sovereign unto himself" misses the point.[25] The professional standard of faculty academic freedom does not confer autonomy on any individual professor, nor does Parate appear to have been seeking it. What academic freedom does guarantee is that faculty experts will participate in deciding who is qualified to teach and that they will employ standards other than the appeasement of administrators. Indeed, by suggesting that the alternative to upholding Isibor's actions would be to declare Parate "a sovereign unto himself," the court appeared to envision the matter in terms of extremes: either concede to administrators the authority to judge faculty performance in any way they like, without regard for professional norms or for faculty input, or deny that faculty performance is subject to review at all.

The *Parate* court's statement that "[t]he administration of the university rests not with the courts, but with the administrators of the institution," while accurate to the point of tautology, is troubling because, in context, it implies that faculty have no role to play in determining who is fit to teach. Similarly, the next sentence—"A nontenured professor does not escape reasonable supervision in the manner in which she conducts her classes or assigns her grades"—illustrates the contrast between the two models of academic freedom by using the word "reasonable" in a way that would raise the eyebrows, and probably the hackles, of most professors.[26] Indeed, the point made throughout this book—that *what* academic freedom is depends on *whose* it is—has rarely been more effectively illustrated than in *Parate*.

In another academic-freedom dispute, *Edwards v. California University of Pennsylvania* (1998), a professional review would probably have reached the same conclusion as did the lawsuit, but by a different route. Dilawar M. Edwards, a tenured professor of education at California University of Pennsylvania, taught a course on instructional media for several years. At first, his sections, like those taught by other faculty in the department, focused on the use of audiovisual and other media as pedagogical tools. Over time, however, he began to place increasing emphasis on such issues as religion, the censorship of religious speech, and the perils of humanism. In response to a student complaint, the university's vice president for academic affairs, Nancy Nelson, instructed Edwards to stop using his instructional media classes to advance a religious view. Edwards appealed to the president of the university, who supported Nelson.

The chair of Edwards's department, David Campbell, brought the matter to a department meeting at which the faculty voted to reinstate an earlier version of the instructional media syllabus. Campbell thereupon cancelled Edwards's book order for an upcoming section of the course. Edwards was later assigned to teach a course on tests and measurements, which he had not taught before. The students complained that he missed classes, left early, and generally failed to provide a reasonable quality of instruction. At an explosive department meeting, Campbell called Edwards an embarrassment to the department and stated that his teaching was better suited to a fundamentalist Christian institution than to a public university. The administration scheduled a meeting to discuss these issues, but when the materials reached Edwards a few days in advance, he protested that he had not had sufficient time to prepare. Nelson put him on paid leave for the rest of the semester. He was scheduled to teach both courses—instructional media and tests and measurements—the following semester.

Edwards sued the university in federal district court on the grounds that his constitutional rights to due process, free speech, and equal protection under the law had been infringed. He also alleged that the university had violated the Establishment Clause of the First Amendment and had retaliated against him for constitutionally protected speech. Unlike most federal cases involving academic freedom, *Edwards* was tried by a jury. In instructing the jury, the judge applied a standard derived from *Hazelwood:* that the university's action had to be reasonably related to a legitimate pedagogical concern. The jury found in favor of the university.

The U.S. Court of Appeals for the Third Circuit agreed. In a decision written by future Supreme Court Justice Samuel Alito, the appeals court declared, "We do not find it necessary to determine whether the district court's instruction adequately defined the 'reasonably related to a legitimate educational interest' standard because, as a threshold matter, we conclude that a public university professor does not have a First Amendment right to decide what will be taught in the classroom." The court continued, "This conclusion is compelled by our decision in *Bradley v. Pittsburgh Board of Education,* where we explained that 'no court has found that teachers' First Amendment rights extend to choosing their own curriculum or classroom management techniques in contravention of school policy or dictates.'"[27] *Bradley,* discussed in Chapter 1, held that K–12 authorities could prevent a teacher from using a classroom-management technique known as Learnball. Elsewhere, the Third Circuit referenced two other K–12 decisions discussed in Chapter 1: *Boring v. Buncombe County Board of Education,* dealing with a drama teacher's choice of a controversial play, and *Kirkland v. Northside Independent School District,* involving a teacher's use of an unapproved reading list. The only university-based precedent cited on this point is *Rosenberger v. Rector and Visitors of the University of Virginia* (1995), which focuses on student speech. Contrasting the speech of students with the speech of the university, the *Rosenberger* Court stated, "When the University determines the content of the education it provides, it is the University speaking, and we have permitted the government to regulate the content of what is or is not expressed when it is the speaker."[28] Without addressing the question of whether K–12 and university education are in fact identical with respect to locus of control in classroom speech, the *Edwards* court proceeded on the assumption that, for First Amendment purposes, the curricular governance of universities is indistinguishable from that of K–12 public schools. In particular, it concluded that the university, not the professor, is the speaker in college classes. Although individual professors do not have a claim to total autonomy even under professional standards of academic freedom, this uncritical application of a K–12 model to the university level illustrates the difference between constitutional and professional norms.

In *Edwards,* the Third Circuit followed the example of other courts in citing the "four essential freedoms of the university" passage from *Sweezy* and *Ewing*'s reference to the inconsistency between "the "independent and uninhibited exchange of ideas among teachers and students" and "autonomous decisionmaking by the academy itself." On this basis, the court stated that "Edwards's reliance on the principle of academic freedom does not affect our conclusion that the University can make content-based decisions when shaping its curriculum. . . . In sum, caselaw from the Supreme Court and this court on academic freedom and the First Amendment compel the conclusion that Edwards does not have a constitutional right to choose curriculum materials in contravention of the University's dictates."[29] As is true of other decisions discussed in this chapter, the primary issue raised by this declaration is not that individual professors are or should be a law unto themselves but that "university" and "academy" are equated with the administration without reference to the faculty as a whole.

Because Edwards's colleagues were involved in evaluating his choice of curricular materials, his failure to prevail in this case does not in itself create tension between institutional and faculty academic freedom. Academic freedom protects the right of the faculty as a whole to carry primary responsibility for academic matters, not the right of an individual professor to be what the *Parate* court called "a sovereign unto himself." In *Edwards,* as in *Ewing* and *Grutter,* protection for administrative action also sustains what the faculty wanted to do. Unlike the other two decisions, however, *Edwards* does not explicitly reference faculty participation as evidence of the academic validity of the university's actions.

Under the principles that apply to academic freedom as a professional standard, the likelihood that Edwards would have prevailed in a professional review was substantially diminished by his colleagues' declaration that the material he was teaching was extraneous to the course. In accord with AAUP policy statements, one of the professional standards to be applied by the faculty as a whole to the teaching of individual professors is the obligation to focus on matters germane to the subject and purpose of the course.

An occasional brief digression would not violate this rule, but it seems likely that a professional review would have determined that Edwards's emphasis on religion permeated a course whose purpose in the program was to accomplish something quite different. To be sure, the department chair's reference to a fundamentalist college might be interpreted as evidence of bias against a religious viewpoint, and if that indeed was the case, then the chair was at fault. Even if he erred in that respect, however, that would not have entitled Edwards to continue dedicating an inordinate amount of class time to subjects only tangentially related, at best, to the material the course was meant to cover. By the same reasoning, it would not have been necessary in a professional review to consider either the Establishment Clause implications of using public-university classes for religious proselytizing or Edwards's constitutional right to the free exercise of his religion. If his sections of the instructional media course were dedicated to a nongermane topic, that would violate professional standards regardless of the specific content of the nongermane material and regardless of his reasons for introducing it. In that situation, his peers would have not only the right but the duty to define and enforce the appropriate content of the course.

Like *Parate*, *Edwards* dealt solely with curriculum-related speech. Another case that arose at California University of Pennsylvania, *Brown v. Armenti* (2001), also raised questions about a professor's academic-freedom right to criticize the university administration. Robert Brown, a tenured professor, gave a failing grade to a student who had attended only three class meetings out of fifteen. The university president, Angelo Armenti, demanded that the grade be changed to an Incomplete. When Brown refused, he was removed from teaching that course. Brown subsequently wrote a critical evaluation of Armenti to be presented to the trustees of the university, and two years later, he was dismissed. He filed a lawsuit accusing the administration of retaliating against him for his refusal to change the grade and for his criticism of the president, both of which, he asserted, constituted protected speech under the First Amendment. In deciding whether summary judgment without a trial was appropriate, the court did not concern itself with the accuracy of Brown's account of his dismissal. Rather, it considered whether, if the university had indeed terminated his employment for those reasons, it would or might have violated his rights under the First Amendment.

Although Brown relied on the Sixth Circuit's decision in *Parate* to support his contention that he could not be forced to change a grade, the Third Circuit found, without explanation, that its decision in *Edwards* represented "a more realistic view of the university-professor relationship." The court also referenced the "four essential freedoms": "Because grading is pedagogic, the assignment of the grade is subsumed under the university's freedom to determine how a course is to be taught. We therefore conclude that a public university professor does not have a First Amendment right to expression via the school's grade assignment procedures."[30] Having found that Brown's speech with respect to the student's grade was not constitutionally protected, the court declared that the university could penalize him for it without violating his First Amendment rights. The court reached the same conclusion with respect to his criticism of President Armenti, citing *Connick v. Myers* (1983) to show that a public employee's criticism of a supervisor's conduct does not enjoy First Amendment protection.

The decision does not indicate whether the university had reasons for terminating Brown's employment other than the dispute about a grade change and his criticism of Armenti, nor does it say whether the university conducted a hearing that included faculty input. Accordingly, this discussion of a hypothetical academic-freedom review based on professional standards concerns only the questions raised in the case. Under those standards, the academic-freedom implications of Brown's memorandum about Armenti would depend, to some extent, on its content. If he criticized the president's method of drinking soup and cast aspersions upon the virtue of his mother, it would be difficult to show that such speech implicated the purposes of academic freedom. If, on the other hand, he questioned Armenti's impact on the intellectual quality of instruction at the university, such a critique might well be considered an extension of faculty expertise in pedagogy and scholarship.

With respect to the failing grade, a professional review would assess Brown's academic justification for issuing it, and under normal grading standards, a student who missed 80 percent of the classwork would indeed fail the course. Reviewers would also consider the fact that if the student had presented a medical or other legitimate excuse for missing most of the course, university administrators could have allowed the student to withdraw. The distinction between withdrawal and the grade of Incomplete favored by Armenti is that a student who withdraws must take the course afresh another semester, whereas a grade of Incomplete implies that the student should be able to earn a passing grade in the section in which he or she was already enrolled. In most instances, satisfying an Incomplete involves something on the order of taking a missed examination or handing in a late paper. By this standard, Brown's decision that an Incomplete was inappropriate when the student had missed 80 percent of the course was not unreasonable.

In the absence of more detailed information about the facts surrounding Brown's dismissal, it is possible only to speculate about the likely outcome of a professional review. The point is that because such reviews are sensitive to substantive academic values and standards, as the courts cannot be, they differ materially from the courts' simple assignment of authority to administrators without attempting to determine whether administrative actions are consistent with widely accepted professional norms for assessing teaching, scholarship, or other faculty speech. As AAUP documents beginning with the 1915 *Declaration* have repeatedly emphasized, if university scholarship and teaching are regulated by administrative whim without reference to the best practices of the profession or to cutting-edge knowledge in each content field, American universities cannot remain intellectually credible, nor can this nation maintain its status as a world leader in higher education.

Legal scholars have long been aware—and in most instances critical—of judicial deference to the judgment of university administrators. Similarly, they have long deplored the use of generic public-employee law in cases involving faculty in public universities. Nevertheless, the discussion of decisions that preceded *Garcetti v. Ceballos* was conducted at a low hum compared with the roar that greeted the application of *Garcetti* to academic-freedom cases. Among other things, *Garcetti*'s emphasis on the authority of supervisors to regulate the speech of employees is not compatible with such values as the promotion of intellectual debate and deference to content-area expertise. The reaction to *Garcetti* and subsequent decisions also reflects the fact that the academic community was, for the most part, taken by surprise. In light of the reasoning underlying such decisions as *Parate, Edwards,* and *Brown,* it ought not to have been. The courts have never provided significant First Amendment protection for the academic freedom of faculty, and the post-*Garcetti* decisions represent a logical progression rather than a dogleg in the conceptualization of constitutional, as opposed to professional, academic-freedom rights.

9

Caution! Paradigms May Shift

In light of *Garcetti* and its progeny, it is more urgent than ever that it be clear that the case for academic freedom is not now written, nor was it ever written, merely on legal litmus paper but in the history of the profession that recognizes universities that deserve to bear the name.

—American Association of University Professors, *Protecting an Independent Faculty Voice: Academic Freedom After Garcetti v. Ceballos*

RICHARD CEBALLOS WAS A DEPUTY DISTRICT attorney in Los Angeles County when, in February 2000, he reviewed an affidavit that had been used to secure a search warrant. Believing that the affidavit, given by a deputy sheriff, contained significant misrepresentations, he wrote a memorandum advising his superiors that the case should be dismissed. When his superiors went ahead with the prosecution, Ceballos shared his reservations with the trial court, which nonetheless found the warrant valid. Ceballos was subsequently reassigned to a less desirable position, transferred to another courthouse, and denied a promotion. He filed suit, asserting that the negative job actions were retaliatory and violated his rights under the First and Fourteenth Amendments. The federal district court ruled against him on the ground that even if his superiors' actions were retaliatory—a contention they denied—Ceballos's rights were not violated, because the speech in question had been undertaken in the course of his official duties and was thus subject to sanction by his superiors.

The U.S. Court of Appeals for the Ninth Circuit overturned the lower court's ruling in 2004. Applying the *Pickering/Connick* test, it found that Ceballos had spoken out on a matter of public concern and that his speech did not disrupt the operations of his office.[1] The court did not attempt to determine whether he had spoken as a citizen. Instead, based on a precedent within that circuit, it found that speech does not lose its First Amendment protection because it occurs in the course of one's duties as a public employee. "The mere fact that a public employee exposes individual wrongdoing or government misdeeds when making a regular as opposed to a special report does not, by itself, result in the denial of First Amendment protection. Whether a job duty is routine or non-routine is a far less important factor for purposes of First Amendment analysis than the content of the public employee's speech."[2] Accordingly, the court found that Ceballos's constitutional rights had been violated.

One of the three judges who heard the case, Diarmuid F. O'Scannlain, concurred in the decision because he agreed that the precedent upon which it was based did indeed apply. Nevertheless, he argued that the precedent had been wrongly decided. In his view, the court was obliged to determine whether Ceballos had spoken as a citizen or in pursuance of his duties as a public employee. While acknowledging that public employees retain their right to speak freely as citizens outside the scope of their employment, Judge O'Scannlain denied that the First Amendment protects speech that fulfills the requirements of a government job.

In a 2006 decision written by Justice Anthony Kennedy and joined by Chief Justice John Roberts and Justices Antonin Scalia, Clarence Thomas, and Samuel Alito, the Supreme Court reversed the decision of the Ninth Circuit. The majority agreed with O'Scannlain that public employees enjoy First Amendment protection only for their speech as citizens outside the scope of their jobs. Commenting on the *Pickering/Connick* test that the Ninth Circuit had applied, the Court noted that although Marvin Pickering's letter to the editor dealt with topics that affected the school district in which he worked, it was not written pursuant to his duties as a teacher. Speech is not automatically barred from First Amendment protection because its topic is in some way connected with the speaker's job, as Pickering's concern about school finances related to his position as a teacher. The operative question is whether the speech is undertaken in the course of fulfilling the job responsibilities for which a public employee is paid.

The Court found that unlike Pickering's letter to the editor, Ceballos's memorandum to his superiors regarding the deputy sheriff's affidavit fell within the responsibilities of his job. According to the Court, "[W]hen pub-

lic employees make statements pursuant to their official duties, the employees are not speaking as citizens for First Amendment purposes, and the
Constitution does not insulate their communications from employer discipline." By this standard, tests involving the content of speech—for instance,
whether it relates to a matter of public concern—yield to a heightened emphasis on the role of the speaker. Moreover, because Ceballos's speech fell
within the scope of what he was paid to do, the Court described his evaluation of the affidavit as something "the employer itself has commissioned or
created" and was thus entitled to regulate.[3]

Particularly troubling to civil libertarians is the Court's declaration that
even if Ceballos's duty required him to state his opinion of the affidavit, he
could nonetheless be penalized if his employers did not like what he said.
"The fact that his duties sometimes required him to speak or write," the
Court found, "does not mean his supervisors were prohibited from evaluating his performance."[4] On its face, this statement appears unexceptionable:
of course employers can evaluate how well employees perform their duties,
including those that involve writing or speaking. In context, however, it does
not distinguish between quality and viewpoint. Employees who are required
to express an opinion on a particular matter could face severe penalties, including loss of employment, for refusing to tailor their reports to fit the preferences of their supervisors even if the only way to comply with that standard would be to falsify their conclusions. This would hold true even if the
report involved a matter of great public concern. The Court noted that whistle-blowing laws might protect the speech of government employees in some
circumstances, but no such laws applied to Ceballos—nor, Justice David
Souter argued in dissent, are they sufficiently extensive in their coverage to
constitute an acceptable solution to this problem.

In the Court's view, the ability of public employees to discuss matters of
public concern outside the scope of their jobs constitutes sufficient exercise
of their First Amendment rights. As the Court observed, "Refusing to recognize First Amendment claims based on government employees' work
product does not prevent them from participating in public debate. The employees retain the prospect of constitutional protection for their contributions to the civic discourse. This prospect of protection, however, does not
invest them with a right to perform their jobs however they see fit." If the
distinction between speech as a citizen and speech as a public employee
were not preserved, the Court asserted, then judges rather than government
employers would be obliged to oversee the work product of employees who

alleged that their speech addressed matters of public concern. In view of the nature of public employment, such claims could be made with some regularity. In the words of the Court, "When an employee speaks as a citizen addressing a matter of public concern, the First Amendment requires a delicate balancing of the competing interests surrounding the speech and its consequences. When, however, the employee is simply performing his or her job duties, there is no warrant for a similar degree of scrutiny. To hold otherwise would be to demand permanent judicial intervention in the conduct of governmental operations to a degree inconsistent with sound principles of federalism and the separation of powers."[5]

Acknowledging that the free expression of ideas by knowledgeable and experienced public employees could be useful within their jobs, the Court pointed out that *Garcetti* said merely that government employers *could* penalize employees for unwelcome speech, not that they had to do so or indeed should do so. As the Court explained, nothing in *Garcetti* prevents government employers from establishing their own policies to protect the free expression of employees. In addition to encouraging valuable input, the Court suggested, such policies might prevent employees from feeling that the safest way to express their concerns would be to reveal them in a public forum outside the range of any activity associated with their jobs.

Recognizing that some government employers might wish to restrict employee speech as much as possible despite the advantages of encouraging free speech among employees, the Court warned employers not to construct excessively broad job descriptions in order to leave as little room as possible for their employees' free expression as citizens. "Formal job descriptions often bear little resemblance to the duties an employee actually is expected to perform, and the listing of a given task in an employee's written job description is neither necessary nor sufficient to demonstrate that conducting the task is within the scope of the employee's professional duties for First Amendment purposes." The Court added one further note to address the impact of this ruling on professors in public universities: "There is some argument that expression related to academic scholarship or classroom instruction implicates additional constitutional interests that are not fully accounted for by this Court's customary employee speech jurisprudence. We need not, and for that reason do not, decide whether the analysis we conduct today would apply in the same manner to a case involving speech related to scholarship or teaching."[6]

Four members of the Court dissented from the majority decision. Justices John Paul Stevens, David Souter (joined by Stevens and Ruth Bader Ginsburg), and Stephen Breyer wrote dissenting opinions suggesting that the majority went too far in its withdrawal of First Amendment protection from the speech of public employees in the course of their duties. In their view, the interest of government employers in regulating the workplace and in providing efficient service to the public must be weighed against the employees' interest in speaking out and the public benefit of having them do so. As Justice Stevens expressed it, "The proper answer to the question 'whether the First Amendment protects a government employee from discipline based on speech made pursuant to the employee's official duties' is 'Sometimes,' not 'Never.' Of course a supervisor may take corrective action when such speech is 'inflammatory or misguided.' But what if it is just unwelcome speech because it reveals facts that the supervisor would rather not have anyone else discover?"[7]

Justice Souter, in his dissent, emphasized the importance of allowing public employees to address serious deficiencies in the policies or operations of their offices without threat of retaliation. In his view, the government employer has the right to pursue "its chosen policy and objectives," and it can demand "competence, honesty, and judgment from employees who speak for it in doing their work. But I would hold that private and public interests in addressing official wrongdoing and threats to health and safety can outweigh the government's stake in the efficient implementation of policy, and when they do public employees who speak on these matters in the course of their duties should be eligible to claim First Amendment protection."[8]

According to the dissenting justices, the value of public employees' speech with respect to matters of public concern is no less, and may well be greater, when such matters arise in the course of their work. Justice Souter pointed out, for instance, that under *Garcetti*, a school principal whose job is to evaluate teacher performance could be fired for saying, no matter how accurately, that the superintendent's daughter is not doing a good job. "Would anyone deny that a prosecutor like Richard Ceballos may claim the interest of any citizen in speaking out against a rogue law enforcement officer, simply because his job requires him to express a judgment about the officer's performance? (But the majority says the First Amendment gives Ceballos no protection, even if his judgment in this case was sound and appropriately expressed.)" Further examples mentioned in Souter's dissent include an auditor who uncovers the embezzlement of public funds, a building inspector who reports an attempted bribe, and a police officer who refuses to obey an order to violate someone's constitutional rights. "The majority, however, places all these speakers beyond the reach of First Amendment protection against retaliation," Souter protested. He also addressed the matter of professors in public universities: "The ostensible domain beyond the pale of the First Amendment is spacious enough to include even the teaching of a public university professor, and I have to hope that today's majority does not mean to imperil First Amendment protection of academic freedom in public colleges and universities, whose teachers necessarily speak and write 'pursuant to official duties.'"[9]

Garcetti brings the story of academic freedom in America full circle. When the fledgling AAUP issued its 1915 *Declaration of Principles on Academic Freedom and Academic Tenure*, it did so in an environment in which the law assumed a master-servant relationship between trustees and faculty. In *Protecting an Independent Faculty Voice: Academic Freedom After Garcetti v. Ceballos* (2009), an AAUP subcommittee explained, "As this was the legal landscape on which the 1915 *Declaration* was mapped, it is not surprising that the drafters drew no support from the law and made no claim on it. Instead, the 1915 *Declaration* addressed the function of the university and so of the role of the faculty within it. The focus was conceptual; the practical consequences were anticipated to play out in institutional policies and practices and in the public's sympathetic understanding—not necessarily in the courts."[10] Following a long and circuitous legal journey that began with the anticommunist cases of the 1950s, *Garcetti* appears to have returned the legal landscape to something close to its 1915 status. Accordingly, *Protecting an Independent Faculty Voice* recommends doing exactly what the Supreme Court suggested in *Garcetti*: developing internal policies to define and protect academic freedom, as constitutional law has never done well and now, arguably, does not do at all.

The Children of *Garcetti*: K–12

As might be expected from the degree of control that school boards have always exercised over classroom speech, *Garcetti* has the potential to make far less of a difference in K–12 schools than in public universities. It would, however, be an exaggeration to say that *Garcetti* is irrelevant to K–12 instruction. To illustrate the impact of *Garcetti* on disputes involving the professional discretion of K–12 teachers, let us consider six lawsuits, two pre-*Garcetti* and four post-*Garcetti*.

The first of these cases, *Givhan v. Western Line Consolidated School District* (1979), was referenced by the Supreme Court as an example of a situation in which a teacher's speech would be protected under *Garcetti*. Bessie Givhan, a junior high school English teacher in Mississippi, complained to the principal that the school's hiring practices were racially biased. When her teaching contract was not renewed, she sued. The federal district court, finding that the failure to renew her contract was the direct result of her criticisms, ordered her reinstated. Reversing this decision, the U.S. Court of Appeals for the Fifth Circuit ruled that Givhan's speech was not constitutionally protected under *Pickering* because she had voiced her complaints in private conversations with the principal rather than in a public discussion. The Supreme Court disagreed. According to the Court, "The First Amendment forbids abridgment of the 'freedom of speech.' Neither the Amendment itself nor our decisions indicate that this freedom is lost to the public employee who arranges to communicate privately with his employer rather than to spread his views before the public. We decline to adopt such a view of the First Amendment."[11]

Givhan is mentioned in *Garcetti* to show that "[t]he First Amendment protects some expressions related to the speaker's job" even if the communication is private and occurs in the workplace. The Court suggested that Givhan's speech would have been protected even under *Garcetti* because, although Givhan spoke with her principal in his office, the topic she discussed —the district's hiring practices—fell outside the scope of her duties. Writing in dissent, Justice John Paul Stevens denied that Givhan's job description had anything to do with the outcome of that case. "Our silence [in *Givhan*] as to whether or not her speech was made pursuant to her job duties demonstrates that the point was immaterial," he protested. "That is equally true today, for it is senseless to let constitutional protection for exactly the same words hinge on whether they fall within a job description." Justice Souter made a similar point. "The difference between a case like *Givhan* and this one is that the subject of Ceballos's speech fell within the scope of his job responsibilities, whereas choosing personnel was not what the teacher was hired to do. The effect of the majority's constitutional line between these two cases, then, is that a *Givhan* schoolteacher is protected when complaining to the principal about hiring policy, but a school personnel officer would not be if he protested that the principal disapproved of hiring minority job applicants. This is an odd place to draw a distinction."[12] Expanding on these arguments, Martha M. McCarthy and Suzanne E. Eckes pointed out that the outcome of a future case along the same lines as *Givhan* would depend on whether the teacher's responsibilities could be construed to encompass an interest in how other teachers were hired. Particularly ironic, McCarthy and Eckes noted, is the fact that "if a public employee's specific role is to uncover wrongdoing, there is no protection for doing so."[13]

A pre-*Garcetti* K–12 case that would unquestionably have been decided differently under *Garcetti* is *Evans-Marshall v. Board of Education of the Tipp City Exempted Village School District* (2005). Shelley Evans-Marshall taught English at Tippecanoe High School in Tipp City, Ohio. During the academic year 2000–2001 she received good evaluations with no unsatisfactory ratings. The same was true of her first evaluation in the fall of 2001. The situation changed following two school board meetings at which members of the public complained about her use of what they described as obscene materials: Hermann Hesse's *Siddhartha*, Ray Bradbury's *Fahrenheit 451*, and Harper Lee's *To Kill a Mockingbird*. The principal, Charles Wray, subsequently gave Evans-Marshall her first negative review, admonishing her to seek the approval of her department chair before using "'[a]ny material containing graphic violence, sexual themes, profanity, suicide, drugs and alcohol." She replied in writing that the books contained no inappropriate material and that they had been selected and purchased by the school board. She later showed her students a film, *Romeo and Juliet*, rated PG-13. According to Evans-Marshall, films with that rating did not have to be cleared in advance with the administration. In March, Wray wrote, "'The evaluation from the first part of the year addressed several areas of concern that has [*sic*] arisen this year. There have been improvements but not enough to recommend a continuing contract.'"[14] When her contract was not renewed, she filed suit in federal district court.

The court rejected the school board's attempt to have the case dismissed, and the U.S. Court of Appeals for the Sixth Circuit upheld that ruling. According to the appeals court, the three novels and the film were, in themselves, constitutionally protected speech that touched on matters of public concern. As an ironic example, the court mentioned the discussion of government censorship in *Fahrenheit 451*. The court further noted, "Evans-Marshall alleges that the three novels 'had been purchased and approved by the Board.' Furthermore, the movie used in class was rated PG-13, and according to Evans-Marshall, could be shown without prior approval. Nonetheless, after a public outcry related to the use of the disputed materials, Evans-Marshall alleges that she was criticized publicly by Wray, received negative evaluations for the first time, and was eventually terminated. Such allegations are sufficient to establish protected First Amendment activity under the *Pickering* test, at least for the purposes of a motion to dismiss."[15]

Since Evans-Marshall's classroom speech clearly fell within the scope of her employment, she would presumably have lost the case under *Garcetti* even if she had been able to show at trial that the materials she was using dealt with matters of public concern and had been purchased and approved by the board. The principal's assertion in March that she had not followed his earlier instructions would have been more than enough to justify adverse job action. Advance notice of what speech is proscribed—held by some courts to be part of the *Hazelwood* test—does not appear to be required under *Garcetti*. Even if Wray had not informed Evans-Marshall of his expectations, *Garcetti* would arguably have allowed school officials to decline to renew her contract by virtue of their authority to penalize teachers for their classroom speech.

Among the K–12 cases decided since *Garcetti*, the most widely discussed is *Mayer v. Monroe County Community School Corporation* (2007). Deborah Mayer, an untenured first-year teacher, taught social studies in Clear Creek Elementary School in Monroe County, Indiana. Each Friday she used a school-approved newsletter, *Time for Kids,* in a current-events class. During a discussion of a newsletter story about protests against the war in Iraq, a student asked whether Mayer approved of peace marches. She replied that whenever she saw a sign saying "Honk for Peace," she honked. To emphasize the importance of finding peaceful solutions to disagreements, she referenced a conflict-resolution initiative at the school. The parents of a student in the class objected to what they saw as Mayer's insertion of her political views into her instruction, and the principal, Victoria Rogers, instructed her not to take sides in a political controversy. Rogers subsequently sent a memorandum to the entire faculty admonishing them not to confuse the school's advocacy of peaceful resolutions of student conflicts with support for peace in Iraq. In the memorandum, she announced the cancellation of the school's annual Peace Month. The protesting parents asked to have their daughter removed from Mayer's class, alleging that she was teaching below grade level, retaliating against their daughter, and continuing to discuss peace. Mayer denied those accusations.

Mayer's difficulties with the administration were not confined to the free-speech dispute. The parents of several children in her class had asked to have them moved to sections taught by other teachers because, they alleged,

Mayer talked down to the students and sometimes demeaned them. School officials also claimed that Mayer's interpersonal skills were poor and that her responses to complaints were unhelpful and unprofessional. When her contract was not renewed, she sued on the ground that the dismissal was impermissible retaliation for her constitutionally protected speech about peace marches. For purposes of the lawsuit, the court assumed that she had indeed been dismissed because of those remarks and set about determining whether they were constitutionally protected. The answer was no. The district court found that although Mayer's comments about peace marches dealt with a matter of public concern, she was speaking as a teacher who could be required to adhere to the school's curriculum. The court concluded, "Teachers, including Ms. Mayer, do not have a right under the First Amendment to express their opinions with their students during the instructional period, particularly if the teacher's supervisors have directed her not to do so. Here, the fact that Ms. Mayer's January 10, 2003, comments were made prior to any prohibitions by school officials does not establish that she had a First Amendment right to make these comments in the first place. Previous judicial holdings have recognized that teachers do not have a First Amendment right to arrogate control of the curricula."[16]

Mayer appealed on the basis of *Pickering/Connick*, but by the time the case reached the U.S. Court of Appeals for the Seventh Circuit, the Supreme Court had decided *Garcetti*. Accordingly, the appeals court ruled that Mayer's employers could penalize her for speech related to her duties as a teacher.

> This is so in part because the school system does not 'regulate' teachers' speech as much as it *hires* that speech. Expression is a teacher's stock in trade, the commodity she sells to her employer in exchange for a salary. A teacher hired to lead a social-studies class can't use it as a platform for a revisionist perspective that Benedict Arnold wasn't really a traitor, when the approved program calls him one; a high-school teacher hired to explicate *Moby-Dick* in a literature class can't use *Cry, The Beloved Country* instead, even if Paton's book better suits the instructor's style and point of view; a math teacher can't decide that calculus is more important than trigonometry and decide to let Hipparchus and Ptolemy slide in favor of Newton and Leibniz.[17]

Rejecting Mayer's contention that academic freedom insulated public-school teachers from *Garcetti*, the court concluded, "It is enough to hold that the First Amendment does not entitle primary and secondary teachers, when conducting the education of captive audiences, to cover topics, or advocate viewpoints, that depart from the curriculum adopted by the school system."[18]

The outcome of *Mayer* has been the subject of widespread and sometimes impassioned discussion. In a 2008 article, Alison Lima protested that the court should not have found that Mayer was at fault for not teaching the curriculum, since she was doing exactly that when she conducted the discussion of the *Time for Kids* newsletter. Responding briefly and on point to a student's curriculum-related question, Lima argued, has nothing to do with refusing to teach the curriculum. While agreeing that a teacher has no right to proselytize or coerce her students to share her opinions, Lima denied that a brief answer to a direct question constituted legitimate grounds for disciplinary action. On the contrary, she maintained, K–12 schools have a responsibility to teach students how to deal with divergent views, and rulings such as *Mayer* will intimidate teachers into avoiding the robust discussions necessary to achieve this goal.[19]

In a 2009 article, Neal H. Hutchens treated *Mayer* as an example of the courts' inappropriate reliance on "simple rhetoric that casts democratically elected school boards versus individualistic teachers seeking to impose their views and values on captive students." In his opinion, such a formulation militates against providing teachers with even modest protection for their speech. As he observed,

> The problem with the rhetoric in a case like *Mayer* concerning the need for school officials to be able to control teachers' in-class speech is equating even modest First Amendment protections for teachers with potential chaos in the curriculum. Even courts sympathetic to teachers' speech have recognized the dominant role of school boards in determining curricular and pedagogical matters. Accordingly, schools are not facing a problem of elementary and secondary teachers armed with extensive First Amendment academic freedoms running amok in the classroom and disregarding the approved curriculum. Instead, the reality confronting courts, and schools for that matter, involves whether teachers should be bereft of even limited First Amendment protections for in-class speech.[20]

Hutchens also argued in favor of a standard, adopted in some decisions based on *Hazelwood*, under which teachers would have to be informed in advance of the school's rules regarding classroom speech. "Far from a battle for control over the classroom between the school board and its teachers, courts, in considering applying *Garcetti* to teachers' classroom speech, must decide whether teachers merit modest First Amendment protection for in-class

communications, namely some kind of reasonable notice that certain categories of speech are prohibited."[21] From this perspective, he argued that the
Mayer court was wrong to disregard the fact that the school district's policy
against pairing the school's peace initiative with the war in Iraq had not been
promulgated when Mayer made her remarks.

Although *Mayer* dealt with in-class speech, the Seventh Circuit was not
concerned with the Supreme Court's suggestion that *Garcetti* might not
"apply in the same manner to a case involving speech related to scholarship
or teaching," because the court interpreted that reservation as pertaining
only to postsecondary education. In *Lee v. York County School Division* (2007),
however, the U.S. Court of Appeals for the Fourth Circuit interpreted the
Court's language more broadly.[22] William Lee, a Spanish teacher, sued the
school district after officials removed religious materials that he had posted
on the bulletin boards in his classroom. The Fourth Circuit ruled in favor of
the school district, but it did so on the basis of *Pickering/Connick* rather than
Garcetti because of uncertainty about whether *Garcetti* applies to classroom
speech at any level.

Another post-*Garcetti* K–12 case, *Williams v. Dallas Independent School District* (2007), relates squarely to the concerns about whistle-blowing expressed
by Justices Stevens and Souter. Gregory Williams, athletic director and head
football coach at Pinkston High School in Dallas, Texas, made repeated attempts to resolve discrepancies in the finances of the athletic program. The
accounts were handled by the office manager, who reported to the principal.
He wrote to both of them complaining about what he considered to be not
only unprofessional accounting practices but misappropriation of funds.
He was thereupon removed from his position as athletic director, and in the
spring term, he was placed on administrative leave and his contract was not
renewed. Shortly afterward, the school district placed the principal and the
office manager on leave pending an investigation of financial irregularities,
but Williams was not reinstated. He filed suit, contending that his speech
about the school officials' handling of the funds allocated to athletics closely
paralleled the protected speech in *Pickering*.

In a pre-*Garcetti* ruling, the district court granted summary judgment in
favor of the school district on the ground that Williams's interactions with
the principal and the office manager constituted a private employee dispute
and not the speech of a citizen on a matter of public concern. For this reason, it is not clear that Williams would have prevailed even if the lawsuit
had been decided on the basis of *Pickering*. By the time the case reached the

U.S. Court of Appeals for the Fifth Circuit, however, *Garcetti* had been decided. The appeals court declared, "Williams's reliance on *Pickering* . . . is
now inapposite. The Supreme Court's recent pronouncement in *Garcetti v.
Ceballos* added a threshold layer to the *Pickering* balancing test. Under
Garcetti, we must shift our focus from the content of the speech to the role
the speaker occupied when he said it. Emphasizing the distinction between
a speaker acting in her role as 'citizen' and her role as 'employee,' *Garcetti*
held that the First Amendment does not protect 'expressions made pursuant
to their official duties.' Even if the speech is of great social importance, it is
not protected by the First Amendment so long as it was made pursuant to
the worker's official duties."[23]

Based on this standard, the court found that Williams's interactions with
the principal and the office manager were undertaken "in the course of performing his job as Athletic Director; thus, the speech contained therein is
not protected by the First Amendment."[24] As Justices Stevens and Souter
had anticipated, the application of *Garcetti* proved to be insensitive to the
social benefit of exposing financial irregularities in the school system, which
are most likely to be recognized by school employees who deal with the affected accounts in the course of their jobs. But since the district court had
already ruled against Williams before *Garcetti* was decided, the same might
be said of the *Pickering* standard on which that decision was based—further
evidence that little protection existed for the free speech of public employees even before *Garcetti* was decided. At a minimum, Williams's failure to
prevail in the district court under *Pickering* raises doubt about *Garcetti*'s impact on the outcome of that case.

No such question exists about the effect of *Garcetti* on *Weintraub v. Board
of Education of the City of New York* (2010). David Weintraub, a teacher in an
elementary school in Brooklyn, filed a union grievance complaining that
school officials had not dealt effectively with a fifth-grade student who threw
books at him on two occasions. School officials later gave him poor performance reviews and accused him of a variety of offenses that he denied, including sexual abuse of a student and assault on another teacher. Finally,
his employment was terminated. He sued, claiming that the school officials
had fired him for filing the union grievance and that the dismissal violated
his First Amendment rights. The school district asked the federal district
court to dismiss the case, but the court declined to do so. Based on *Pickering*, the court found that "it cannot seriously be contested that the content
of speech questioning an administrative response, or lack thereof, to disci-

pline problems in the classroom relates to a matter of public concern, regardless of whether that speech comes from a elected official, citizen, or
teacher."[25]

After the Supreme Court decided *Garcetti*, the federal district court re-
considered its decision in *Weintraub* at the request of the school district. It
found that "*Garcetti* works an innovation upon the law by transmuting this
principle, formerly a simple corollary to the proposition that a state employee's speech must concern a matter of public interest in order to enjoy
First Amendment protection, into a new and independent element of a
claim of First Amendment retaliation—that the public employee's speech
was made in the employee's capacity as a private citizen rather than as an
employee, a criterion that is never satisfied when the employee speech at
issue was made pursuant to the employee's official duties."[26] On this basis,
the court reversed its earlier ruling and dismissed the case, except that Weintraub was free to pursue a complaint based on retaliation for his private conversations with fellow teachers.

The U.S. Court of Appeals for the Second Circuit upheld this ruling in
2010. Among the issues it considered was a point raised in *Garcetti*: the difficulty of determining the scope of an employee's job responsibilities. Weintraub argued that his job description did not include filing union grievances
against school officials, but the court, employing a broader standard, considered whether the action in question was undertaken within the framework of the employee's job. According to the court, "[U]nder the First
Amendment, speech can be 'pursuant to' a public employee's official job
duties even though it is not required by, or included in, the employee's job
description, or in response to a request by the employer. In particular, we
conclude that Weintraub's grievance was 'pursuant to' his official duties because it was 'part-and-parcel of his concerns' about his ability to 'properly ex-
ecute his duties' as a public school teacher—namely, to maintain classroom
discipline, which is an indispensable prerequisite to effective teaching and
classroom learning."[27] The court also noted that Weintraub was able to file
the union grievance only because he was an employee of the school district.
Unlike writing a letter to a newspaper or speaking at a public meeting, filing a union grievance against school officials has no parallel among the options open to citizens in general.

As the comparison of pre-*Garcetti* and post-*Garcetti* rulings demonstrates,
the primary effect of that decision on K–12 schools, where curricular decisions have always rested with boards of education, is that it allows school of-

ficials to penalize teachers for anything they say in the course of their employment. Such distinctions as whether a teacher's speech deals with a matter of public concern or whether a school official's action serves a legitimate pedagogical purpose now play an even more limited role than they did before. Under *Garcetti*, a teacher's on-the-spot response to a student question may be penalized, regardless of its content, even if the teacher had no way of knowing that school officials would disapprove of it. To anyone familiar with the real world of K–12 teaching and the behavior of students at that level—as the courts sometimes appear not to be—that places teachers in an impossible situation. The chilling effect on discussions of ideas between teachers and students is too obvious to require amplification, and as Kevin G. Welner pointed out, an educational system that ties teachers absolutely to prefabricated board-approved messages cannot be expected to foster critical thinking or facility in dealing with diverse views. Moreover, what Karen Daly called the "infantilization" of teachers and Neal Hutchens described as the lack of even modest protection for teachers as professionals is widely viewed as a factor in the destructively high turnover among teachers.[28] Thus, although *Garcetti* is generally associated with the academic freedom of university professors and has the potential to make a greater difference there than in K–12 education, its relevance to cases involving K–12 teachers is not negligible.

The Children of *Garcetti:* Public Universities

On behalf of the *Garcetti* majority, Justice Kennedy wrote: "Justice Souter suggests today's decision may have important ramifications for academic freedom, at least as a constitutional value. There is some argument that expression related to academic scholarship or classroom instruction implicates additional constitutional interests that are not fully accounted for by this Court's customary employee-speech jurisprudence. We need not, and for that reason do not, decide whether the analysis we conduct today would apply in the same manner to a case involving speech related to scholarship or teaching."[29] This reservation about how, or indeed whether, the reasoning of *Garcetti* applies to the speech of faculty is henceforth referred to as the *Garcetti* caveat.

To explore the practical implications of the *Garcetti* caveat, let us consider four post-*Garcetti* lawsuits involving faculty in public universities. Justice Kennedy's use of the phrase *"related to scholarship or teaching"* (emphasis added) is particularly important to three of these cases because they deal with situations in which faculty who were not engaged in research or teaching expressed views based on their pedagogical or scholarly expertise. The fourth case concerns classroom instruction as such.

The first of these lawsuits to reach a federal district court arose from a dispute between Kevin Renken, a tenured associate professor of mechanical engineering at the University of Wisconsin-Milwaukee, and William Gregory, the dean of his college. Renken was the principal investigator (PI) on a grant from the National Science Foundation (NSF), which provided $66,499 over three years toward the establishment of a thermal engineering laboratory. The purpose was to improve undergraduate education by adding laboratory work to courses that did not already include it. The university agreed to contribute the equivalent of $222,667 to the project as its share of the costs. Part of the university's contribution was to take the form of providing laboratory space and releasing faculty from teaching duties to provide time for grant-related activities.

In May 2002, Gregory sent a letter to Renken and John Reisel, another faculty member working on the grant, asking them to sign off on certain provisions for the university's cost-sharing. Renken and Reisel replied that the dean's proposal did not include enough laboratory space, and they objected to its allocation of funds to be spent on laboratories and release time from teaching. In their view, the dean's proposal allocated NSF funds to cover part of what should have been the university's contribution, and they refused to sign the letter. When they complained that student workers were not being paid and purchasing orders were not being processed, the dean responded that no account could be activated to fund the grant activities until they signed off on the letter.

In July 2002, Dean Gregory sent a revised letter omitting the previous reference to laboratory space. The letter indicated that Renken and Reisel knew that no funds would be paid from the grant until they signed, and it warned that if they did not sign, the university would cancel the grant. Renken declined to sign, but he asked to be released from teaching a course in accord with the terms of the grant. In August 2002, Gregory told Renken and Reisel that the grant funds would be returned to the NSF. The following November, the dean of the Graduate School presented them with a compromise proposal, which they rejected. The university then returned the grant funds to the NSF.

Renken sued, alleging that the university had violated his First and Fourteenth Amendment rights by reducing his pay, denying him a merit raise, defaming him, and otherwise discriminating against him because of his opposition to their plan for the NSF grant. In a pre-*Garcetti* ruling in 2005, the district court dismissed all the allegations except his claim that his First Amendment rights had been violated. In 2007, following *Garcetti*, the court dismissed the First Amendment claim on the ground that Renken's protests against the administration's handling of the grant constituted speech undertaken in the course of his official duties. Moreover, the court stated, even if the speech were that of a citizen, it would still not be protected, because he spoke in connection with a private interest—his teaching and research —and not on a matter of public concern.

The U.S. Court of Appeals for the Seventh Circuit upheld the district court's decision. In *Renken v. Gregory* (2008), the appeals court said that Renken was not entitled to First Amendment protection, because he spoke in the course of his public employment. Despite his assertion that his work on the grant was done at his discretion "'*while* in the course of his job and not as a *requirement* of his job,'" the court found that when he complained about the university's handling of the grant funds, he "was speaking as a faculty employee, and not as a private citizen, because administering the grant as a PI fell within the teaching and service duties that he was employed to perform." Even if Renken was not explicitly required to apply for grants, or for that particular grant, he had done so in the course of fulfilling his work-related obligations. "Renken made his complaints regarding the University's use of NSF funds pursuant to his official duties as a University professor," the decision states. "Therefore, his speech was not protected by the First Amendment."[30] Although the Seventh Circuit clearly identified Renken's grant activities as part of his teaching obligation, it did not mention the *Garcetti* caveat. Rather, the court acted on the assumption that university professors may be penalized for any and all speech undertaken in the course of their jobs.

A more complex case involving alleged retaliation for arguments with administrators arose when Juan Hong, a professor in the Department of Chemical Engineering and Materials Science at the University of California, Irvine (UCI), did not receive a merit raise. Hong claimed that four incidents had led to the retaliatory denial of the raise. The first occurred in 2002, when he participated in the review of a colleague, Professor Ying Chang. Chang's accomplishments included the acquisition of a $400,000 research grant, and Hong reported a rumor that her husband's company had donated half that amount in equipment, thus qualifying her for a matching grant from the university. Hong argued at a faculty meeting that if the rumor proved to be true, she should not be given credit for having won a competitive grant, and he sought the approval of the department chair, Professor Stanley Grant, to investigate.[31] After Chang resigned, Hong asked UCI officials to insert a letter from him into her file and then send the file to the dean.

In 2003, Hong complained to Grant about the use of department funds to pay part-time lecturers for teaching courses that should, he felt, have been taught by regular faculty. Grant subsequently made an effort to reduce the use of lecturers. In the same year, Professor Farghalli Mohamed applied for an accelerated merit raise, and Hong voted against it and wrote a letter dissenting from the positive recommendation that Mohamed received. At a faculty meeting, Hong alleged that Mohamed had improperly included two doctoral students from outside the university in his list of supervised students and that he had mischaracterized two conference papers as refereed publications. When Mohamed received the salary increase and sent an e-mail thanking the department for its support, Hong called for an investigation to determine whether Grant and other UCI administrators had acted inappropriately in approving the raise. Hong's final clash with administrators prior to the lawsuit occurred in 2004, when Grant extended an informal job offer to a candidate pending approval by the department. Hong protested that by acting in advance of the department vote, Grant had violated faculty self-governance as practiced at UCI.

Hong was scheduled to be evaluated for a merit raise in 2003, but he asked to defer it for a year because his research productivity had been insufficient. When he applied for the raise in 2004, he wrote a self-advocacy statement which, according to the court, "listed his success in attracting extramural grants as 'zero.' He described his participation in peer-reviewed publications as 'average' and 'minimal.'"[32] Hong presented no awards, honors, or other evidence of recognition in his field. University officials informed Hong that his research was inadequate to justify the raise, and Grant was instructed to assign him additional teaching because he was not doing enough scholarship to justify the reduced teaching load of a research professor.

Asserting that these actions constituted retaliation for his criticisms with respect to Chang, Mohamed, the prospective hire, and the use of lecturers, Hong filed a Whistleblower Retaliation Complaint with the university's Board of Regents. The board rejected it because, among other things, "there was ample evidence to support the denial of Mr. Hong's merit increase, an increased teaching load and a proposed change in series from full Professor."[33] Hong then filed a lawsuit pro se—that is, acting as his own attorney —alleging that Grant and other UCI officials had violated his First Amendment rights. The administrators responded that the decision to deny the merit raise was based on Hong's record as a scholar, not on his criticism of colleagues and university officials. They added that even if the court found that retaliation had been involved, Hong's suit would still have no merit because the speech in question had been undertaken pursuant to his duties as a faculty member and made him subject to discipline by university authorities.

Like the courts that decided pre-*Garcetti* cases involving academic freedom, the federal district court made no attempt to adjudicate the academic merits of the dispute—in this instance, Hong's eligibility for a merit raise. Rather, it concerned itself with defining locus of control with respect to faculty speech. As the basis for making this determination, the court found that "[w]hile Mr. Hong's professional responsibilities undoubtedly include teaching and research, they also include a wide range of academic, administrative and personnel functions in accordance with UCI's self-governance principle. . . . As an active participant in his institution's self-governance, Mr. Hong has a professional responsibility to offer feedback, advice and criticism about his department's administration and operation from his perspective as a tenured, experienced professor. UCI allows for expansive faculty involvement in the interworkings of the University, and it is therefore the professional responsibility of the faculty to exercise that authority."[34]

To Hong, "professional responsibility to offer feedback, advice, and criticism" meant that he was entitled to do so without fear of retaliation. The court, however, cited *Garcetti* to the effect that speech undertaken in the course of a public employee's job is commissioned by the employer and is subject to the employer's control. Accordingly, the court said of Professor Chang's review, "UCI 'commissioned' Mr. Hong's involvement in the peer review process and his participation is therefore part of his official duties as a faculty member. The University is free to regulate statements made in the course of that process without judicial interference." Similarly, in discussing Professor Mohamed's review, the court stated, "This type of feedback and criticism was 'commissioned' by UCI when it established the faculty's integral role in peer evaluations. As such, it was within Mr. Hong's official duties as a faculty member and is not protected."[35]

In these passages, as elsewhere in *Hong v. Grant* (2007), the court treated UCI's governance structure as a corporate hierarchy. By contrast, the AAUP maintains that "[i]nstitutional rules or policies providing for faculty participation do not delegate authority to subordinates in a hierarchy; they recognize the faculty as a body of cognate authority whose individual and collective counsel should be sought, even whose approval must be secured in some matters before institutional policies may be adopted or actions taken."[36] Thus defined, the role of professors in public universities is inconsistent with the assumption that their participation in university governance constitutes speech hired or commissioned by administrators who are entitled to penalize the expression of views that deviate from a corporate orthodoxy.

Pursuing its view of the relationship between university faculty and administrators, the court stated, with presumably unintended irony, that university officials must have "wide latitude" to regulate faculty speech "if UCI is to accomplish its very important educational and research mission."[37] In reality, the educational and research mission of a public university can be achieved only if faculty are free to provide candid expert advice independent of what the administration might wish to hear. A related irony, or perhaps a paradox, is that under *Hong*, UCI's commitment to including professors in academic decisionmaking reduces the range of faculty speech protected by the First Amendment. If a university values faculty input enough to make it part of a professor's job, as UCI does, the consequence is to render the faculty subject to discipline if what they say displeases the administration.

Hong appealed his case to the U.S. Court of Appeals for the Ninth Circuit, and at the time of this writing, it has yet to be heard. In support of his appeal, the AAUP and the Thomas Jefferson Center for the Protection of Free Expression filed an amicus curiae brief arguing, among other things, that the *Garcetti* caveat concerning "speech related to scholarship or teaching" extends to Hong's comments on the qualifications of colleagues and the staffing practices of his department.[38] By this reasoning, the district court should not have acted on the assumption that *Garcetti* applies to such speech, since the Supreme Court has reserved judgment on that point. The authors of the brief also wrote that faculty in public universities cannot fulfill their social function if the only statements that enjoy First Amendment protection are those "that fall so far beyond the speaker's field of expertise as to be valueless to the general public, lawmakers, and others who depend upon scholarly guidance and counsel."[39]

As these arguments suggest, the real significance of the Ninth Circuit's impending decision is not what it will say about Professor Hong's merit raise but how it will affect the academic freedom of the faculty as a whole. Hong himself delayed his merit review for a year because of a scholarly performance he acknowledged to be "minimal," and just as he participated in Mohamed's merit-raise review, his colleagues were presumably consulted about his. Accordingly, it is by no means clear that the denial of the merit raise constituted retaliation for his speech, nor is a federal court the appropriate venue for a substantive review of a faculty member's academic achievements. The question before the Ninth Circuit is whether a master-servant relationship exists between the faculty and the administration such that professors share their expert opinions at their own risk.

The U.S. Court of Appeals for the Third Circuit addressed the same question when it decided *Gorum v. Sessoms* in March 2009. The dispute that led to *Gorum* began in 2004, when an irregularity in the record of a student at Delaware State University (DSU) sparked an audit of grade changes.[40] The audit revealed that the chair of the Mass Communications Department, Professor Wendell Gorum, had changed other instructors' grades without their knowledge or consent. To be sure, decisions such as *Parate v. Isibor* (1989) and *Edwards v. California University of Pennsylvania* (1998) upheld the right of university administrators to change grades given by faculty, but Professor Gorum undertook this action on his own without authorization from the dean or the central administration. An investigation by a disciplinary committee found that he had given students, particularly athletes, passing grades in courses that they had failed, had never attended, or had dropped. In all, the committee identified forty-eight grade changes that, in its view, "undermine[d] the very tenets of the educational profession and [rose] to a level deserving condemnation by the academic community." Nevertheless, the committee stopped short of recommending dismissal. Gorum contended that a generally lax atmosphere existed at DSU within which rules were not enforced and administrators were not held accountable for their conduct, and the committee agreed. Its report suggested that Gorum's actions represented the "tip of the iceberg" and that he himself was "the scapegoat (albeit a blamable scapegoat)."[41] Accordingly, the committee recommended that he be removed from his chairmanship, suspended for two years without pay, and put on probation on his return.

The president of DSU, Allen L. Sessoms, rejected the committee's recommendation and asked the board of trustees to fire Gorum. He denied knowledge of any misbehavior at DSU comparable to Gorum's and vowed to penalize any administrator found to have committed similar infractions. The board dismissed Gorum in 2005, and he filed suit in 2006, claiming that he was being penalized for his repeated criticism of Sessoms. Three incidents, he alleged, had led to the termination of his employment. First, he had spoken before the Faculty Senate to oppose offering the DSU presidency to Sessoms. Second, he had vigorously defended a football player who had brought a gun to campus, and when Sessoms suspended the student, Gorum had hired and paid an attorney to represent him. Third, in his capacity as chair of a speakers committee, he had derailed an attempt to have the president speak at a fraternity prayer breakfast.

Citing *Garcetti*, the attorneys representing DSU argued that Gorum's speech was not constitutionally protected, because it was that of a public employee acting within the duties of his position. They also contended that the decision to dismiss him had not been based on his opposition to Sessoms and that he would have been fired even if the events he cited had never occurred. The district court granted summary judgment in favor of DSU, and the Third Circuit upheld the decision. According to the appeals court, Gorum's opposition to the hiring of Sessoms, his defense of the gun-carrying student athlete, and his participation in the choice of a speaker for the fraternity prayer breakfast were all undertaken in the course of his professional duties. Moreover, based on a precedent involving the Delaware State Police, the court applied a standard of general public-employee law that is particularly inapposite to the culture of public universities: that employees are subject to discipline for speech based on specialized knowledge acquired in the course of their jobs. This formulation is fundamentally incompatible with academic freedom, which protects faculty speech from constraint precisely because of the professional expertise and experience on which that speech is based.

Unlike the courts in *Renken* and *Hong*, the Third Circuit took note of the *Garcetti* caveat relating to the speech of professors in public universities, but it found that the caveat did not apply to Gorum's speech.

> In determining that Gorum did not speak as a citizen when engaging in his claimed protected activities, we are aware that the Supreme Court did not answer in *Garcetti* whether the "official duty" analysis "would apply in the same manner to a case involving speech related to scholarship or teaching." We recognize as well that "There is some argument that expression related to academic scholarship or classroom instruction implicates additional con-

stitutional interests that are not fully accounted for by . . . customary employee-speech jurisprudence." But here we apply the official duty test because Gorum's actions so clearly were not "speech related to scholarship or
teaching," and because we believe that such a determination here does not
"imperil First Amendment protection of academic freedom in public colleges and universities."[42]

Consistent with the limitations placed on faculty speech elsewhere in the
decision, the court's interpretation of the *Garcetti* caveat reflected a narrow
understanding of "speech related to scholarship or teaching." Under a
broader interpretation, Gorum's work with the fraternity and with the student who brought a gun to campus could be considered related to his teaching, and his evaluation of Sessoms as a candidate for the presidency could
be classified as a conclusion reached on the basis of his expertise as a teacher
and a scholar.

Having placed Gorum's speech within a wide range of faculty expression
subject to control by the administration, the Third Circuit went on to rule
that the three incidents Gorum cited were not the cause of his dismissal.
Although the DSU administration could presumably have fired Gorum for
his speech, the court found that it had not in fact done so. "Gorum's arguments are, we deem, makeweight attempts to counter his dismissal for doc-
toring student grades. Gorum violated a key part of the academic code, and
this justified his termination notwithstanding the normal protections of
tenure."[43]

The Third Circuit's determination that the *Garcetti* caveat did not apply to
Gorum was based on the finding that Gorum's expression was not "speech
related to scholarship or teaching." By contrast, *Sheldon v. Dhillon* (2009)
dealt squarely with the relevance of the *Garcetti* caveat to an instructor's
classroom speech. June Sheldon was an adjunct instructor in the San José/
Evergreen Community College District, where she had taught biology and
microbiology since 1986. In the summer of 2007, a student in a course on
human heredity asked about the genetic basis of homosexuality. According
to Sheldon, she "answered the student's question by noting the complexity
of the issue, providing a genetic example mentioned in the textbook, and
referring students to the perspective of a German scientist," Dr. Gunter
Dorner. She also "mentioned that Dr. Dorner's views were only one set of
theories in the 'nature versus nurture' debate" and "briefly described what
the students would learn later in the course, that 'homosexual behavior
may be influenced by both genes and environment.'" A student who was

offended by Sheldon's response filed a complaint alleging that she had "made 'offensive and unscientific' statements, including that there 'aren't any real lesbians' and that 'there are hardly any gay men in the Middle East because the women are treated very nicely.'"[44]

Officials in the community college district conducted an investigation that included consultation with full-time biology professors, although the extent to which the faculty concurred in the outcome is in dispute. The administration concluded "that Sheldon was teaching misinformation as science, and that the statements were grievous enough to warrant withdrawing her course assignments for the spring semester."[45] Sheldon's name was removed from the seniority list of adjunct instructors, and with the approval of the board of trustees, her employment with the district was terminated.

Represented by attorneys from the Alliance Defense Fund and the Pacific Justice Institute, Sheldon sued in federal district court, claiming that her classroom speech was protected by the First Amendment. The community college district responded that under *Garcetti*, the First Amendment did not apply, because "when engaging in classroom instruction, the teacher is performing her duties as a public employee and not speaking as a private citizen."[46] Focusing on the *Garcetti* caveat, the court pointed out that the Supreme Court had not yet decided whether, or to what extent, the reasoning of *Garcetti* extends to classroom speech. Accordingly, the court opted to decide *Sheldon* under a pre-*Garcetti* standard.

Since California is in the Ninth Circuit, the district court examined that circuit's earlier decisions and found a precedent that had been decided on the basis of a test derived from *Hazelwood v. Kuhlmeier* (1988): whether the regulation of speech by school officials is "reasonably related to legitimate pedagogical concerns."[47] Based on this standard, the court found that if Sheldon's "instructional speech was within the parameters of the approved curriculum and within academic norms," then "the defendants' actions were not reasonably related to legitimate pedagogical concerns."[48] Because the professional competence of Sheldon's speech was in dispute, as were other key facts, the court rejected the district's motion to dismiss her complaint without a trial. To be sure, her status as an adjunct faculty member hired semester by semester meant that she was a temporary employee, but the court found that "[e]ven though Sheldon could have been discharged for no reason whatsoever, and had no constitutional right to a hearing prior to the decision not to rehire her, she may nonetheless establish a claim to reinstatement if the decision not to rehire her was made by reason of her exercise of constitutionally protected First Amendment freedoms."[49] At the time of this writing, a trial is pending.

Mending the Constitutional Fence

As the AAUP points out in the 1915 *Declaration,* if university faculty are to fulfill their duty to the public, the expert conclusions that they reach must be their own and must be widely recognized as their own. A department promotion and tenure committee, for instance, cannot serve its crucial purpose as a gatekeeper unless its members are free to express truthfully their opinion of each candidate's work. As highly educated and experienced experts in the candidate's field, it is their right and their obligation to represent accurately the degree to which the candidate's teaching and scholarship are sound, original, and valuable. Similarly, broader faculty committees whose members may not be experts in the same discipline are responsible for determining the extent to which the candidate's work, as evaluated by experts in his or her field, has met the standards for retention, promotion, or a merit raise at that institution. Without that information, which can be tendered only by faculty who are free to speak their minds, no university can adequately assess the achievements of the people it retains to conduct the scholarship and teaching that justify its existence.

For these reasons, *Hong* is perhaps the most troubling of the post-*Garcetti* decisions because it explicitly states that administrators, having assigned faculty to provide an expert review of a colleague's work, are free to penalize any professor who says something that they do not like. Although it is not uncommon for administrators to have the authority to reject the faculty's recommendations, there is a significant difference between openly overruling the faculty and creating a climate in which what professors say is not, or may not be, what they think. Even if faculty genuinely agree with administrators in a particular instance, that agreement would be useless as a scholarly validation of administrative actions if a pervasive atmosphere of intimidation tainted every faculty recommendation with the suspicion of sycophancy and self-interest. The same reasoning applies to faculty involvement in decisions having to do with program development, course assignment policies, grant management, curriculum, grading standards, admission to academic programs, and a host of other matters directly and indirectly related to scholarship and teaching. It is not an exaggeration to say that without candid expert input into academic decisionmaking related to, but separate from, teaching and scholarship, American public universities would stand no chance of remaining competitive in the world market.

A final consideration relates to the differences between public universities and other public workplaces. The reasoning underlying not only *Garcetti* but also earlier decisions, such as *Pickering* and *Connick,* is that without control over employee speech, government employers cannot preserve order in the workplace and facilitate the efficient delivery of services to the public. Accordingly, when speaking and writing fall within an employee's job description, that work product is deemed to constitute speech for hire commissioned by the government to convey, not the employee's message, but the government's. Therein lies the most fundamental flaw in the application of generic public-employee law to faculty in public universities. Paradoxical as it may seem, a public university would violate, not fulfill, its public duty if it interfered with the free production of the teaching and scholarship that are not merely the means of achieving its goal but the goal itself. To be sure, university administrators are entitled and indeed obligated to evaluate the quality of faculty work, but "quality" must mean meeting the standards of the field as collectively defined by its experts, not conforming to administrative or public preconceptions. Far from being a disruption to the work of a university or an obstacle to its ability to serve the public, controversial speech is its heart's blood.

As the Supreme Court pointed out in *Garcetti,* even if faculty academic freedom is not protected by the First Amendment, that does not mean that it cannot be protected at all. In reality, it has never enjoyed much constitutional protection despite ringing rhetoric affirming its value, usually in cases that were decided on some other basis. Accordingly, two questions remain to be answered. Is it possible and desirable to provide First Amendment protection for faculty academic freedom? And how might it be protected otherwise?

As a means of clarifying the constitutional issues affecting academic freedom, Robert M. O'Neil cited the Supreme Court's decision in *Rust v. Sullivan* (1991), which concerned the right of doctors providing government-funded health services to discuss abortion with their patients. In that case, the Court declared that the government was entitled to fund only speech that conveyed its own message. Nevertheless, O'Neil pointed out, the government may also provide funding whose purpose is served not by mandating the dissemination of a governmental message but by enabling the speech of others. "One could differentiate, for example, between workplace situations in which government control of the employee's message is integral to the agency's responsibility for management of the workplace and those in which such government power or control is incidental to performance of the tasks and functions of the workplace," he wrote.[50]

A situation in which government control of employee speech was deemed inconsistent with the function of a government agency arose in *Polk County v. Dodson* (1981), in which the Supreme Court ruled that although public defenders are public employees, their speech cannot be controlled by the state. Because the reasoning of *Polk County* is based on the attorney-client relationship, it does not apply directly to university faculty. More broadly, however, the decision effectively concedes that the government may employ people to carry out tasks that are constitutionally inconsistent with adherence to a government-approved message. At a minimum, *Polk County* acknowledges that public workplaces differ among themselves with respect to the relationship between government control of employee speech and the agency's ability to perform its intended function.

Based on the premise that the speech of professors in public universities is not that of the state, Sheldon Nahmod has suggested that although public universities may penalize faculty for failing to meet legitimate quality standards, they may not engage in viewpoint discrimination. In his words, a public university class is "an intentionally created educational forum for the enabling of professorial (and student) speech, per the rationale of *Rosenberger*. University classroom speech is thus not government speech. Similarly, professorial scholarship is an intentionally created metaphorical educational forum for the dissemination of knowledge by academics. It, too, is not government speech. The First Amendment consequence is that the government should not be allowed to engage in viewpoint discrimination by punishing faculty because of what they say in the classroom or write in their scholarship."[51] An analogy may be found in extracurricular programs in which public schools and universities recognize and support a wide range of student clubs for the purpose of providing opportunities for student speech. None of this speech is controlled by or attributable to the institution, whose educational aims are served by facilitating the speech of others.

By far the most sweeping plan for reframing constitutional law as it pertains to academic freedom was presented by Judith Areen in a *Georgetown Law Review* article that the Third Circuit cited in *Gorum*. Noting that the courts have been willing to consider the government in different roles, such as sovereign and employer, she proposed the new category of government-as-educator. Among other things, such an approach would allow the courts to take account of the differences between public universities and other government workplaces. As Areen explained, "Debate that might be viewed as disruptive in other public agencies is an accepted, and even necessary, part of the production of new knowledge and its dissemination in classrooms. So, too, employee criticism that might seem insubordinate in other public agencies may be a necessary part of fulfilling the governance responsibilities of a faculty member in a college or university."[52] If the role of government-as-educator were adopted, public universities would continue to function as employers when dealing with nonacademic matters, such as parking and health benefits, and in their relationship with nonfaculty employees. With respect to academic matters, however, they would not be bound by the rules that the government must observe in its role as sovereign or as employer.

Under Areen's proposal, any discipline imposed on professors as a result of their speech would have to be clearly justified. One possible justification, and indeed an excellent one, would be to show that the disciplinary action was endorsed by a faculty body on academic grounds. Because the locus of control in academic freedom is assigned to the faculty as a whole, an individual professor who challenges a faculty-approved action in court would have to show that the action fell so far outside established academic norms as to be unjustifiable as a professional decision. Continuing this line of argument, Areen questioned how courts could justify deference to academic judgments made by trustees or administrators without faculty involvement. While endorsing the right of each public university to establish its own governance system, she suggested that the cost of excluding faculty from academic decisionmaking might be an adverse result if a professor challenged an administrative action in court. "Colleges and universities would remain free to decide whether and how much to involve faculty in making academic decisions," she proposed. But "[i]f faculty were not consulted about a particular academic decision that was later challenged in court, the institution would have the burden of showing that the challenged decision was made on academic grounds."[53]

In addition to proposing constitutional remedies for the present state of academic-freedom cases in the federal courts, legal scholars have been considering ways to strengthen and extend academic freedom through the use of such documents as collective bargaining agreements and faculty handbooks, whose provisions are enforceable as a matter of employment or contract law. The authors of *Protecting an Independent Faculty Voice*, while recognizing the importance of filing amicus curiae briefs in lawsuits involving academic freedom, emphasized the need to develop effective internal policies, which in turn necessitates educating trustees and administrators about the "risks to institutional health and to higher education generally if they use the *Hong-Renken-Sessoms* doctrine to curtail intramural faculty speech."[54]

To be sure, constitutional and professional remedies are not mutually exclusive, and a blending of the two might seem to represent the most robust approach to protecting academic freedom. Seeking judicial remedies of any kind, however, is a two-edged sword. Unlike the professional standards that are primarily responsible for making academic freedom a reality in American higher education, constitutional law is shaped by nonacademics, who may change it at any time in ways that might not reflect the best academic practices. A single 5–4 decision of the Supreme Court is sufficient to redefine any constitutional theory or practice, no matter how well established it had been thought to be. When cases do not reach the Supreme Court, conflicting decisions among circuit courts may result in regional differences in the extent to which academic freedom is protected—differences that have no principled basis with respect to academic freedom as a professional standard.

Shaped by constituencies that understand the centrality of academic freedom to the goals, intellectual integrity, academic quality, and reputation of a university, in-house policies have the potential to be more nuanced and better tailored to the needs of each institution than constitutional tests could ever be. Moreover, as internal statements of the terms of appointment at a particular university, such documents eliminate the need either to adapt general public-employee law to the university culture or to justify treating one class of public employees differently from all others. Perhaps most significantly, policies and procedures established by universities are able to provide what the courts cannot: meaningful assessments of the substantive quality of academic speech, as opposed to the simple assignment of authority that is characteristic of legal decisions. The efficacy of academic-freedom policies at private universities, where constitutional protection was never an issue, augurs well for a renewed reliance, among public universities, on professional standards that were once the only protection for academic freedom and that remain its best hope.

Afterword

> Not that it is solely, or chiefly, to form great thinkers, that freedom of think-ing is required. On the contrary, it is as much and even more indispensable, to enable average human beings to attain the mental stature which they are capable of. There have been, and may again be, great individual thinkers, in a general atmosphere of mental slavery. But there never has been, nor ever will be, in that atmosphere, an intellectually active people.
> —John Stuart Mill, *On Liberty*

NOT FAR BENEATH THE SURFACE OF SOME disputes in K–12 schools and pub-lic universities lies a subtextual debate over the value of controversy in its own right. The actions taken by university administrators when faculty sug-gested a causal link between race and intelligence, for instance, reflected not only a rejection of that conclusion but also a determination to prevent controversy from boiling up on campus. The same is true of the repeated ef-forts of Salt Lake City school officials to marginalize a particular view of sex-ual orientation. There, too, the motivating factor was not merely a desire to suppress disfavored ideas but a conviction that the debate itself was de-structive. In each instance, discomfort with controversy went beyond sim-ple disagreement with certain ideas. It evinced the belief that the correct an-swer was, literally, *unquestionably* true. Viewed from that perspective, a vigorous exchange of ideas has nothing to offer, since disputation makes sense only if we agree that the full truth may not yet be known. Otherwise, far from representing a positive value, entertainment of debate may appear to be a denial or a betrayal of the truth. A facile dismissal of this behavior as "politically correct" in the one instance and "homophobic" in the other misses the point because it focuses on the specific issues of race and sexual orientation. More important are the forces underlying the administrators' responses—forces that might emerge in constituencies of any political persuasion with respect to their own flashpoint issues.

Resistance to controversy, which manifests itself in public discussions in a wide variety of venues, is particularly destructive in the context of public schools and universities because it is antithetical to their core functions. The American system of public education as a whole undoubtedly has a responsibility to convey information and to promote critical thinking with respect to academic disciplines. Beyond that, however, it must prepare students to understand the *purposes* of controversy and to think beyond the wall of their preconceived ideas. Public education must, in fact, help students to outdo previous generations in mastering these skills if they are to function effectively amid the diversity, polarization, and internationalization of the twenty-first century. That goal is ambitious, and it may be unattainable. Certainly, the administrative and judicial responses to the disputes discussed throughout this book are not promising.

To make any real difference, an understanding of the management and importance of controversial expression must permeate the educational system. Treating it as an instructional outcome would be futile; it must be woven into the fabric of public schools and universities. It cannot be compartmentalized into an advanced placement course in high school or into an orientation program in a university. Nor can it be reduced to an item on a curricular checklist, subject to assessment by means of multiple-choice questions on a standardized test. Each of the specific disagreements discussed in this book might be capable of a practical solution, at least in the short term, but the larger issues that those case studies illustrate can be addressed by nothing less than a revolution in thinking.

Although most of the K–12 and university disputes used as examples in this discussion date from the late twentieth and early twenty-first centuries, the argument I am making about the value of controversy reflects much older ideas. This continuity of thought is suggested by epigraphs taken from works by Galileo, John Milton, and John Stuart Mill, who represent a long tradition of thinkers including, among many others, Socrates, Thomas Aquinas, and Charles Darwin. As a fitting close to this discussion, I offer some brief reflections on one of the Mill's arguments as it applies to the current state of academic freedom.

On Liberty was published in the same year as *On the Origin of Species*, and like Darwin, Mill has been lionized and demonized. In particular, critics complain that in his enthusiasm for the social utility of rational debate, he took an overly optimistic and even naïve view of the extent to which the public good is served by the open expression of ideas—the more unpopular, the better. Nevertheless, one aspect of his work is particularly thought-provoking: his conceptualization of a cycle that begins with a new idea passionately maintained in the face of resistance from defenders of the then-prevailing orthodoxy. If that idea takes root, gains strength, and in time becomes the orthodoxy, it loses in intensity what it gains in breadth of acceptance. Indeed, the idea itself, as understood by complacent adherents who take it for granted, is in some subtle way not the same idea that was once championed by its embattled initiators. In Mill's words, "[N]ot only the grounds of the opinion are forgotten in the absence of discussion, but too often the meaning of the opinion itself. The words which convey it, cease to suggest ideas, or suggest only a small portion of those they were originally employed to communicate. Instead of a vivid conception and a living belief, there remain only a few phrases retained by rote; or, if any part, the shell and husk only of the meaning is retained, the finer essence being lost."[1]

When, in the early years of the twentieth century, professors were being fired for expressing ideas that displeased administrators and trustees, the fledgling AAUP's generation of support for academic freedom corresponded with the first stage of Mill's cycle. At that point, ideas are "full of meaning and vitality to those who originate them, and to the direct disciples of the originators. Their meaning continues to be felt in undiminished strength, and is perhaps brought out into even fuller consciousness, so long as the struggle lasts to give the doctrine or creed an ascendancy over other creeds." Once a belief has become established, however, "those who hold it have generally inherited, not adopted it. . . . Instead of being, as at first, constantly on the alert either to defend themselves against the world, or to bring the world over to them, they have subsided into acquiescence, and neither listen, when they can help it, to arguments against their creed, nor trouble dissentients (if there be such) with arguments in its favour. From this time may usually be dated the decline in the living power of the doctrine."

Scholars of higher education, including Michael Bérubé, Marc Bousquet, and Cary Nelson, have been protesting for years about the difficulty of mobilizing university faculty to deal effectively with such issues as the increasingly corporate culture of university administrations, the subordination of academic values to the generation of revenue, and the excessive use of contingent faculty.[2] Most frustrating of all, as Cary Nelson observed in *No University Is an Island* (2010), is "the truth . . . that faculty members *have* the power they need to save higher education's key roles if they choose to exercise it collectively."[3] Instead, too many professors take pride in focusing on their scholarship—a tendency that university administrations encourage for a variety of reasons. Far from demanding their right to participate in shared governance, faculty profess themselves to be too involved in research to undertake mundane service work, such as participating in promotion reviews or serving on search committees. Then, when the thinking of career administrators and professional staff begins to dominate the institution, faculty who remain unwilling to take the time to engage in institutional decisionmaking complain that it should be done by people like themselves. Speaking from the perspective of thirty years as a professor in a public university, I do not believe that academic control has been wrenched from the bleeding hands of a desperately struggling faculty. Too many of us have been unwilling to do what it takes to hold on to it.

Mill's suggestion that "[b]oth teachers and learners go to sleep at their post as soon as there is no enemy in the field" may provide both an explanation for faculty disengagement and a reason to hope that *Garcetti* and its progeny will spark a new stage of this cycle. After writing at length about the problems posed by these decisions, I dare to suggest that they may also generate renewed vigor in support of academic freedom and the values it represents and fosters. Important among these is an increased appreciation of the importance of controversial expression, not only among ourselves and our students but also at other levels of public education. Together with K–12 teachers, professors in public universities have an obligation to look beyond our individual teaching and research, and even beyond the shared governance of our own institutions, toward making American education safe for controversy.

NOTES

Chapter 1. A Seat at the Table

1. Because a college may be either a freestanding institution of higher education or a unit within a university, and because the repeated use of "colleges and universities" would be awkward, the word "university" is used throughout this book to refer to higher education in general.

2. Michael A. Olivas, "Reflections on Professorial Academic Freedom: Second Thoughts on the Third 'Essential Freedom,'" *Stanford Law Review* 45 (1993): 1855–56.

3. The National Academy of Sciences, according to its Web site, is "an honorific society of distinguished scholars engaged in scientific and engineering research, dedicated to the furtherance of science and technology and to their use for the general welfare." http://www.nasonline.org. The American Association for the Advancement of Science is "an international non-profit organization dedicated to advancing science around the world by serving as an educator, leader, spokesperson and professional association." http://www.aaas.org. Among other things, it publishes the journal *Science*. The National Center for Science Education was founded to "educate the press and public about the scientific, educational, and legal aspects of the creation and evolution controversy, and supply needed information and advice to defend good science education at local, state, and national levels." http://ncse.com.

4. Founded by the television evangelist Pat Robertson and headed by Jay Sekulow, the American Center for Law and Justice "is specifically dedicated to the ideal that religious freedom and freedom of speech are inalienable, God-given rights. The Center's purpose is to educate, promulgate, conciliate, and where necessary, litigate, to ensure that those rights are protected under the law." http://www.aclj.org.

5. *LeVake v. Independent School District #656*, 625 N.W.2d 502, 509 (2001).

6. American Association of University Professors (henceforth AAUP) Web site, http://www.aaup.org.

7. AAUP, *Declaration of Principles on Academic Freedom and Academic Tenure* (1915), available at http://www.aaup.org.

8. For further information on the history of academic freedom in America, see Richard Hofstadter and Walter P. Metzger, *The Development of Academic Freedom in the United States* (New York: Columbia University Press, 1955); Neil Hamilton, *Zealotry and Academic Freedom: A Legal and Historical Perspective* (New Brunswick, N.J.: Transaction Publishers, 1995); Walter P. Metzger, "A Stroll Along the New Frontiers of Academic Freedom," in Peggie J. Hollingsworth, ed., *Unfettered Expression: Freedom in American Intellectual Life* (Ann Arbor: University of Michigan Press, 2000), 73–97; Walter P. Metzger, "The 1940 Statement of Principles on Academic Freedom," in William W. Van Alstyne, ed., *Freedom and Tenure in the Academy* (Durham, N.C.: Duke University Press, 1993), 3–77; and David Rabban, "A Functional Analysis of 'Individual' and 'Institutional' Academic Freedom Under the First Amendment," in Van Alstyne, *Freedom and Tenure in the Academy*, 227–301. Matthew W. Finkin and Robert C. Post provide an excellent discussion of the principles of academic freedom enunciated by the AAUP in Finkin and Post, *For the Common Good: Principles of American Academic Freedom* (New Haven: Yale University Press, 2008). This work also demonstrates the relationship between early cases of faculty dismissals opposed by the AAUP and contemporary challenges to academic freedom.

9. Ronald Dworkin, "We Need a New Interpretation of Academic Freedom," in Louis Menand, ed., *The Future of Academic Freedom* (Chicago: University of Chicago Press, 1996), 185.

10. Louis Menand, "The Limits of Academic Freedom," in Menand, *Future of Academic Freedom*, 10.

11. Louis Menand, "Culture and Advocacy," in Patricia Meyer Spacks, ed., *Advocacy in the Classroom: Problems and Possibilities* (New York: Palgrave Macmillan, 1996), 119.

12. Cary Nelson, *Manifesto of a Tenured Radical* (New York: New York University Press, 1997), 2. For examples of the arguments on the other side, see the most recent edition of Roger Kimball's *Tenured Radicals: How Politics Has Corrupted Our Higher Education*, 3rd ed. (Chicago: Ivan R. Dee, 2008).

13. Gertrude Himmelfarb, "The New Advocacy and the Old," in Spacks, *Advocacy in the Classroom*, 97, 99.

14. Joan W. Scott, "Academic Freedom as an Ethical Practice," in Menand, *Future of Academic Freedom*, 169, 172.

15. Menand, "Limits of Academic Freedom," 14.

16. Harris Mirkin, "The Pattern of Sexual Politics: Feminism, Homosexuality, and Pedophilia," *Journal of Homosexuality* 37 (1999).

17. Donald F. Uerling, "Academic Freedom in K–12 Education," *Nebraska Law Review* 79 (2000): 961.

18. Kevin G. Welner, "Locking Up the Marketplace of Ideas and Locking Out School Reform: Courts' Imprudent Treatment of Controversial Teaching in America's Public Schools," *UCLA Law Review* 50 (2003): 1029.

19. Uerling, "Academic Freedom in K–12 Education," 975.

20. Karen C. Daly, "Balancing Act: Teachers' Classroom Speech and the First Amendment," *Journal of Law and Education* 30 (2001): 31.

21. In brief, although the subject of the sentence is "Congress," the Free Speech Clause as interpreted by the courts prevents any arm of government from interfering with the free expression of individuals unless the speech falls within a stated exception, such as perjury or fraud. Among these exceptions to the First Amendment's protection of free speech, two are particularly relevant here: the right of K–12 school administrators to place reasonable limits on the speech of students and the authority of government employers to regulate the speech of their employees.

22. *Miles v. Denver Public Schools,* 733 F. Supp. 1410, 1411 (1990).

23. *Hazelwood v. Kuhlmeier,* 484 U.S. 260, 273 (1988).

24. *Miles v. Denver Public Schools,* 944 F.2d 773, 776, 777, 779 (1991).

25. *Ward v. Hickey,* 996 F.2d 448, 452, 453 (1993).

26. *Ward,* 996 F.2d at 453, 454.

27. *Lacks v. Ferguson Reorganized School District District R-2,* 147 F.3d 718, 724 (1998).

28. Neal H. Hutchens, "Silence at the Schoolhouse Gate: The Diminishing First Amendment Rights of Public School Employees," *Kentucky Law Journal* 97 (2008–9): 67.

29. Daly, "Balancing Act," 16.

30. *Pickering v. Board of Education,* 391 U.S. 563, 568, 572 (1968).

31. *Pickering,* 391 U.S. at 574.

32. *Pickering,* 391 U.S. at 573, 570.

33. *Kirkland v. Northside Independent School District,* 890 F.2d 794, 797 (1989).

34. *Kirkland,* 890 F.2d at 800.

35. *Boring v. Buncombe County Board of Education,* 136 F.3d 364, 367, 370, 368 (1998).

36. *Bradley v. Pittsburgh Board of Education,* 910 F.2d 1172, 1174 (1990).

37. *Bradley,* 910 F2d at 1176, 1177.

38. Nadine Strossen," First Amendment and Civil Liberties Traditions of Academic Freedom," in Spacks, *Advocacy in the Classroom,* 72.

39. AAUP, *Joint Statement on Rights and Freedoms of Students,* available at http://www .aaup.org/aaup/pubsres/policydocs/contents/stud-rights.htm.

40. 20 USC 4071 (a).

41. For a discussion of distinctions between the free-speech rights of students in secondary school and the rights of students in universities, see Karyl Roberts Martin, "Demoted to High School: Are College Students' Free Speech Rights the Same as Those of High School Students?" *Boston College Law Review* 45 (December 2003).

42. *The Papers of Benjamin Franklin,* vol. 1, ed. Leonard Larabee (New Haven: Yale University Press, 1959), 27.

Chapter 2. Freedom and (or) Equality

1. Jonathan Arac, *Huckleberry Finn as Idol and Target: The Functions of Criticism in Our Time,* The Wisconsin Project on American Writers (Madison: University of Wisconsin Press, 1997), 80.

2. "The Concord Library's Banning of *Huckleberry Finn,*" in Laurie Champion, ed., *Critical Responses to Mark Twain's "Huckleberry Finn,"* Critical Responses in Arts and Letters Series, no. 1 (New York: Greenwood Press, 1991), 15.

3. Robert Moran and Connie Langland, "Pennsylvania NAACP Opposes 'Huck Finn' Requirement," *Buffalo News*, February 4, 1998.

4. Arthur Magida, "Huck's Unvarnished Truth," *Christian Science Monitor*, March 2, 2000, available at http://www.encyclopedia.com/doc/1G1-59700104.html.

5. Moran and Langland, "Pennsylvania NAACP Opposes 'Huck Finn' Requirement."

6. *Monteiro v. Tempe Union High School District*, 158 F.3d 1022, 1024 (1998).

7. *Monteiro*, 158 F3d. at 1026, 1029, 1030.

8. John H. Wallace, "The Case Against *Huck Finn*," in James S. Leonard, Thomas A. Tenney, and Thadious M. Davis, eds., *Satire or Evasion? Black Perspectives on Huckleberry Finn* (Durham, N.C.: Duke University Press, 1992), 16, 23.

9. Jocelyn Chadwick-Joshua, *The Jim Dilemma: Reading Race in Huckleberry Finn* (Jackson: University Press of Mississippi, 1998), xiv.

10. Arac, *Huckleberry Finn as Idol and Target*, 218.

11. Jocelyn Chadwick-Joshua, "'Blame de pint! I reck'n I knows what I knows': Ebonics, Jim, and New Approaches to Understanding *The Adventures of Huckleberry Finn*," in James S. Leonard, ed., *Making Mark Twain Work in the Classroom* (Durham, N.C.: Duke University Press, 1999), 177.

12. Jim Knippling, "Censorship and African American Literature," in Jean Brown, ed., *Preserving Intellectual Freedom: Fighting Censorship in Our Schools* (Urbana, Ill.: National Council of Teachers of English, 1994), 74.

13. Liz Leyden, "Story Hour Didn't Have a Happy Ending," *Washington Post*, December 3, 1998.

14. Lynette Holloway, "Teacher in Book Dispute Starts New Job in Queens School," *New York Times*, December 5, 1998.

15. Lynette Holloway, "Author of Disputed Book Is Criticized in Brooklyn," *New York Times*, December 9, 1998.

16. Lynette Holloway, "School Officials Support Teacher on Book That Parents Call Racially Insensitive," *New York Times*, November 25, 1998.

17. Lynette Holloway, "Author of Disputed Book Is Criticized in Brooklyn," *New York Times*, December 9, 1998.

18. For discussions of racial insensitivity, see Richard Mulcahy, "A Full Circle: Advocacy and Academic Freedom in Crisis," in Patricia Meyer Spacks, ed., *Advocacy in the Classroom: Problems and Possibilities* (New York: Palgrave Macmillan, 1996), 142–60; Ronald Dworkin, "We Need a New Interpretation of Academic Freedom," in Louis Menand, ed., *The Future of Academic Freedom* (Chicago: University of Chicago Press, 1996), 181–98; and Thomas Sowell, *Inside American Education: The Decline, the Deception, the Dogmas* (New York: Free Press, 1993).

19. Jill Nelson, "Vilifying White Teacher Won't Erase Black Self-Hatred," *Houston Chronicle*, December 2, 1998.

20. Dinitia Smith, "Furor Over Book Brings Pain and Pride to Its Author," *New York Times*, November 25, 1998.

21. Clyde Haberman, "An Ignorant Cry of Racism Makes All Knees Jerk," *New York Times*, December 4, 1998.

22. Carolivia Herron's Web site, http://www.carolivia.org/nappyhair/.

23. *Doe v. University of Michigan*, 721 F. Supp. 852, 854 (1989).

24. *Doe*, 721 F. Supp. at 856.
25. *Doe*, 721 F. Supp. at 858, 859, 867.
26. Robert M. O'Neil, *Free Speech in the College Community* (Bloomington: Indiana University Press, 1997),16–17.
27. Donald Alexander Downs, *Restoring Free Speech and Liberty on Campus* (Oakland, Calif.: Independent Institute; Cambridge, England: Cambridge University Press, 2005), 270.
28. *UWM Post v. Board of Regents of the University of Wisconsin System*, 774 F. Supp. 1163, 1165 (1991).
29. *UWM Post*, 774 F. Supp. at 1165.
30. In most discussions of speech codes it is assumed that restrictions on faculty speech would be more objectionable, and would create a greater furor with respect to academic freedom, than would restrictions on the nonacademic speech of students. Nevertheless, it is arguable that because academic freedom is tied to the functions of the university, speech that does not further any educational purpose could be deemed to lie outside its scope. For discussions of this issue, see Ronald Dworkin, "We Need a New Interpretation of Academic Freedom," in Menand, *Future of Academic Freedom*, 181–98; and Louis Menand, "The Limits of Academic Freedom," in Menand, *Future of Academic Freedom*, 3–20.
31. *UWM Post*, 774 F. Supp. at 1173.
32. *Chaplinsky v. New Hampshire*, 315 U.S. 568, 569, 573 (1942).
33. *Chaplinsky*, 315 U.S. at 572.
34. *UWM Post*, 774 F. Supp. at 1165.
35. *Corry v. The Leland Stanford Junior University*, Case No. 740309, Superior Court, State of California, County of Santa Clara, February 27, 1995, 1.
36. *Corry*, at 8.
37. *Corry*, at 30, 34–35.
38. Gerhard Casper, "Statement on *Corry v. Stanford University*," available at http://www.stanford.edu/dept/pres-provost/president/speeches/950309corry.html.
39. Stanley Fish, *There's No Such Thing as Free Speech, and It's a Good Thing, Too* (New York: Oxford University Press, 1994), 115.
40. Herbert Marcuse, "Repressive Tolerance," in Robert Paul Wolff, Barrington Moore, Jr., and Herbert Marcuse, *A Critique of Pure Tolerance* (Boston: Beacon Press, 1969), 95–137, available at http://www.marcuse.org.
41. Mari J. Matsuda, Charles R. Lawrence III, Richard Delgado, and Kimberle Williams Crenshaw, *Words That Wound: Critical Race Theory, Assaultive Speech, and the First Amendment* (Boulder, Colo.: Westview Press, 1993), 7.
42. Matsuda et al., *Words That Wound*, 35, 44.
43. Matsuda et al., *Words That Wound*, 80.
44. To provoke discussion among college students about the problems associated with policies that reflect only majoritarian perspectives, Richard Delgado joined with Jean Stefancic in writing *Understanding Words That Wound* (2004). Formatted as a textbook of critical race theory, it illustrates each of the themes of Matsuda et al.'s *Words That Wound* with discussion questions, class exercises, and recommended readings.

45. Henry Louis Gates, Jr., "Critical Race Theory and Freedom of Speech," in Menand, *Future of Academic Freedom*, 120.

46. Gates, "Critical Race Theory," 141.

47. Gates, "Critical Race Theory," 147. Critical race theory has also been discussed in conjunction with other forms of hate speech. Martin P. Golding, for instance, has offered a systematic legal analysis of the balancing required when universities seek to curb racist, sexist, and anti-Semitic speech. See Golding, *Free Speech on Campus* (Lanham, Md.: Rowman and Littlefield, 2000).

48. Alan Charles Kors and Harvey A. Silverglate, *The Shadow University: The Betrayal of Liberty on America's Campuses* (New York: Free Press, 1998), 3, 75.

49. Foundation for Individual Rights in Education (FIRE) Web site, http://www.the fire.org/about/mission/.

50. FIRE Web site, http://www.thefire.org/.

51. AAUP, "On Freedom of Expression and Campus Speech Codes" (1994), available at http://www.aaup.org/AAUP/pubsres/policydocs/contents/speechcodes.htm.

52. For additional material supporting speech codes, see Thomas P. Hustoles and Walter B. Connolly, Jr., eds., *Regulating Racial Harassment on Campus: A Legal Compendium* (Washington, D.C.: National Association of College and University Attorneys, 1990); and John K. Wilson, *The Myth of Political Correctness: The Conservative Attack on Higher Education* (Durham, N.C.: Duke University Press, 1995). On the other side of the debate, a chapter entitled "The New Censorship" provides a conservative's critique of the University of Michigan's speech code, in Dinesh D'Souza, *Illiberal Education: The Politics of Race and Sex on Campus* (New York: Free Press, 1991). Additional arguments against the regulation of hate speech may be found in Andrew Peyton Thomas, *The People v. Harvard Law: How America's Oldest Law School Turned Its Back on Free Speech* (San Francisco: Encounter Books, 2005); Jeffrey Toobin, "Speechless: Free Expression and Civility Clash at Harvard," *New Yorker*, January 27, 2003, 32; Les Csorba III, ed., *Academic License: The War on Academic Freedom* (Evanston, Ill.: UCA Books, 1988); William Van Alstyne and Nicholas Wolfson, *Hate Speech, Sex Speech, Free Speech* (Westport, Conn.: Praeger, 1997); and Henry Louis Gates, Jr., et al., *Speaking of Race, Speaking of Sex: Hate Speech, Civil Rights, and Civil Liberties* (New York: New York University Press, 1994). Timothy C. Shiell, in *Campus Hate Speech on Trial* (Lawrence: University Press of Kansas, 1998), provides an in-depth history and analysis of the development of campus speech codes and the legal challenges they have faced. Martin P. Golding, in *Free Speech on Campus* (Lanham, Md.: Rowman and Littlefield, 2000), discusses the development of campus speech codes with particular attention to the philosophical arguments underlying them. For a historical perspective, see a discussion of the academic-freedom issues raised by 1960s racial strife at Cornell in Donald Alexander Downs, *Cornell '69: Liberalism and the Crisis of the American University* (Ithaca, N.Y.: Cornell University Press, 1999). Collections of essays giving both sides of the debate include Paul Berman, ed., *Debating P.C.: The Controversy over Political Correctness on College Campuses* (New York: Dell, 1992); and Patricia Aufderheide, ed., *Beyond P.C.: Toward a Politics of Understanding* (St. Paul, Minn.: Graywolf Press, 1992).

Chapter 3. Price-Fixing in the Free Marketplace of Ideas

1. Richard Lynn, *The Science of Human Diversity: A History of the Pioneer Fund* (Lanham, Md.: University Press of America, 2001), 409, 409–10.
2. *Levin v. Harleston,* 770 F. Supp. 895, 900-901 (1991).
3. *Levin,* 770 F. Supp. at 901.
4. *Levin,* Trial Transcript, 241.
5. *Levin,* Transcript, 260, 262.
6. *Levin,* Transcript, 233.
7. *Levin,* 770 F. Supp. at 902.
8. *Levin,* 770 F. Supp. at 908.
9. *Levin,* Transcript, 14.
10. *Levin v. Harleston,* 770 F. Supp. 895 (1991), at 914.
11. *Levin,* 770 F. Supp. at 911.
12. *Levin,* 770 F. Supp. at 913, 920.
13. *Levin,* Transcript, 391.
14. The Center for Individual Rights specializes in litigation involving free speech and civil rights. For additional information, see its Web site, http://www.cir-usa .org/.
15. *Levin,* 770 F. Supp. at 915, 917.
16. *Levin,* 770 F. Supp. at 921, 925.
17. Robert M. O'Neil, *Free Speech in the College Community* (Bloomington: Indiana University Press, 1997), 37.
18. *Jeffries v. Harleston,* 21 F.3d 1238, 1242 (1994) .
19. *Jeffries v. Harleston,* 820 F. Supp. 736, 738 (1993).
20. *Jeffries v. Harleston,* 828 F. Supp. 1066, 1092 (1993).
21. Denise K. Magner, "Controversial City College Professor Is a Study in Contradictions," *Chronicle of Higher Education,* December 18, 1991.
22. *Jeffries* 828 F. Supp. at 1071.
23. Massimo Calabresi, "Skin Deep 101," *Time,* February 14, 1994, 16.
24. For additional material on the Levin case, together with further examples of racially controversial faculty speech, see O'Neil, *Free Speech;* Alan Charles Kors and Harvey A. Silverglate, *The Shadow University: The Betrayal of Liberty on America's Campuses* (New York: Free Press, 1998); Timothy C. Shiell, *Campus Hate Speech on Trial* (Lawrence: University Press of Kansas, 1998); Perry A. Zirkel, "Academic Freedom Revisited," *Academe* 74 (September 1992); and Nathan Glazer, "Levin, Jeffries, and the Fate of Academic Autonomy," *William and Mary Law Review* 36 (1995).
25. Pioneer Fund Web site, http://www.pioneerfund.org.
26. Unless otherwise indicated, all primary documents quoted in this discussion of the Pioneer Fund controversy are located in the files of the University of Delaware chapter of the AAUP.
27. The Pioneer Fund's account of its history and goals, together with summaries of the work of Pioneer Fund recipients, appear in Richard Lynn, *The Science of Human Diversity: A History of the Pioneer Fund* (Lanham, Md.: University Press of America, 2001).

28. By way of full disclosure, let me say that at the time of this writing I have been president of the University of Delaware chapter of the AAUP since January 1, 2009. I held no leadership role during the Pioneer Fund dispute and cannot remember whether I was even a member at that time—probably so, but I wouldn't swear to it.

29. Ron Kaufman, "U. Delaware Reaches Accord on Race Studies," *Scientist* 6 (1992), 3.

30. Stalking the Wild Taboo, at L. R. Andrews, Inc., http://www.lrainc.com/swtaboo /stalkers/sheriff.html.

31. Edward M. Miller, unpublished letter to *The Driftwood*, August 14, 1996, available at http://www.lrainc.com/swtaboo/stalkers/em_drif1.html.

32. Denise K. Magner, "Professor's Comments on Race and Intelligence Create a Furor," *Chronicle of Higher Education*, November 1, 1996.

33. For further reading on the controversy over race-based intelligence theory, see O'Neil, *Free Speech*; Kors and Silverglate, *Shadow University*; Jonathan Marks, "Race Across the Physical-Cultural Divide in American Anthropology," in Henrika Kuklick, ed., *A New History of Anthropology* (New York: Blackwell, 2007); Richard Mulcahy, "A Full Circle: Advocacy and Academic Freedom in Crisis," in Patricia Meyer Spacks, ed., *Advocacy in the Classroom: Problems and Possibilities* (New York: Palgrave Macmillan, 1996); "Professor Linda Gottfredson: Another Academic Advocate of Racial Differences in Intelligence," *Journal of Blacks in Higher Education* 26 (Winter 1999–2000); Adam Miller, "The Pioneer Fund: Bankrolling the Professors of Hate," *Journal of Blacks in Higher Education* 6 (Winter 1994–95); Thomas Short, "Big Brother in Delaware: Women and Minority Oversensitivity Obstructs Academic Freedom at University of Delaware," *National Review*, March 18, 1991, available at http://findarticles.com/p/articles/mi_m1282/is_n4_v43/ai_10519801; and Morton Hunt, *The New Know-Nothings: The Political Foes of the Scientific Study of Human Nature* (New Brunswick, N.J.: Transaction Publishers, 1999).

Chapter 4. Rainbow Before the Storm

1. *Downs v. Los Angeles Unified School District*, 228 F.3d 1003, 1007 (2000).

2. *Downs*, 228 F. 3d at 1011, 1012, 1016–17.

3. "Children of the Rainbow—First Grade," 372. This unpublished curriculum guide was accessed in 1994 at the offices of the New York City affiliate of the American Civil Liberties Union.

4. The author of *Heather Has Two Mommies* removed the text dealing with artificial insemination from a later edition because the controversy it engendered had proven to be a distraction from the book's primary message.

5. Leslea Newman, "A Note from Heather's Mom to Parents and Teachers," http://www.alyson.com/html/00_files/00_ednote/0400/0400heather10_01_ int.html (printout in author's possession).

6. Leslea Newman, *Heather Has Two Mommies* (Boston: Alyson Wonderland, 1989).

7. Michael Willhoite, *Daddy's Roommate* (Boston: Alyson Wonderland, 1990).

8. George Will, "Don't Blur Tolerance, Indifference," *Chicago Sun-Times*, December 6, 1992.

9. Newman, "Note from Heather's Mom."

10. Notes on the school-board candidates' questionnaires were taken in 1994 from copies on file in the offices of the New York City affiliate of the American Civil Liberties Union. All quotations from candidates' questionnaires are taken from this source.

11. Will, "Don't Blur Tolerance," 53.

12. "The Parents Rebel—IV," *Wall Street Journal*, December 7, 1992.

13. Mary Jordan, "Guidance on Gays Divides Parents," *Washington Post*, December 8, 1992.

14. Among the more intriguing attachments to the questionnaires was a photograph of a male candidate bearing the caption "[This candidate] is a father of all the children in District 16."

15. "Parents Rebel."

16. Sam Roberts, "Politics and the Curriculum Fight," *New York Times*, December 15, 1992.

17. Sam Dillon, "Tension on Queens School Board That Fought Fernandez," *New York Times*, February 19, 1994.

18. For another controversy involving *Heather Has Two Mommies* and *Daddy's Roommate*, see *Sund v. City of Wichita Falls*, 121 F. Supp. 2d 530 (2000). The two books, which were shelved in the children's section of a Texas public library, drew fire from a small but vocal group led by a local pastor. Opponents pressured the city council into enacting a resolution that allowed adult holders of library cards to petition for the removal of any book from the children's section. Removal required the signatures of 300 of the town's 100,000 residents. In striking down this regulation, the court observed that it gave "vocal minorities veto power over any children's book with which they disagree" (p. 534) while leaving opponents of the removal with no recourse. Similarly, in *Parker v. Hurley*, 474 F. Supp. 2d 261 (2007), a federal district court dismissed a lawsuit filed by Massachusetts parents who objected to the public schools' use of a children's book entitled *King and King* (New York: Tricycle Books, 2003). Written by Linda de Haan and Stern Nijland, it relates the story of two princes who marry each other.

19. When a decision is appealed to a higher court, a majority of votes is needed to overturn it. A tie vote has the effect of upholding the lower court's ruling.

20. *Tinker v. Des Moines Independent Community School District*, 393 U.S. 503, 506 (1969).

21. *Tinker*, 393 U.S. 503 at 508, 510.

22. *Bethel School District No. 403 v. Fraser*, 478 U.S. 675, 687, 678 (1986).

23. *Bethel*, 478 U.S. at 682, 683.

24. For a brief explanation of public-forum law, see the University of Missouri–Kansas City Law School Web site, http://www.law.umkc.edu/faculty/projects/ftrials/conlaw/designatedforum.htm.

25. *Hazelwood v. Kuhlmeier*, 484 U.S. 260, 270-71 (1988).

26. *Hazelwood*, 484 U.S. at 273.

27. According to the Christian Legal Society's Web site, http://www.clsnet.org/society/about-cls/purpose, its mission is "[t]o inspire, encourage, and equip lawyers and law students, both individually and in community, to proclaim, love and serve Jesus Christ through the study and practice of law, the provision of legal assis-

tance to the poor, and the defense of religious freedom & sanctity of human life."

28. For an extended discussion of Justice Clarence Thomas's dissent in *Morse v. Frederick*, see David Blacker, "An Unreasonable Argument Against Student Free Speech," *Educational Theory* 59 (2009).

29. *Saxe v. State College Area School District*, 240 F.3d 200, 202 (2001).

30. *Saxe*, 240 F.3d at 203.

31. *Saxe*, 240 F. 3d at 203, 204.

32. *Saxe*, 240 F. 3d at 204, 217.

33. 20 USC 4071 (a).

34. Author's interview with Kay Peterson, April 3, 1998, at East High School, Salt Lake City, Utah. Unless otherwise indicated, all quotations from Peterson are from this interview.

35. *East High Gay/Straight Alliance v. Board of Education of Salt Lake City School District*, Complaint, March 19, 1998, p. 6.

36. The Eagle Forum, founded by the conservative activist Phyllis Schlafly, opposes globalism, feminism, homosexuality, and abortion, among other things. More information is available on its Web site, http://www.eagleforum.org/.

37. Editorial, "Merry Gay Bashing," *Salt Lake Tribune*, December 27, 1995.

38. Tom Barberi, guest column, *Salt Lake Tribune*, January 14, 1996.

39. Letter to the editor, *Deseret News*, February 2, 1996.

40. *Congressional Record*, vol. 130, June 27, 1984, p. 19248.

41. Minutes, Board of Education of Salt Lake City, Public Hearing and Board Meeting, February 20, 1996, 6.

42. Marjorie Cortez, "Board Votes to Ban All Non-Curricular Clubs," *Deseret News*, February 21, 1996.

43. Jason Swenson, "School Board Meets to 'Self-Evaluate,'" *Deseret News*, February 26, 1996.

44. Louis Sahagun, "Utah Board Bans All School Clubs in Anti-Gay Move," *Los Angeles Times*, February 22, 1996.

45. Lambda Legal, formerly the Lambda Legal Defense and Education Fund, describes itself as "the oldest national organization pursuing high-impact litigation, public education and advocacy on behalf of equality and civil rights for lesbians, gay men, bisexuals, transgender people and people with HIV." Further information is available on its Web site, http://www.lambdalegal.org/. The Rutherford Institute states that its purpose is "to provide legal services in the defense of religious and civil liberties and to educate the public on important issues affecting their constitutional freedoms." Additional information is available at http://www.rutherford.org/.

46. *East High Gay/Straight Alliance v. Board of Education of Salt Lake City School District*, Complaint, March 19, 1998, 7.

47. *East High Gay/Straight Alliance v. Board of Education of Salt Lake City School District*, 81 F. Supp. 2d 1199, 1204 (1999).

48. *Board of Education of the Westside Community Schools v. Mergens*, 496 U.S. 226, 239-40 (1990).

49. Other lawsuits in which federal courts ordered school officials to recognize the Gay-Straight Alliance as part of the extracurricular program include *Colin v. Or-*

ange Unified School District, 83 F. Supp. 2d 1135 (2000); and *Gay-Straight Alliance of Okeechobee High School v. School Board of Okeechobee County*, 483 F. Supp. 2d 1224 (2007). A subsequent ruling in *Okeechobee* prevented school officials from inquiring "about the sexual orientation of any club participant, the names of anonymous participants, and participants' personal lives outside the school." *Gay-Straight Alliance of Okeechobee High School v. School Board of Okeechobee County*, 242 F.R.D. 644, 644 (2007).

50. *East High School PRISM Club v. Seidel*, 95 F. Supp. 2d 1239, 1243, 1242 (2000).
51. *East High School PRISM Club*, 95 F. Supp. 2d at 1243.
52. *East High School PRISM Club*, 95 F. Supp. 2d at 1246.
53. For legal analyses of the status of gay-friendly clubs in public schools, see Brian Berkley, "Making Gay Straight Alliance Student Groups Curriculum-Related: A New Tactic for Schools Trying to Avoid the Equal Access Act," *Washington and Lee Law Review* 61 (Fall 2004); Carolyn Pratt, "Protecting the Marketplace of Ideas in the Classroom: Why the Equal Access Act and the First Amendment Require the Recognition of Gay/Straight Alliances in America's Public Schools," *First Amendment Law Review* 5 (Spring 2007); Alice Riener, "Pride and Prejudice: The First Amendment, the Equal Access Act, and the Legal Fight for Gay Student Groups in High Schools," *American University Journal of Gender, Social Policy, and the Law* 14 (2006).
54. A heckler is an audience member whose interruptions interfere with the speaker's ability to convey his or her message. The term "heckler's veto" means that the speaker is silenced because of disruptions caused by those who disagree. During the civil rights era, for instance, opponents of racial desegregation first rioted and then used the riots to suggest that racial integration should be terminated for the sake of maintaining public order.
55. *Gay Lesbian Bisexual Alliance v. Pryor*, 110 F.3d 1543, 1545 (1997).
56. Joan Biskupic, "Justices Uphold Campus Fees," *Washington Post*, March 23, 2000.
57. *Board of Regents of the University of Wisconsin System v. Southworth*, 529 U.S. 217, 223 (2000).
58. *Southworth*, 529 U.S. at 229.
59. *Southworth*, 529 U.S. at 229, 233.
60. *Southworth*, 529 U.S. at 235.
61. *Southworth v. Wisconsin*, 376 F. 3d 757, 773 (2004).
62. *Christian Legal Society v. Walker*, 453 F.3d 853, 868 (2006).
63. For an overview of the debate over CLS student chapters, see Christian A. Malanga, "Expressive Association: Student Organizations' Right to Discriminate: A Look at Public Law Schools' Nondiscrimination Policies and Their Application to Christian Legal Society Student Chapters," *Western New England Law Review* 29 (2007).
64. *Christian Legal Society v. Kane*, 2006 U.S. Dist. LEXIS 27347 (2009), p. 80.

Chapter 5. Here Comes Darwin

1. This theory has since been amended to say that even if a variation is merely neutral, not actively helpful or harmful, it may persist and continue to develop. In time, as conditions change, it may come to serve a useful function.

2. William W. Van Alstyne, "Academic Freedom and the First Amendment in the Supreme Court of the United States: An Unhurried Historical Review," in Van Alstyne, ed., *Freedom and Tenure in the Academy* (Durham, N.C.: Duke University Press, 1993), 98.

3. "Thomas Henry Huxley (1825–1895)," University of California Museum of Paleontology, http://www.ucmp.berkeley.edu/history/thuxley.html.

4. George E. Webb, *The Evolution Controversy in America* (Lexington: University Press of Kentucky, 1994), 11.

5. Webb, *Evolution Controversy in America*, 137. Agassiz also suggested that each race of humans had been created by a separate act—a theory that was soon adopted as a creationist justification for racism.

6. Asa Gray, *Darwiniana: Essays and Reviews Pertaining to Darwinism* (New York: D. Appleton, 1887), 379.

7. Charles Darwin, *Autobiography*, ed. Gavin de Beer (1887; Oxford: Oxford University Press, 1974), 50, 54.

8. W. S. Lilly, "Materialism and Morality," *Popular Science Monthly* 30 (February 1887), 477, 488. Some evolutionists later denigrated religion just as Agassiz and Lilly had disparaged Darwinism.

9. Joseph LeConte, "The Relation of Evolution to Materialism," *Popular Science Monthly* 33 (May 1888), 80.

10. James R. Moore, *The Post-Darwinian Controversies: A Study of the Protestant Struggle to Come to Terms with Darwin in Great Britain and America, 1870–1900* (London: Cambridge University Press, 1979), 245.

11. W. D. Le Sueur, "Evolution Bounded by Theology," *Popular Science Monthly* 29 (June 1886), 159.

12. Andrew Dickson White, "New Chapters in the Warfare of Science," *Popular Science Monthly* 32 (February 1888), 441.

13. White, "New Chapters," 601.

14. LeConte, "Relation of Evolution to Materialism," 79.

15. For a highly readable account of the Scopes trial interspersed with a personal memoir, see Matthew Chapman, *Trials of the Monkey: An Accidental Memoir* (New York: Picador USA, 2001). For a contemporary account that includes much of the trial transcript, see Leslie H. Allen, ed., *Bryan and Darrow at Dayton: The Record and Documents of the "Bible-Evolution Trial"* (New York: Russell and Russell, 1925).

16. Public Acts of the State of Tennessee, 64th General Assembly (1925), Chapter 27, House Bill No. 185, available at http://www.law.umkc.edu/faculty/projects/ftrials/scopes/tennstat.htm.

17. Edward J. Larson, *Summer for the Gods: The Scopes Trial and America's Continuing Debate Over Science and Religion* (New York: Basic Books, 1997), 102.

18. H. L. Mencken, "Mencken Finds Daytonians Full of Sickening Doubts About Value of Publicity," *Baltimore Evening Sun*, July 9, 1925, available at http://www.positiveatheism.org/hist/menck01.htm.

19. H. L. Mencken, "Yearning Mountaineers' Souls Need Reconversion Nightly, Mencken Finds," *Baltimore Evening Sun*, July 13, 1925, available at http://www.positiveatheism.org/hist/menck02.htm#SCOPES5.

20. H. L. Mencken, "Mencken Likens Trial to Religious Orgy, with Defendant a Beelzebub," *Baltimore Evening Sun,* July 11, 1925, available at http://www.positive atheism.org/hist/mencko2.htm#SCOPES4.

21. L. Sprague de Camp, *The Great Monkey Trial* (Garden City, N.Y.: Doubleday, 1968), 170.

22. *The World's Most Famous Court Trial: Tennessee Evolution Case,* 3rd ed. (Cincinnati: National Book Company, 1925), 281.

23. *World's Most Famous Court Trial,* 65.

24. *World's Most Famous Court Trial,* 297.

25. *World's Most Famous Court Trial,* 137.

26. John Thomas Scopes, "Reflections—Forty Years After" (1965), available at the University of Missouri–Kansas City School of Law Web site, http://www.law.umkc .edu/faculty/projects/ftrials/scopes/scopesreflections.html.

27. *World's Most Famous Court Trial,* 299, 304.

28. *Tennessee Evolution Case,* 338–39.

29. William Jennings Bryan, *Seven Questions in Dispute* (New York: Revell, 1924), 154.

30. Edward L. Rice, "Darwin and Bryan—A Study in Method," *Science,* March 6, 1925, 245, 247.

31. *Epperson v. Arkansas,* 393 U.S. 97, 99 (n. 3)(1968).

32. Randy Moore, *Evolution in the Courtroom: A Reference Guide* (Santa Barbara, Calif.: ABC-CLIO, 2002), 44.

33. Moore, *Evolution in the Courtroom,* 47.

34. Susan Epperson, "Teaching in the Bible Belt," in Peter Irons, ed., *The Courage of Their Convictions: Sixteen Americans Who Fought Their Way to the Supreme Court* (New York: Penguin, 1990), 223.

35. Randall Bezanson, *How Free Can Religion Be?* (Champaign: University of Illinois Press, 2006), 91.

36. *Epperson v. Arkansas,* 393 U.S. at 103, 106, 107.

37. Ark.Stat.Ann. § 80–1663, et seq. (1981 Supp.).

38. Marcel C. LaFollette, ed., *Creationism, Science, and the Law: The Arkansas Case* (Cambridge: MIT Press, 1983), 5.

39. Moore, *Evolution in the Courtroom,* 82.

40. Brief for the American Jewish Congress and the Synagogue Council of America as Amici Curiae at 46, *Edwards v. Aguillard* 482 U.S. 578 (1987).

41. Many of the documents in this case, including the complaint and transcripts of testimony, may be found at the AntiEvolution.org Web site, http://www.antievolution .org/projects/mclean/new_site/index.htm.

42. *McLean v. Arkansas,* 529 F. Supp. 1255, 1261, 1264 (1982).

43. *McLean,* 529 F. Supp. at 1260, 1270.

44. *McLean,* 529 F. Supp. at 1274.

45. Jurisdictional Statement at 25, *Edwards v. Aguillard* 482 U.S. 578 (1987).

46. Frances Frank Marcus, "Elation, Relief and Sadness in Louisiana as Fight Ends," *New York Times,* June 20, 1987.

47. Brief for Appellees at 18, *Edwards v. Aguillard,* 482 U.S. 578 (1987).

48. Paul Reidinger, "Creationism in the Classroom," *ABA Journal,* 72 December 1, 1986, 66.

49. Al Kamen, "Creationism Case Raises Issues of Faith, 'Freedom,'" *Washington Post*, December 10, 1986.

50. *Aguillard v. Treen*, 420 F. Supp. 426, 428 (1985).

51. *Edwards v. Aguillard*, 765 F. 2d 1251, 1257 (1985).

52. *Edwards*, 765 F. 2d at 1257 (1985).

53. Brief for the American Association of University Professors and the American Council on Education as Amici Curiae at 5, 12, 13, *Edwards v. Aguillard*, 482 U.S. 578 (1987).

54. Brief for the American Federation of Teachers, AFL-CIO as Amicus Curiae at 10, *Edwards v. Aguillard*, 482 U.S. 578 (1987).

55. Brief for the National Academy of Sciences as Amicus Curiae at 4, 14–15, *Edwards v. Aguillard*, 482 U.S. 578 (1987).

56. Brief for National Academy at 21.

57. Brief for 72 Nobel Laureates, 17 State Academies of Science, and 7 other Scientific Organizations as Amici Curiae at 4, *Edwards v. Aguillard*, 482 U.S. 578 (1987).

58. Brief of the Rabbinical Alliance of America, the Catholic Center, the Free Methodist Church of North America, Robert K. Dornan, William Dannemeyer, Patrick L. Swindall, and the Committee on Openness in Science as Amici Curiae at 5, *Edwards v. Aguillard*, 482 U.S. 578 (1987).

59. Brief of Rabbinical Alliance at 7.

60. Oral argument, December 10, 1986, at 24, 25, *Edwards v. Aguillard*, 482 U.S. 578 (1987).

61. *Edwards*, Oral argument at 27.

62. *Edwards*, Oral argument at 33, 34.

63. *Edwards v. Aguillard*, 482 U.S. 578, 586, 586 n. 6 (1987).

64. *Edwards*, 482 U.S. at 592, 583 (1987).

Chapter 6. And Yet It Moves

1. For additional information on Behe's arguments, see Michael Behe, *Darwin's Black Box: The Biochemical Challenge to Evolution* (New York: Free Press, 1996); and Behe, *The Edge of Evolution: A Search for the Limits of Darwinism* (New York: Free Press, 2008).

2. Edward Humes, *Monkey Girl: Evolution, Education, Religion, and the Battle for America's Soul* (New York: Ecco, 2007), 2. This book is a highly readable and thorough discussion of the Dover case.

3. Trial Transcript, Day 8 AM, at 15, *Kitzmiller v. Dover Area School District*, 400 F. Supp. 2d 707 (2005). All trial transcripts are available at http://ncse.com.

4. *Kitzmiller v. Dover Area School District*, 400 F. Supp. 2d 707, 751, 752 (2005).

5. As the name suggests, Americans United for Separation of Church and State identifies itself as "a nonpartisan organization dedicated to preserving the constitutional principle of church-state separation as the only way to ensure religious freedom for all Americans." www.au.org.

6. Web site of the Thomas More Law Center, http://www.thomasmore.org/qry/page .taf?id=23. Laurie Goodstein, "In Pennsylvania, It Was Religion vs. Science, Pastor vs. Ph.D., Evolution vs. the Half-Fish," *New York Times*, September 30, 2005,

notes that Thompson was the former Michigan prosecutor who had lost his position after repeatedly failing to convict Dr. Jack Kevorkian.

7. Trial Transcript, Day 16 AM, at 9, *Kitzmiller v. Dover Area School District*, 400 F. Supp. 2d 707 (2005).

8. *Kitzmiller*, 400 F. Supp. at 754.

9. Trial Transcript, Day 16 AM, at 129, *Kitzmiller v. Dover Area School District*, 400 F. Supp. 2d 707 (2005).

10. Trial Transcript, Day 7 AM, at 145, *Kitzmiller v. Dover Area School District*, 400 F. Supp. 2d 707 (2005).

11. Trial Transcript, Day 14 PM, at 19, *Kitzmiller v. Dover Area School District*, 400 F. Supp. 2d 707 (2005).

12. *Kitzmiller*, 400 F. Supp. at 709.

13. Trial Transcript, Day 13 PM, at 45, *Kitzmiller v. Dover Area School District*, 400 F. Supp. 2d 707 (2005).

14. Trial Transcript, Day 13 PM, at 39, *Kitzmiller v. Dover Area School District*, 400 F. Supp. 2d 707 (2005).

15. *Kitzmiller*, 400 F. Supp. 2d at 761.

16. In psychology, "locus of control" refers to an individual's perception of events as having internal or external causes. As the term is used here, it designates the place, point, or center of control—that is, the ability of one or more constituencies to make decisions in a particular situation.

17. For a more detailed account of the scientific arguments in *Kitzmiller*, see Joan DelFattore, "Speaking of Evolution: The Historical Context of *Kitzmiller v. Dover Area School District*," *Rutgers Journal on Law and Religion* (Fall 2007), available at http://www.law andreligion.com/articles/DelFattore.pdf. In addition to works mentioned elsewhere in this chapter, books summarizing the arguments in favor of ID include John Angus Campbell and Stephen C. Meyer, eds., *Darwinism, Design, and Public Education* (East Lansing: Michigan State University Press, 2003); William A. Dembski, *Uncommon Dissent: Intellectuals Who Find Darwinism Unconvincing* (Wilmington, Del.: ISI Books, 2004); Phillip E. Johnson, *Darwin on Trial* (Washington, D.C.: Regnery Gateway, 1991); and Thomas Woodward, *Doubts About Darwin: A History of Intelligent Design* (Grand Rapids, Mich.: Baker Books, 2003). Evolutionist rebuttals of ID may be found in Kenneth Miller, *Finding Darwin's God: A Scientist's Search for Common Ground Between God and Evolution* (New York: Cliff Street Books, 1999); Matt Young and Taner Edis, eds., *Why Intelligent Design Fails: A Scientific Critique of the New Creationism* (New Brunswick, N.J.: Rutgers University Press, 2004); Niall Shanks, *God, the Devil, and Darwin: A Critique of Intelligent Design Theory* (New York: Oxford University Press, 2004); and Eugenie C. Scott, *Evolution vs. Creationism: An Introduction* (Westport, Conn.: Greenwood Press, 2004). Histories of the debate and collections of essays on both sides include Michael Ruse, *The Evolution-Creation Struggle* (Cambridge: Harvard University Press, 2005); Robert T. Pennock, *Intelligent Design Creationism and Its Critics: Philosophical, Theological, and Scientific Perspectives* (Cambridge: MIT Press, 2001); and George E. Webb, *The Evolution Controversy in America* (Lexington: University Press of Kentucky, 1994).

18. National Academy of Sciences, *Teaching About Evolution and the Nature of Science* (1998), available at http://books.nap.edu/openbook.php?record_id=5787&page=27.

19. Expert Report of Michael Behe at 8, *Kitzmiller v. Dover Area School District,* 400 F. Supp. 2d 707 (2005). All expert reports are available at http://ncse.com.
20. Trial Transcript, Day 11 PM, at 38, *Kitzmiller v. Dover Area School District,* 400 F. Supp. 2d 707 (2005).
21. Behe, *Darwin's Black Box,* quoted in Trial Testimony of Michael Behe, Day 11, at 100.
22. Trial Transcript, Day 20 PM, at 47, *Kitzmiller v. Dover Area School District,* 400 F. Supp. 2d 707 (2005).
23. Expert Report of Kevin Padian at 3, *Kitzmiller v. Dover Area School District,* 400 F. Supp. 2d 707 (2005).
24. Behe, *Darwin's Black Box,* quoted in Trial Transcript, Day 12 AM, at 59, *Kitzmiller v. Dover Area School District,* 400 F. Supp. 2d 707 (2005).
25. Expert Report of Scott Minnich, at 7 (note), *Kitzmiller v. Dover Area School District,* 400 F. Supp. 2d 707 (2005).
26. Trial Transcript, Day 12 AM, at 104, *Kitzmiller v. Dover Area School District,* 400 F. Supp. 2d 707 (2005).
27. Expert Report of Kenneth Miller at 12, *Kitzmiller v. Dover Area School District,* 400 F. Supp. 2d 707 (2005).
28. Trial Transcript, Day 12 PM, at 22–23, *Kitzmiller v. Dover Area School District,* 400 F. Supp. 2d 707 (2005).
29. Expert Report of Kevin Padian, at 5.
30. Analysis of Kenneth Miller's Statement by Michael Behe at 5, *Kitzmiller v. Dover Area School District,* 400 F. Supp. 2d 707 (2005).
31. Trial Transcript, Day 20 PM, at 56, *Kitzmiller v. Dover Area School District,* 400 F. Supp. 2d 707 (2005).
32. National Academy of Sciences, *Teaching About Evolution,* 58.
33. Trial Transcript, Day 11 PM, at 112, *Kitzmiller v. Dover Area School District,* 400 F. Supp. 2d 707 (2005).
34. Trial Transcript, Day 21 PM, at 89, *Kitzmiller v. Dover Area School District,* 400 F. Supp. 2d 707 (2005).
35. Trial Transcript, Day 20 PM, at 33, *Kitzmiller v. Dover Area School District,* 400 F. Supp. 2d 707 (2005) (assent to question as framed by plaintiffs' attorney).
36. Trial Transcript, Day 11 PM, at 36, *Kitzmiller v. Dover Area School District,* 400 F. Supp. 2d 707 (2005).
37. Plaintiffs' Findings of Fact and Conclusions of Law at 29, *Kitzmiller v. Dover Area School District,* 400 F. Supp. 2d 707 (2005).
38. Trial Transcript, Day 11 PM, at 72, *Kitzmiller v. Dover Area School District,* 400 F. Supp. 2d 707 (2005).
39. Expert Report of Kenneth Miller, at 20.
40. Expert Report of Kevin Padian, at 11.
41. Expert Report of Kevin Padian, at 12.
42. Trial Transcript, Day 9 PM, at 88, *Kitzmiller v. Dover Area School District,* 400 F. Supp. 2d 707 (2005).
43. In a book published after the conclusion of *Kitzmiller,* Behe reiterated his belief in the common descent of humans and animals, and he further distanced himself from the creationist-based element of intelligent design by denying that the earth was created only a few thousand years ago. See Behe, *Edge of Evolution.*

44. Brief in Support of Plaintiffs' Proposed Findings of Fact and Conclusions of Law at 60, *Kitzmiller v. Dover Area School District*, 400 F. Supp. 2d 707 (2005).

45. A full account of Forrest's findings on the Discovery Institute and her analysis of *Pandas* appear in Barbara Forrest and Paul R. Gross, *Creationism's Trojan Horse: The Wedge of Intelligent Design* (New York: Oxford University Press, 2004).

46. Expert Report of Michael Behe, at 7.

47. For an extended discussion of the evolution-creation controversy as a clash between two comparably evangelical world-views, see Michael Ruse, *The Evolution Wars: A Guide to the Debates* (Santa Barbara, Calif.: ABC-CLIO, 2000).

48. Richard Dawkins, *The Blind Watchmaker: Why the Evidence of Evolution Reveals a Universe Without Design* (New York: W. W. Norton, 1996), 6.

49. Trial Transcript, Day 11 PM, at 104, *Kitzmiller v. Dover Area School District*, 400 F. Supp. 2d 707 (2005).

50. Trial Transcript, Day 6 PM, at 90, *Kitzmiller v. Dover Area School District*, 400 F. Supp. 2d 707 (2005).

51. *Kitzmiller*, 400 F. Supp 2d at 718–19.

52. *Kitzmiller*, 400 F. Supp 2d at 720.

53. *Kitzmiller*, 400 F. Supp 2d at 721.

54. *Kitzmiller*, 400 F. Supp 2d at 747.

55. *Kitzmiller*, 400 F. Supp 2d at 755.

56. *Kitzmiller*, 400 F. Supp 2d at 745.

57. *Kitzmiller*, 400 F. Supp 2d at 722.

58. *Kitzmiller*, 400 F. Supp 2d at 725, 738.

59. *Kitzmiller*, 400 F. Supp 2d at 738.

60. Trial Transcript, Day 18 PM, at 23, *Kitzmiller v. Dover Area School District*, 400 F. Supp. 2d 707 (2005).

61. *Kitzmiller*, 400 F. Supp. 2d at 756.

62. For a discussion of charges of judicial activism, see Joan DelFattore, *The Fourth R: Conflicts Over Religion in America's Public Schools* (New Haven: Yale University Press, 2004), 156–60, 303–5.

63. Phyllis Schlafly, "Judge's Unintelligent Rant Against Design," January 6, 2006, available at the Eagle Form Web site, http://www.eagleforum.org/column/2006 /jan06/06-01-04.html.

64. Amy Worden, "Judge in Dover Case Still Fighting," *Philadelphia Inquirer*, June 5, 2006.

65. Additional disputes over intelligent design are discussed in Bruce E. Johansen, *Silenced! Academic Freedom, Scientific Inquiry, and the First Amendment Under Siege in America* (Westport, Conn.: Praeger, 2007), chap. 2.

66. *Freiler v. Tangipahoa Parish Board of Education*, 975 F. Supp. 819, 821 (1997).

67. *Freiler*, 975 F. Supp. at 821.

68. *Freiler*, 975 F. Supp. at 823.

69. *Freiler*, 975 F. Supp. at. 829, 830.

70. *Freiler v. Tangipahoa Parish Board of Education*, 185 F.3d 337, 346 (1999).

71. *Selman v. Cobb County School District*, 390 F. Supp. 2d 1286, 1290 (2005).

72. *Selman*, 390 F. Supp. 2d, at 1292.

73. *Selman*, 390 F. Supp. 2d, at 1307.

74. The Creation Science Association for Mid-America describes itself as a "non-de-

nominational, independent, non-profit, educational and research corporation whose members are concerned about the widespread false teaching called 'evolution.'" http://www.csama.org/.

75. Colleen M. McGrath, "Redefining Science to Accommodate Religious Beliefs: The Constitutionality of the 1999 Kansas Science Education Standards," *New York Law School Law Review* 45 (2001): 318, 325.

76. Jacques Steinberg, "Evolution Struggle Shifts to Kansas School Districts," *New York Times,* August 25, 1999.

77. "Opinions of Candidates on Teaching Creationism Alarm Some Scientists," *St. Louis Post-Dispatch,* August 27, 1999.

78. Steve Kraske, "Creationism Evolves into Campaign Topic," *Kansas City Star,* September 2, 1999.

79. Cornelia Dean, "Believing Scripture but Playing by Science's Rules," *New York Times,* February 12, 2007.

80. Lehigh University Department of Biological Sciences, "Department Position on Evolution and 'Intelligent Design,'" available at http://www.lehigh.edu/~inbios/news/evolution.htm.

81. Robert M. O'Neil, *Free Speech in the College Community* (Bloomington: Indiana University Press, 1997), xii.

82. Ronald Dworkin, "We Need a New Interpretation of Academic Freedom," in Louis Menand, ed., *The Future of Academic Freedom* (Chicago: University of Chicago Press, 1996), 189.

Chapter 7. The Mote and the Beam

1. David Horowitz's extensive writings include, among others, *Party of Defeat,* cowritten with Ben Johnson (Dallas: Spence, 2008); *Indoctrination U.: The Left's War Against Academic Freedom* (New York: Encounter Books, 2007); and *The Professors: The 101 Most Dangerous Academics in America* (Washington, D.C.: Regnery, 2006). Online, his work may be found at *FrontPageMag.com,* an online journal he founded (http://frontpagemag.com/), among other places.

2. Entitled "Is Intellectual Diversity an Endangered Species on America's College Campuses?" the hearing took place before the U.S. Senate Health, Education, Labor, and Pensions Committee on October 29, 2003. It featured speakers from the American Council of Trustees and Alumni and the Foundation for Individual Rights in Education, as well as a professor and a student who claimed to have been negatively affected by leftist bias on campus. No ABR opponent was invited to speak, and only the committee's Republican members—who were then in the majority—attended the hearing. The full transcript of the hearing is available online at the U.S. Government Printing Office Web site at http://frwebgate.access.gpo.gov/cgi-bin/getdoc.cgi?dbname=108_senate_hearings&docid=90–304.

3. See the testimony of Anne D. Neal of ACTA at a hearing before the Select Committee on Academic Freedom in Higher Education of the Pennsylvania House of Representatives on January 10, 2006, available at http://www.studentsforacademicfreedom.org/news/1297/AnneNealACTATestimonyPaatTemple011706.htm. See also the testimony of Joan Wallach Scott before the Select Committee on Student Academic Freedom of the Pennsylvania House of Representatives on Novem-

ber 9, 2005, available at http://www.aacu.org/meetings/annualmeeting/AM06
/LawrenceWhiteScottTestimonyonAcaBillofRights.htm.

4. Michael Bérubé's objections to the ABR may be found in Bérubé, *What's Liberal About the Liberal Arts? Classroom Politics and "Bias" in Higher Education*
   (New York: W. W. Norton, 2006). From 2004 to 2007, he maintained a weblog,
   http://www.michaelberube.com/index.php/weblog, where, among other things,
   he debated with Horowitz. Links to weblog entries on academic freedom by John
   K. Wilson are available at http://collegefreedom.org/search/node/wilson. His interview with Horowitz appears at the Students for Academic Freedom Web site,
   http://www.studentsforacademicfreedom.org/news/2450/david-horowitz-and-
   john-wilson-exchange-over-academic-freedom, and his views are summarized in
   Wilson, *Patriotic Correctness: Academic Freedom and Its Enemies* (Boulder, Colo.:
   Paradigm, 2008), chap. 3. Wilson is also the author of *The Myth of Political Correctness: The Conservative Attack on Higher Education* (Durham, N.C.: Duke University Press, 1995), among others. The debate between Horowitz and Graham
   Larkin is discussed and reproduced in Stephen H. Aby, ed., *The Academic Bill of
   Rights Debate: A Handbook* (Westport, Conn.: Praeger, 2007), chap. 4; also included are essays by advocates on both sides of the controversy and key documents relating to it.

5. ACTA describes itself as "an independent, non-profit organization committed to
   academic freedom, excellence, and accountability at America's colleges and universities." In defining its commitment to academic freedom, it emphasizes what
   it sees as the threat to academic freedom posed by "politically correct" policies and
   faculty. Its mission and history are at its Web site, http://www.goacta.org/about
   /mission-and-history.cfm.

6. William Buckley, *God and Man at Yale: The Superstitions of "Academic Freedom"*
   (Washington, D.C.: Regnery, 1951), xv–xvi. For an analysis of Buckley's book in the
   context of the debate over the ABR, see Bruce L. R. Smith, Jeremy D. Mayer, and
   A. Lee Fritschler, *Closed Minds? Politics and Ideology in American Universities*
   (Washington, D.C.: Brookings Institution Press, 2008).

7. In *What's Liberal?* Bérubé points out that state funding of public universities has
   dropped precipitately in recent years, to the point where it represents a very small
   percentage of many universities' budgets. "[T]he real scandal of public universities," he wrote, "is that they have become increasingly beholden to right-wing
   demagoguery with respect to 'the public' (as in, 'why should your taxes pay the
   salaries of these America-hating liberals') even as right-wing demagogues in
   elected office have managed to cut our funding from the states. . . . It's a neat
   trick, invoking the public with one hand and privatizing the enterprise with the
   other" (283).

8. Buckley, *God and Man at Yale*, 185; David Horowitz, "Campus Blacklist," April 18,
   2003, available at the Students for Academic Freedom Web site, http://www
   .studentsforacademicfreedom.org/news/1914/blacklist.html.

9. Buckley, *God and Man at Yale*, xiv.

10. Buckley, *God and Man at Yale*, 114.

11. Buckley, *God and Man at Yale*, 185.

12. Buckley, *God and Man at Yale*, , 175.

13. Buckley, *God and Man at Yale*, 181.

14. Buckley, *God and Man at Yale*, 194.
15. Ben Shapiro, *Brainwashed: How Universities Indoctrinate America's Youth* (Nashville, Tenn.: Thomas Nelson, 2004), xv. Among the many other books expressing similar sentiments are Charles J. Sykes, *Prof Scam: Professors and the Demise of Higher Education* (New York: St. Martin's Press, 1990); Dinesh D'Souza, *Illiberal Education: The Politics of Race and Sex on Campus* (New York: Free Press, 1991); and David Horowitz, *One Party Classroom: How Radical Professors at America's Top Colleges Indoctrinate Students and Undermine Our Democracy* (New York: Crown Forum, 2009).
16. Horowitz, "Campus Blacklist."
17. The American Enterprise Institute for Public Policy Research supports research by conservative scholars dealing with economics, foreign relations, and social policy. Among the recent publications listed on its Web site are books that criticize Medicare and foreign aid and that advocate deregulation; see http://www.aei.org/bookmain.
18. American Enterprise Institute, "The Shame of America's One-Party Campuses," *American Enterprise* (September 2002), 18.
19. American Enterprise Institute, "Shame of America's One-Party Campuses," 18.
20. David Horowitz and Eli Lehrer, "Political Bias in the Administrations and Faculties of 32 Elite Colleges and Universities," August 28, 2003, available at http://www.studentsforacademicfreedom.org/news/1898/lackdiversity.html.
21. Horowitz and Lehrer, "Political Bias."
22. Smith, Mayer, and Fritschler, *Closed Minds?* 19.
23. Contrary to the beliefs underlying the selection of "liberal" departments in the surveys conducted by the American Enterprise Institute and the Center for the Study of Popular Culture, Smith, Mayer, and Fritschler, in *Closed Minds?*, found that faculty in the hard sciences do not differ significantly in political ideology from those in the social sciences. See also Stanley Rothman, S. Robert Lichter, and Neil Nevitte, "Politics and Professorial Advancement Among College Faculty," *Forum* 3 (2005), art. 2.
24. Martin Plissner, "Flunking Statistics: The Right's Disinformation About Faculty Bias," *American Prospect*, December 30, 2002, 16.
25. Bérubé, *What's Liberal?* 42.
26. Bérubé, *What's Liberal?* 91.
27. Testimony by Robert Moore Before the Pennsylvania General Assembly's House Select Committee on Student Academic Freedom, November 9, 2005, available at http://www.aaup.org/AAUP/GR/state/Academic+Bill+of+Rights-State+Level/mooretestimony.htm.
28. Smith, Mayer, and Fritschler, *Closed Minds?* 177.
29. Mark Bauerlein, "Liberal Groupthink Is Anti-Intellectual," *Chronicle of Higher Education*, November 12, 2004, available at http://chronicle.com/article/Liberal-Groupthink-Is/6278.
30. AAUP, *Joint Statement on Rights and Freedoms of Students*, available at http://www.aaup.org/aaup/pubsres/policydocs/contents/stud-rights.htm; AAUP, *Statement on Graduate Students*, available at http://www.aaup.org/aaup/pubsres/policydocs/contents/statementongraduatestudents.htm.
31. Horowitz, "Campus Blacklist."

32. For a detailed discussion of the fight over the ABR in Pennsylvania, together with background on Horowitz and the ABR movement, see Smith, Mayer, and Fritschler, *Closed Minds?*

33. Mary Beth Marklein, "Ex-Liberal Navigates Right," *USA Today,* May 31, 2006, available at http://www.usatoday.com/.

34. Ken Kesey, *One Flew Over the Cuckoo's Nest* (1962; New York: Penguin, 2003), 9.

35. Lewis Carroll, *Through the Looking-Glass* (London: Branden Books, 1873), 102.

36. Douglas Adams, *The Hitchhiker's Guide to the Galaxy* (New York: Pocket Books, 1979), 50.

37. Academic Bill of Rights, available at http://www.studentsforacademicfreedom.org/documents/1925/abor.html.

38. AAUP, *Statement of Principles on Academic Freedom and Tenure* (1940), available at http://www.aaup.org/aaup/pubsres/policydocs/contents/1940statement.htm.

39. AAUP, *Statement* (1940), note 2.

40. AAUP, *Freedom in the Classroom* (2007), available at http://www.aaup.org/aaup/comm/rep/A/class.htm.

41. Academic Bill of Rights.

42. AAUP, *Freedom in the Classroom.*

43. Bérubé, *What's Liberal?* 125.

44. Academic Bill of Rights.

45. Academic Bill of Rights.

46. Academic Bill of Rights.

47. AAUP, Letter to the Missouri Senate, available at http://www.aaup.org/aaup/GR/state/MOsenlet.htm.

48. Testimony of Robert M. O'Neil before the Pennsylvania General Assembly's House Select Committee on Student Academic Freedom, Philadelphia, Pennsylvania, January 9, 2006, available at http://www.aaup.org/AAUP/GR/state/Academic+Bill+of+Rights-State+Level/oneiltestimony.htm.

49. "Diversity Facilitation Training" (handout), Curricular Approach to Residence Life, University of Delaware, August 2007. The full document is available at the Foundation for Individual Rights in Education Web site, http://www.thefire.org/public/pdfs/730a8163b35b360f8edd2b889c832ce9.pdf?direct.

50. Student Life Committee of the Faculty Senate, University of Delaware, "Assessment on the Curricular Approach to Residence Life," February 22, 2008, available at http://www.facsen.udel.edu/sites/Student%20Life/studentlifeassessmentreport.htm.

51. "University of Delaware Requires Students to Undergo Ideological Reeducation," available at http://www.thefire.org/article/8555.html.

52. Patrick Harker, President, "A Message to the University of Delaware Community," *UDaily,* November 1, 2007, available at http://www.udel.edu/PR/UDaily/2008/nov/letter110107.html.

53. Student Life Committee of the Faculty Senate, "Assessment."

54. Residence Life, "Competencies."

55. Student Life Committee of the Faculty Senate, "Assessment."

56. Open Letter from Adam Kissel to University of Delaware Faculty, available at http://www.facsen.udel.edu/sites/Student%20Life/studentlifeassessmentreport.htm.

57. Adam Kissel, "University of Delaware ResLife Misappropriates UD Environmental Sustainability Initiative for Student Activism," May 2, 2008, available at http://www.thefire.org/article/9265.html.

58. Jennifer Hayes, "Faculty Senate Postpones ResLife Proposal Decision," *The Review,* May 6, 2008, available at http://www.thefire.org/public/pdfs/28ee4d974eb9 9a8e219c71870c191f80.pdf.

59. Meeting Minutes, Regular Meeting of the University of Delaware Faculty Senate, May 12, 2008, available at http://www.facsen.udel.edu/sites/agendas%5CFACSEN Minutes2008May12.htm.

60. National Association of Social Workers, "Code of Ethics," revised 2008, available at http://www.socialworkers.org/pubs/code/code.asp.

61. Office of the Provost, Missouri State University, "School of Social Work Site Visit Report," March 29, 2007, available at http://www.missouristate.edu/provost/social work.htm.

62. For a defense of advocacy as a crucial element of the social work profession, see Elizabeth J. Clark, "Advocacy: Profession's Cornerstone," *NASW News* (July 2007), available at http://www.socialworkers.org/pubs/news/2007/07/clark.asp. Dr. Clark is the executive director of the National Association of Social Workers.

63. House Bill No. 1315, Second Regular Session, 94th General Assembly, Missouri House of Representatives, available at http://www.house.mo.gov/billtracking /bills081/biltxt/intro/HB1315I.htm.

Chapter 8. All Roads Lead to *Garcetti*

1. *Garcetti v. Ceballos,* 547 U.S. 410 (2006).

2. AAUP, *Declaration of Principles on Academic Freedom and Academic Tenure* (1915), available at http://www.aaup.org/aaup/pubsres/policydocs/contents/1915.htm. All quotations from the 1915 *Declaration* are from this source. Its authors, many of whom were social scientists and all of whom were products of the Darwinian age and its attitudes, spoke in terms of science and scientific thought. Nevertheless, the principles of academic freedom articulated in this document apply with equal force to any subject of inquiry or debate without regard for departmental boundaries.

3. For a detailed discussion of pre–Civil War American colleges and their governance systems, see Richard Hofstadter, *Academic Freedom in the Age of the College* (1955; New Brunswick, N.J.: Transaction Publishers, 1996). A similar discussion of post–Civil War higher education may be found in Walter P. Metzger, *Academic Freedom in the Age of the University* (New York: Columbia University Press, 1955). The two combined make up Hofstadter and Metzger, *The Development of Academic Freedom in the United States* (New York: Columbia University Press, 1955).

4. Matthew C. Finkin and Robert W. Post, *For the Common Good: Principles of American Academic Freedom* (New Haven: Yale University Press, 2009), 150, 154.

5. *Statement of Principles on Academic Freedom and Tenure* (1940), available at http://www.aaup.org/AAUP/pubsres/policydocs/contents/1940statement.htm.

6. *Statement on Government of Colleges and Universities,* available at http://www.aaup .org/AAUP/pubsres/policydocs/contents/governancestatement.htm.

7. Finkin and Post, *For the Common Good*, 124, 125.

8. AAUP, *Protecting an Independent Faculty Voice: Academic Freedom After Garcetti v. Ceballos*, available at http://www.aaup.org/.

9. AAUP, *On the Relationship of Faculty Governance to Academic Freedom*, in *AAUP Policy Documents and Reports*, 10th ed. (Washington, D.C.: AAUP, 2006), 141.

10. AAUP, *On the Relationship of Faculty Governance to Academic Freedom*, 143.

11. *Wieman v. Updegraff*, 344 U.S. 183, 196-7 (1952).

12. *Sweezy v. New Hampshire*, 354 U.S. 234, 250 (1957).

13. *Sweezy*, 354 U.S. at 262.

14. Judith Areen, "Government as Educator: A New Understanding of First Amendment Protection of Academic Freedom and Governance," *Georgetown Law Journal* 97 (2009).

15. *Keyishian v. Board of Regents*, 385 U.S. 589, 599, 602 (1967).

16. *Keyishian*, 385 U.S. at 603, 604.

17. *Regents of the University of Michigan v. Ewing*, 474 U.S. 214, 225 (1985).

18. *Ewing*, 474 U.S. at 226, 226n12.

19. *Grutter v. Bollinger*, 539 U.S. 306, 329 (2003).

20. *Parate v. Isibor*, 868 F.2d 821, 825 (1989).

21. *Parate*, 868 F.2d, at 826, 830.

22. *Parate*, 868 F.2d, at 826, 831.

23. Michael A. Olivas, "Reflections on Professorial Academic Freedom: Second Thoughts on the Third 'Essential Freedom,'" *Stanford Law Review* 45 (1993): 1851.

24. *Parate v. Isibor*, 868 F.2d 821 (1989), p. 827.

25. *Parate*, 868 F.2d, at 827.

26. *Parate*, 868 F.2d, at 827.

27. *Edwards v. California University of Pennsylvania*, 156 F.3d 488, 491 (1998).

28. *Edwards*, 156 F.3d, at 491.

29. *Edwards*, 156 F.3d, at 492.

30. *Brown v. Armenti*, 247 F.3d 69, 75 (2001). Kevin A. Rosenfield, arguing that the courts have erred in granting administrations too much authority to regulate professors' speech, suggests applying a *Hazelwood*-like test such that a professor's right to grade would be protected unless the administration's reason for wanting a change was reasonably related to a legitimate educational objective. See Rosenfeld, "*Brown v. Armenti* and the First Amendment Protection of Teachers and Professors in Grading Their Students," *Northwestern University Law Review* 97 (2003).

Chapter 9. Caution! Paradigms May Shift

1. A discussion of the *Pickering/Connick* test appears in Chapter 1.

2. *Ceballos v. Garcetti*, 361 F. 3d 1168, 1177 (2004).

3. *Garcetti v. Ceballos*, 547 U.S. 410, 421, 422 (2006).

4. *Garcetti*, 547 U.S. 410, at 422.

5. *Garcetti*, 547 U.S. 410, at 422, 423.

6. *Garcetti*, 547 U.S. 410, at 424–25, 425.

7. *Garcetti*, 547 U.S. 410, at 426.

8. *Garcetti*, 547 U.S. 410, at 428.

9. *Garcetti,* 547 U.S. 410, at 431–32, 433, 438.

10. AAUP, *Protecting an Independent Faculty Voice: Academic Freedom After Garcetti v. Ceballos,* available at http://www.aaup.org/.

11. *Givhan v. Western Line Consolidated School District,* 439 U.S. 410, 415-16 (1979).

12. *Garcetti,* 547 U.S. 410, at 421, 427, 430.

13. Martha M. McCarthy and Suzanne E. Eckes, "Silence in the Hallways: The Impact of *Garcetti v. Ceballos* on Public School Educators," *Boston University Public Interest Law Journal* 17 (Spring 2008): 230.

14. *Evans-Marshall v. Board of Education of Tipp City,* 428 F.3d 223, 227 (2005).

15. *Evans-Marshall,* 428 F.3d, at 231–32.

16. *Mayer v. Monroe County Community School Corporation,* 1:04-CV-1695-SEB-VSS, U.S. District Court for the Southern District of Indiana, Indianapolis Division (2006), 37.

17. *Mayer v. Monroe County Community School Corporation,* 474 F.3d 477, 479 (2007).

18. *Mayer* 474 F. 3d at 479 (2007) .

19. Alison Lima, "Casenote and Comment: Shedding First Amendment Rights at the Classroom Door? The Effects of *Garcetti* and *Mayer* on Education in Public Schools," *George Mason Law Review* 16 (Fall 2008).

20. Neal H. Hutchens, "Silence at the Schoolhouse Gate: The Diminishing First Amendment Rights of Public School Employees," *Kentucky Law Journal* 97 (2008–9): 74–75, 74.

21. Hutchens, "Silence at the Schoolhouse Gate," 76.

22. *Garcetti,* 547 U.S. 410, at 425; *Lee,* 484 F.3d 687 (2007).

23. *Williams v. Dallas Independent School District,* 480 F.3d 689, 692 (2007).

24. *Williams,* 480 F.3d at 694.

25. *Weintraub v. Board of Education of the City of New York,* 423 F. Supp. 2d 38, 52 (2006).

26. *Weintraub v. Board of Education of the City of New York,* 489 F. Supp. 2d 209, 214 (2006).

27. *Weintraub v. Board of Education of the City School District of the City of New York,* 07-2376-cv (Second Circuit, January 27, 2010), 17; 2010 U.S. App. LEXIS 1782, p. 17.

28. Kevin G. Welner, "Locking Up the Marketplace of Ideas and Locking Out School Reform: Courts' Imprudent Treatment of Controversial Teaching in America's Public Schools," *UCLA Law Review* 50 (2003); Karen C. Daly, "Balancing Act: Teachers' Classroom Speech and the First Amendment," *Journal of Law and Education* 30 (2001): 16; Hutchens, "Silence at the Schoolhouse Gate."

29. *Garcetti,* 547 U.S. 410, at 425.

30. *Renken v. Gregory,* 541 F.3d 769, 773, 774, 775 (2008).

31. The department Web site now lists Hong as professor emeritus. Professor Stanley Grant, identified here as the department chair, no longer holds that position.

32. *Hong v. Grant,* 516 F. Supp. 2d 1158, 1164 (2007).

33. *Hong,* 516 F. Supp. 2d, at 1164.

34. *Hong,* 516 F. Supp. 2d, at 1167.

35. *Hong,* 516 F. Supp. 2d, at 1167, 1168.

36. AAUP, *Protecting an Independent Faculty Voice.*

37. *Hong,* 516 F. Supp. 2d, at 1161.

38. The Thomas Jefferson Center defines itself as "a unique organization, devoted

solely to the defense of free expression in all its forms. . . . It is as concerned with the musician as with the mass media, with the painter as with the publisher, and as much with the sculptor as the editor." Among its best-known activities is the annual announcement of the Jefferson Muzzle Awards, given to individuals or groups that have perpetrated "especially egregious or ridiculous affronts to free expression." http://www.tjcenter.org/about/.

39. Brief for the Thomas Jefferson Center for the Protection of Free Expression and the American Association of University Professors as Amici Curiae, at 19, available at http://www.tjcenter.org/wp-content/uploads/JuanHongvStanleyGrant SACV06-0134CJC(RNBx).pdf.

40. My home institution is the University of Delaware, not Delaware State University. I am not acquainted with any of the participants in *Gorum v. Sessoms*.

41. *Gorum v. Sessoms*, 561 F.3d 179,183 (2009).

42. *Gorum*, 561 F.3d , at 186.

43. *Gorum*, 561 F.3d, at 188.

44. *Sheldon v. Dhillon*, C-08-03438 RMW (N.D. California, November 25, 2009), 3.

45. *Sheldon*, 4.

46. *Sheldon*, 5.

47. *Hazelwood v. Kuhlmeier*, 484 U.S. 260, 273 (1988).

48. *Sheldon*, 7.

49. *Sheldon*, 8 (n. 2).

50. Robert M. O'Neil, "Academic Speech in the Post-*Garcetti* Environment," 7 *First Amendment Law Review* 1 (Fall 2008): 16.

51. Sheldon Nahmod, "Academic Freedom and the Post-*Garcetti* Blues," 7 *First Amendment Law Review* 54 (Fall 2008): 69. In *Rosenberger v. Rector and Visitors of the University of Virginia* (1995), the Supreme Court stated that the university could not declare a student religious publication ineligible for funding because of the viewpoint it expressed.

52. Judith Areen, "Government as Educator: A New Understanding of First Amendment Protection of Academic Freedom and Governance," 97 *Georgetown Law Journal* 945 (2009): 990.

53. Areen, "Government as Educator," 997.

54. AAUP, *Protecting an Independent Faculty Voice*.

Afterword

1. John Stuart Mill, *On Liberty*, available at http://www.bartleby.com/.130/2.html. All quotations from Mill are from this source.

2. The term "contingent faculty" refers broadly to people who fulfill faculty functions without holding full-time, tenured, or tenure-track positions. Contingent faculty may work full-time or part-time, and they may be on continuing or temporary appointments. Many contingent faculty are hired and paid by the course, and such arrangements may continue for decades. June Sheldon, whose case is discussed in Chapter 9, is an example of a contingent faculty member.

3. Cary Nelson, *No University Is an Island: Saving Academic Freedom* (New York: New York University Press, 2010), 77.

INDEX

AAUP. *See* American Association of University Professors

abortion, 15–16, 168, 195–96, 264

Abrams, Steve, 171

Academic Bill of Rights, x, 180–213

academic freedom: conceptual development of, 214–24; content expertise and, 4–6, 80, 117, 125, 138, 153, 155–56, 165, 174–78, 196–97, 217–20, 237; defined as a constitutional right, 144–46, 224–38; definition of, 1–2, 4–5, 8–10, 73, 83, 177, 229; ideological bias and, 199–213; idiosyncratic definitions of, 135–46, 169; limited by *Garcetti v. Ceballos*, 253–67; locus of control of, 3–4, 179–80, 183–84, 190, 231–33, 235–37, 257–59, 266–67, 287n16; public employee law and, 65–66, 238–46; race-based intelligence and, 56–84; related to universities' missions, 7–8, 264–69; students' rights and, 180–93, 197–99, 277n30; universities' institutional right to, 45, 224–38, 277n30. *See also* American Association of University Professors; evolution; freedom of expression; universities; *specific institutions, legal decisions, and people*

ACLU. *See* American Civil Liberties Union

Adams, Douglas, 193

Adler v. New York, 225–26

Adventures of Huckleberry Finn, The (Twain), 29–34, 39

affirmative action, 57–60, 69–70, 74, 190, 201

AFL-CIO, 181

African American studies, 64–66, 188, 194, 196

Agassiz, Louis, 120–23, 147, 158

Aguillard, Don, 141

Alito, Samuel, 234, 240

Alliance Defense Fund, 209, 262

American Anti-Evolution Association, 132

American Association for the Advancement of Science, 6, 273n3

American Association of University Professors (AAUP): definition of academic freedom and, 7–12, 69, 81, 178, 194–97, 214–22, 244; publications of, 10, 24, 53, 76, 194, 196–98, 212–22, 235, 238–39, 244, 264, 266; role of, in protecting academic freedom, 74–76, 142–43, 154, 156, 165, 181, 191, 200, 211, 257, 270; speech codes and, 53

American Association of University Women, 133

American Center for Law and Justice, 6, 101

299